Object-Oriented Programming with Borland® Pascal 7

Object-Oriented Programming with Borland® Pascal 7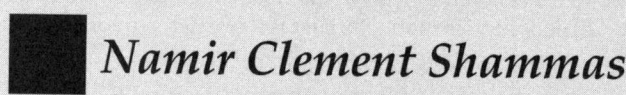

Namir Clement Shammas

PUBLISHING

A Division of Prentice Hall Computer Publishing
11711 North College, Carmel, Indiana, 46032 USA

To my son Joseph.

Copyright © 1993 by Sams Publishing

All rights reserved. No part of this book shall be reproduced, stored in a retrieval system, or transmitted by any means, electronic, mechanical, photocopying, recording, or otherwise, without written permission from the publisher. No patent liability is assumed with respect to the use of the information contained herein. Although every precaution has been taken in the preparation of this book, the publisher and author assume no responsibility for errors or omissions. Neither is any liability assumed for damages resulting from the use of the information contained herein. For information, address Sams Publishing, 11711 N. College Ave., Carmel, IN 46032.

International Standard Book Number: 0-672-30333-7

Library of Congress Catalog Card Number: 93-83483

96 95 94 93   4 3 2 1

Interpretation of the printing code: the rightmost double-digit number is the year of the book's printing; the rightmost single-digit, the number of the book's printing. For example, a printing code of 93-1 shows that the first printing of the book occurred in 1993.

Trademarks

All terms mentioned in this book that are known to be trademarks or service marks have been appropriately capitalized. Sams Publishing cannot attest to the accuracy of this information. Use of a term in this book should not be regarded as affecting the validity of any trademark or service mark. Borland is a registered trademark of Borland International, Inc.

Composed in Palatino and MCPdigital by Prentice Hall Computer Publishing

Printed in the United States of America

Publisher
Richard K. Swadley

Acquisitions Manager
Jordan Gold

Acquisitions Editor
Gregory S. Croy

Development Editor
Phillip Paxton

Production Editor
Erik Dafforn

Copy Editors
Anne Clarke Barrett
Melba Hopper
Joe Williams

Editorial Coordinators
Bill Whitmer
James R. Welter II

Editorial Assistant
Sharon Cox

Technical Editor
Scott Palmer

Cover Designer
Tim Amrhein

Director of Production and Manufacturing
Jeff Valler

Production Manager
Corinne Walls

Imprint Manager
Kelli Widdifield

Book Designer
Michele Laseau

Production Analyst
Mary Beth Wakefield

Proofreading/Indexing Coordinator
Joelynn Gifford

Graphics Image Specialists
Tim Montgomery
Dennis Sheehan
Sue VandeWalle

Production
Christine Cook
Mitzi Foster Gianakos
Dennis Clay Hager
Carla Hall-Batton
Howard Jones
Sean Medlock
Juli Pavey
Angela M. Pozdol
Tonya Simpson
Dennis Wesner
Donna Winter
Lillian Yates
Alyssa Yesh

Indexers
John Sleeva
Suzanne G. Snyder

Overview

Introduction

- 1   OOP Basics
- 2   Constructors and Destructors
- 3   Overriding Methods
- 4   Object Types as Extendible Records
- 5   Abstract Object Types
- 6   Generic Object Types
- 7   Metamorphic Object Types
- 8   Containment
- 9   Privileged Instances and Pseudo-Private Methods
- 10   Disabled Instances
- 11   Disciplined Instances
- 12   Emulating C++ Static Members
- 13   The Oberon Solution
- 14   Turbo Vision Collections
- 15   Persistent Objects and Streams

Appendix A   Disk Contents

Index

Contents

Introduction

1	**OOP Basics**	**1**
	The Legacy of Structured Programming	2
	The OOP Approach	2
	Classes and Objects	3
	Methods that Alter the Object's State	4
	Inheritance	4
	Polymorphism	5
	Borland Pascal OOP Features	6
	Static vs. Virtual Methods	14
	Dynamic Objects	21
	Summary	24
2	**Constructors and Destructors**	**25**
	The Default Constructor	26
	Multiconstructor Object Types	32
	The Copy Constructor	42
	Invoking Constructors of Parent Object Types	49
	Virtual Destructors	58
	Handling Constructor Errors	58
	Summary	65
3	**Overriding Methods**	**67**
	Overriding Static Methods	68
	Overriding Virtual Methods	74
	Summary	87
4	**Object Types As Extendible Records**	**89**
	Simulating Extendible Records	90
	Extendible Records in an Object-Type Hierarchy	95
	Summary	103
5	**Abstract Object Types**	**105**
	Basic Rules for Abstract Object Types	106
	Abstract Object Types as Base Types	106
	Abstract Objects in Subhierarchies	118
	The TArray Object Type	127

Object-Oriented Programming with Borland Pascal 7

        The TAbsSortArray Object Type 128
        The TSortArray Object Type 129
        The TNocaseSortArray Object Type 129
    Summary 134

6   Generic Object Types   135

    Overview of Generic Programming..136
    The Elements of Generic Programming 137
    Building Generic Routines 139
    The Generic Linear-Search Function 140
    The Generic Stack Object Type 143
    Summary 156

7   Metamorphic Object Types   159

    Metamorphic Object Types 160
    An Array-Queue-Stack Example 161
        The TStrArray Object Type 162
        The TStrFixedQue Object Type 163
        The TStrFixedStack Object Type 165
    Test Program to Test Object
       Types in the Metamorf Library Unit 172
    Summary 177

8   Containment   179

    The Basics of Containment 180
    Containment and Extendible Records 181
    Containment in Object-Type Hierarchies 188
    Modular Objects 195
    Direct Access to Components of Modular Objects 201
    Multiple Inheritance: What If? 208
    Summary 213

9   Privileged Instances and Pseudo-Private Methods   215

    Privileged Instances 216
        The TUArray Object Type 217
        The TFlexUArray Object Type 219
        The TUArray_IO Object Type 219
        The TFlexUArray_IO Object Type 220
        The TOArray Object Type 220
        The TFlexOArray Object Type 221
        The TOArray_IO Object Type 221

        The TFlexOArray_IO Object Type 221
    Testing Privileged Instances 232
        Testing Object Type TUArray 232
        Testing Object Type TUArray_IO 233
        Testing Object Type TFlexUArray 233
        Testing Object Type TFlexUArray_IO 234
    Using Privileged Instances 241
    Pseudo-Private Methods 256
        The TUArray Object Type 258
        The TFlexUArray Object Type 258
        The TUArray_IO Object Type 258
        The TFlexUArray_IO Object Type 259
        The TOArray Object Type 259
        The TFlexOArray Object Type 259
        The TFlexOArray_IO Object Type 259
    Testing the Polymrf4 Library Unit 270
    Summary 276

10   Disabled Instances   277

    Basics of Disabled Instances 278
    Disabled Single Instances 278
    Disabling Contained Instances 288
    Summary 293

11   Disciplined Instances   295

    The Basics of Disciplined Instances 296
    A Basic Statistics Example 297
    Summary 308

12   Emulating C++ Static Members   309

    Basics of Static Members 310
    Implementing Static Members 311
    An Instance-Counting Example 312
    A Shared Data Example 318
    Summary 323

13   The Oberon Solution   325

    Extendible Records in Oberon 326
    Emulating Methods in Oberon 326
    Emulating the Oberon Solution 327
    An Array Example 328

		Summary 342	
14	**Turbo Vision Collections**		**343**
		Unordered Collections 344	
		Sorted Collections 358	
		Sorted String Collections 365	
		Unsorted String Collections 369	
		Summary 374	
15	**Persistent Objects and Streams**		**375**
		The Features of Streams 376	
		The TStream Subhierarchy 377	
		The Load and Store Methods 383	
		Object-Type Registration 386	
		Sequential Stream I/O 388	
		Random-Access Stream I/O 396	
		Polymorphic Streams 399	
		Streams and Collections 409	
		Summary 418	
A	**Disk Contents**		**421**
		Generic Pascal Classes Library 422	
		TechnoJock Object Toolkit 422	
		TechnoJock Turbo Toolkit 423	
		Dialog Design 424	
		Boilerplate 424	
Index			**425**

Acknowledgments

I would like to acknowledge the participation of the many people who made this book possible. I wish to thank Greg Croy and Phil Paxton for putting their knowledge and vision into this book. Many thanks also to the editors, Erik Dafforn and Anne Clarke, for their patience and skill. In addition, I would like to thank Scott Palmer for his valuable technical review and recommendations; it is always appreciated when a fellow author takes the time to review a manuscript. Finally, I would like to thank the fine Production, Proofreading, and Indexing Departments at Sams Publishing.

Introduction

This book is aimed at programmers who work with Borland/Turbo Pascal 7.0 and use (or wish to use) its object-oriented language extensions. The book assumes an average knowledge of the non-object-oriented aspects of Borland/Turbo Pascal and some familiarity with Turbo Vision. The topics covered by this book show you how to extend the object-oriented features of Borland Pascal. I hope that many of the programming tricks open new doors on how you view object-oriented programming and its components. (Note: Several chapters in this book contain program listings followed by their output. When the screen clears during the execution of a program, the phrase *The Screen Clears* appears on the page.)

The book contains 15 chapters. The chapters are modular and can be read in any order. If you are new to object-oriented programming, I suggest that you first read Chapters 1 and 2.

Chapter 1 introduces you to the basic notions of object-oriented programming (OOP) and presents the OOP extensions to Pascal as implemented in Borland Pascal 7.0.

Chapter 2 looks at constructors and destructors and the role they play in instantiating and removing instances of the object types. This chapter also discusses special constructors and how to handle constructor errors.

Chapter 3 discusses overriding static and virtual methods. The chapter also shows the impact of overriding methods on the design of object type hierarchies.

Chapter 4 shows you how to use object types as extendible records. The chapter presents two examples. The first shows object types acting as extendible records in a non-OOP program. The second example shows how to integrate extendible records with other object types in an OOP program.

Chapter 5 presents abstract object types. This chapter discusses the rules for declaring and using abstract object types in an object type hierarchy. The chapter also presents the two main types of abstract object types.

Chapter 6 discusses generic object types. The chapter presents the basic principles of generic programming and how to integrate these principles with object-oriented programming. As an example, the chapter presents an object type that models a generic stack.

Chapter 7 presents metamorphic object types and shows you how these types change context in an object type hierarchy. The example offered by the chapter

looks at a single object type hierarchy that implements dynamic arrays, fixed queues, and fixed stacks as metamorphic object types.

Chapter 8 discusses containment as a method commonly used in designing object type hierarchies. The chapter looks at containment in extendible records, in object type hierarchies, and in modular objects. The chapter also discusses multiple inheritance.

Chapter 9 looks at programming tricks to implement privileged instances and pseudo-private methods. The chapter shows how you can replace an object type hierarchy with a single object type that supports privileged instances. The chapter also shows you how to implement an object type hierarchy with pseudo-private methods that can be made practically private or public in the descendant object types.

Chapter 10 discusses how to implement disabled instances to model malfunctioning objects. The chapter presents the principle of implementing disabled instances and shows how these principles apply to a single instance and to contained instances.

Chapter 11 looks at disciplined instances that represent state engine objects. The chapter gives an example of a linear regression object which implements a state engine.

Chapter 12 presents a programming trick to emulating C++ static members. The chapter discusses the concepts behind static members and how these members can be used. The examples offered by the chapter include an instance-counting object type and a data-sharing object type.

Chapter 13 discusses a programming trick to emulate deferred binding (in other words, very late binding) as inspired by the Oberon programming language. The chapter illustrates how this technique works in binding the sorting and searching method of an object type which models dynamic arrays.

Chapter 14 looks at the versatile Turbo Vision collections. The chapter discusses the advantages of using the collections structure and presents unordered collections, sorted collections, sorted string collections, and unsorted string collections.

Chapter 15 presents the topics of creating and using persistent objects and streams. The chapter looks at the features of streams and how they are implemented in the TStream hierarchy (in Turbo Vision). The chapter also discusses how to make an object streamable, and discusses sequential stream I/O, random-access stream I/O, polymorphic streams, and how to use streams with collections.

The book includes a companion disk that contains the Pascal listings. The listings are collected in a self-extracting archive file. To unpack the files, see the instructions in the very back of this book (on the page facing the disk).

OOP Basics

Welcome to the world of object-oriented programming! Your journey into this fascinating world of a new programming paradigm has just started. This chapter looks at the basic concepts of OOP and how they are applied to Borland Pascal 7.0. You'll learn about the following:

- The basic concepts of classes and objects
- Manipulating objects with methods
- Inheritance among classes
- Polymorphic behavior of a class hierarchy
- The basic, object-oriented programming features of Borland Pascal

Object-Oriented Programming with Borland Pascal 7

The Legacy of Structured Programming

Before heading on into the world of object-oriented programming (OOP) let's briefly look back down the road. Structured programming promotes order separately in the code and data structures of a program. This order includes the notion of reusable code and highly independent routines. Interestingly, the Pascal language itself (including Borland's Turbo Pascal) has played a major part in promoting structured programming in academic circles.

Structured programming fosters a primarily procedural approach to developing software. Data structures take second place. The popular top-down software development method requires that you break an application into major tasks, and then repeatedly divide these tasks into smaller and smaller subtasks. In general, data manipulation takes place in the lower-level subtasks.

The OOP Approach

The appeal of structured programming is that it emulates the world of objects we live in. Just look around you! This book is an object, and so is your chair. Your computer system is an object made up of smaller objects: the screen, the keyboard, the disk drives, the motherboard, and so forth. Some objects are highly animated and some are not. Even inactive objects (such as things in your garage or attic) occupy space and must be taken into account.

Object-oriented programming was conceived by computer scientists who viewed the world as populated by objects acting and interacting with each other according to their nature. The procedures applied to the objects are of secondary importance because they depend on the objects themselves. For example, you cannot print a car, or drive a light bulb, or wash your computer—these actions are inappropriate because they are not part of the object's normal functionality.

Object-oriented programming offers a paradigm shift in software development. This approach goes beyond simply making data structures primary and procedures secondary. The next section begins to clarify the basics of object-oriented programming that make it very different from structured programming. For now, just remember that object-oriented programming picks up where structured programming left off. OOP offers more real-world logic with which to organize the modeling of an object and better coordinate the spin-off of child objects.

Classes and Objects

The digital clock that sits near my computer's screen is a good illustration of the concept of classes and objects. My clock—a CASINO-65—is the simplest type of mass-produced digital clock (see Figure 1.1). It displays the time and has a few buttons that enable me to change or adjust the time.

My clock is by no means unique! It's one particular clock from an assembly line. It belongs to a class of clocks that represents a specific clock model, the CASINO-65. All CASINO-65 clocks have the same physical features and functionality. Thus, the clock model represents a *class of objects* that have the same characteristics and functionality. My clock is merely an *instance* of the CASINO-65 model.

Although it has a lot in common with other CASINO-65 clocks, this instance of a CASINO-65 has its own *state*: the particular time setting and rate of deviation from the actual time (perhaps attributable to the particular set of batteries running it). A clock's time setting and deviation rate could be thought of as data fields, defining the state of the clock object. Classes encapsulate, or combine, the *functionality* of the modeled object and *data fields* that define the object's state.

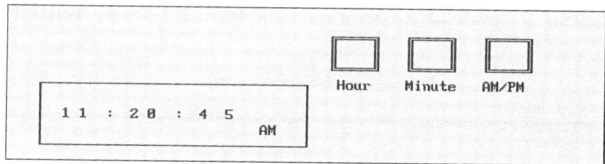

Figure 1.1. The CASINO-65 clock.

A *class* is a category of objects that encapsulate and share the same characteristics and functionality.

An *object* is an instance of a class. Each object has its own particular state.

The *state* of an object depends on the values of its *data fields*.

Object-Oriented Programming with Borland Pascal 7

Methods that Alter the Object's State

The state of my CASINO-65 clock is indicated by the displayed time. When I want to adjust the time (for example, after a power failure) I press the buttons on the front panel. Each button changes the display in a particular way: the hour button advances the hours, the minute button advances the minutes, and the AM/PM button toggles between the AM and PM indicators. By using these buttons, I send to the clock's circuits electrical signals to alter its state and, consequently, change the displayed time. In object-oriented programming terms, the clock buttons correspond to *methods* that alter the clock's state.

We may now add to our definition of classes: classes combine the functionality of the modeled object, data fields that define the object's state, and the *methods* that alter these fields.

These methods—the buttons—implement the functionality of my clock. The electrical signals generated by pressing the clock buttons represent, in object-oriented programming terms, messages that I'm sending to the clock as an object. The clock responds to these messages. Again, in object-oriented programming terms, we say that the clock object is the *owner* of the messages. The notion of ownership becomes more relevant when dealing with a class hierarchy, as we do in a moment.

> The *message* represents what is being done to an object.
>
> The *method* is how the message is being carried out.

Inheritance

Suppose that the makers of my CASINO-65 clock decide to introduce a new model, the CASINO-66, which has the same features of the 65, plus an alarm. Because the clock manufacturer is more likely to build on the 65 model than to start from scratch, the new CASINO-66 model is a refinement of the CASINO-65, with a new set of buttons to set the alarm and turn it on or off. In OOP terms, the CASINO-66 has *inherited* the features of the model 65 and introduced new functionality. The CASINO-66 is a *subclass* of the CASINO-65 clocks.

Suppose that, sometime later, the CASINO clock makers plan to offer the CASINO-100, which has a clock, an alarm, and a radio. The CASINO-100 would be designed by starting with the CASINO-66 model. In object-oriented terms, the CASINO-100 is a subclass of CASINO-66; the radio feature represents the new functionality of the class of CASINO-100 clocks.

The *hierarchy* of CASINO clocks is shown here:

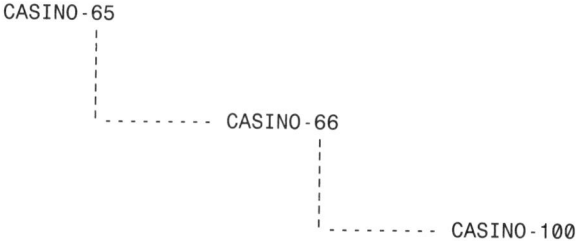

The concept of *inheritance* is important to object-oriented programming. Inheritance enables the spin-off of a new class from an existing one. The new class is called the *subclass* and the parent class is called the *superclass*. The first ancestor class (that is, the parent of all other classes in a hierarchy) is called the *base* class. The CASINO-65 may be considered the base class of the CASINO clocks and the parent of the CASINO-66 clocks.

The significance of inheritance comes from the fact that the new subclass need not reinvent the wheel by redeclaring all the data fields and procedures of the parent class. Instead, only new data fields require declaration.

While the subclass can declare new methods, methods also can be inherited. In addition, the subclass can declare what inherited methods are to be overridden. These abilities enable you to adjust the functionality of a subclass to suit its purpose.

Polymorphism

The term *polymorphism* is important in object-oriented programming. Derived from the Greek for "multiple shapes," polymorphism can perhaps be best translated as *message abstraction*: the ability to send a message without worrying about the specific method that will execute the message.

The CASINO clocks can help illustrate polymorphism. The CASINO-66 inherited the time features of the CASINO-65. The manufacturer probably uses the same

exterior button for both clock models. Suppose that the designer of the CASINO-66 had to modify the internal electrical circuits to accommodate both the time and alarm systems. The owner of the CASINO-65 and CASINO-66 clocks would operate the time setting buttons in exactly the same way, without realizing (or caring) that the time-regulating circuits are different. In object-oriented terms, the time buttons of the CASINO-66 model exhibit *polymorphic behavior*: they perform the same overall task as those of the CASINO-65 using different circuits.

The example can be extended to include the CASINO-100 model, where the physical time and alarm buttons of the CASINO-66 are reused but a new internal circuit is utilized to manage the interaction between the radio and the alarm system. The time and alarm buttons show polymorphic behavior, because they perform the same overall job as in the CASINO-66 model while using different internal circuits. This polymorphic behavior gives the time button of the three CASINO models a certain level of abstraction.

Polymorphism allows each class to own custom versions of methods that maintain a unified response within a class hierarchy.

Borland Pascal OOP Features

The first object-oriented extensions to the Pascal language were implemented by Apple Computer, Inc., with the help of Nicklaus Wirth, the father of Pascal. The Borland Pascal OOP features find their roots in the Apple implementation. Classes are declared as follow:

```
className = OBJECT ¦ OBJECT(parentClass>)

     [PUBLIC]
            <list of public data fields>
            <headers for public methods>
     [PRIVATE
            <list of private data fields>
            <headers for private methods>]
     END;
```

The keyword OBJECT first was used by Apple Computer's Object Pascal and is inherited by Borland Pascal. The OBJECT keyword led the Borland Pascal manual to call classes "objects," because the OBJECT keyword is used. Other object-oriented Pascal implementations also use the OBJECT keyword, but recognize the data types defined as classes. All other object-oriented languages (including Borland's Turbo C++) define classes as the template data types for objects. The best way to deal with this dual system of nomenclature in this book is as follows:

OOP Basics

1. The term *object type* refers to the Borland Pascal OBJECT data type.
2. The term *object variable* refers to the Borland Pascal variable of type OBJECT.
3. The term *class* is used when discussing classes in general.
4. The term *object* refers to the instance of a class in general.

Keep these rules in mind as you read the following explanation of the components of an object type:

- The record-like data fields that belong to an object type define the state of the object variables.
- The headers for methods are equivalent to FORWARD declarations for different functions and procedures, which are encapsulated in the object type to provide the desired functionality. You cannot include the code body in the declaration of an object type.

Object-oriented programming discourages the direct access of data fields. Instead, define user-defined object types to offer access methods to set and query the values of various data fields. This access scheme allows controlled access to the data fields and a more robust object type. Some data fields can be set and queried, others can only be queried, and still others are strictly for internal use and cannot be accessed. Borland Pascal 7.0 offers the keywords PRIVATE and PUBLIC, which allow data fields and methods to be declared as private and public, respectively. The PUBLIC is optional: data fields are public by default. Using the PRIVATE and PUBLIC keywords, you can place intermittent declarations of public and private data fields and headers in the declaration of an object type.

An example of an object-type hierarchy is shown in Listing 1.1. The object types in this listing model the following simple geometric shapes:

- The TCircle object type models a simple circle and is declared as follows:

```
TCircle = OBJECT
  PRIVATE
    Radius : REAL;
  PUBLIC
    PROCEDURE SetRadius(R : REAL { input   });
    FUNCTION GetRadius : REAL;
    FUNCTION Area : REAL;
    FUNCTION Circumference : REAL;
END;
```

The TCircle object type has one data field (the Radius) in which to store the radius of the circle. This field is declared as private, and all the methods as public. Two methods, SetRadius and GetRadius, set and query

the value of the Radius data field, respectively. These methods enforce the object-oriented programming disciplines, which foster the controlled access of data fields. The Area and Circumference methods return the area and circumference of the circle, respectively. TCircle is the base object type for the geometric-shape hierarchy.

- The TSphere object type models a sphere, and is declared as follows:

```
TSphere = OBJECT(TCircle)
    FUNCTION Area : REAL;
    FUNCTION Volume : REAL;
END;
```

The TSphere object type is declared a descendent of TCircle by placing the name of the parent object type in parentheses after the keyword OBJECT. The method Area overrides the Area method inherited from TCircle to calculate the surface area of the sphere. The method Volume returns the volume of the sphere. The Radius data field and the methods GetRadius, SetRadius, and Circumference are inherited from TCircle. The GetRadius and SetRadius methods serve the TSphere object type adequately.

- The TCylinder object type models a solid cylinder, and is declared as follows:

```
TCylinder = OBJECT(TCircle)
  PRIVATE
    Height : REAL;
  PUBLIC
    PROCEDURE SetHeight(H : REAL { input  });
    FUNCTION GetHeight : REAL;
    FUNCTION Area : REAL;
    FUNCTION BaseArea : REAL;
    FUNCTION Volume : REAL;
END;
```

The TCylinder object type is another descendent of TCircle. Because a cylinder has a circular base and a height, the object type modeling it requires radius and height data fields. The Radius data field is inherited from TCircle. The TCylinder object type declares the required Height data field as a private field. The TCylinder object type also declares the methods SetHeight and GetHeight, which set and query, respectively, the values of Height. Like TSphere, the TCylinder object type overrides the inherited Area method to declare its own version. This new version calculates the total surface area as being equal to the lateral area plus twice the base area. The base area is returned by method BaseArea. The volume of the solid cylinder is obtained by method Volume.

- The THollowCylinder object type models a hollow cylinder, and is declared as follows:

```
THollowCylinder = OBJECT(TCylinder)
  PRIVATE
    InnerRadius : REAL;
  PUBLIC
    PROCEDURE SetInnerRadius(R : REAL { input });
    FUNCTION GetInnerRadius : REAL;
    FUNCTION Area : REAL;
    FUNCTION BaseArea : REAL;
END;
```

The THollowCylinder object type, a descendent of TCylinder, presents a refinement of the solid cylinder. The hollow cylinder has two radii and a height. The data fields for the outer radius and the height are inherited from TCylinder. The THollowCylinder object type declares the required InnerRadius data field (again, as a private field), and declares the methods SetInnerRadius and GetInnerradius to set and query, respectively, InnerRadius. The THollowCylinder object type defines its own versions of methods Area and BaseArea. The method Volume is inherited from its parent object type TCylinder, because the volume of a hollow cylinder also is equal to the product of the base area and the cylinder height.

As you look at Listing 1.1, notice the following regarding the various methods:

- All methods are defined outside the object-type declaration. This declaration is mandated by the Borland Pascal compiler.

- Each method is qualified by the name of the owner object type. This qualification tells the Borland Pascal compiler two things:

    First, it tells the Borland Pascal compiler that the routine is part of an object type.

    Second, it associates methods with their respective object types. This association certainly removes the ambiguity of associating methods like Area, BaseArea, and Volume with their proper object types.

- The methods access the data fields without the need for additional qualifiers. The same is said about accessing other methods that belong to the same object-type hierarchy. Traditional implementations of object-oriented Pascal require that you employ the identifier SELF, a reference to the object type itself, to access the various data fields and methods. Thus, for example, Self.Radius, is used to access the Radius data field. The

Object-Oriented Programming with Borland Pascal 7

implementors of Borland Pascal have chosen to simplify matters greatly by placing an invisible WITH Self DO inside each method. This implicit WITH statement absolves you from explicitly qualifying the data fields and methods with SELF.

 When you examine the code in Listing 1.1, you'll notice the keyword INHERITED. This keyword specifies the use of the inherited method without explicitly stating the name of the parent object type. Borland introduced this keyword in Borland Pascal Version 7.0 to be more compatible with Object Pascal.

Listing 1.1. The source code for the PRGMSHAP.PAS program.

```
Program Shapes;

Uses Crt;

TYPE
    TCircle = OBJECT
      PRIVATE
        Radius : REAL;
      PUBLIC
        PROCEDURE SetRadius(R : REAL { input });
        FUNCTION GetRadius : REAL;
        FUNCTION Area : REAL;
        FUNCTION Circumference : REAL;
    END;

    TSphere = OBJECT(TCircle)
        FUNCTION Area : REAL;
        FUNCTION Volume : REAL;
    END;

    TCylinder = OBJECT(TCircle)
      PRIVATE
        Height : REAL;
      PUBLIC
        PROCEDURE SetHeight(H : REAL { input });
        FUNCTION GetHeight : REAL;
        FUNCTION Area : REAL;
        FUNCTION BaseArea : REAL;
        FUNCTION Volume : REAL;
    END;

    THollowCylinder = OBJECT(TCylinder)
      PRIVATE
        InnerRadius : REAL;
      PUBLIC
```

```
            PROCEDURE SetInnerRadius(R : REAL { input  });
            FUNCTION GetInnerRadius : REAL;
            FUNCTION Area : REAL;
            FUNCTION BaseArea : REAL;
        END;

PROCEDURE TCircle.SetRadius(R : REAL { input  });
BEGIN
    Radius := R
END;

FUNCTION TCircle.GetRadius : REAL;
BEGIN
    GetRadius := Radius
END;

FUNCTION TCircle.Area : REAL;
BEGIN
    Area := Pi * SQR(Radius);
END;

FUNCTION TCircle.Circumference : REAL;
BEGIN
    Circumference := 2 * Pi * Radius
END;

FUNCTION TSphere.Area : REAL;
BEGIN
    Area := 4 * INHERITED Area
END;

FUNCTION TSphere.Volume : REAL;
BEGIN
    Volume := 4 / 3 * Pi * SQR(Radius) * Radius
END;

PROCEDURE TCylinder.SetHeight(H : REAL { input  });
BEGIN
    Height := H
END;

FUNCTION TCylinder.GetHeight : REAL;
BEGIN
    GetHeight := Height
END;

FUNCTION TCylinder.Area : REAL;
BEGIN
    Area := 2 * BaseArea + INHERITED Circumference * Height;
END;
```

continues

Listing 1.1. continued

```pascal
FUNCTION TCylinder.BaseArea : REAL;
BEGIN
    BaseArea := INHERITED Area
END;

FUNCTION TCylinder.Volume : REAL;
BEGIN
    Volume := BaseArea * Height
END;

PROCEDURE THollowCylinder.SetInnerRadius(R : REAL { input });
BEGIN
    InnerRadius := R
END;

FUNCTION THollowCylinder.GetInnerRadius : REAL;
BEGIN
    GetInnerRadius := InnerRadius
END;

FUNCTION THollowCylinder.Area : REAL;
BEGIN
    Area := 2 * BaseArea + INHERITED Circumference * Height
END;

FUNCTION THollowCylinder.BaseArea : REAL;
BEGIN
    BaseArea := Pi * (SQR(Radius) - SQR(InnerRadius))
END;

VAR Circle : TCircle;
    Sphere : TSphere;
    Cylinder : TCylinder;
    Hollow : THollowCylinder;
    AKey : CHAR;

BEGIN
    ClrScr;
    Circle.SetRadius(1);
    WRITELN('Circle Radius        = ', Circle.GetRadius);
    WRITELN('Circle Circumference = ', Circle.Circumference);
    WRITELN('Circle Area          = ', Circle.Area);
    WRITELN;
    Sphere.SetRadius(1);
    WRITELN('Sphere Radius        = ', Sphere.GetRadius);
    WRITELN('Sphere Area          = ', Sphere.Area);
    WRITELN('Sphere Volume        = ', Sphere.Volume);
    WRITELN;
    Cylinder.SetRadius(1);
```

```
        Cylinder.SetHeight(10);
        WRITELN('Cylinder Radius     = ', Cylinder.GetRadius);
        WRITELN('Cylinder Height     = ', Cylinder.GetHeight);
        WRITELN('Cylinder Base Area  = ', Cylinder.BaseArea);
        WRITELN('Cylinder Area       = ', Cylinder.Area);
        WRITELN('Cylinder Volume     = ', Cylinder.Volume);
        WRITELN;
        Hollow.SetRadius(1);
        Hollow.SetInnerRadius(0.5);
        Hollow.SetHeight(10);
        WRITELN('Hollow Radius       = ', Hollow.GetRadius);
        WRITELN('Hollow Inner Radius = ', Hollow.GetInnerRadius);
        WRITELN('Hollow Height       = ', Hollow.GetHeight);
        WRITELN('Hollow Base Area    = ', Hollow.BaseArea);
        WRITELN('Hollow Area         = ', Hollow.Area);
        WRITELN('Hollow Volume       = ', Hollow.Volume);
        WRITELN;
        AKey := ReadKey;
END.
```

The program in Listing 1.1. declares four object variables—Circle, Sphere, Cylinder, and Hollow, one for each object type (TCircle, TSphere, TCylinder, and THollowCylinder). The various messages are sent to these objects using the record-like reference syntax. For example, the expression Circle.SetRadius(1) sends a SetRadius message to object variable Circle (an instance of the object type TCircle) with an argument of 1.

Here's the screen output for program PRGMSHAP.PAS:

[BEGIN Output]

```
Circle Radius        = 1.0000000000E+00
Circle Circumference = 6.2831853072E+00
Circle Area          = 3.1415926536E+00

Sphere Radius        = 1.0000000000E+00
Sphere Area          = 1.2566370614E+01
Sphere Volume        = 4.1887902048E+00

Cylinder Radius      = 1.0000000000E+00
Cylinder Height      = 1.0000000000E+01
Cylinder Base Area   = 3.1415926536E+00
Cylinder Area        = 6.9115038379E+01
Cylinder Volume      = 3.1415926536E+01

Hollow Radius        = 1.0000000000E+00
Hollow Inner Radius  = 5.0000000000E-01
Hollow Height        = 1.0000000000E+01
Hollow Base Area     = 2.3561944902E+00
```

```
Hollow Area        = 6.7544242052E+01
Hollow Volume      = 3.1415926536E+01
[END Output]
```

Static vs. Virtual Methods

If you examine the output of Listing 1.1, you see that the volumes of the similarly dimensioned solid and hollow cylinders are the same! This result is an error, because the value for the hollow cylinder must be less than that of the solid cylinder. Where did the program go wrong?

The answer lies with the Volume method the object type THollowCylinder inherits from TCylinder. The TCylinder object type declares the method Volume as follows:

```
FUNCTION TCylinder.Volume : REAL;
BEGIN
    Volume := BaseArea * Height
END;
```

When the Hollow object variable receives the Volume message it invokes the inherited TCylinder.Volume method. If you single-step through the statement that has Hollow.Volume, you'll find that the method TCylinder.Volume calls the TCylinder.BaseArea method and *not* THollowCylinder.BaseArea. This is the source of the error. You might ask: why did the compiler ignore THollowCylinder.BaseArea even though it existed? The answer lies in the types of methods supported by Borland Pascal.

Borland Pascal supports two kinds of methods: *static* and *virtual*. Each type uses a different way of resolving nested method calls.

The compiler resolves nested static methods at compile time. Basically, this is the traditional manner in which Pascal nested-routine calls are resolved. When the program starts executing, the run-time system has all the nested calls figured out and set. Executing the program is a matter of systematically following routine calls. For example, in Listing 1.1 the inherited TCylinder.Volume calls BaseArea. The Borland Pascal compiler resolves this call by invoking TCylinder.BaseArea. This sequence is applied to both Cylinder.Volume and Hollow.Volume messages.

Virtual methods offer a more sophisticated and accurate way to resolve nested method calls. In fact, polymorphism cannot be easily and efficiently achieved without virtual methods. Virtual methods guarantee that the messages sent to object variables are properly interpreted. This occurs because the nested methods are resolved at runtime instead of at compile-time. Thus, if methods `TCylinder.BaseArea` and `THollowCylinder.BaseArea` are made virtual, the program in Listing 1.1 calculates the correct volume for the hollow cylinder. How and why does this happen? The following steps explain the sequence of events:

1. The message `Volume` is sent to object variable `Hollow`.

2. The runtime system attempts to find a `TCylinder.Volume` method. Because none is declared, it looks at the methods of the parent object type, `TCylinder`.

3. A `TCylinder.Volume` method is found. It contains a call to the virtual method `BaseArea`.

4. The runtime system looks at the virtual methods of the original message handler, variable `Hollow`. A matching virtual `BaseArea` method is found and is used with `TCylinder.Volume`.

5. The result of method `TCylinder.Volume` produces the correct response to the `Volume` message.

Making methods virtual therefore causes the runtime system to carry out the additional work of resolving nested method calls in a smarter way.

Now that you've seen the advantages of using virtual methods, let's focus on how to set them up. The basic idea is that the compiler needs to keep track of the virtual methods of the various object types. A special table, called the Virtual Method Table (VMT), is established for this purpose. Borland Pascal requires the following rules to be observed when dealing with virtual methods:

- The object type that uses virtual methods must declare at least one constructor. A *constructor* is a special procedure that performs two major tasks:

  First, the constructor tells the compiler that the compiler needs to set up a VMT table.

  Second, the constructor performs object-variable initialization. Attempting to send a message before invoking the constructor causes your system to hang. An object type is permitted multiple constructors to facilitate various ways of initializing the instances of object types. The typical constructor name is `Init`.

- The keyword `VIRTUAL` is used to declare methods as virtual. It is placed in a separate statement after the routine heading inside the object-type declaration.

Object-Oriented Programming with Borland Pascal 7

> **WARNING:**
>
> The VIRTUAL keyword *must not* appear in the method definition.

- Once a method is declared virtual in an object type, it remains virtual in all the descendants of that object type. A method can start as a static member and can be overridden by a virtual method of a descendant object type. The following diagram illustrates the second case:

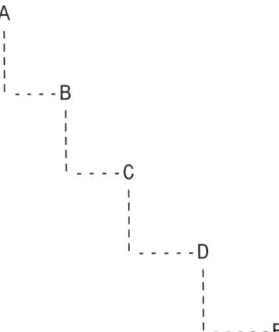

    Assume that all the objects in the hierarchy have a method, M. Object A declares method M as static. Object B declares method M as virtual. Now all objects following B in the hierarchy (C, D, and E) also must declare method M to be virtual (if they use method M).

- Although the parameter list of static methods can be changed by descendant object types, the parameter list of a virtual method cannot.

- A destructor is needed to remove the instance of the object type and eliminate the associated VMT table. A destructor must be called if dynamic allocation was carried out by the object instance.

    Destructors have no parameter lists. Only one destructor should be called for an object type. The typical destructor name is Done.

- The instances of object types with virtual methods are placed in the heap area instead of in the program's data segment.

> The parameter list of static methods can be altered by descendant object types. The parameter list of virtual methods cannot be altered by descendant object types.

OOP Basics

Listing 1.2 uses virtual methods to re-create the geometric object types of Listing 1.1. Notice that the TCylinder and THollowCylinder object types declare their BaseArea methods as virtual. In addition, these object types use a constructor and a destructor. In the case of TCylinder, the constructor SetHeight replaces the procedure SetHeight. Similarly, the constructor SetInnerRadius replaces procedure SetInnerRadius in the THollowCylinder object type. The destructors for these two classes do nothing; their main purpose is to indicate to the runtime system that the corresponding VMT tables no longer are needed. Other changes between Listing 1.1 and Listing 1.2 are as follows:

- The object types are placed in a library unit. This enables various applications to create instances of these object types.

- The data fields of the object types are placed in PRIVATE clauses to make them inaccessible to the object variables of client programs. (You'll find more information about PRIVATE data members and methods in the next chapter.)

Listing 1.2. The source code for the SHAPES library unit.

```
Unit Shapes;

INTERFACE

TYPE
    TCircle = OBJECT
      PRIVATE
        Radius : REAL;
      PUBLIC
        PROCEDURE SetRadius(R : REAL { input });
        FUNCTION GetRadius : REAL;
        FUNCTION Area : REAL;
        FUNCTION Circumference : REAL;
    END;

    TSphere = OBJECT(TCircle)
        FUNCTION Area : REAL;
        FUNCTION Volume : REAL;
    END;

    TCylinder = OBJECT(TCircle)
      PRIVATE
        Height : REAL;
      PUBLIC
        CONSTRUCTOR SetHeight(H : REAL { input });
```

continues

Listing 1.2. continued

```
      DESTRUCTOR Done;
      FUNCTION GetHeight : REAL;
      FUNCTION Area : REAL;
      FUNCTION BaseArea : REAL; VIRTUAL;
      FUNCTION Volume : REAL;
    END;

    THollowCylinder = OBJECT(TCylinder)
      PRIVATE
        InnerRadius : REAL;
      PUBLIC
        CONSTRUCTOR SetInnerRadius(R : REAL { input });
        DESTRUCTOR Done;
        FUNCTION GetInnerRadius : REAL;
        FUNCTION Area : REAL;
        FUNCTION BaseArea : REAL; VIRTUAL;
    END;

IMPLEMENTATION

PROCEDURE TCircle.SetRadius(R : REAL { input });
BEGIN
    Radius := R
END;

FUNCTION TCircle.GetRadius : REAL;
BEGIN
    GetRadius := Radius
END;

FUNCTION TCircle.Area : REAL;
BEGIN
    Area := Pi * SQR(Radius);
END;

FUNCTION TCircle.Circumference : REAL;
BEGIN
    Circumference := 2 * Pi * Radius
END;

FUNCTION TSphere.Area : REAL;
BEGIN
    Area := 4 * INHERITED Area
END;

FUNCTION TSphere.Volume : REAL;
BEGIN
    Volume := 4 / 3 * Pi * SQR(Radius) * Radius
END;
```

OOP Basics

```
CONSTRUCTOR TCylinder.SetHeight(H : REAL { input });
BEGIN
    Height := H
END;

DESTRUCTOR TCylinder.Done;
BEGIN
END;

FUNCTION TCylinder.GetHeight : REAL;
BEGIN
    GetHeight := Height
END;

FUNCTION TCylinder.Area : REAL;
BEGIN
    Area := INHERITED Area + INHERITED Circumference * Height;
END;

FUNCTION TCylinder.BaseArea : REAL;
BEGIN
    BaseArea := INHERITED Area
END;

FUNCTION TCylinder.Volume : REAL;
BEGIN
    Volume := BaseArea * Height
END;

CONSTRUCTOR THollowCylinder.SetInnerRadius(R : REAL { input });
BEGIN
    InnerRadius := R
END;

DESTRUCTOR THollowCylinder.Done;
BEGIN
END;

FUNCTION THollowCylinder.GetInnerRadius : REAL;
BEGIN
    GetInnerRadius := InnerRadius
END;

FUNCTION THollowCylinder.Area : REAL;
BEGIN
    Area := BaseArea + INHERITED Circumference * Height
END;

FUNCTION THollowCylinder.BaseArea : REAL;
BEGIN
```

continues

Listing 1.2. continued

```
    BaseArea := Pi * (SQR(Radius) - SQR(InnerRadius))
END;

END.
```

Listing 1.3. shows TSSHAPE1.PAS, a test program for the SHAPES.PAS library unit. The program resembles the main program body of Listing 1.1—notice that Done messages are sent to the Cylinder and Hollow object variables.

Listing 1.3. The source code for the test program TSSHAPE1.PAS.

```
Program TestShapes;

Uses Crt, Shapes;

VAR Circle : TCircle;
    Sphere : TSphere;
    Cylinder : TCylinder;
    Hollow : THollowCylinder;
    AKey : CHAR;

BEGIN
    ClrScr;
    Circle.SetRadius(1);
    WRITELN('Circle Radius        = ', Circle.GetRadius);
    WRITELN('Circle Circumference = ', Circle.Circumference);
    WRITELN('Circle Area          = ', Circle.Area);
    WRITELN;
    Sphere.SetRadius(1);
    WRITELN('Sphere Radius        = ', Sphere.GetRadius);
    WRITELN('Sphere Area          = ', Sphere.Area);
    WRITELN('Sphere Volume        = ', Sphere.Volume);
    WRITELN;
    Cylinder.SetRadius(1);
    Cylinder.SetHeight(10);
    WRITELN('Cylinder Radius      = ', Cylinder.GetRadius);
    WRITELN('Cylinder Height      = ', Cylinder.GetHeight);
    WRITELN('Cylinder Base Area   = ', Cylinder.BaseArea);
    WRITELN('Cylinder Area        = ', Cylinder.Area);
    WRITELN('Cylinder Volume      = ', Cylinder.Volume);
    WRITELN;
    Cylinder.Done;
    Hollow.SetRadius(1);
    Hollow.SetInnerRadius(0.5);
```

OOP Basics

```
        Hollow.SetHeight(10);
        WRITELN('Hollow Radius        = ', Hollow.GetRadius);
        WRITELN('Hollow Inner Radius  = ', Hollow.GetInnerRadius);
        WRITELN('Hollow Height        = ', Hollow.GetHeight);
        WRITELN('Hollow Base Area     = ', Hollow.BaseArea);
        WRITELN('Hollow Area          = ', Hollow.Area);
        WRITELN('Hollow Volume        = ', Hollow.Volume);
        WRITELN;
        Hollow.Done;
        AKey := ReadKey;
END.
```

Here's the output generated by the program in Listing 1.3:

```
[BEGIN Output]
Circle Radius          =   1.0000000000E+00
Circle Circumference   =   6.2831853072E+00
Circle Area            =   3.1415926536E+00

Sphere Radius          =   1.0000000000E+00
Sphere Area            =   1.2566370614E+01
Sphere Volume          =   4.1887902048E+00

Cylinder Radius        =   1.0000000000E+00
Cylinder Height        =   1.0000000000E+01
Cylinder Base Area     =   3.1415926536E+00
Cylinder Area          =   6.5973445725E+01
Cylinder Volume        =   3.1415926536E+01

Hollow Radius          =   1.0000000000E+00
Hollow Inner Radius    =   5.0000000000E-01
Hollow Height          =   1.0000000000E+01
Hollow Base Area       =   2.3561944902E+00
Hollow Area            =   6.5188047562E+01
Hollow Volume          =   2.3561944902E+01
[END Output]
```

Dynamic Objects

You can use pointers to object types to create dynamic instances of objects, called *dynamic objects*. The New and Dispose intrinsics (that is, predefined or built-in routines) are used for this purpose. Borland Pascal has extended the syntax of the New and Dispose statements to include calls to constructors and destructors. Here is the general form for the extended New syntax:

```
New(objectPointer, constructorName(<arguments_list>));
```

This has the same effect as:

```
New(objectPointer);
objectPointer^.constructorName(<argument_list>);
```

Here is the general form for the extended `Dispose` syntax:

```
Dispose(objectPointer, destructorName);
```

This replaces the following two statements:

```
objectPointer^.destructorName;
Dispose(objectPointer);
```

Listing 1.4 contains a version of Listing 1.3 that uses pointers to object types instead of to object variables. The dynamic objects for the `TCircle` and `TSphere` object types are created and removed using the standard-syntax `New` and `Dispose` statements. The dynamic objects for the `TCylinder` and `THollowCylinder` use the extended syntax with the `New` and `Dispose` statements.

Listing 1.4. The TSSHAPE2.PAS test program, which uses dynamic objects.

```
Program TestShapes2;

Uses Crt, Shapes;

VAR Circle : ^TCircle;
    Sphere : ^TSphere;
    Cylinder : ^TCylinder;
    Hollow : ^THollowCylinder;
    AKey : CHAR;

BEGIN
    ClrScr;
    New(Circle);
    Circle^.SetRadius(1);
    WRITELN('Circle Radius        = ', Circle^.GetRadius);
    WRITELN('Circle Circumference = ', Circle^.Circumference);
    WRITELN('Circle Area          = ', Circle^.Area);
    WRITELN;
    Dispose(Circle);
    New(Sphere);
    Sphere^.SetRadius(1);
    WRITELN('Sphere Radius        = ', Sphere^.GetRadius);
    WRITELN('Sphere Area          = ', Sphere^.Area);
    WRITELN('Sphere Volume        = ', Sphere^.Volume);
    WRITELN;
```

OOP Basics

```
        Dispose(Sphere);
        New(Cylinder, SetHeight(10));
        Cylinder^.SetRadius(1);
        WRITELN('Cylinder Radius      = ', Cylinder^.GetRadius);
        WRITELN('Cylinder Height      = ', Cylinder^.GetHeight);
        WRITELN('Cylinder Base Area   = ', Cylinder^.BaseArea);
        WRITELN('Cylinder Area        = ', Cylinder^.Area);
        WRITELN('Cylinder Volume      = ', Cylinder^.Volume);
        WRITELN;
        Dispose(Cylinder, Done);
        New(Hollow, SetInnerRadius(0.5));
        Hollow^.SetRadius(1);
        Hollow^.SetHeight(10);
        WRITELN('Hollow Radius        = ', Hollow^.GetRadius);
        WRITELN('Hollow Inner Radius  = ', Hollow^.GetInnerRadius);
        WRITELN('Hollow Height        = ', Hollow^.GetHeight);
        WRITELN('Hollow Base Area     = ', Hollow^.BaseArea);
        WRITELN('Hollow Area          = ', Hollow^.Area);
        WRITELN('Hollow Volume        = ', Hollow^.Volume);
        WRITELN;
        Dispose(Hollow, Done);
        AKey := ReadKey;
END.
```

Here's the output generated by the program in Listing 1.4:

```
[BEGIN Output]
Circle Radius         =  1.0000000000E+00
Circle Circumference  =  6.2831853072E+00
Circle Area           =  3.1415926536E+00

Sphere Radius         =  1.0000000000E+00
Sphere Area           =  1.2566370614E+01
Sphere Volume         =  4.1887902048E+00

Cylinder Radius       =  1.0000000000E+00
Cylinder Height       =  1.0000000000E+01
Cylinder Base Area    =  3.1415926536E+00
Cylinder Area         =  6.5973445725E+01
Cylinder Volume       =  3.1415926536E+01

Hollow Radius         =  1.0000000000E+00
Hollow Inner Radius   =  5.0000000000E-01
Hollow Height         =  1.0000000000E+01
Hollow Base Area      =  2.3561944902E+00
Hollow Area           =  6.5188047562E+01
Hollow Volume         =  2.3561944902E+01
[END Output]
```

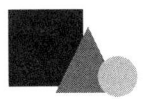

Summary

This chapter introduced you to the basics of object-oriented programming (OOP) and the OOP features of Borland Pascal. You learned about the basic concepts of OOP:

- *Classes* encapsulate the data fields and operations of objects.

- *Objects* are instances of classes. The *state* of an object is defined by the combination of values in the *data fields* of that object. Objects interact with each other by sending *messages*.

- *Methods* manipulate an object by changing the state of that object. When an object receives a message, the object invokes the proper method to respond to that message

- *Inheritance* allows the creation of new classes from existing ones. Inheritance enables the development of a class *hierarchy*. Each descendant class refines the operations and characteristics of its parent class. Descendant classes inherit the data fields and methods of the ancestor classes. In addition, descendant classes define new methods and may also define new data fields, when needed.

- Descendant classes also can *override* an inherited method by declaring their own versions of methods. The ability to override inherited methods enables descendent classes to respond properly to messages.

- *Polymorphism* enables the instances of various classes in a hierarchy to correctly respond to the same message—each instance in its own way.

    Polymorphic behavior of a class hierarchy supports a level of abstraction in dealing with messages. Polymorphism enables the instances of various classes in a hierarchy to correctly respond to the same message—each instance in its own way.

- Borland Pascal builds on Object Pascal, which was developed by Apple Computer, Inc. and Nicklaus Wirth. The Borland Pascal object types encapsulate both data fields and the declaration of special functions and procedures. These routines support the operations of an object type.

    The Borland Pascal implementation extends the OOP syntax by supporting *private* and *public* data fields and methods. In addition, object types include special routines called *constructors* and *destructors*, which create and remove instances of an object type. These routines are intended for use with object types that declare *virtual methods*. Virtual methods play a vital role in supporting polymorphic behavior in objects.

Chapter 2

Constructors and Destructors

Constructors create instances of an object type, especially instances that use virtual methods. Destructors are responsible for removing these instances and regaining any dynamic memory. Understanding how constructors and destructors work is important, especially when you design a complex hierarchy of object types. In this chapter you'll learn about the following topics:

- The default constructor
- The multiconstructor object type
- The copy constructor

- The invocation of constructors of parent object types
- Virtual destructors
- Handling constructor errors

The Default Constructor

The *default constructor* is a term borrowed from C++ to indicate a constructor with no parameter list. Such constructors are common in initializing empty instances of an object type. Examples of this kind of object type include such data structures as stacks, lists, and trees. The default constructor essentially sets up the instance but does not insert any data.

Let's look at a simple example. Listing 2.1 shows the program STACK1.PAS, which manipulates the stack of long integers. STACK1.PAS implements dynamic stacks of long integers using a linked list. The program declares the `StackRec` record, the `StackPtr` pointer type, and the `TStack` object type. The types `StackRec` and `StackPtr` manage the nodes of the dynamic linked list.

The object type `TStack` declares the constructor `Init`, the destructor `Done`, three private data fields, and the following set of methods:

- The Boolean function `GetAllocateError`, which returns True if there is an error in pushing a data item onto the stack. Otherwise, the function returns False.

- The Boolean function `IsEmpty`, which returns True if the stack is empty. Otherwise, the function returns False.

- The virtual procedure `Push`, which pushes a long integer onto the stack. The procedure actually inserts the new data item into the linked list that emulates the stack.

- The virtual Boolean function `Pop`, which returns True when it pops a long integer off the stack. The reference parameter X passes the popped value. If the stack is empty, the function returns False.

- The virtual procedure `Clear`, which empties the stack.

I declare the methods `Push`, `Pop`, and `Clear` as virtual to justify the use of a constructor and destructor. These methods represent operations that work on a specific storage scheme. Should you create a descendant of `TStack`, you may need to define a new set of methods `Push`, `Pop`, and `Clear`.

Constructors and Destructors

The `TStack` object type declares the data fields `Top`, `Height`, and `AllocateError`. The data field `Top` is the pointer to the top of the stack. The data field `Height` stores the current number of items in the stack. The Boolean data field `AllocateError` stores the status of dynamic allocation error.

The constructor `Init` is a default constructor: it has no parameters. As such, `Init` merely initializes the data fields of the instance. The method `Push` is the one responsible for pushing the data onto the stack.

The main section of the program declares the dynamic stack `S`. The program creates the instance `S` by invoking the default constructor `Init`. The program uses the `WHILE` loop and the `Push` method to push a few integers onto the dynamic stack. The program uses the `Pop` method in a `WHILE` loop to pop numbers off the stack.

> The far function `HeapErrorHandler` returns the value of 1. This value causes the runtime system to assign the pointer `NIL` to a pointer in a `New` or a `GetMem` statement when dynamic allocation fails. This type of assignment prevents runtime errors that stop the program. To activate the `HeapErrorHandler`, the program assigns the address of the function to the predefined pointer `HeapError`.

Listing 2.1. The program STACK1.PAS, which manipulates the stack of long integers.

```
Program Stack;

{
  This program manipulates the stack of long integers.
}

{$M 8192, 0, 655350}

Uses Crt;

TYPE
    StackPtr = ^StackRec;
    { stack node type }
    StackRec = RECORD
        DataItem : LONGINT;
        NextLink : StackPtr
    END;

    { object type that models stack of long integers }
```

continues

Listing 2.1. continued

```
    TStack = OBJECT
        CONSTRUCTOR Init;
        DESTRUCTOR Done; VIRTUAL;
        FUNCTION GetAllocateError : BOOLEAN;
        FUNCTION IsEmpty : BOOLEAN;
        PROCEDURE Push(X : LONGINT { input  }); VIRTUAL;
        FUNCTION Pop(VAR X : LONGINT { input  }) : BOOLEAN; VIRTUAL;
        PROCEDURE Clear; VIRTUAL;
      PRIVATE
        Top            : StackPtr; { pointer to the top of the stack }
        Height         : WORD;     { height of stack                 }
        AllocateError  : BOOLEAN;  { dynamic allocation error        }
    END;

{---------------------------------------- HeapErrorHandler ----------}

FUNCTION HeapErrorHandler(Size : WORD { input  }) : INTEGER; FAR;

BEGIN
    HeapErrorHandler := 1
END;

{------------------------------------------------ Init ------------}

CONSTRUCTOR TStack.Init;
{ construct instance of TStack }
BEGIN
    { initialize fields of object type }
    Height := 0;
    AllocateError := FALSE;
    Top := NIL
END;

{------------------------------------------------ Done ------------}

DESTRUCTOR TStack.Done;
{ remove instance of TStack }
BEGIN
    Clear
END;

{------------------------------------------------ IsEmpty ------------}

FUNCTION TStack.IsEmpty : BOOLEAN;
{ return TRUE if stack is empty. Otherwise returns FALSE. }
BEGIN
    IsEmpty := Height = 0
END;

{-------------------------------------- GetAllocateError ------------}
```

Constructors and Destructors

```
FUNCTION TStack.GetAllocateError : BOOLEAN;
{ returns the status of dynamic allocation for the
last Pop message sent to the object. }
BEGIN
    GetAllocateError := AllocateError
END;


{---------------------------------------------- Push -----------}

PROCEDURE TStack.Push(X : LONGINT { input  });

{ pushes the data X onto the stack. }

VAR p : StackPtr;

BEGIN
    AllocateError := FALSE;
    IF Top <> NIL THEN BEGIN
        New(p); { allocate new stack element }
        IF p = NIL THEN BEGIN
            AllocateError := TRUE;
            Exit;
        END;
        p^.DataItem := X;
        p^.NextLink := Top;
        Top := p
    END
    ELSE BEGIN
        New(Top);
        IF Top = NIL THEN BEGIN
            AllocateError := TRUE;
            Exit;
        END;
        Top^.DataItem := X;
        Top^.NextLink := NIL
    END;
    INC(Height)
END;


{---------------------------------------------- Pop -----------}

FUNCTION TStack.Pop(VAR X : LONGINT { input  }) : BOOLEAN;

{ pops the top of the stack and returns a Boolean value. }

VAR p : StackPtr;

BEGIN
```

continues

Listing 2.1. continued

```
    IF Height > 0 THEN BEGIN
        X := Top^.DataItem;
        p := Top;
        Top := Top^.NextLink;
        Dispose(p); { deallocate stack node }
        DEC(Height);
        Pop := TRUE { return function value }
    END
    ELSE
        Pop := FALSE { return function value }
END;

{------------------------------------------------- Clear ------------}

PROCEDURE TStack.Clear;

{ clears the stack object. }

VAR x : LONGINT;

BEGIN
    WHILE Pop(x) DO
        { do nothing };
END;

VAR L : LONGINT;
    S : TStack;
    AKey : Char;
    NoError : BOOLEAN;

BEGIN
    HeapError := @HeapErrorHandler;
    ClrScr;
    { construct the stack object variable }
    S.Init;
    L := 1;
    NoError := TRUE;
    { loop to push data into the stack }
    WHILE (L <= 512) AND NoError DO BEGIN
      WRITELN('Pushing ', L:3, ' in the stack');
      { push data in stack }
      S.Push(L);
      { update dynamic allocation error status }
      NoError := NOT S.GetAllocateError;
      IF NoError THEN
         L := 2 * L
      ELSE BEGIN
```

Constructors and Destructors

```
        WRITELN;
        WRITELN('Error in allocating stack space');
        WRITELN;
      END;
    END;
    WRITELN;
    WRITE('Press any key to pop the stack');
    AKey := ReadKey;
    WRITELN; WRITELN;
    { loop to pop off data from the stack }
    WHILE S.Pop(L) DO
      WRITELN('Popping off ', L:3, ' from the stack');
    WRITELN;
    WRITE('Press any key to end the program');
    AKey := ReadKey;
    { remove the TStack instance }
    S.Done;
END.
```

Here's a sample output for the program in Listing 2.1:

```
[BEGIN OUTPUT]
Pushing   1 in the stack
Pushing   2 in the stack
Pushing   4 in the stack
Pushing   8 in the stack
Pushing  16 in the stack
Pushing  32 in the stack
Pushing  64 in the stack
Pushing 128 in the stack
Pushing 256 in the stack
Pushing 512 in the stack

Press any key to pop the stack

Popping off 512 from the stack
Popping off 256 from the stack
Popping off 128 from the stack
Popping off  64 from the stack
Popping off  32 from the stack
Popping off  16 from the stack
Popping off   8 from the stack
Popping off   4 from the stack
Popping off   2 from the stack
Popping off   1 from the stack

Press any key to end the program
[END OUTPUT]
```

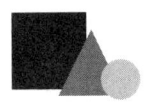

Multiconstructor Object Types

Borland Pascal allows you to use multiple constructors in an object type. These constructors allow you to:

- Fine-tune the creation of the instances
- Use alternate methods for creating the instances of an object type

Let's look at an example. Listing 2.2 shows the program ARRAY1.PAS, which creates dynamic arrays of REALs using multiple constructors. ARRAY1.PAS declares the object type TRealArray to model dynamic arrays of REALs. The object type declares three constructors: Init, Init2, and Init3. Each constructor fine-tunes the creation of an instance; more about these constructors later. The TRealArray object type also declares a destructor and the following methods:

- The function GetSize, which returns the number of array elements in an instance of TRealArray.
- The Boolean function GetAllocateError, which returns True if an error occurs in the dynamic allocation of the array. Otherwise, the function returns False.
- The Boolean function Store, which saves a floating-point number in array element number Index. (The index of the first array element is 0.) The function returns True and stores the argument of parameter X in the array when the argument of parameter Index is valid. If the argument of parameter Index is not valid, the function returns False and no data is stored in the array.
- The Boolean function Recall, which retrieves a floating-point number from the array element number Index. The function returns True and passes the fetched value through reference parameter X when the argument of parameter Index is valid. When the argument of parameter Index is not valid, the function returns False and no data is recalled from the array.

The TRealArray object type declares the data fields DataPtr, Size, and AllocateError. The data field DataPtr is the pointer to the dynamic array. The data field Size stores the number of array elements. The data field AllocateError stores the error status of the dynamic allocation.

The three constructors of the object type (Init, Init2, and Init3) vary in the number of parameters:

- The constructor Init has the single parameter ArraySize. As the name suggests, this parameter specifies the size of the dynamic array. The instance of TRealArray stores the argument of ArraySize in the data field Size. You can create an array with a default size using the DEFAULT_SIZE constant. You also can create a default-size array by passing the argument 0 to the constructor. The constructor assigns the constant DEFAULT_SIZE to the data field Size if the latter is 0 (after receiving a copy of the value in parameter ArraySize). The constructor Init uses a FOR loop to assign zeros to the elements of the dynamic array.

- The constructor Init2 has two parameters: ArraySize and FillVal. The first parameter plays the same role as in constructor Init. The parameter FillVal specifies the value used to initialize every element of the dynamic array. The program declares the constant DEFAULT_FILLVAL to provide a default fill value.

  The statements in constructor Init2 are similar to the ones in constructor Init. The only difference is that the FOR loop in constructor Init2 assigns FillVal to every array element.

- The constructor Init3 adds another level of sophistication in initializing an array with data patterns. The program declares the enumerated data type TFillPattern to list the various kinds of data fill patterns. The enumerated values of TFillPattern are as follows:

  The enumSameVal value, which specifies that the array elements are assigned the same value

  The enumIncVal value, which indicates that the array elements are assigned a sequence of numbers that change in increments

  The enumScaleVal value, which specifies that the array elements are assigned a sequence of numbers that change by a multiplicative factor

  The enumRandVal value, which indicates that the array elements are assigned a sequence of random numbers

The parameters FillVal and ChangeVal provide the values used in the patterns of initializations. The constructor uses the pattern specified by the argument for the parameter FillPatrn. In the case of the enumerated value enumSameVal, the constructor assigns the value of the FillVal parameter to the array elements. This action produces the same effect as the constructor Init2.

In the case of the enumerated value enumIncVal, the parameter FillVal provides the base value for the assigned numbers. The parameter ChangeVal supplies the increments in the sequence of assigned numbers. Thus, the constructor assigns

FillVar to the first array element, FillVal + ChangeVal to the second element, FillVal + 2 * ChangeVal to the third element, and so on.

In the case of the enumerated value enumScaleVal, the parameter FillVal provides the base value for the assigned numbers. The parameter ChangeVal supplies the factor in the sequence of assigned numbers. Thus, the constructor assigns FillVar to the first array element, FillVal * ChangeVal to the second element, FillVal * ChangeVal * ChangeVal to the third element, and so on.

In the case of the enumerated value enumRandVal, the parameter FillVal specifies the minimum random value generated. The ChangeVal parameter designates the range of random numbers. Thus, the random numbers generated are in the range of FillVal to FillVal + ChangeVal - 1.

The ARRAY1.PAS in Figure 2.2 program declares the constants DEFAULT_CHANGEVAL and DEFAULT_FILL_PATTERN, which provide default values for the ChangeVal and FillPatrn parameters.

The main section of the program declares five instances of TRealArray, Ar1 to Ar5. The program creates these instances, as follows:

1. The program creates the Ar1 instance using the constructor Init. This instance has ten elements, all of which are set to 0.

2. The program creates the Ar2 instance using constructor Init2. This instance has ten elements which are initialized to 2.5.

3. The program creates the Ar3 instance using constructor Init3. This instance has ten elements, which are initialized using an increment pattern. The pattern starts at 1 and increases the assigned value to every other element by 1.

4. The program creates the Ar4 instance using constructor Init3. This instance has ten elements which are initialized using a multiplicative factor pattern. The pattern starts at 1 and multiplies the assigned value to every other element by 2.

5. The program creates the Ar5 instance using constructor Init3. This instance has ten elements, which are initialized with random numbers (using the enumerated value enumRandVal). The random numbers range from 0 to 999.

Once the ARRAY1.PAS program creates the various instances of TRealArray, it uses the procedure ShowArray to display the initialized instances. Finally, the program invokes the destructor on each instance to remove it.

Listing 2.2. The program ARRAY1.PAS, which creates dynamic arrays of REALS using one multiple constructor.

```
Program Array1;

{
  This program creates dynamic arrays of REALs using a variety
  of constructors.
}

{$X+,R-}
{$M 8192, 0, 655350}

Uses Crt;

TYPE
  TFillPattern = ( enumSameVal,   { same value in every element }
                   enumIncVal,    { increasing/decreasing values }
                   enumScaleVal,  { scaled up/down values }
                   enumRandVal    { assign random numbers }
                 );
  OneArray = ARRAY[0..0] OF REAL;
  ArrayPtr = ^OneArray;

  TRealArray = OBJECT
    CONSTRUCTOR Init(ArraySize : WORD { input });
    CONSTRUCTOR Init2(ArraySize : WORD; { input }
                      FillVal   : REAL  { input });
    CONSTRUCTOR Init3(ArraySize : WORD;          { input }
                      FillVal,                   { input }
                      ChangeVal : REAL;          { input }
                      FillPatrn : TFillPattern { input });
    DESTRUCTOR Done; VIRTUAL;

    FUNCTION GetSize : WORD;
    FUNCTION GetAllocateError : BOOLEAN;
    FUNCTION Store(X     : REAL; { input }
                   Index : WORD  { input }) : BOOLEAN;
    FUNCTION Recall(VAR X   : REAL; { output }
                    Index : WORD  { input }) : BOOLEAN;
  PRIVATE
    DataPtr : ArrayPtr;
    Size : WORD;
    AllocateError : BOOLEAN;
  END;

CONST DEFAULT_SIZE = 10;
      DEFAULT_FILLVAL = 1;
      DEFAULT_CHANGEVAL = 1;
      DEFAULT_FILL_PATTERN : TFillPattern = enumSameVal;
```

continues

Listing 2.2. continued

```pascal
{---------------------------------- HeapErrorHandler ----------}

FUNCTION HeapErrorHandler(Size : WORD { input }) : INTEGER; FAR;

BEGIN
    HeapErrorHandler := 1
END;

{------------------------------------------- Init -----------}

CONSTRUCTOR TRealArray.Init(ArraySize : WORD { input });
{ construct instance of TRealArray }

VAR i : WORD;

BEGIN
  Size := ArraySize;
  IF Size = 0 THEN
    Size := DEFAULT_SIZE;
  GetMem(DataPtr, Size * SizeOf(REAL));
  AllocateError := DataPtr = NIL;
  IF NOT AllocateError THEN
    FOR i := 0 TO Size - 1 DO
      DataPtr^[i] := 0

END;

{---------------------------------------------- Init2 -----------}

CONSTRUCTOR TRealArray.Init2(ArraySize : WORD; { input }
                             FillVal   : REAL  { input });
{ construct instance of TRealArray and assign a fill value
  to the elements of the array                              }

VAR i : WORD;

BEGIN
  Size := ArraySize;
  IF Size = 0 THEN
    Size := DEFAULT_SIZE;
  GetMem(DataPtr, Size * SizeOf(REAL));
  AllocateError := DataPtr = NIL;
  { allocation successful? }
  IF NOT AllocateError THEN
    FOR i := 0 TO Size - 1 DO
      DataPtr^[i] := FillVal
END;

{---------------------------------------------- Init3 -----------}
```

Constructors and Destructors   2

```
CONSTRUCTOR TRealArray.Init3(
                    ArraySize : WORD;       { input }
                    FillVal,                { input }
                    ChangeVal : REAL;       { input }
                    FillPatrn : TFillPattern { input });
{ construct instance of TRealArray and assign values in the
  specified pattern                                        }

VAR i : WORD;
    x : REAL;

BEGIN
  Size := ArraySize;
  IF Size = 0 THEN
    Size := DEFAULT_SIZE;
  IF ChangeVal = 0 THEN
    ChangeVal := DEFAULT_CHANGEVAL;
  GetMem(DataPtr, Size * SizeOf(REAL));
  AllocateError := DataPtr = NIL;
  { allocation successful? }
  IF NOT AllocateError THEN
    CASE FillPatrn OF
      enumSameVal :
                  FOR i := 0 TO Size - 1 DO
                    DataPtr^[i] := FillVal;
      enumIncVal :
                  BEGIN
                    x := FillVal;
                    FOR i := 0 TO Size - 1 DO BEGIN
                      DataPtr^[i] := x;
                      x := ChangeVal + x;
                    END;
                  END;
      enumScaleVal :
                  BEGIN
                    x := FillVal;
                    FOR i := 0 TO Size - 1 DO BEGIN
                      DataPtr^[i] := x;
                      x := ChangeVal * x;
                    END;
                  END;
      enumRandVal :
                  BEGIN
                    Randomize;
                    FOR i := 0 TO Size - 1 DO
                      DataPtr^[i] := FillVal +
                              Random(Trunc(ChangeVal));
                  END;
    END;
END;
```

continues

Listing 2.2. continued

```
{------------------------------------------ Done ------------}

DESTRUCTOR TRealArray.Done;
{ remove instance of TRealArray }
BEGIN
  IF DataPtr <> NIL THEN
    FreeMem(DataPtr, Size * SizeOf(REAL))
END;

{------------------------------------------ GetSize ------------}

FUNCTION TRealArray.GetSize : WORD;
{ return the size of the array }
BEGIN
  GetSize := Size
END;

{------------------------------------ GetAllocateError ------------}

FUNCTION TRealArray.GetAllocateError : BOOLEAN;
{ get the allocation error status }
BEGIN
  GetAllocateError := AllocateError
END;

{------------------------------------------ Store ------------}

FUNCTION TRealArray.Store(X     : REAL; { input }
                         Index : WORD  { input }) : BOOLEAN;
{ store an array element }
BEGIN
  IF Index < Size THEN BEGIN
    DataPtr^[Index] := X;
    Store := TRUE;
  END
  ELSE
    Store := FALSE;
END;

{------------------------------------------ Recall ------------}

FUNCTION TRealArray.Recall(VAR X    : REAL; { output }
                           Index : WORD  { input }) : BOOLEAN;
{ recall the contents of an array element }
BEGIN
  IF Index < Size THEN BEGIN
    X := DataPtr^[Index];
    Recall := TRUE;
  END
```

```
    ELSE
       Recall := FALSE;
END;

{*************************** MAIN *****************************}

VAR Ar1, Ar2, Ar3, Ar4, Ar5 : TRealArray;

PROCEDURE ShowArray(    NewScrn : BOOLEAN;   { input }
                        Msg     : STRING;    { input }
                    VAR A       : TRealArray { input });

VAR i : WORD;
    x : REAL;

BEGIN
  IF NewScrn THEN ClrScr;
  WRITELN(Msg); WRITELN;
  FOR i := 0 TO A.GetSize - 1 DO
    IF A.Recall(x, i) THEN
      WRITELN(x)
    ELSE
      WRITELN('Index ', i, ' is out of range');
END;

PROCEDURE PressKey;
BEGIN
   WRITELN;
   WRITE('Press any key...');
   ReadKey;
END;

BEGIN
    HeapError := @HeapErrorHandler;
   { create instances of TRealArray }
   Ar1.Init(10);
   Ar2.Init2(10, 2.5);
   Ar3.Init3(10, 1, 1, enumIncVal);
   Ar4.Init3(10, 1, 2, enumScaleVal);
   Ar5.Init3(10, 0, 1000, enumRandVal);

   { display arrays }
   ShowArray(TRUE, 'Array 1 contains the following data:', Ar1);
   PressKey;
   ShowArray(TRUE, 'Array 2 contains the following data:', Ar2);
   PressKey;
   ShowArray(TRUE, 'Array 3 contains the following data:', Ar3);
   PressKey;
   ShowArray(TRUE, 'Array 4 contains the following data:', Ar4);
   PressKey;
```

continues

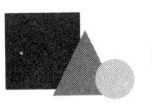

Listing 2.2. continued

```
    ShowArray(TRUE, 'Array 5 contains the following data:', Ar5);
    PressKey;

    { remove instances of TRealArray }
    Ar1.Done;
    Ar2.Done;
    Ar3.Done;
    Ar4.Done;
    Ar5.Done;
END.
```

Here's a sample output for the program in Listing 2.2:

```
[BEGIN OUTPUT]
Array 1 contains the following data:

 0.0000000000E+00
 0.0000000000E+00
 0.0000000000E+00
 0.0000000000E+00
 0.0000000000E+00
 0.0000000000E+00
 0.0000000000E+00
 0.0000000000E+00
 0.0000000000E+00
 0.0000000000E+00

Press any key...
```

The screen clears

```
Array 2 contains the following data:

 2.5000000000E+00
 2.5000000000E+00
 2.5000000000E+00
 2.5000000000E+00
 2.5000000000E+00
 2.5000000000E+00
 2.5000000000E+00
 2.5000000000E+00
 2.5000000000E+00
 2.5000000000E+00

Press any key...
```

Constructors and Destructors

The screen clears

```
Array 3 contains the following data:

   1.0000000000E+00
   2.0000000000E+00
   3.0000000000E+00
   4.0000000000E+00
   5.0000000000E+00
   6.0000000000E+00
   7.0000000000E+00
   8.0000000000E+00
   9.0000000000E+00
   1.0000000000E+01

Press any key...
```

The screen clears

```
Array 4 contains the following data:

   1.0000000000E+00
   2.0000000000E+00
   4.0000000000E+00
   8.0000000000E+00
   1.6000000000E+01
   3.2000000000E+01
   6.4000000000E+01
   1.2800000000E+02
   2.5600000000E+02
   5.1200000000E+02

Press any key...
```

The screen clears

```
Array 5 contains the following data:

   7.9200000000E+02
   3.4400000000E+02
   4.0000000000E+02
   1.4300000000E+02
   3.0300000000E+02
   1.8400000000E+02
   6.1600000000E+02
   1.9200000000E+02
   7.9400000000E+02
   3.1000000000E+01

Press any key...
[END OUTPUT]
```

The Copy Constructor

The constructors presented in Listing 2.2 create instances of an array by specifying various parameters, such as size, fill value, and fill pattern. There are many cases when you need to create a new instance as a duplicate of an existing instance. You might use the copy as a kind of backup within the program, or you may need to create an instance of comparable size and specifications, where the copied data isn't important. In the latter case, the source instance becomes a kind of mold for creating other instances.

The copy constructor performs the task of creating the instances of an object type using existing instances. Naturally, the object type needs at least one other constructor to create instances from scratch, so to speak.

The process of copying instances involves duplicating both the data structures and the data—in other words, duplicating both form and content. I recommend that you employ a separate method to copy instances. You then can use the instance-duplicator method and the copy constructor together to create new instances directly from existing instances.

Let's look at an example that puts the above techniques to work. Listing 2.3 shows the program ARRAY2.PAS, which uses the copy constructor to duplicate instances of an object type. The program in Listing 2.3 has a number of elements in common with the program in Listing 2.2.

The object type TRealArray also models dynamic arrays of REALs. The object type has two constructors: Init and InitCopy. The constructor Init creates instances of TRealArray by specifying their sizes. This constructor is identical to the Init constructor in Listing 2.2. The constructor InitCopy creates an instance of TRealArray using the existing instance specified by the parameter AnArray. If you examine the statements in the constructor InitCopy, you notice that the constructor assigns NIL to the DataPtr data field and then invokes the Boolean function CopyArray. The constructor passes the parameter AnArray to the function CopyArray.

The function CopyArray copies one existing instance into another. The function returns True if the duplication is successful, or False if not successful. The function CopyArray deallocates any existing dynamic space and allocates new dynamic space for the duplicate instance.

The main program section declares the instances Ar1 and Ar2 and performs the following tasks:

1. Creates the instance Ar1 using the constructor Init. The constructor invocation specifies the default array size using the constant DEFAULT_SIZE.

2. Displays the newly created instance Ar1 by calling the procedure ShowArray.

3. Assigns values to array Ar1 and displays the contents of the array.

4. Creates the instance Ar2 as a copy of instance Ar1, using the copy constructor InitCopy.

5. Displays the contents of instance Ar2 (which match those of instance Ar1).

6. Alters the values in instance Ar1 and displays the contents of the array.

7. Copies the instance Ar1 to Ar2 and displays the contents of the array Ar2.

8. Destroys the instances Ar1 and Ar2.

Listing 2.3. The program ARRAY2.PAS, which uses the copy constructor to duplicate instances of an object type.

```
Program Array2;

{
  This program creates dynamic arrays of REALs using a variety
  of constructors, including a copy constructor.
}
{$X+,R-}
{$M 8192, 0, 655350}

Uses Crt;

CONST DEFAULT_SIZE = 8;

TYPE
  OneArray = ARRAY[0..0] OF REAL;
  ArrayPtr = ^OneArray;

  TRealArray = OBJECT
    CONSTRUCTOR Init(ArraySize : WORD { input });
    CONSTRUCTOR InitCopy(VAR AnArray : TRealArray { input });
    DESTRUCTOR Done; VIRTUAL;
```

continues

Listing 2.3. continued

```pascal
    FUNCTION GetSize : WORD;
    FUNCTION GetAllocateError : BOOLEAN;
    FUNCTION Store(X     : REAL; { input }
                   Index : WORD  { input }) : BOOLEAN;
    FUNCTION Recall(VAR X     : REAL; { output }
                        Index : WORD  { input  }) : BOOLEAN;
    FUNCTION CopyArray(VAR AnArray : TRealArray { input }) : BOOLEAN;
  PRIVATE
    DataPtr : ArrayPtr;
    Size : WORD;
    AllocateError : BOOLEAN;
  END;

{--------------------------------------- HeapErrorHandler ----------}

FUNCTION HeapErrorHandler(Size : WORD { input  }) : INTEGER; FAR;

BEGIN
    HeapErrorHandler := 1
END;

{------------------------------------------------ Init ------------}

CONSTRUCTOR TRealArray.Init(ArraySize : WORD { input });
{ construct instance of TRealArray }

VAR i : WORD;

BEGIN
  Size := ArraySize;
  IF Size = 0 THEN
    Size := DEFAULT_SIZE;
  GetMem(DataPtr, Size * SizeOf(REAL));
  AllocateError := DataPtr = NIL;
  { allocation successful? }
  IF NOT AllocateError THEN
    FOR i := 0 TO Size - 1 DO
      DataPtr^[i] := 0
END;

{------------------------------------------------ InitCopy ------------}

CONSTRUCTOR TRealArray.InitCopy(VAR anArray : TRealArray { input });
{ create an instance using an existing instance }
BEGIN
  DataPtr := NIL;
  CopyArray(AnArray); { ignore function result }
END;
```

Constructors and Destructors

```
{---------------------------------------------- Done -----------}

DESTRUCTOR TRealArray.Done;
{ remove instance of TRealArray }
BEGIN
  IF DataPtr <> NIL THEN
    FreeMem(DataPtr, Size * SizeOf(REAL))
END;

{------------------------------------------- GetSize -----------}

FUNCTION TRealArray.GetSize : WORD;
{ return the size of the array }
BEGIN
  GetSize := Size
END;

{--------------------------------------- GetAllocateError ------------}

FUNCTION TRealArray.GetAllocateError : BOOLEAN;
{ get the allocation error status }
BEGIN
  GetAllocateError := AllocateError
END;

{-------------------------------------------- Store -----------}

FUNCTION TRealArray.Store(X     : REAL; { input }
                         Index : WORD  { input }) : BOOLEAN;
{ store an array element }
BEGIN
  IF Index < Size THEN BEGIN
    DataPtr^[Index] := X;
    Store := TRUE;
  END
  ELSE
    Store := FALSE;
END;

{-------------------------------------------- Recall -----------}

FUNCTION TRealArray.Recall(VAR X    : REAL; { output }
                           Index : WORD  { input }) : BOOLEAN;
{ recall the contents of an array element }
BEGIN
  IF Index < Size THEN BEGIN
    X := DataPtr^[Index];
    Recall := TRUE;
  END
```

continues

Listing 2.3. continued

```
  ELSE
    Recall := FALSE;
END;

{---------------------------------------- CopyArray ------------}

FUNCTION TRealArray.CopyArray(VAR AnArray : TRealArray { input })
                                         : BOOLEAN;
{ copy the contents of an array AnArray to the targeted array }
VAR i : WORD;

BEGIN
  { deallocate existing data }
  IF DataPtr <> NIL THEN
    FreeMem(DataPtr, Size * SizeOf(REAL));
  Size := AnArray.Size;
  GetMem(DataPtr, Size * SizeOf(REAL));
  AllocateError := DataPtr = NIL;
  { copy array elements? }
  IF NOT AllocateError THEN
    FOR i := 0 TO Size - 1 DO
      DataPtr^[i] := AnArray.DataPtr^[i];
  CopyArray := NOT AllocateError;
END;

{***************************** MAIN *****************************}

VAR Ar1, Ar2 : TRealArray;
    I : WORD;
    X : REAL;

PROCEDURE ShowArray(    NewScrn : BOOLEAN;    { input }
                        Msg     : STRING;     { input }
                    VAR A       : TRealArray { input });

VAR i : WORD;
    x : REAL;

BEGIN
  IF NewScrn THEN ClrScr;
  WRITELN(Msg); WRITELN;
  FOR i := 0 TO A.GetSize - 1 DO
    IF A.Recall(x, i) THEN
      WRITELN(x)
    ELSE
      WRITELN('Index ', i, ' is out of range');
END;
```

Constructors and Destructors

```
PROCEDURE PressKey;
BEGIN
   WRITELN;
   WRITE('Press any key...');
   ReadKey;
   WRITELN;
END;

BEGIN
   HeapError := @HeapErrorHandler;
   Ar1.Init(DEFAULT_SIZE);
   ShowArray(TRUE, 'New Array 1 is:', Ar1);
   PressKey;
   X := 1;
   FOR I := 0 TO Ar1.GetSize - 1 DO BEGIN
     Ar1.Store(X, I);
     X := 2.5 * X;
   END;
   ShowArray(TRUE, 'Updated Array 1 is:', Ar1);
   PressKey;
   Ar2.InitCopy(Ar1);
   ShowArray(FALSE, 'Array 2 (copy of Array1) is:', Ar2);
   PressKey;
   FOR I := 0 TO Ar1.GetSize - 1 DO BEGIN
     Ar1.Recall(X, I);
     X := X + 1000;
     Ar1.Store(X, I);
   END;
   ShowArray(TRUE, 'Updated Array 1 is:', Ar1);
   PressKey;
   Ar2.CopyArray(Ar1);
   ShowArray(FALSE, 'Array 2 (copy of Array1) is:', Ar2);
   PressKey;

   { remove instances of TRealArray }
   Ar1.Done;
   Ar2.Done;
END.
```

Here's a sample output for the program in Listing 2.3:

```
[BEGIN OUTPUT]
New Array 1 is:

 0.0000000000E+00
 0.0000000000E+00
 0.0000000000E+00
 0.0000000000E+00
 0.0000000000E+00
 0.0000000000E+00
 0.0000000000E+00
```

47

```
0.0000000000E+00
0.0000000000E+00

Press any key...
```

The screen clears

```
Updated Array 1 is:

 1.0000000000E+00
 2.5000000000E+00
 6.2500000000E+00
 1.5625000000E+01
 3.9062500000E+01
 9.7656250000E+01
 2.4414062500E+02
 6.1035156250E+02

Press any key...
Array 2 (copy of Array1) is:

 1.0000000000E+00
 2.5000000000E+00
 6.2500000000E+00
 1.5625000000E+01
 3.9062500000E+01
 9.7656250000E+01
 2.4414062500E+02
 6.1035156250E+02

Press any key...
```

The screen clears

```
Updated Array 1 is:

 1.0010000000E+03
 1.0025000000E+03
 1.0062500000E+03
 1.0156250000E+03
 1.0390625000E+03
 1.0976562500E+03
 1.2441406250E+03
 1.6103515625E+03

Press any key...
Array 2 (copy of Array1) is:

 1.0010000000E+03
 1.0025000000E+03
 1.0062500000E+03
```

```
1.0156250000E+03
1.0390625000E+03
1.0976562500E+03
1.2441406250E+03
1.6103515625E+03

Press any key...
[END OUTPUT]
```

Invoking Constructors of Parent Object Types

The main advantage of object-oriented programming over structured programming is the ability to extend classes by adding new data fields and methods, and by reusing inherited data fields and methods. This programming advantage certainly is true for constructors. It's rather common to have the constructor of a child object type invoke the constructor of the parent object type. Typically, the constructor of a descendant object type first invokes the constructor of its parent and then performs additional initialization. This approach enables the descendant object type to fine-tune the creation of instances.

Let me demonstrate this language feature with the next program. Listing 2.4 shows the program ARRAY3.PAS, which uses the constructors of the parent object types in the constructors of the child object type. The program deals with dynamic arrays of integers. These arrays are similar to the floating-point arrays presented earlier. The program declares the following small hierarchy of object types:

- The TIntArray object type, which models dynamic arrays which store integers. The TIntArray type greatly resembles the TRealArray type in Listing 2.3. The constructor TIntArray.Init creates instances of this object type by assigning zeros to the array elements.

- The TRandIntArray object type, a descendant of TIntArray, which represents dynamic arrays which store integers. The constructor TRandIntArray.Init creates instances of this object type by assigning random numbers to the array elements.

- The TSortedRandIntArray object type, a descendant of TRandIntArray, which models *read-only* dynamic arrays of integers. The constructor TSortedRandIntArray.Init creates instances of this object type by assigning random numbers to the array elements and then sorting these elements.

The object types TRandIntArray and TSortedRandIntArray are more suitable for applications that involve simulation. I chose to make the latter object type read-only in order to enable its instances to retain the ordered sequence of random numbers.

Now that you've been introduced to the various object types, let's focus on their constructors. The constructor TIntArray.Init has a single parameter, ArraySize, which specifies the size of the dynamic array. The statements in this constructor are similar to the ones in the TRealArray.Init constructor of Listings 2.2 and 2.3. The main difference is that the dynamic array stores integers instead of floating-point numbers.

The constructor TRandIntArray.Init has three parameters: ArraySize, FirstVal, and LastVal. The ArraySize parameter specifies the size of the dynamic array. The parameters FirstVal and LastVal define the range of random numbers that fill the elements of the dynamic array. The constructor first invokes the constructor of the parent object type. This invocation uses the INHERITED keyword. If you replace the current statement with TIntArray.Init(Array), you perform the same task. After invoking the parent's constructor, TRandIntArray.Init randomizes the seed of the random-number generator and then uses a FOR loop to store random numbers in the elements of the dynamic array.

The constructor TSortedRandIntArray.Init has the same three parameters of constructor TRandIntArray. The first statement in the constructor invokes the constructor TRandIntArray.Init and supplies it with the arguments ArraySize, FirstVal, and LastVal. The constructor TSortedRandIntArray.Init then uses the private CombSort method to sort the elements of the dynamic array. If you trace the execution of the constructor TSortedRandIntArray.Init, you see that the program invokes the constructors of the object types TRandIntArray and TIntArray.

To make the instances of TSortedRandIntArray read-only, I declare a new version of the virtual method Store. This new version simply returns False and ignores the arguments of the parameters X and Index.

The main program section declares instance of three object types and performs the following tasks:

1. Creates IntArr as an instance of TIntArray. This instance has ten elements.

2. Creates RandIntArr as an instance of TRandIntArray. The instance has ten elements, each of which contain random numbers between 0 and 1000.

3. Creates SortedRandIntArr as an instance of TSortedRandIntArray. The instance has ten elements, which contain sorted random numbers between 0 and 1000.

Constructors and Destructors

4. Displays the instances IntArr, RandIntArr, and SortedRandIntArr by calling the procedure ShowArray. Notice that this procedure has the parameter of type TIntArray. Consequently, ShowArray is able to accept arguments that are instances of the descendants of TIntArray.

5. Removes instances IntArr, RandIntArr, and SortedRandIntArr using their destructors.

Listing 2.4. The program ARRAY3.PAS, which uses constructors of the parent object types in the constructors of the child object type.

```
Program Array3;

{
  This program demonstrates using the inherited constructors
  in a small hierarchy that models dynamic arrays of integers.
}
{$X+,R-}
{$M 8192, 0, 655350}

Uses Crt;

CONST DEFAULT_SIZE = 10;

TYPE

  OneArray = ARRAY[0..0] OF INTEGER;
  ArrayPtr = ^OneArray;

  TIntArray = OBJECT
    CONSTRUCTOR Init(ArraySize : WORD { input });
    DESTRUCTOR Done; VIRTUAL;

    FUNCTION GetSize : WORD;
    FUNCTION GetAllocateError : BOOLEAN;
    FUNCTION Store(X     : INTEGER; { input }
                   Index : WORD     { input }) : BOOLEAN; VIRTUAL;
    FUNCTION Recall(VAR X : INTEGER; { output }
                    Index : WORD     { input })
                          : BOOLEAN; VIRTUAL;
  PRIVATE
    DataPtr : ArrayPtr;
    Size : WORD;
    AllocateError : BOOLEAN;
  END;
```

continues

Listing 2.4. continued

```pascal
  TRandIntArray = OBJECT(TIntArray)
    CONSTRUCTOR Init(ArraySize : WORD;    { input }
                    FirstVal,             { input }
                    LastVal   : INTEGER { input });
    DESTRUCTOR Done; VIRTUAL;
  END;

  TSortedRandIntArray = OBJECT(TRandIntArray)
    CONSTRUCTOR Init(ArraySize : WORD;    { input }
                    FirstVal,             { input }
                    LastVal   : INTEGER { input });
    DESTRUCTOR Done; VIRTUAL;
    FUNCTION Store(X     : INTEGER; { output }
                   Index : WORD     { input  })
                         : BOOLEAN; VIRTUAL;
  PRIVATE
    PROCEDURE CombSort;
  END;

{------------------------------------- HeapErrorHandler ----------}

FUNCTION HeapErrorHandler(Size : WORD { input }) : INTEGER; FAR;

BEGIN
    HeapErrorHandler := 1
END;

{------------------------------------------------ Init -----------}

CONSTRUCTOR TIntArray.Init(ArraySize : WORD { input });
{ construct instance of TIntArray }

VAR i : WORD;

BEGIN
  Size := ArraySize;
  IF Size = 0 THEN
    Size := DEFAULT_SIZE;
  GetMem(DataPtr, Size * SizeOf(INTEGER));
  AllocateError := DataPtr = NIL;
  IF NOT AllocateError THEN
    FOR i := 0 TO Size - 1 DO
      DataPtr^[i] := 0

END;
{------------------------------------------------ Done -----------}
```

Constructors and Destructors

```
DESTRUCTOR TIntArray.Done;
{ remove instance of TIntArray }
BEGIN
  IF DataPtr <> NIL THEN
    FreeMem(DataPtr, Size * SizeOf(INTEGER))
END;

{---------------------------------------- GetSize -----------}

FUNCTION TIntArray.GetSize : WORD;
{ return the size of the array }
BEGIN
  GetSize := Size
END;

{---------------------------------- GetAllocateError -----------}

FUNCTION TIntArray.GetAllocateError : BOOLEAN;
{ get the allocation error status }
BEGIN
  GetAllocateError := AllocateError
END;

{---------------------------------------- Store -----------}

FUNCTION TIntArray.Store(X     : INTEGER; { input }
                        Index : WORD     { input }) : BOOLEAN;
{ store an array element }
BEGIN
  IF Index < Size THEN BEGIN
    DataPtr^[Index] := X;
    Store := TRUE;
  END
  ELSE
    Store := FALSE;
END;

{---------------------------------------- Recall -----------}

FUNCTION TIntArray.Recall(VAR X : INTEGER; { output }
                         Index : WORD     { input }) : BOOLEAN;
{ recall the contents of an array element }
BEGIN
  IF Index < Size THEN BEGIN
    X := DataPtr^[Index];
    Recall := TRUE;
  END
  ELSE
    Recall := FALSE;
END;
```

continues

Listing 2.4. continued

```pascal
{----------------------------------------- Init -----------}

CONSTRUCTOR TRandIntArray.Init(ArraySize : WORD;   { input }
                               FirstVal,           { input }
                               LastVal   : INTEGER { input });
{ create the instance of array with random integers }
VAR i : WORD;

BEGIN
  INHERITED Init(ArraySize);
  Randomize;
  FOR i := 0 TO Size - 1 DO
    DataPtr^[i] := FirstVal + Random(LastVal - FirstVal + 1);

END;

{----------------------------------------- Done -----------}

DESTRUCTOR TRandIntArray.Done;
{ remove the instance of TRandIntArray }
BEGIN
  INHERITED Done;
END;

{----------------------------------------- Init -----------}

CONSTRUCTOR TSortedRandIntArray.Init(
                 ArraySize : WORD;   { input }
                 FirstVal,           { input }
                 LastVal   : INTEGER { input });
{ create instance of read-only array of integers }
BEGIN
  INHERITED Init(ArraySize, FirstVal, LastVal);
  { sort the array }
  CombSort;
END;

{----------------------------------------- Done -----------}

DESTRUCTOR TSortedRandIntArray.Done;
{ remove instance of TSortedRandIntArray }
BEGIN
  INHERITED Done;
END;

{----------------------------------------- Store -----------}
```

```
FUNCTION TSortedRandIntArray.Store(
                      X     : INTEGER; { output }
                      Index : WORD     { input  })
                            : BOOLEAN;
{ disable inherited Store method }
BEGIN
  Store := FALSE;
END;

{---------------------------------------- CombSort -----------}

PROCEDURE TSortedRandIntArray.CombSort;

{ sort the array of random numbers using the Comb sort method }

VAR i, j, offset : WORD;
    temp, i1, i2 : INTEGER;
    inOrder : BOOLEAN;

BEGIN
  offset := Size;
  REPEAT
    offset := (offset * 8) DIV 11;
    IF offset = 0 THEN offset := 1;
    inOrder := TRUE;
    FOR i := 0 TO Size - 1 - offset DO BEGIN
      j := i + offset;
      IF DataPtr^[i] > DataPtr^[j] THEN BEGIN
        temp := DataPtr^[i];
        DataPtr^[i] := DataPtr^[j];
        DataPtr^[j] := temp;
        inOrder := FALSE;
      END;
    END;
  UNTIL (offset = 1) AND inOrder;
END;

{*************************** MAIN ******************************}

VAR IntArr : TIntArray;
    RandIntArr : TRandIntArray;
    SortedRandIntArr : TSortedRandIntArray;

PROCEDURE ShowArray(    NewScrn : BOOLEAN; { input }
                        Msg     : STRING;  { input }
                    VAR A       : TIntArray { input });

VAR i : WORD;
    x : INTEGER;
```

continues

Listing 2.4. continued

```pascal
BEGIN
  IF NewScrn THEN ClrScr;
  WRITELN(Msg); WRITELN;
  FOR i := 0 TO A.GetSize - 1 DO
    IF A.Recall(x, i) THEN
      WRITELN(x)
    ELSE
      WRITELN('Index ', i, ' is out of range');
END;

PROCEDURE PressKey;
BEGIN
   WRITELN;
   WRITE('Press any key...');
   ReadKey;
   WRITELN;
END;

BEGIN
   HeapError := @HeapErrorHandler;
   { create the instances of TIntArray, TRandIntArray,
     and TSortedRandIntArray.                           }
   IntArr.Init(10);
   RandIntArr.Init(10, 0, 1000);
   SortedRandIntArr.Init(10, 0, 1000);
   ShowArray(TRUE, 'Simple integer array is initialized as:',
             IntArr);
   PressKey;
   ShowArray(TRUE, 'Random-number array is initialized as:',
             RandIntArr);
   PressKey;
   ShowArray(TRUE, 'Sorted random-number array is initialized as:',
             SortedRandIntArr);
   PressKey;
   { remove the instances of TIntArray, TRandIntArray,
     and TSortedRandIntArray.                           }
   IntArr.Done;
   RandIntArr.Done;
   SortedRandIntArr.Done;
END.
```

Here's a sample output for the program in Listing 2.4:

Constructors and Destructors

```
[BEGIN OUTPUT]
Simple integer array is initialized as:

0
0
0
0
0
0
0
0
0
0

Press any key...
```

The screen clears

```
Random-number array is initialized as:

20
76
347
127
846
227
793
592
314
992

Press any key...
```

The screen clears

```
Sorted random-number array is initialized as:

20
76
127
227
314
347
592
793
846
992

Press any key...
[END OUTPUT]
```

Virtual Destructors

You may have noticed that the various object types in this chapter declare *virtual destructors*. Why? Declaring virtual destructors ensures that dynamic instances of an object type are removed properly using the correct destructor. Otherwise, runtime errors may occur, with unpredictable effects.

Handling Constructor Errors

The process of creating instances of object types is not error-proof, yet the failure of an object type has consequences ranging from severe to fatal. Therefore, the effectiveness of any constructor is critical. The programs presented earlier in this chapter use a Boolean data field to signal one kind of failure (a dynamic allocation error) that might occur in creating instances. The Boolean function GetAllocateError (which I implemented in every object type) can report the failure of the dynamic allocation. Because I was confident that the constructor would not fail in the previous programs, I did not use the function GetAllocateError.

Borland Pascal enables you to handle constructor errors on two fronts:

- First, the constructor must perform a cleanup operation to remove the dynamic memory it just created for the new instance.
- Second, the constructor should be able to signal to the program that an error is occurring.

When the program execution reaches the BEGIN clause in a constructor, it creates the new instance and allocates dynamic memory for the runtime system. These steps are handled automatically by the compiler-generated code. The statements you place in a constructor should detect runtime errors, such as dynamic allocation error and file I/O error. If your constructors detect such errors, they must perform a combination of the following tasks:

- Deallocate any dynamic memory.
- Close any opened files.
- Reverse any other critical initialization steps.

After performing any or all of the above tasks, the constructor should invoke the special procedure Fail. This procedure deallocates dynamic memory that previously was allocated by the runtime system. In addition, the procedure `Fail` enables the program to detect constructor errors. Borland Pascal allows you to invoke `Fail` only inside a constructor.

Detecting a constructor error in a program depends on whether the instance created is static or dynamic. (Static and dynamic instances are discussed in Chapter 1.) For static instances, the constructor acts as a Boolean function that returns True when it succeeds and False when it fails. Consequently, use an IF statement to detect the success of a constructor. Here's the general form for using the constructor's result with a static instance:

```
IF staticInstance.Init THEN BEGIN
    staticInstance.Method1;
    staticInstance.Method2;
    ...
    staticInstance.Done;
END;
```

In the case of a dynamic instance, the runtime system assigns NIL to the pointer managing the instance when the constructor fails. Here's the general form for using a pointer to manage a dynamic instance:

```
dynamicInstance^.Init;
IF dynamicInstance <> NIL THEN BEGIN
    dynamicInstance^.Method1;
    dynamicInstance^.Method2;
    ...
    dynamicInstance^.Done;
END;
```

Let's look at an example. Listing 2.5 shows the program ARRAY4.PAS, which uses constructor-error handling mechanisms. The program declares the object type TIntArray, which models dynamic integer arrays. The object type is based on the one that appears in Listing 2.4. The main difference in this version of TIntArray is in the constructor Init. This constructor adds an ELSE clause to the IF statement and invokes the Fail procedure when the data field AllocateError is True.

The main program section creates two large instances of TIntArray: one static and the other dynamic. The program creates the static instance Ar1, which stores 32,000 elements. The program places the constructor call in an IF statement. When the constructor is successful in creating the large array, the program performs the following tasks:

1. Displays a message informing you that the program created a static instance.

2. Fills the instance with random numbers.

3. Calls the procedure ShowStat to calculate and display the mean value and standard deviation for the values in the static instance Ar1.

4. Removes the static instance Ar1 using the destructor.

If the constructor fails, the program executes the ELSE clause of the IF statement and displays an error message.

The ARRAY4.PAS program also creates a dynamic instance using the pointer pAr1. This instance stores 32,000 elements. The program creates a dynamic instance using the New statement. The program then invokes the constructor Init. The program next employs an IF statement to determine if the pointer pAr1 is not NIL. If this condition is true, the program performs the following tasks:

1. Displays a message informing you that the program created a dynamic instance.

2. Fills the instance with random numbers.

3. Calls the procedure ShowStat to calculate and display the mean value and standard deviation for the values in the dynamic instance pAr1.

4. Removes the dynamic instance pAr1 using the destructor.

If the constructor fails, the program executes the ELSE clause of the IF statement and displays an error message.

Listing 2.5. The program ARRAY4.PAS, which uses constructor-error handling mechanisms.

```
Program Array4;

{
  This program demonstrates constructor-error handling mechanisms.
}

{$X+,R-}
{$M 8192, 0, 655350}

Uses Crt;

CONST DEFAULT_SIZE = 10;
      BIG_INSTANCE = 32000;
      MAX_RAND = 100;

TYPE
  OneArray = ARRAY[0..0] OF INTEGER;
  ArrayPtr = ^OneArray;
```

Constructors and Destructors 2

```
   TIntArray = OBJECT
     CONSTRUCTOR Init(ArraySize : WORD { input });
     DESTRUCTOR Done; VIRTUAL;

     FUNCTION GetSize : WORD;
     FUNCTION GetAllocateError : BOOLEAN;
     FUNCTION Store(X     : INTEGER; { input }
                    Index : WORD     { input })
                          : BOOLEAN; VIRTUAL;
     FUNCTION Recall(VAR X : INTEGER; { output }
                     Index : WORD    { input })
                          : BOOLEAN; VIRTUAL;
   PRIVATE
     DataPtr : ArrayPtr;
     Size : WORD;
     AllocateError : BOOLEAN;
   END;

{---------------------------------------- HeapErrorHandler ----------}

FUNCTION HeapErrorHandler(Size : WORD { input }) : INTEGER; FAR;

BEGIN
    HeapErrorHandler := 1
END;

{------------------------------------------------ Init -----------}

CONSTRUCTOR TIntArray.Init(ArraySize : WORD { input });
{ construct instance of TIntArray }

VAR i : WORD;

BEGIN
  Size := ArraySize;
  IF Size = 0 THEN
    Size := DEFAULT_SIZE;
  GetMem(DataPtr, Size * SizeOf(INTEGER));
  AllocateError := DataPtr = NIL;
  IF NOT AllocateError THEN
    FOR i := 0 TO Size - 1 DO
      DataPtr^[i] := 0
  ELSE
    Fail;
END;

{-------------------------------------------- Done -----------}

DESTRUCTOR TIntArray.Done;
{ remove instance of TIntArray }
```

continues

Listing 2.5. continued

```pascal
BEGIN
  IF DataPtr <> NIL THEN
    FreeMem(DataPtr, Size * SizeOf(INTEGER))
END;

{--------------------------------------- GetSize -----------}

FUNCTION TIntArray.GetSize : WORD;
{ return the size of the array }
BEGIN
  GetSize := Size
END;

{------------------------------------ GetAllocateError -----------}

FUNCTION TIntArray.GetAllocateError : BOOLEAN;
{ get the allocation error status }
BEGIN
  GetAllocateError := AllocateError
END;

{----------------------------------------- Store -----------}

FUNCTION TIntArray.Store(X     : INTEGER; { input }
                        Index : WORD     { input }) : BOOLEAN;
{ store an array element }
BEGIN
  IF Index < Size THEN BEGIN
    DataPtr^[Index] := X;
    Store := TRUE;
  END
  ELSE
    Store := FALSE;
END;

{----------------------------------------- Recall -----------}

FUNCTION TIntArray.Recall(VAR X  : INTEGER; { output }
                          Index : WORD     { input }) : BOOLEAN;
{ recall the contents of an array element }
BEGIN
  IF Index < Size THEN BEGIN
    X := DataPtr^[Index];
    Recall := TRUE;
  END
  ELSE
    Recall := FALSE;
END;
```

Constructors and Destructors

```
{*************************** MAIN ****************************}

VAR Ar1, Ar2 : TIntArray;
    pAr1 : ^TIntArray;
    I : WORD;
    X : INTEGER;

PROCEDURE ShowStat(VAR A : TIntArray { input  });

{ display mean and standard deviation statistics for
  the random numbers stored in instance A }

VAR i, n : WORD;
    x : INTEGER;
    sumx, sumxx, mean, sdev : REAL;

BEGIN
  sumx := 0;
  sumxx := 0;
  FOR i := 0 TO A.GetSize - 1 DO BEGIN
    A.Recall(x, i);
    sumX := sumX + x;
    sumXX := sumXX + x * x;
  END;
  n := A.GetSize;
  mean := sumX / n;
  sdev := SQRT((sumXX - SQR(sumX) / n)/(n - 1));
  WRITELN('Number of elements = ', n);
  WRITELN('Mean = ', mean : 5:2);
  WRITELN('Std. Dev. = ', sdev : 5:2);
END;

PROCEDURE PressKey;
BEGIN
   WRITELN;
   WRITE('Press any key...');
   ReadKey;
   WRITELN;
END;

BEGIN
   HeapError := @HeapErrorHandler;
   ClrScr;
   Randomize;
   { is the static instance created? }
   IF Ar1.Init(BIG_INSTANCE) THEN BEGIN
     WRITELN('Created static instance');
     WRITELN;
     FOR I := 0 TO Ar1.GetSize - 1 DO
       Ar1.Store(1 + Random(MAX_RAND), i);
```

continues

Listing 2.5. continued

```
    ShowStat(Ar1);
    PressKey;
    Ar1.Done;
  END
  ELSE BEGIN
    WRITELN;
    WRITE('Error: Cannot create static instance with ');
    WRITELN(BIG_INSTANCE, ' elements');
    WRITELN;
  END;

  New(pAr1);
  pAr1^.Init(BIG_INSTANCE);
  { was the dynamic instance created? }
  IF pAr1 <> NIL THEN BEGIN
    WRITELN;
    WRITELN('Created dynamic instance');
    WRITELN;
    FOR I := 0 TO pAr1^.GetSize - 1 DO
      pAr1^.Store(1 + Random(MAX_RAND), i);
    ShowStat(pAr1^);
    PressKey;
    pAr1^.Done;
  END
  ELSE BEGIN
    WRITELN;
    WRITE('Error: Cannot create dynamic instance with');
    WRITELN(BIG_INSTANCE, ' elements');
    WRITELN;
  END;
  Dispose(pAr1);
END.
```

Here's a sample output for the program in Listing 2.5:

```
[BEGIN OUTPUT]
Created static instance

Number of elements = 32000
Mean = 50.67
Std. Dev. = 28.91

Press any key...

Created dynamic instance
```

```
Number of elements = 32000
Mean = 50.36
Std. Dev. = 28.86

Press any key...
[END OUTPUT]
```

Summary

This chapter discussed the workings of constructors and destructors. You learned about the following topics:

- The *default constructor* is a parameterless constructor that initializes instances that are empty of information.

- Multiple constructors support different ways of creating object type instances. Some of these constructors may offer different ways of creating instances, while others may provide refinement of each other.

- The *copy constructor* allows the creation of an instance from an existing instance. Copy constructors usually work with an instance-duplicating method. This approach allows you to copy both new and existing instances.

- The invocation of constructors of parent object types enables you to build on the action of these constructors. Typically, the constructor of a descendant object type first calls the constructor of its parent object type and then carries out additional initialization.

- Virtual destructors ensure that dynamic instances of an object type are properly removed using the correct destructor.

- Borland Pascal supports a mechanism to handle constructor errors. The mechanism uses the special procedure Fail to deallocate special dynamic memory used for a new instance. In addition, the Fail procedure causes the constructor to return a value of False (as though it were a function) when used with a static instance. In the case of a dynamic instance, the constructor assigns NIL to the pointer that manages the instance.

Chapter 3

Overriding Methods

The ability to override inherited methods is an important feature in object-oriented languages. This feature enables classes to define new methods that offer more specialized ways for responding to messages. These methods (along with the new methods) implement the specialization offered by the descendant object type. This chapter discusses:

- Overriding static and virtual methods.
- How this process affects the design of object types.

Overriding Static Methods

Borland Pascal allows you to override private static methods in descendant object types that are declared in the same program module as the parent object types. The overriding method may declare a parameter list that differs from that of the inherited method. There are two general approaches for overriding inherited static methods:

- The overriding method builds on the inherited methods by offering additional statements. These statements fine-tune the action of the inherited method, for example, to manipulate or update data fields in the descendant object type. In the majority of the cases, a descendant object type builds on the parent's method. However, you still can build on an ancestor's method if needed.

- The overriding method uses a new set of statements to implement the needed response. In this case, the inherited method isn't used because it lacks the proper response on which the descendant object type can build.

Let's look at a program that illustrates both of the above schemes for overriding inherited methods. Listing 3.1 shows the program DATE1.PAS, which illustrates overriding static methods. The DATE1.PAS program declares a hierarchy of two object types: TDate and its descendant TFrmtDate.

The TDate object type models an unformatted date. The TDate type has three private data fields: fDay, fMonth, and fYear. These data fields store the day, month, and year, respectively. The TDate object type declares the following three methods:

1. The Boolean function AssignVals assigns values to the data fields. The function returns True if the following conditions are true:

    - The argument for parameter aDay is in the range of 1 to 31.
    - The argument for parameter aMonth is in the range of 1 to 12.
    - The argument for parameter aYear is in the range of 1900 to 3000, after normalization. Normalization adds the value 1900 to the year argument if the argument initially is less than 1900.

The preceding date validation is, of course, not foolproof.

2. The procedure `RecallDate` retrieves the values in the data fields. The reference parameters `aDay`, `aMonth`, and `aYear` return the values stored in the data fields of the `TDate` instance.

3. The function `CompareDate` compares the date of an instance with that of parameter `aDate`. This parameter is also an instance of type `TDate`. The function returns the following values:

   - +1 when the date of the instance comes after the date of `aDate`.
   - −1 when the date of the instance comes before the date of `aDate`.
   - 0 when the dates of the instance and parameter `aDate` are the same.

The program also declares the object type `TFrmtDate` as a descendant of `TDate`. The descendant object type declares no new data fields. The type `TFrmtDate` declares the new method `ShowDate` and the overriding methods `AssignVals` and `RecallDate`. The `ShowDate` method displays the date using the data in the inherited fields `fDay`, `fMonth`, and `fYear`. The method uses the MM/DD/YYYY format to display the date.

The `AssignVals` method overrides the inherited `AssignVals` method. Both versions of method `AssignVals` use the same parameter list. The `TFrmtDate.AssignVals` method implements a new feature that allows it to obtain the system date (using the `GetDate` procedure exported by the `Dos` library unit) if either one of its arguments is 0. If neither of the arguments is 0, the method invokes the inherited `AssignVals` method.

The `RecallDate` method overrides the inherited `RecallDate` method. The overriding method has four parameters, compared to three in method `TDate.RecallDate`. The additional parameter returns a string with the formatted date. The method uses the MM/DD/YYYY date format. In addition to declaring a different parameter list, for the sake of illustration, I purposely coded the `RecallDate` method to avoid calling the inherited method.

The program also declares the procedure `TestDates` to compare two instances of `TFrmtDate` and display a message indicating the outcome of the comparison.

The main program section declares two `TFrmtDate` instances: `Day1` and `Day2`. The program compares three arbitrary dates for these variables. Each comparison involves sending the `AssignVals` messages to the instances `Day1` and `Day2`. When both messages return True, the program invokes the `TestDate` procedure to compare the dates and display the result of the comparison.

Listing 3.1. The program DATE1.PAS, which illustrates overriding static methods.

```pascal
Program Date1;

{ Program shows how to override static methods }

{$X+}

Uses Dos, Crt;

TYPE
  TDate = OBJECT
    FUNCTION AssignVals(aDay,         { input }
                        aMonth,       { input }
                        aYear : WORD { input }) : BOOLEAN;
    PROCEDURE RecallDate(VAR aDay,          { output }
                             aMonth,        { output }
                             aYear : WORD { output });
    FUNCTION CompareDate(VAR aDate : TDate { input })
                                  : INTEGER;

  PRIVATE
    fDay : WORD;
    fMonth : WORD;
    fYear : WORD;
  END;

  TFrmtDate = OBJECT(TDate)
    FUNCTION AssignVals(aDay,         { input }
                        aMonth,       { input }
                        aYear : WORD { input }) : BOOLEAN;
    PROCEDURE RecallDate(VAR aDay,           { output }
                             aMonth,         { output }
                             aYear : WORD;  { output }
                         VAR DateStr : STRING { output });
    PROCEDURE ShowDate;
  END;

{------------------------------------------- AssignVals -----------}

FUNCTION TDate.AssignVals(aDay,         { input }
                          aMonth,       { input }
                          aYear : WORD { input })
                                  : BOOLEAN;
{ assign components of date to data fields }
BEGIN
  fDay := aDay;
  fMonth := aMonth;
  fYear := aYear;
  IF fYear < 1900 THEN INC(fYear, 1900);
```

```
    AssignVals := (fDay IN [1..31]) AND
                  (fMonth IN [1..12]) AND
                  (fYear >= 1900) AND
                  (fYear <= 3000);
END;

{------------------------------------------- RecallDate -----------}

PROCEDURE TDate.RecallDate(VAR aDay,      { output }
                              aMonth,     { output }
                              aYear  : WORD { output });
{ get date components }
BEGIN
  aDay := fDay;
  aMonth := fMonth;
  aYear := fYear;
END;

{------------------------------------------- CompareDate -----------}

FUNCTION TDate.CompareDate(VAR aDate : TDate { input })
                              : INTEGER;
{ compare dates. Return:

       +1 when self > aDate
        0 when self = aDate
       -1 when self < aDate
}
BEGIN
  IF fYear > aDate.fYear THEN
    CompareDate := +1
  ELSE IF fYear < aDate.fYear THEN
    CompareDate := -1
  ELSE BEGIN
    IF fMonth > aDate.fMonth THEN
      CompareDate := +1
    ELSE IF fMonth < aDate.fMonth THEN
      CompareDate := -1
    ELSE BEGIN
      IF fDay > aDate.fDay THEN
        CompareDate := +1
      ELSE IF fDay < aDate.fDay THEN
        CompareDate := -1
      ELSE
        CompareDate := 0; { dates are the same! }
    END
  END;
END;
```

continues

Listing 3.1. continued

```
{---------------------------------------- AssignVals ------------}

FUNCTION TFrmtDate.AssignVals(aDay,          { input }
                              aMonth,        { input }
                              aYear : WORD   { input })
                                  : BOOLEAN;
VAR dummy : WORD;

BEGIN
  If (aDay = 0) OR (aMonth = 0) OR (aYear = 0) THEN BEGIN
    GetDate(fYear, fMonth, fDay, dummy);
    AssignVals := TRUE;
  END
  ELSE
    AssignVals := INHERITED AssignVals(aDay, aMonth, aYear);
END;

{---------------------------------------- RecallDate ------------}

PROCEDURE TFrmtDate.RecallDate(VAR aDay,             { output }
                                   aMonth,          { output }
                                   aYear : WORD;    { output }
                               VAR DateStr : STRING { output });
{ recall data field and return string image of date }

VAR s : STRING;

BEGIN
  aDay := fDay;
  aMonth := fMonth;
  aYear := fYear;
  { build string image of date }
  IF aMonth < 10 THEN BEGIN
    Str(aMonth:1, s);
    DateStr := '0' + s;
  END
  ELSE
    Str(aMonth:2, DateStr);
  IF aDay < 10 THEN BEGIN
    Str(aDay:1, s);
    DateStr := DateStr + '/0' + s;
  END
  ELSE BEGIN
    Str(aDay:2, s);
    DateStr := DateStr + '/' + s;
  END;
  Str(aYear:4, s);
  DateStr := DateStr + '/' + s;
END;
```

Overriding Methods 3

```
{---------------------------------------- ShowDate -----------}

PROCEDURE TFrmtDate.ShowDate;

VAR s : STRING;
    dummy1, dummy2, dummy3 : WORD;

BEGIN
  RecallDate(dummy1, dummy2, dummy3, s);
  WRITE(s);
END;

{******************** MAIN ********************}

VAR Day1, Day2 : TFrmtDate;
    Result : INTEGER;

PROCEDURE TestDates(VAR Date1,              { input }
                        Date2 : TFrmtDate { input });
BEGIN
  Result := Date1.CompareDate(Date2);
  Date1.ShowDate;
  IF Result > 0 THEN
    WRITE(' is after ')
  ELSE IF Result < 0 THEN
    WRITE(' is before ')
  ELSE
    WRITE(' is the same as ');
  Date2.ShowDate;
  WRITELN;
  WRITELN;
END;

BEGIN
  ClrScr;
  IF Day1.AssignVals(1, 1, 1994) AND
     Day2.AssignVals(4, 2, 1995) THEN
     TestDates(Day1, day2);

  IF Day1.AssignVals(10, 3, 1994) AND
     Day2.AssignVals(4, 2, 1994) THEN
     TestDates(Day1, day2);

  IF Day1.AssignVals(0, 0, 0) AND
     Day2.AssignVals(0, 0, 0) THEN
     TestDates(Day1, day2);
  WRITELN;
  WRITE('Press any key to end the program...');
  ReadKey;
END.
```

Here's a sample output for the program in Listing 3.1:

```
[BEGIN OUTPUT]
01/01/1994 is before 02/04/1995

03/10/1994 is after 02/04/1994

02/04/1993 is the same as 02/04/1993


Press any key to end the program...
[END OUTPUT]
```

Overriding Virtual Methods

Overriding virtual methods support polymorphic behaviors in an object-type hierarchy. Borland Pascal (as well as all other OOP languages) dictates that the parameter list of an overriding virtual method must be the same as the inherited one. As with static methods, the overriding virtual method may or may not invoke the inherited method. This decision depends on the particular application.

Borland Pascal allows you to override private virtual methods in descendant object types that are declared in the same program module as the parent object types.

Let's look at an example that illustrates overriding virtual methods: a library unit and a test program that deal with dynamic arrays of strings. Listing 3.2 shows the library unit PolyMorf, which illustrates overriding virtual methods. The library declares the TStrArray object type and its descendant, TVirtStrArray.

The TStrArray object type models heap-based dynamic arrays of string. The object type declares the following data fields:

- The MaxSize data field specifies the total number of array elements.
- The WorkSize data field contains the number of elements that store meaningful data. The constructor assigns 0 to the WorkSize field of a new instance.
- The DataPtr data field is the pointer to the dynamic array.
- The InOrder Boolean data field is a flag that monitors the order of the array.

Overriding Methods 3

The constructor `Init` creates an instance with a number of elements specified by parameter `ArraySize`. The constructor fills the array elements with empty strings. The destructor `Done` regains the dynamic memory allocated for the array.

The `TStrArray` object type declares the following methods:

- The virtual Boolean function `Store` writes a string at a specified array index. The function returns True if the argument for parameter `Index` is in the range of 1 to `MaxSize`. Otherwise, the function returns False. If the valid argument of `Index` is greater than the data field `WorkSize`, the function updates `WorkSize` with the value of `Index`. The function assigns False to the data field `InOrder` because storing a string in the array most likely will corrupt any existing sort order. You can add more statements in function `Store` to test whether or not the stored element actually corrupts the order of the array (if the array already is sorted).

- The virtual Boolean function `Recall` retrieves a string from the array element number `Index`. The function returns True when the argument of parameter `Index` is in the range of 1 to `WorkSize`. Otherwise, the function returns False. The reference parameter `X` passes the accessed array element to the caller.

- The private virtual procedure `UnSafeStore` performs a quick storage of a string in an array element. This method is a version of function `Store` that *assumes* that the argument for parameter `Index` is in the range of 1 to `WorkSize`. I declared this method as private to speed up the operations of the methods `Sort`, while denying its access to the instances of `TStrArray`.

- The private virtual procedure `UnSafeRecall` performs a quick retrieval of a string from an array element. This method is a version of function Recall that *assumes* that the argument for parameter `Index` is in the range of 1 to `WorkSize`. I declared this method as private to speed up the operations of the methods `Sort` and `Search`, while denying its access to the instances of `TStrArray`.

- The function `GetWorkSize` returns the value in the `WorkSize` data field. This result tells you how many meaningful strings there are in an instance of `TStrArray`.

- The function `GetMaxSize` returns the value in the `MaxSize` data field.

- The procedure `Sort` sorts the first `WorkSize` array elements in ascending order. The procedure uses the Shell-Metzner algorithm and sends `UnSafeRecall` and `UnSafeStore` messages to read and write the array elements. Because the methods `UnSafeStore` and `UnSafeRecall` are virtual, the descendant object types can inherit the Sort method and use with their own versions of UnSafeStore and UnSafeRecall. Thus, the Sort method supports polymorphic behavior.

- The function Search performs a binary search for a string in the array. The method sorts the array by sending a Sort message when the InOrder data field is False. The function returns the index of the matching element, or returns the constant NOT_FOUND (which is 0) when no match is found. The Search method uses the UnSafeRecall method to quickly retrieve data from the array elements. Because the method UnSafeRecall is virtual, the descendant object types can inherit the Search method and use it with their own versions of UnSafeRecall. Thus, the Search method supports polymorphic behavior.

The Polymorf library unit declares the TVirtStrArray object type. This type models dynamic disk-based arrays of strings. The descendant object type declares the data field FileVar to act as the handle for the supporting data file. The TVirtStrArray object type declares a constructor, destructor, and the virtual methods Store, Recall, UnSafeStore, and UnSafeRecall.

The TVirtStrArray.Init constructor has the parameters ArraySize and aStrFile. The ArraySize indicates the maximum number of strings in the disk-based array. The parameter aStrFile specifies the name of the supporting file. If the constructor cannot open the file specified by the aStrFile parameter, it prompts you to enter a new filename. The destructor Done first closes the supporting data file and then deletes it.

The TVirtStrArray object type inherits the Sort, Search, GetWorkSize, and GetMaxSize methods. TVirtStrArray also inherits the data fields MaxSize, WorkSize, DataPtr, and InOrder. In this case, the descendant object type has no use for the data field DataPtr because it stores its data in a file and not in the heap. The virtual methods Store, Recall, UnSafeStore, and UnSafeRecall override the inherited ones and use the file I/O procedures Seek, READ, and WRITE to access the string from the data file. The overriding methods do not invoke the inherited ones because the two sets of methods support different storage schemes. The inherited methods Sort and Search properly work with the instance of TVirtStrArray thanks to the private virtual methods UnSafeStore and UnSafeRecall.

> The polymorphic behavior in methods Sort and Search comes at the cost of additional overhead due to calling the methods UnSafeStore and UnSafeRecall. Fortunately, the overhead in this case is slight, which

> makes inheritance and polymorphism viable. However, in applications where the overhead of calling virtual methods is high, you might be better off implementing different versions of methods such as Sort and Search to gain much needed speed.

Listing 3.2. The library unit `PolyMorf`, which illustrates overriding virtual methods.

```
UNIT Polymorf;

{ This library implements polymorphic arrays.}

{************************************************************}
{*********************} INTERFACE {**********************}
{************************************************************}

{$X+}

CONST STRING_SIZE = 80;
      NOT_FOUND = 0;

TYPE
  LSTRING = STRING[STRING_SIZE];
  OneString = ARRAY [1..1] OF LSTRING;
  OneStringPtr = ^OneString;
  TFILE = FILE OF LSTRING;

  TStrArray = OBJECT
     CONSTRUCTOR Init(ArraySize : WORD { input  });
     DESTRUCTOR Done;
     FUNCTION Store(aStr  : LSTRING; { input   }
                    Index : WORD     { input  })
                          : BOOLEAN; VIRTUAL;
     FUNCTION Recall(VAR aStr   : LSTRING; { output }
                         Index  : WORD     { input  })
                           : BOOLEAN; VIRTUAL;
     FUNCTION GetWorkSize : WORD;
     FUNCTION GetMaxSize : WORD;
     PROCEDURE Sort;
     FUNCTION Search(SearchStr : LSTRING { input  }) : WORD;
   PRIVATE
     MaxSize,
     WorkSize { current size } : WORD;
     DataPtr : OneStringPtr;
     InOrder : BOOLEAN;
```

continues

Listing 3.2. continued

```pascal
      PROCEDURE UnSafeStore(aStr  : LSTRING; { input  }
                           Index : WORD    { input  });
                                    VIRTUAL;
      PROCEDURE UnSafeRecall(VAR aStr  : LSTRING; { output }
                                 Index : WORD    { input  });
                                    VIRTUAL;
  END;

  TVirtStrArray = OBJECT(TStrArray)
      CONSTRUCTOR Init(ArraySize : WORD;   { input  }
                       aStrFile : LSTRING  { input  });
      FUNCTION Store(aStr  : LSTRING; { input  }
                     Index : WORD    { input  })
                          : BOOLEAN; VIRTUAL;
      FUNCTION Recall(VAR aStr  : LSTRING; { output }
                          Index : WORD    { output })
                          : BOOLEAN; VIRTUAL;
      DESTRUCTOR Done;
    PRIVATE
      FileVar : TFILE;
      PROCEDURE UnSafeStore(aStr  : LSTRING; { input  }
                            Index : WORD    { input  });
                                    VIRTUAL;
      PROCEDURE UnSafeRecall(VAR aStr  : LSTRING; { output }
                                 Index : WORD    { input  });
                                    VIRTUAL;
  END;

{************************************************************}
{*******************} IMPLEMENTATION {*******************}
{************************************************************}

{$R-}

{----------------------------------------- HeapErrorHandler ----------}

FUNCTION HeapErrorHandler(Size : WORD { input  }) : INTEGER; FAR;

BEGIN
    HeapErrorHandler := 1
END;

{------------------------------------------------ Init -----------}

CONSTRUCTOR TStrArray.Init(ArraySize : WORD { input  });
{ create instance of TStrArray }
BEGIN
  { allocate dynamic memory }
  GetMem(DataPtr, ArraySize * STRING_SIZE);
```

Overriding Methods

```
    IF DataPtr = NIL THEN BEGIN
      Fail;
      EXIT;
    END;
    MaxSize := ArraySize;
    WorkSize := 0;
    InOrder := FALSE;
    { assign null strings to dynamic array }
    WHILE ArraySize > 0 DO BEGIN
        Store('', ArraySize);
        DEC(ArraySize)
    END;
END;

{---------------------------------------------- Done -----------}

DESTRUCTOR TStrArray.Done;
{ remove instance of TStrArray }
BEGIN
  IF DataPtr <> NIL THEN
    FreeMem(DataPtr, MaxSize * STRING_SIZE);
END;

{---------------------------------------------- Sort -----------}

PROCEDURE TStrArray.Sort;
{ sort array using Shell-Metzner method }
VAR offset, i, j : WORD;
    strI, strJ : LSTRING;

BEGIN
  IF WorkSize < 2 THEN EXIT;
  offset := WorkSize;
  WHILE offset > 1 DO BEGIN
    offset := offset div 2;
    REPEAT
      InOrder := TRUE;
      FOR j := 1 TO WorkSize - offset DO BEGIN
        i := j + offset;
        UnSafeRecall(strJ, j);
        UnSafeRecall(strI, i);
        IF strI < strJ THEN BEGIN
          UnSafeStore(strI, j);
          UnSafeStore(strJ, i);
          InOrder := FALSE
        END; { IF }
      END; { FOR }
    UNTIL InOrder;
  END; { WHILE }
END;
```

continues

Listing 3.2. continued

```
{--------------------------------------------- Search -----------}

FUNCTION TStrArray.Search(SearchStr : LSTRING { input  }) : WORD;
{ perform binary search for SearchStr in array }
VAR low, high, median : WORD;
    strMedian : LSTRING;

BEGIN
  { array needs to be sorted? }
  IF NOT InOrder THEN
    Sort;
  { set initial search limits }
  low := 1;
  high := WorkSize;
  { search for data }
  REPEAT
    median := (low + high) div 2;
    UnSafeRecall(strMedian, median);
    IF SearchStr < strMedian THEN
      high := median - 1
    ELSE
      low := median + 1;
  UNTIL (SearchStr = strMedian) OR (low > high);
  { found a match? }
  IF SearchStr = strMedian THEN
    Search := median
  ELSE
    Search := NOT_FOUND;
END;

{--------------------------------------------- Store -----------}

FUNCTION TStrArray.Store(aStr  : LSTRING; { input  }
                         Index : WORD     { input  })
                                : BOOLEAN;
{ store string aStr at element number Index }
BEGIN
  IF Index <= MaxSize THEN BEGIN
    IF Index > WorkSize THEN
      WorkSize := Index;
    DataPtr^[Index] := aStr;
    InOrder := FALSE;
    Store := TRUE
  END
  ELSE
    Store := FALSE
END;
```

Overriding Methods 3

```
{---------------------------------------- Recall -----------}

FUNCTION TStrArray.Recall(VAR aStr  : LSTRING; { output }
                              Index : WORD    { output })
                                    : BOOLEAN;
{ recall string from element number Index }
BEGIN
  IF Index <= WorkSize THEN BEGIN
    aStr := DataPtr^[Index];
    Recall := TRUE
  END
  ELSE
    Recall := FALSE
END;

{---------------------------------------- UnSafeStore -----------}

PROCEDURE TStrArray.UnSafeStore(aStr  : LSTRING; { input  }
                                Index : WORD    { input  });
{ store string aStr at element number Index }
BEGIN
  DataPtr^[Index] := aStr;
END;

{---------------------------------------- UnSafeRecall -----------}

PROCEDURE TStrArray.UnSafeRecall(VAR aStr  : LSTRING; { output }
                                     Index : WORD    { input  });
{ recall string from element number Index }
BEGIN
    aStr := DataPtr^[Index];
END;

{---------------------------------------- GetWorkSize -----------}

FUNCTION TStrArray.GetWorkSize : WORD;
{ return working size of array }
BEGIN
  GetWorkSize := WorkSize;
END;

{---------------------------------------- GetMaxSize -----------}

FUNCTION TStrArray.GetMaxSize : WORD;
{ return maximum size of array }
BEGIN
  GetMaxSize := MaxSize;
END;
```

continues

Listing 3.2. continued

```pascal
{---------------------------------------------- Init -----------}

CONSTRUCTOR TVirtStrArray.Init(ArraySize : WORD;   { input }
                               aStrFile  : LSTRING { input });
{ create an instance of TVirtStrArray }
VAR ok : BOOLEAN;

BEGIN
  { loop until a valid filename is provided }
  REPEAT
    Assign(FileVar, aStrFile);
    {$I-} Rewrite(FileVar); {$I+}
    ok := IOResult = 0;
    IF NOT ok THEN BEGIN
      WRITELN;
      WRITELN('Cannot open file ', aStrFile);
      WRITELN;
      WRITELN('Enter filename -> ');
      READLN(aStrFile); WRITELN;
    END;
  UNTIL ok;
  MaxSize := ArraySize;
  WorkSize := 0;
  InOrder := FALSE;
  { assign null strings to dynamic array }
  Seek(FileVar, 0);
  aStrFile := '';
  WHILE ArraySize > 0 DO BEGIN
    WRITE(FileVar, aStrFile);
    DEC(ArraySize)
  END;
END;

{---------------------------------------------- Done -----------}

DESTRUCTOR TVirtStrArray.Done;
{ remove instance of TVirtStrArray by closing
  and deleting the supporting data file }
BEGIN
  Close(FileVar);
  {$I+} Erase(FileVar); {$I-}
END;

{---------------------------------------------- Store -----------}

FUNCTION TVirtStrArray.Store(aStr  : LSTRING; { input }
                             Index : WORD    { input })
                                   : BOOLEAN;
{ store string aStr at element number Index }
```

```
      BEGIN
        IF Index <= MaxSize THEN BEGIN
          IF Index > WorkSize THEN
            WorkSize := Index;
          Seek(FileVar, Index-1);
          WRITE(FileVar, aStr);
          InOrder := FALSE;
          Store := TRUE
        END
        ELSE
          Store := FALSE
      END;

      {---------------------------------------------- Recall -----------}

      FUNCTION TVirtStrArray.Recall(VAR aStr   : LSTRING; { output }
                                        Index : WORD     { input  })
                                              : BOOLEAN;
      { recall string from element number Index }
      BEGIN
        IF Index <= WorkSize THEN BEGIN
          Seek(FileVar, Index - 1);
          READ(FileVar, aStr);
          Recall := TRUE
        END
        ELSE
          Recall := FALSE
      END;

      {---------------------------------------- UnSafeStore -----------}

      PROCEDURE TVirtStrArray.UnSafeStore(aStr   : LSTRING; { input }
                                          Index : WORD     { input });
      { store string aStr at element number Index }
      BEGIN
          Seek(FileVar, Index-1);
          WRITE(FileVar, aStr);
      END;

      {---------------------------------------- UnSafeRecall -----------}

      PROCEDURE TVirtStrArray.UnSafeRecall(VAR aStr   : LSTRING; { output }
                                               Index : WORD     { input });
      { recall string from element number Index }
      BEGIN
          Seek(FileVar, Index - 1);
          READ(FileVar, aStr);
      END;

      BEGIN
        HeapError := @HeapErrorHandler;
      END.
```

The program ARRAY5.PAS, shown in Listing 3.3, tests the `PolyMorf` library unit. The program uses the $DEFINE, $IFDEF, $ELSE, and $ENDIF compiler directives to perform conditional compilation. This approach enables me to use a single listing instead of two very similar ones. The current version in Listing 3.3 uses disk-based arrays. If you remove the $ character from the $DEFINE directive, the program compiles to use heap-based arrays. In either case, the test program performs the same tasks, thanks to polymorphism.

The test program performs the following relevant tasks:

1. Defines the `VM_ARRAY` macro.

2. Declares the `TARGET_FILE` constant (which stores the name of the supporting data file) and the `AnArray` variable (an instance of the `TVirtStrArray` object type) if the `VM_ARRAY` macro is defined. Otherwise, the program declares `AnArray` as an instance of the object type `TStrArray`.

3. Creates the instance `AnArray`. The actual creation process depends on whether or not the macro `VM_ARRAY` is defined. If `VM_ARRAY` is defined, the program invokes the `TVirtStrArray.Init` constructor. Otherwise, the program uses the `TStrArray.Init` constructor.

4. Prompts you to enter `TEST_SIZE` number of strings. The program stores your input in the dynamic array by sending the `Store` message to the instance `AnArray`.

5. Sorts the contents of the array by sending the `Sort` message to the instance `AnArray`.

6. Repeatedly displays the array elements (by sending the `Recall` message to instance `AnArray`) and prompts you to enter a search string or to press the Enter key to end the search process. If you enter a string, the program uses the input with the `Search` message. The program sends this message to the instance `AnArray` and stores the result in variable `I`. The program then compares the value in variable `I` with the constant `NOT_FOUND`. If the two values are different, the program displays the index of the matching array element. Otherwise, the program writes a no-match message.

7. Destroys the instance `AnArray` using the destructor `Done`.

Listing 3.3. The program ARRAY5.PAS, which tests the `PolyMorf` library unit.

```
Program Array5;
{
    This program tests polymorphic virtual arrays.
}
```

```
Uses Crt, PolyMorf;

{ remove the $ from the next comment to use
  the heap-based dynamic arrays }
{$DEFINE VM_ARRAY}

CONST TEST_SIZE = 5;
{$IFDEF VM_ARRAY}
      TARGET_FILE = 'VM.DAT';
VAR AnArray : TVirtStrArray;
{$ELSE}
VAR AnArray : TStrArray;
{$ENDIF}
    I : WORD;
    S : LSTRING;

BEGIN
    ClrScr;
    { test the AnArray object }
{$IFDEF VM_ARRAY}
    AnArray.Init(TEST_SIZE, TARGET_FILE);
{$ELSE}
    AnArray.Init(TEST_SIZE);
{$ENDIF}
    FOR I := 1 TO TEST_SIZE DO BEGIN
        WRITE('Enter string # ',I,' ? ');
        READLN(S);
     IF NOT AnArray.Store(S, I) THEN
        WRITELN('Out of bound index');
    END;
    AnArray.Sort; { sort the array }
    REPEAT
     ClrScr;
     WRITELN('Sorted array is:'); WRITELN;
     FOR I := 1 TO TEST_SIZE DO BEGIN
            IF WhereY > 22 THEN BEGIN
                WRITELN;
                WRITE('Press any key to continue...');
                ReadKey;
                ClrScr;
            END;
         IF AnArray.Recall(S, I) THEN
           WRITELN(I:2,'   ',S);
        END;
    WRITELN;
    WRITE('Search for string (press [Enter] to exit) -> ');
    READLN(S);
       WRITELN;
     IF S <> '' THEN BEGIN
         I := AnArray.Search(S);
```

continues

Listing 3.3. continued

```
            IF I <> NOT_FOUND THEN
              WRITELN('Matches element ', I)
            ELSE
              WRITELN('Has no match');
            WRITELN;
            WRITE('Press space bar to continue...');
            ReadKey;
      END;
      WRITELN;
   UNTIL S = '';
   AnArray.Done; { deallocate dynamic memory }
   WRITELN;
   WRITE('Press any key to end the program...');
   ReadKey;
END.
```

Here is a sample output for the program in Listing 3.3:

```
[BEGIN OUTPUT]
Enter string # 1 ? CA
Enter string # 2 ? WA
Enter string # 3 ? VA
Enter string # 4 ? MI
Enter string # 5 ? NY
```

The screen clears

```
Sorted array is:

   1   CA
   2   MI
   3   NY
   4   VA
   5   WA


Search for string (press [Enter] to exit) -> CA

Matches element 1

Press space bar to continue...
[END OUTPUT]
```

Summary

This chapter discussed overriding static and virtual methods. You learned about the following:

- Borland Pascal allows you to override static methods in descendant object types. The overriding method may declare a parameter list that differs from that of the inherited method. The overriding inherited static methods may call the inherited method to build on their action, or completely bypass them. The latter case occurs when the inherited methods are too cumbersome or unsuitable for use by the descendant object type.

- Overriding virtual methods supports polymorphic behaviors in an object-type hierarchy. Borland Pascal dictates that the parameter list of an overriding virtual method must be the same as that of the inherited one. As with static methods, the overriding method may or may not invoke the inherited method. This decision depends on the particular application.

Chapter 4

Object Types As Extendible Records

Structured programming in Pascal fosters the declaration of structures using the RECORD types. Object-oriented programming introduces classes that are super-records, containing both data fields and methods. Thus, conceptually, classes extend records in a manner similar to the way a descendant class extends its parent. Consequently, classes are able to behave just like structures.

This chapter discusses how object types in Borland Pascal can act as extendible records. You'll learn about the following topics:

- Object types as extendible, non-OOP records
- Simulating extendible records
- Object types as extendible records in a hierarchy of object types

Simulating Extendible Records

Pascal records provide structures that include logically related data fields. Such fields often include previously declared records. The problem with nested records is the need to use multiple dot access operators to access the nested data fields. Here's an example:

```
TYPE
    TimeRec = RECORD
        fHour : BYTE;
        fMin  : BYTE;
        fSec  : BYTE;
    END;

    DateTimeRec = RECORD
        fYear  : WORD;
        fMonth : BYTE;
        fDay   : BYTE;
        fTime  : TimeRec;
    END;

VAR DT : DateTimeRec;

BEGIN
    DT.fYear := 1994;
    DT.fMonth := 2;
    DT.fDay := 5;
    DT.fTime.fHour := 9;
    DT.fTime.fMinute := 29;
    DT.fTime.fSec := 45;
    DisplayDateTime(DT);
END;
```

The variable DT is a DateTimeRec record structure. Accessing the fYear, fMonth, and fDay data fields requires one dot operator, as shown in the previous sample

Object Types As Extendible Records

assignments. By contrast, accessing the data fields fHour, fMin, and fSec in the nested record fTime requires two dot operators. Using the WITH statement can somewhat relieve the problem, as shown below:

```
BEGIN
    WITH DT DO BEGIN
       fYear := 1994;
       fMonth := 2;
       fDay := 5;
       WITH fTime DO BEGIN
          fHour := 9;
          fMinute := 29;
          fSec := 45;
       END;
    END;
    DisplayDateTime(DT);
END;
```

Using object types enables you to extend records by adding new data fields that have the same access level (that is, require the same number of dot operators for access). Applying object types to the preceding example, you can write the records TimeRec and DateTimeRec as:

```
TYPE
    TimeRec = OBJECT
        fHour : BYTE;
        fMin  : BYTE;
        fSec  : BYTE;
    END;

    DateTimeRec = OBJECT(TimeRec)
        fYear  : WORD;
        fMonth : BYTE;
        fDay   : BYTE;
    END;

VAR DT : DateTimeRec;

BEGIN
    DT.fYear := 1994;
    DT.fMonth := 2;
    DT.fDay := 5;
    DT.fHour := 9;
    DT.fMinute := 29;
    DT.fSec := 45;
    DisplayDateTime(DT);
END;
```

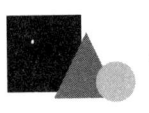

Notice that the new version of DateTimeRec has no fTime data field because it inherits the data fields fHour, fMin, and fSec from the parent object type. In addition, notice that the same assignment uses a single dot operator to access the data fields of the variable DT.

The previous example shows that you can use object types to emulate extendible records. As such, these object types lack any methods and must declare all their data fields as public.

> **NOTE**
>
> An *extendible record* is an object type with only public data fields. Inheritance enables you to create a hierarchy of extendible records, where descendants add new data fields to their inherited data fields.

Let me present an example that uses object types to simulate a small hierarchy of extendible records. Listing 4.1 shows the program RECOBJ1.PAS, which declares the object types NameRec, MailingRec, and ContactRec. These object types emulate extendible records. Each extendible record builds on the data fields inherited from its parent extendible record (thanks to inheritance). The program uses these object types strictly as extendible records.

The NameRec object type declares three public data fields: LastName, FirstName, and MiddleInit. The MailingRec object type is a descendant of NameRec. MailingRec inherits the preceding data fields and adds the Street, City, State, and Zip public data fields. Likewise, ContactRec, a descendant of MailingRec, inherits all of the preceding data fields and adds the Company, Title, Phone, and Fax public data fields.

The RECOBJ1.PAS program declares the array of ContactRec, named Contacts, and the array of ContactRec constants, named dB. This constant contains a miniature database. The program performs the following tasks:

1. Copies the elements of array dB into array Contacts.

2. Sorts the elements of array Contacts using the (uhm...) bubble sort method.

3. Uses the elements of the unordered array dB to search for matching elements in the sorted array Contacts. Once the program finds a match, it displays the index of the matching array as well as the matching record.

Listing 4.1. The program RECOBJ1.PAS, which simulates extendible records using object types.

```pascal
Program RecObj1;

{
  This program uses objects containing only data fields to
    simulate extendible records.
}

{$X+}

Uses Crt;

CONST MAX_CONTACTS = 5;

TYPE
  STRING40 = STRING[40];
  STRING14 = STRING[14];
  STRING2  = STRING[2];

  NameRec = OBJECT
    LastName   : STRING40;
    FirstName  : STRING40;
    MiddleInit : CHAR;
  END;

  MailingRec = OBJECT(NameRec)
    Street : STRING40;
    City   : STRING40;
    State  : STRING2;
    Zip    : STRING40;
  END;

  ContactRec = OBJECT(MailingRec)
    Company : STRING40;
    Title   : STRING40;
    Phone   : STRING14;
    Fax     : STRING14;
  END;

VAR Contacts : ARRAY[1..MAX_CONTACTS] OF ContactRec;
    Temp : ContactRec;
    I, J : WORD;
    NotFound : BOOLEAN;
```

continues

Listing 4.1. continued

```
CONST dB : ARRAY[1..MAX_CONTACTS] OF ContactRec =
      ((LastName : 'Shanes'; FirstName : 'John'; MiddleInit : 'C';
        Street : '123 Lothus Way'; City : 'Richmond'; State: 'IN';
        Zip : '46232'; Company : 'ESSO'; Title : 'Programmer';
        Phone : '(317) 555-1234'; Fax : '(317) 555-1235'),
       (LastName : 'Barnes'; FirstName : 'James'; MiddleInit : 'A';
        Street : '13 Tree Ln'; City : 'River'; State: 'MI';
        Zip : '48132'; Company : 'LCDEX'; Title : 'Manager';
        Phone : '(313) 555-5434'; Fax : '(313) 555-5436'),
       (LastName : 'Williams'; FirstName : 'Joe'; MiddleInit : 'F';
        Street : '33 River Rd'; City : 'Paris'; State: 'VA';
        Zip : '22134'; Company : 'HARDEX'; Title : 'Manager';
        Phone : '(703) 555-9988'; Fax : '(703) 555-9987'),
       (LastName : 'Salinas'; FirstName : 'Ronald'; MiddleInit : 'A';
        Street : '52 Cyprus Ln'; City : 'San Diego'; State: 'CA';
        Zip : '98231'; Company : 'CARITEX'; Title : 'Manager';
        Phone : '(619) 555-7778'; Fax : '(619) 555-7779'),
       (LastName : 'Rollins'; FirstName : 'Beth'; MiddleInit : 'J';
        Street : '24 Oaktree Ln'; City : 'Atlanta'; State: 'GA';
        Zip : '48231'; Company : 'PEACHPRO'; Title : 'Writer';
        Phone : '(404) 555-5555'; Fax : '(404) 555-5556')
       );

BEGIN
  FOR I := 1 TO MAX_CONTACTS DO
    Contacts[i] := dB[I];

  FOR I := 1 TO MAX_CONTACTS - 1 DO
    FOR J := I + 1 TO MAX_CONTACTS DO
      IF Contacts[I].LastName > Contacts[J].LastName THEN BEGIN
        Temp := Contacts[I];
        Contacts[I] := Contacts[J];
        Contacts[J] := Temp;
      END;

  FOR I := 1 TO MAX_CONTACTS DO BEGIN
    ClrScr;
    WRITELN('Searching for ', db[I].LastName);
    WRITELN;
    J := 1;
    NotFound := TRUE;
    WHILE NotFound AND (J <= MAX_CONTACTS) DO
      IF db[I].LastName <> Contacts[J].LastName THEN
        INC(J)
      ELSE
        NotFound := FALSE;

    IF NOT NotFound THEN BEGIN
      WRITELN('Found at index ', J);
      WRITELN;
```

```
      WITH Contacts[J] DO BEGIN
        WRITELN(FirstName, ' ', MiddleInit, '. ', LastName);
        WRITELN(Title);
        WRITELN(Company);
        WRITELN(Street);
        WRITELN(City, ', ' , State, ' ', Zip);
        WRITELN;
        WRITELN('Tel: ', Phone);
        WRITELN('Fax: ', Fax);
      END;
    END
    ELSE
      WRITELN('No match found');
    WRITELN;
    IF I < MAX_CONTACTS THEN
      WRITE('Press any key to continue...')
    ELSE
        WRITE('Press any key to end the program...');
    ReadKey;
  END;
END.
```

Here's a sample output for the program in Listing 4.1:

```
[BEGIN OUTPUT]
Searching for Barnes

Found at index 1

James A. Barnes
Manager
LCDEX
13 Tree Ln
River, MI 48132

Tel: (313) 555-5434
Fax: (313) 555-5436

Press any key to continue...
[END OUTPUT]
```

Extendible Records in an Object-Type Hierarchy

The last section focused on using object types as extendible records in non-OOP applications. In this section, I illustrate how to incorporate extendible records in the design of an object-type hierarchy.

Object-Oriented Programming with Borland Pascal 7

The general guidelines for an object-type hierarchy with extendible records are as follows:

- The root of the object-type hierarchy and at least one descendant object type must be object types that act as extendible records.
- The extendible records must be declared before the typical object types.
- The extendible records declare their data fields as private.
- The maximum number of extendible records in an object-type hierarchy is equal to N + 1, where N is the number of object-type branches in the hierarchy.

Figure 4.1 shows a schema for such an object-type hierarchy.

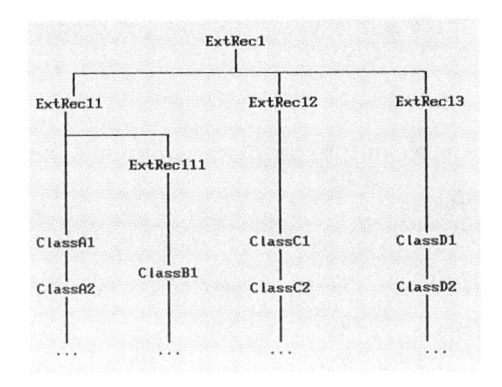

Figure 4.1. A typical object-type hierarchy using extendible records in an object-type hierarchy.

Let's look at an example. Listing 4.2 shows the program RECOBJ2.PAS, which illustrates extendible records in an object-type hierarchy. I created this program using the NameRec and MailingRec extendible records in Listing 4.1. I renamed these object types as TName and TMailing. These object types declare their data fields as private.

The program declares the object types TNameObj and TMailingObj as descendants of TName and TMailing. The TNameObj object type has the following four methods:

- The procedure SetVals assigns values to the inherited data fields LastName, FirstName, and MiddleInit.
- The procedure GetVals returns the values in data fields LastName, FirstName, and MiddleInit, using reference parameters.

Object Types As Extendible Records

- The Boolean function IsSameLastName compares the LastName data field with that of the parameter aName. The function returns True if the two fields are equal. Otherwise, the function returns False.

- The procedure Show displays the full name on the same line.

The RECOBJ2.PAS program also declares the object type TMailingObj, which has the following four methods:

- The procedure SetVals assigns values to the inherited data fields LastName, FirstName, MiddleInit, Company, Street, City, State, and Zip.

- The procedure GetVals returns the values in data fields LastName, FirstName, MiddleInit, Company, Street, City, State, and Zip, using reference parameters.

- The Boolean function IsSameLastName compares the LastName data field with that of the parameter aName. The function returns True if the two fields are equal. Otherwise, the function returns False.

- The procedure Show displays the full name and address.

The RECOBJ2.PAS program also declares the procedures CompareNames and CompareMailings to compare instances of TNameObj and TMailingObj, respectively. Both procedures display their parameters, using the TNameObj.Show and TMailingObj.Show methods, and comment on how these parameters compare.

The program also declares three instances of TNameObj and three instances of TMailingObj. After assigning values to these instances, using the SetVals methods, the program invokes the CompareNames and CompareMailings procedures to compare the various instances.

Listing 4.2. The program RECOBJ2.PAS, which illustrates extendible records in an object-type hierarchy.

```
Program RecObj2;

{
  This program uses extendible records in an object-type hierarchy.
}

{$X+}

Uses Crt;

CONST ARRAY_SIZE = 3;
```

continues

Listing 4.2. continued

```
TYPE
  STRING40 = STRING[40];
  STRING14 = STRING[14];
  STRING2 = STRING[2];

  TName = OBJECT
   PRIVATE
    LastName   : STRING40;
    FirstName  : STRING40;
    MiddleInit : CHAR;
  END;

  TNameObj = OBJECT(TName)
    PROCEDURE SetVals(aLastName,                  { input }
                      aFirstName  : STRING40; { input }
                      aMiddleInit : CHAR      { input });
    PROCEDURE GetVals(VAR aLastName,                  { output }
                          aFirstName  : STRING40; { output }
                      VAR aMiddleInit : CHAR      { output });
    FUNCTION IsSameLastName(VAR aName : TNameObj { input })
                                      : BOOLEAN;
    PROCEDURE Show;
  END;

  TMailing = OBJECT(TName)
   PRIVATE
    Street : STRING40;
    City   : STRING40;
    State  : STRING2;
    Zip    : STRING40;
  END;

  TMailingObj = OBJECT(TMailing)
    PROCEDURE SetVals(aLastName,                  { input }
                      aFirstName  : STRING40; { input }
                      aMiddleInit : CHAR;     { input }
                      aStreet,                    { input }
                      aCity       : STRING40; { input }
                      aState      : STRING2;  { input }
                      aZip        : STRING40  { input });
    PROCEDURE GetVals(VAR aLastName,                  { output }
                          aFirstName  : STRING40; { output }
                      VAR aMiddleInit : CHAR;     { output }
                      VAR aStreet,                    { output }
                          aCity       : STRING40; { output }
                      VAR aState      : STRING2;  { output }
                      VAR aZip        : STRING40  { output });
    FUNCTION IsSameLastName(VAR aMailing : TMailingObj { input })
                                         : BOOLEAN;
```

Object Types As Extendible Records

```
    PROCEDURE Show;
  END;

{---------------------------------------- SetVals ----------}

PROCEDURE TNameObj.SetVals(aLastName,              { input }
                          aFirstName  : STRING40;  { input }
                          aMiddleInit : CHAR       { input });
BEGIN
  LastName := aLastName;
  FirstName := aFirstName;
  MiddleInit := aMiddleInit;
END;

{---------------------------------------- GetVals ----------}

PROCEDURE TNameObj.GetVals(VAR aLastName,              { output }
                              aFirstName  : STRING40;  { output }
                          VAR aMiddleInit : CHAR       { output });
BEGIN
  aLastName := LastName;
  aFirstName := FirstName;
  aMiddleInit := MiddleInit;
END;

{---------------------------------------- IsSameLastName ----------}

FUNCTION TNameObj.IsSameLastName(VAR aName : TNameObj { input })
                                                : BOOLEAN;
BEGIN
  IsSameLastName := LastName = aName.LastName;
END;

{---------------------------------------- Show ----------}

PROCEDURE TNameObj.Show;
BEGIN
  WRITE(FirstName, ' ', MiddleInit, '. ', LastName);
END;

{---------------------------------------- SetVals ----------}

PROCEDURE TMailingObj.SetVals(
                     aLastName,              { input }
                     aFirstName  : STRING40; { input }
                     aMiddleInit : CHAR;     { input }
                     aStreet,                { input }
                     aCity       : STRING40; { input }
                     aState      : STRING2;  { input }
                     aZip        : STRING40  { input });
```

continues

Listing 4.2. continued

```pascal
BEGIN
  LastName := aLastName;
  FirstName := aFirstName;
  MiddleInit := aMiddleInit;
  Street := aStreet;
  City := aCity;
  State := aState;
  Zip := aZip;
END;

{------------------------------------------ GetVals ----------}

PROCEDURE TMailingObj.GetVals(
                      VAR aLastName,              { output }
                          aFirstName : STRING40;  { output }
                      VAR aMiddleInit : CHAR;     { output }
                      VAR aStreet ,               { output }
                          aCity      : STRING40;  { output }
                      VAR aState     : STRING2;   { output }
                      VAR aZip       : STRING40   { output });
BEGIN
  aLastName := LastName;
  aFirstName := FirstName;
  aMiddleInit := MiddleInit;
  aStreet := Street;
  aCity := City;
  aState := State;
  aZip := Zip;
END;

{---------------------------------- IsSameLastName ----------}

FUNCTION TMailingObj.IsSameLastName(
                        VAR aMailing : TMailingObj { input })
                                     : BOOLEAN;
BEGIN
  IsSameLastName := LastName = aMailing.LastName;
END;

{-------------------------------------------- Show ----------}

PROCEDURE TMailingObj.Show;

VAR x : BYTE;
```

```
BEGIN
  x := WhereX;
  WRITE(FirstName, ' ', MiddleInit, '. ', LastName);
  GotoXY(x, WhereY + 1); WRITE(Street);
  GotoXY(x, WhereY + 1); WRITE(City, ', ', State, ' ', Zip);
END;

{---------------------- program procedures -------------------}

PROCEDURE CompareNames(VAR Name1,                { input }
                          Name2  : TNameObj { input });
BEGIN
  Name1.Show;
  IF Name1.IsSameLastName(Name2) THEN
    WRITE(' has the same last name as ')
  ELSE
    WRITE(' does not have the same last name as ');
  Name2.Show;
  WRITELN;
  WRITELN;
END;

PROCEDURE CompareMailings(VAR Name1,              { input }
                             Name2  : TMailingObj { input });
BEGIN
  ClrScr;
  WRITELN('The following mailings:');
  WRITELN;
  Name1.Show;
  WRITELN;
  WRITELN;
  WRITELN('And');
  WRITELN;
  Name2.Show;
  WRITELN;
  WRITELN;
  IF Name1.IsSameLastName(Name2) THEN
    WRITELN('have the same last name.')
  ELSE
    WRITELN('do not have the same last name.');
  WRITELN;
  WRITE('Press any key to continue');
  ReadKey;
END;

VAR Name1, Name2, Name3 : TNameObj;
    Mail1, Mail2, Mail3 : TMailingObj;
```

continues

Listing 4.2. continued

```
BEGIN
  ClrScr;
  Name1.SetVals('Sams', 'Jeff', 'C');
  Name2.SetVals('Rollins', 'David', 'A');
  Name3.SetVals('Rollins', 'Keith', 'V');
  CompareNames(Name1, Name2);
  CompareNames(Name1, Name3);
  CompareNames(Name2, Name3);
  WRITELN;
  WRITE('Press any key to continue');
  ReadKey;

  Mail1.SetVals('Carl', 'Jeff', 'C', '123 River Rd',
                'Richmond', 'IN', '46323');
  Mail2.SetVals('Rogers', 'David', 'B', '45 Ridgeway',
                'Tulsa', 'OK', '54837');
  Mail3.SetVals('Rogers', 'Malcom', 'C', '98 Borland way',
                'Santa Cruz', 'CA', '98101');
  CompareMailings(Mail1, Mail2);
  CompareMailings(Mail1, Mail3);
  CompareMailings(Mail2, Mail3);
END.
```

Here is a sample output for the program in Listing 4.2 comparing names:

```
[BEGIN OUTPUT]
Jeff C. Sams does not have the same last name as David A. Rollins

Jeff C. Sams does not have the same last name as Keith V. Rollins

David A. Rollins has the same last name as Keith V. Rollins


Press any key to continue
[END OUTPUT]
```

Here's a sample output for the program in Listing 4.2 comparing mailings:

```
[BEGIN OUTPUT]
The following mailings:

Jeff C. Carl
123 River Rd
Richmond, IN 46323

And
```

Object Types As Extendible Records

```
Malcom C. Rogers
98 Borland way
Santa Cruz, CA 98101

do not have the same last name.

Press any key to continue
[END OUTPUT]
```

Summary

This chapter discussed how to emulate extendible records using object types. You learned about the following:

- An *extendible record* is an object type with only public data fields. Inheritance enables you to create a hierarchy of extendible records, where descendants add new data fields to the data fields they inherited.

- Object types can be used as extendible records in a hierarchy of object types. The general guidelines for such an object-type hierarchy are as follows:

    The root of the object-type hierarchy and at least one descendant object type must be object types that act as extendible records.

    The extendible records must be declared before the typical object types.

    The extendible records declare their data fields as private.

Chapter 5

Abstract Object Types

Abstraction is an analysis tool that removes details from an examined system. Abstraction allows you to focus on what happens to the system and to ignore how the changes happen. Object-oriented analysis and design methods use abstraction as an effective way to study the domain of the problem and examine the operations of the classes involved. This chapter discusses abstract object types and their role in the design of an object-type hierarchy. You'll learn about the following:

- Basic rules for declaring abstract object types
- Abstract object types as base types in hierarchies
- Abstract object types as base types in subhierarchies

Basic Rules for Abstract Object Types

When you design an object-type hierarchy, you can specify the common operations in that hierarchy using an abstract object type. The latter type enables you to specify *what* happens to the instances of the various descendant object types. The descendants themselves fill in the details on *how* to carry out the operations of an object type.

Abstract object types fall into two categories: *purely abstract* and *partially functioning*. Purely abstract object types specify the public and private methods common to the descendants in the object-type hierarchy. Implementations of these methods contain no statements. (Thus, abstract object types are completely nonfunctional.)

Partially functioning abstract object types specify the public and private methods along with data fields that are common to all or most descendants. In addition, they implement some of the methods common to all or most of the descendants.

Both types of abstract object types have the following aspects in common:

- You must declare all of the object type's methods and data fields as private. This kind of declaration prevents a client program from creating nondummy instances of the abstract object types.

- The methods not implemented by the abstract object type must be declared virtual. This kind of declaration ensures that the descendants also declare these methods as virtual and use the same parameter list. The benefit of a consistent parameter list is the support of polymorphic behavior. Such behavior supports consistent operations among various descendant classes. Partially functioning abstract object types benefit more from this feature than do purely abstract object types.

Abstract Object Types as Base Types

The most common place for an abstract object type in an object-type hierarchy is at the root of the hierarchy. When the hierarchy is simple, consisting of a single chain of inheritance, a single abstract object type suffices. When the object-type hierarchy has many branches, you may end up with several abstract object types. Figure 5.1 shows the schema of an object-type hierarchy that contains several abstract object types. The `AbsType1` object type is common to all the hierarchy branches. Each branch then has an additional abstract object type to specify more operations particular to that branch.

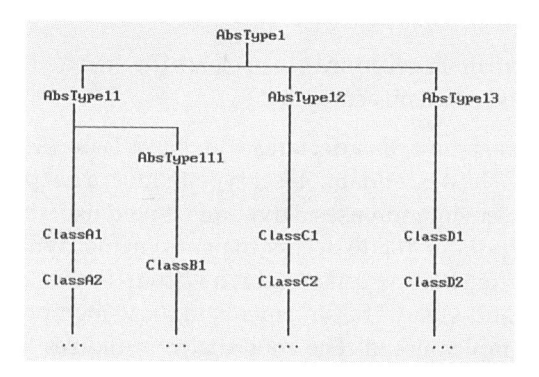

Figure 5.1. An object-type hierarchy that contains abstract object types.

Let's look at an example. Listing 5.1 shows the `AbsStack` library unit, which implements a stack object-type hierarchy using an abstract object type. The library unit supports stacks of strings with the following basic operations:

- Clearing a stack
- Pushing data onto a stack
- Popping data off a stack

The library declares a hierarchy of three object types: `TAbsStack`, `TStrStack`, and `TVMStrStack`. The `TAbsStack`, as the name might suggest, is an abstract object type. It declares all of its data fields and methods as private. We know the object type is a partially functioning abstract type because it declares data fields and contains a few functioning (or implemented, if you prefer) methods. The data fields `Height` and `AllocateError` maintain the stack height and data allocation status, respectively. The object type declares the following methods:

- The dummy constructor and destructor. I included these special methods because of the virtual methods `Push`, `Pop`, and `Clear`.
- The Boolean function `GetAllocateError` returns the value in the `AllocateError` data field.
- The Boolean function `IsEmpty` returns True when the `Height` data field is 0. Otherwise, the function returns False.

- The virtual procedure Push pushes a string onto the stack. This method has no statements in this object type.

- The virtual Boolean function Pop pops a string off the stack. This method has no statements in this object type.

- The virtual procedure Clear clears the stack. This method has no statements in this object type.

The library unit also declares the object type TStrStack as a descendant of TAbsStack. The descendant object type models a heap-based stack of strings. The actual implementation uses a dynamic linked list. The TStrStack object type declares the pointer Top to access the supporting dynamic linked list. TStrStack declares a functioning constructor, a virtual destructor, and the virtual methods Push, Pop, and Clear. The statements in these methods specify how stack operations are implemented. The constructor initializes the stack by initializing the supporting dynamic linked list. The destructor clears the supporting linked list.

The library unit also declares the object type TVMStrStack as another descendant of TAbsStack. This descendant object type models a disk-based stack of strings. The actual implementation uses a random-access file. The TVMStrStack object type declares the DataBuffer, ErrorMessage, and VFile data fields. The object type declares a functioning constructor, a virtual destructor, and the virtual methods Push, Pop, and Clear. The statements in these methods specify how stack operations are implemented—with the help of the supporting file. The constructor opens the supporting random-access data file. The destructor first closes the file and then deletes it.

Listing 5.1. The AbsStack library unit, which implements a stack object-type hierarchy using an abstract object type.

```
UNIT AbsStack;

{ This library implements classes of generic stacks with the following
set of operations:

    + Push
    + Pop
    + Clear
}

{*****************************************************************}
{************************} INTERFACE {***************************}
{*****************************************************************}
```

Abstract Object Types 5

```
{$V-}

TYPE
    { ********************* Abstract Stack *************** }
    TAbsStack = OBJECT
      PRIVATE
        Height        : WORD;        { height of stack            }
        AllocateError : BOOLEAN;     { dynamic allocation error   }
        { ************* State Manipulation Methods ************* }
        CONSTRUCTOR Init;
        DESTRUCTOR Done; VIRTUAL;

        { ***************** State Query Methods **************** }
        FUNCTION GetAllocateError : BOOLEAN;
        FUNCTION IsEmpty : BOOLEAN;

        { ************* Object Manipulation Methods ************ }
        PROCEDURE Push(X : STRING { input   }); VIRTUAL;
        FUNCTION Pop(VAR X : STRING { output  })
                         : BOOLEAN; VIRTUAL;
        PROCEDURE Clear; VIRTUAL;
    END;

    StrStackPtr = ^StrStackRec;
    StrStackRec = RECORD
        NodeData : STRING;
        NextLink : StrStackPtr
    END;

    TStrStack = OBJECT(TAbsStack)
        { ************* State Manipulation Methods ************* }
        CONSTRUCTOR Init;
        DESTRUCTOR Done; VIRTUAL;

        { ************* Object Manipulation Methods ************ }
        PROCEDURE Push(X : STRING { input   }); VIRTUAL;
        FUNCTION Pop(VAR X : STRING { output  })
                         : BOOLEAN; VIRTUAL;
        PROCEDURE Clear; VIRTUAL;
      PRIVATE
        Top : StrStackPtr; { STRING to the top of the stack }
    END;

    TVMStrStack = OBJECT(TAbsStack)
        { ************* State Manipulation Methods ************* }
        CONSTRUCTOR Init(Filename : STRING { input   });
        DESTRUCTOR Done; VIRTUAL;
```

continues

Listing 5.1. continued

```
      { ***************** State Query Methods **************** }
      FUNCTION GetErrorMessage : STRING;

      { ************** Object Manipulation Methods ************ }
      PROCEDURE Push(X : STRING { input  }); VIRTUAL;
      FUNCTION Pop(VAR X : STRING { output })
                      : BOOLEAN; VIRTUAL;
      PROCEDURE Clear; VIRTUAL;
    PRIVATE
      DataBuffer,               { data buffer }
      ErrorMessage   : STRING;  { error message }
      VMfile         : FILE;    { virtual file handle }
  END;

{*****************************************************************}
{**********************} IMPLEMENTATION {*************************}
{*****************************************************************}


{------------------------------------- HeapErrorHandler ----------}

FUNCTION HeapErrorHandler(Size : WORD { input  }) : INTEGER; FAR;

BEGIN
    HeapErrorHandler := 1
END;


{------------------------------------------------ Init -----------}

CONSTRUCTOR TAbsStack.Init;

BEGIN
    { do nothing }
END;


{------------------------------------------------ Done -----------}

DESTRUCTOR TAbsStack.Done;
{ destructor used to clear the stack. }
BEGIN
    { do nothing }
END;


{----------------------------------------------- IsEmpty ---------}

FUNCTION TAbsStack.IsEmpty : BOOLEAN;
{ logical function that queries the empty-state of the stack. }
BEGIN
    IsEmpty := Height = 0
END;
```

Abstract Object Types 5

```
{--------------------------------------------- Push -----------}

PROCEDURE TAbsStack.Push(X : STRING { input  });
BEGIN
END;

{--------------------------------------------- Pop  -----------}

FUNCTION TAbsStack.Pop(VAR X : STRING { output  }) : BOOLEAN;
BEGIN
  Pop := FALSE;
END;

{--------------------------------- GetAllocateError  -----------}

FUNCTION TAbsStack.GetAllocateError : BOOLEAN;
{ returns the status of dynamic allocation for the last Pop
message sent to the object. Function returns TRUE if the dynamic
allocation failed, otherwise, returns FALSE. }
BEGIN
    GetAllocateError := AllocateError
END;

{--------------------------------------------- Clear -----------}

PROCEDURE TAbsStack.Clear;
BEGIN
  { do nothing }
END;



{--------------------------------------------- Init  -----------}

CONSTRUCTOR TStrStack.Init;
{ constructor to initialize generic stack. }
BEGIN
    Height := 0;
    AllocateError := FALSE;
    Top := NIL
END;

{--------------------------------------------- Done  -----------}

DESTRUCTOR TStrStack.Done;
{ destructor used to clear the stack. }
BEGIN
    Clear
END;
```

continues

Listing 5.1. continued

```pascal
{---------------------------------------------- Push ------------}

PROCEDURE TStrStack.Push(X : STRING { input  });
{ pushes the data accessed by STRING X onto the stack.}

VAR p : StrStackPtr;

BEGIN
    AllocateError := FALSE;
    IF Top <> NIL THEN BEGIN
        New(p); { allocate new stack element }
        IF p = NIL THEN BEGIN
            AllocateError := TRUE;
            Exit;
        END;
        p^.NodeData := X;
        p^.NextLink := Top;
        Top := p
    END
    ELSE BEGIN
        New(Top);
        IF Top = NIL THEN BEGIN
            AllocateError := TRUE;
            Exit;
        END;
        Top^.NodeData := X;
        Top^.NextLink := NIL
    END;
    INC(Height)
END;

{---------------------------------------------- Pop ------------}

FUNCTION TStrStack.Pop(VAR X : STRING { input  }) : BOOLEAN;
{ pops the top of the stack and returns a Boolean value.
  Function returns TRUE if the operation was successful. A
  FALSE value is returned if the Pop message is sent to an empty
  stack. }

VAR p : StrStackPtr;

BEGIN
    IF Height > 0 THEN BEGIN
        X := Top^.NodeData;
        p := Top;
        Top := Top^.NextLink;
        Dispose(p); { deallocate stack node }
        DEC(Height);
        Pop := TRUE { return function value }
    END
```

Abstract Object Types

```
    ELSE
        Pop := FALSE { return function value }
END;

{---------------------------------------------- Clear -----------}

PROCEDURE TStrStack.Clear;
{ clears the generic stack object. }

VAR x : STRING;

BEGIN
    WHILE Pop(x) DO
        { do nothing };
END;

{---------------------------------------------- Init -----------}

CONSTRUCTOR TVMStrStack.Init(Filename : STRING { input });

{ constructor to initialize generic stack. }
BEGIN
    Height := 0;
    Assign(VMfile, Filename);
    {$I-} Rewrite(VMfile, SizeOf(STRING)); {$I+}
    IF IOresult <> 0 THEN BEGIN
        ErrorMessage := 'Cannot open file ' + Filename;
        Exit
    END;
    AllocateError := FALSE;
    ErrorMessage := ''
END;

{---------------------------------------------- Done -----------}

DESTRUCTOR TVMStrStack.Done;
{ destructor used to clear the stack. }
BEGIN
    Clear;
END;

{-------------------------------------- GetErrorMessage -----------}

FUNCTION TVMStrStack.GetErrorMessage : STRING;
{ returns the error message }
BEGIN
    GetErrorMessage := ErrorMessage
END;
```

continues

Listing 5.1. continued

```
{------------------------------------------------- Push -----------}

PROCEDURE TVMStrStack.Push(X : STRING { input });
{ pushes the data accessed by parameter X onto the stack. }
BEGIN
    INC(Height);
    Seek(VMfile, Height-1);
    BlockWrite(VMfile, X, 1);
END;

{------------------------------------------------- Pop ------------}

FUNCTION TVMStrStack.Pop(VAR X : STRING { output }) : BOOLEAN;
{ pops the top of the stack and returns a Boolean value. }
BEGIN
    IF Height > 0 THEN BEGIN
        DEC(Height);
        Seek(VMfile, Height);
        BlockRead(VMfile, X, 1);
        Pop := TRUE
    END
    ELSE
        Pop := FALSE;
END;

{------------------------------------------------- Clear ----------}

PROCEDURE TVMStrStack.Clear;
{ clears the generic stack object. }
BEGIN
    Height := 0;
    {$I-}
    Close(VMfile);
    Erase(VMfile);
    {$I+}
END;

BEGIN
    HeapError := @HeapErrorHandler
END.
```

Let's look at a test program for the AbsStack library unit. Listing 5.2 contains the program STACK2.PAS, which tests the AbsStack library unit presented in Listing 5.1. The program declares S as the instance of TStrStack and VS as the instance of TVMStrStack. The program performs the following relevant tasks:

Abstract Object Types 5

1. Instantiates the instance S with the constructor TStrStack.Init.
2. Uses a FOR loop to push onto the stack S the elements of the constant string array StringArray. The program sends a Push message to the instance S to push each string.
3. Pops the strings off the stack S. The program sends the Pop message to the instance S in a WHILE loop. The loop iterates as long as there is an item popped off the stack. The body of the WHILE loop displays the popped string.
4. Removes the instance S by using the destructor.
5. Instantiates the instance VS with the constructor TVMStrStack.Init. This step specifies the file VS.DAT as the supporting file.
6. Uses a FOR loop to push onto the stack VS the elements of the constant string array StringArray. The program sends a Push message to the instance VS to push each string.
7. Pops the strings off the stack VS. The program sends the Pop message to the instance VS and uses a WHILE loop. This loop iterates as long as there's an item popped off the stack. The body of the WHILE loop displays the popped string.
8. Removes the instance VS by using the destructor. This task closes and deletes the file VS.DAT.

Listing 5.2. The program STACK2.PAS, which tests the AbsStack library unit.

```
Program Stack2;

{
    This program tests stacks of strings.
}
{$M 8192, 0, 655350}

Uses Crt, AbsStack;

CONST WAIT = 1000;
      MAX_STRINGS = 10;
```

continues

Listing 5.2. continued

```pascal
CONST StringArray : ARRAY [1..MAX_STRINGS] OF STRING =
                      ('California', 'Virginia', 'Michigan',
                       'New York', 'Washington', 'Nevada',
                       'Alabama', 'Alaska', 'Florida', 'Maine');

VAR S : TStrStack;
    VS : TVMStrStack;
    AString : STRING;
    I : BYTE;

BEGIN
    ClrScr;
    WRITELN('Testing heap-based stacks objects');
    S.Init;
    FOR I := 1 TO MAX_STRINGS DO BEGIN
        WRITELN('Pushing ', StringArray[I]:12, ' into the stack');
        S.Push(StringArray[I]);
        Delay(WAIT);
    END;
    WRITE('Press any key to continue... ');
    ReadKey;
    WRITELN;

    WHILE S.Pop(AString) DO BEGIN
        WRITELN('Popping off ', AString:12, ' from the stack');
        Delay(WAIT);
    END;
    WRITELN;
    WRITE('Press any key to continue... ');
    ReadKey;
    S.Done;

    ClrScr;
    WRITELN('Testing virtual stacks objects');
    VS.Init('VS.DAT');
    FOR I := MAX_STRINGS DOWNTO 1 DO BEGIN
        WRITELN('Pushing ', StringArray[I]:12, ' into the stack');
        VS.Push(StringArray[I]);
        Delay(WAIT);
    END;
    WRITE('Press any key to continue... ');
    ReadKey;
    WRITELN;

    WHILE VS.Pop(AString) DO BEGIN
        WRITELN('Popping off ', AString:12, ' from the stack');
        Delay(WAIT);
    END;
    WRITELN;
    WRITE('Press any key to end the program...');
```

Abstract Object Types 5

```
    ReadKey;
    VS.Done;
END.
```

Here's a sample output for the program in Listing 5.2:

```
[BEGIN OUTPUT]
Testing heap-based stacks objects
Pushing    California into the stack
Pushing      Virginia into the stack
Pushing      Michigan into the stack
Pushing      New York into the stack
Pushing    Washington into the stack
Pushing        Nevada into the stack
Pushing       Alabama into the stack
Pushing        Alaska into the stack
Pushing       Florida into the stack
Pushing         Maine into the stack
Press any key to continue...
Popping off            Maine from the stack
Popping off          Florida from the stack
Popping off           Alaska from the stack
Popping off          Alabama from the stack
Popping off           Nevada from the stack
Popping off       Washington from the stack
Popping off         New York from the stack
Popping off         Michigan from the stack
Popping off         Virginia from the stack
Popping off       California from the stack

Press any key to continue...
```

The screen clears

```
Testing virtual stacks objects
Pushing         Maine into the stack
Pushing       Florida into the stack
Pushing        Alaska into the stack
Pushing       Alabama into the stack
Pushing        Nevada into the stack
Pushing    Washington into the stack
Pushing      New York into the stack
Pushing      Michigan into the stack
Pushing      Virginia into the stack
Pushing    California into the stack
Press any key to continue...
Popping off       California from the stack
Popping off         Virginia from the stack
Popping off         Michigan from the stack
Popping off         New York from the stack
Popping off       Washington from the stack
```

continues

Listing 5.2. continued

```
Popping off       Nevada from the stack
Popping off      Alabama from the stack
Popping off       Alaska from the stack
Popping off      Florida from the stack
Popping off        Maine from the stack

Press any key to end the program...
[END OUTPUT]
```

Abstract Objects in Subhierarchies

You also can use abstract object types as the base classes in subhierarchies. In other words, such abstract object types have nonabstract object type parents. This kind of abstract object type occurs more often in sophisticated object-type hierarchies, such as Turbo Vision. Figure 5.2 shows an object-type hierarchy that contains internal abstract object types.

Conceptually, both kinds of abstract object types are similar. The kind of abstract object type presented in the last section is concentrated at the root of the hierarchy. The kind of abstract object type presented here is located well inside the object-type hierarchy. In addition, this genre of classes tends to be partially functioning. Of course, declaring all of the data fields and methods as private ensures that client programs do not use this type accidentally.

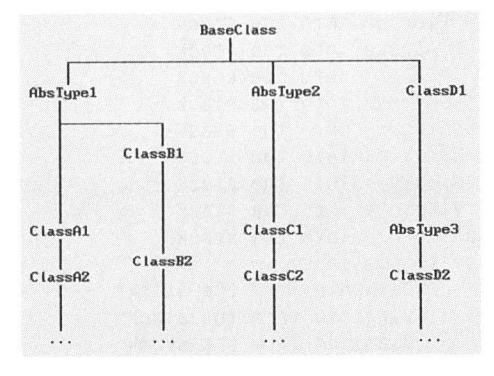

Figure 5.2. An object-type hierarchy that contains internal abstract object types.

Let's look at a program that illustrates an abstract object type at the root of a subhierarchy. Listing 5.3 shows the library unit `AbsArray`, which contains the example. The library declares the following object types:

- The `TArray` object type models an unordered dynamic array of strings.
- The abstract object type `TAbsSortArray`, a descendant of `TArray`, defines operations for the next object type.
- The `TSortArray` object type, a descendant of `TAbsSortArray`, models ordered arrays. This object type supports case-sensitive sorting and searching.
- The `TNocaseSortArray` object type, another descendant of `TAbsSortArray`, models ordered arrays. This object type supports case-insensitive sorting and searching.

The object types `TSortArray` and `TNocaseSortArray` offer two sample variations of ordered arrays. You can add more sibling object types (for example, to sort and search by specific portions of a string or to arrange arrays in descending order).

Listing 5.3. The library unit `AbsArray`, which contains abstract object types inside an object-type hierarchy.

```
Unit AbsArray;

{ This library implements arrays with an abstract object type }

{*****************************************************************}
{************************} INTERFACE {***************************}
{*****************************************************************}

{$V-,R-}

CONST NOT_FOUND = 0;
      DEFAULT_SIZE = 10;
      MAX_CHARS = 20;

TYPE
    LeString = STRING[MAX_CHARS];
    OneArray = ARRAY[1..1] OF LeString;
    ArrayPtr = ^OneArray;
```

continues

Listing 5.3. continued

```
TArray = OBJECT
  CONSTRUCTOR Init(ArraySize : WORD);
  DESTRUCTOR Done; VIRTUAL;
  FUNCTION GetMaxSize : WORD;
  FUNCTION GetWorkSize : WORD;
  FUNCTION GetAllocateError : BOOLEAN;

  FUNCTION Store(X     : LeString; { input }
                 Index : WORD      { input })
                       : BOOLEAN; VIRTUAL;
  FUNCTION Recall(VAR X   : LeString; { output }
                  Index : WORD      { output })
                        : BOOLEAN; VIRTUAL;
  FUNCTION Search(Key : LeString { input }): WORD; VIRTUAL;
 PRIVATE
   DataPtr : ArrayPtr;
   MaxSize,
   WorkSize : WORD;
   AllocateError : BOOLEAN;
END;

TAbsSortArray = OBJECT(TArray)
 PRIVATE
  InOrder : BOOLEAN;
  CONSTRUCTOR Init(ArraySize : WORD);
  DESTRUCTOR Done; VIRTUAL;

  FUNCTION Store(X     : LeString; { input }
                 Index : WORD      { input })
                       : BOOLEAN; VIRTUAL;
  FUNCTION Search(Key : LeString { input }): WORD; VIRTUAL;
  PROCEDURE Sort; VIRTUAL;
END;

TSortArray = OBJECT(TAbsSortArray)
  CONSTRUCTOR Init(ArraySize : WORD { input });
  DESTRUCTOR Done; VIRTUAL;
  FUNCTION Search(Key : LeString { input }): WORD; VIRTUAL;
  PROCEDURE Sort; VIRTUAL;
END;

TNocaseSortArray = OBJECT(TAbsSortArray)
  CONSTRUCTOR Init(ArraySize : WORD { input });
  DESTRUCTOR Done; VIRTUAL;
  FUNCTION Search(Key : LeString { input }): WORD; VIRTUAL;
  PROCEDURE Sort; VIRTUAL;
END;
```

Abstract Object Types

```
{************************************************************************}
{***********************} IMPLEMENTATION {***************************}
{************************************************************************}

{------------------------------------- HeapErrorHandler ----------}

FUNCTION HeapErrorHandler(Size : WORD { input  }) : INTEGER; FAR;

BEGIN
    HeapErrorHandler := 1
END;

FUNCTION UpCaseStr(S : LeString { input }) : LeString;

VAR i : BYTE;

BEGIN
  FOR i := 1 TO Length(S) DO
    S[I] := UpCase(S[I]);
  UpCaseStr := S;
END;

{-------------------------------------------- Init -----------}

CONSTRUCTOR TArray.Init(ArraySize : WORD { input });
{ construct instance of TArray }

VAR i : WORD;

BEGIN
  MaxSize := ArraySize;
  IF MaxSize = 0 THEN
    MaxSize := DEFAULT_SIZE;
  WorkSize := 0;
  GetMem(DataPtr, MaxSize * SizeOf(LeString));
  AllocateError := DataPtr = NIL;
  IF NOT AllocateError THEN
    FOR i := 1 TO MaxSize DO
      DataPtr^[i] := '';
END;

{-------------------------------------------- Done -----------}

DESTRUCTOR TArray.Done;
{ remove instance of TArray }
BEGIN
  IF DataPtr <> NIL THEN
    FreeMem(DataPtr, MaxSize * SizeOf(LeString))
END;
```

continues

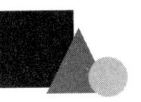

Listing 5.3. continued

```
{---------------------------------------- GetMaxSize -----------}

FUNCTION TArray.GetMaxSize : WORD;
{ return the maximum size of the array }
BEGIN
  GetMaxSize := MaxSize
END;

{---------------------------------------- GetWorkSize -----------}

FUNCTION TArray.GetWorkSize : WORD;
{ return the working size of the array }
BEGIN
  GetWorkSize := WorkSize
END;

{-------------------------------------- GetAllocateError -----------}

FUNCTION TArray.GetAllocateError : BOOLEAN;
{ get the allocation error status }
BEGIN
  GetAllocateError := AllocateError
END;

{---------------------------------------------- Store -----------}

FUNCTION TArray.Store(X     : LeString; { input }
                     Index : WORD      { input }) : BOOLEAN;
{ store an array element }
BEGIN
  IF (Index > 0) AND (Index <= MaxSize) THEN BEGIN
    IF Index > WorkSize THEN
      WorkSize := Index;
    DataPtr^[Index] := X;
    Store := TRUE;
  END
  ELSE
    Store := FALSE;
END;

{---------------------------------------------- Recall -----------}

FUNCTION TArray.Recall(VAR X     : LeString; { output }
                          Index : WORD      { input }) : BOOLEAN;
{ recall the contents of an array element }
```

Abstract Object Types 5

```
    BEGIN
      IF (Index > 0) AND (Index <= WorkSize) THEN BEGIN
        X := DataPtr^[Index];
        Recall := TRUE;
      END
      ELSE
        Recall := FALSE;
    END;

{---------------------------------------------- Search -----------}

    FUNCTION TArray.Search(Key : LeString { input }) : WORD;

    VAR notFound : BOOLEAN;
        i : WORD;

    BEGIN
      notFound := TRUE;
      i := 1;
      WHILE notFound AND (i <= WorkSize) DO
        IF Key <> DataPtr^[i] THEN
          INC(i)
        ELSE
          notFound := FALSE;

      IF notFound THEN
        Search := NOT_FOUND
      ELSE
        Search := i;
    END;

{---------------------------------------------- Init -----------}

    CONSTRUCTOR TAbsSortArray.Init(ArraySize : WORD { input });
    BEGIN
    END;

{---------------------------------------------- Done -----------}

    DESTRUCTOR TAbsSortArray.Done;
    BEGIN
    END;

{---------------------------------------------- Store -----------}

    FUNCTION TAbsSortArray.Store(X     : LeString; { input }
                                 Index : WORD      { input }) : BOOLEAN;
    { store an array element }
```

continues

123

Listing 5.3. continued

```
VAR result : BOOLEAN;

BEGIN
  result := INHERITED Store(X, Index);
  IF result THEN InOrder := FALSE;
END;

{---------------------------------------------- Search -----------}

FUNCTION TAbsSortArray.Search(Key : LeString { input }) : WORD;
BEGIN
  Search := NOT_FOUND;
END;

{---------------------------------------------- Sort -----------}

PROCEDURE TAbsSortArray.Sort;
BEGIN
END;

{---------------------------------------------- Init -----------}

CONSTRUCTOR TSortArray.Init(ArraySize : WORD { input });
{ construct instance of TSortArray }

VAR i : WORD;

BEGIN
  TArray.Init(ArraySize);
  InOrder := FALSE;
END;

{---------------------------------------------- Done -----------}

DESTRUCTOR TSortArray.Done;
{ remove instance of TSortArray }
BEGIN
  IF DataPtr <> NIL THEN
    FreeMem(DataPtr, MaxSize * SizeOf(LeString))
END;

{---------------------------------------------- Search -----------}

FUNCTION TSortArray.Search(Key : LeString { input }) : WORD;

VAR lo, hi, median : WORD;
    i : WORD;
```

Abstract Object Types 5

```
  BEGIN
    IF NOT InOrder THEN
      Sort;
    lo := 1;
    hi := WorkSize;
    REPEAT
      median := (lo + hi) DIV 2;
      IF Key > DataPtr^[median] THEN
        lo := median + 1
      ELSE
        hi := median - 1;
    UNTIL (lo > hi) OR (Key = DataPtr^[median]);

    IF Key = DataPtr^[median] THEN
      Search := median
    ELSE
      Search := NOT_FOUND;
END;

{-------------------------------------------- Sort -----------}

PROCEDURE TSortArray.Sort;
{ sort the array using the entire strings }

VAR i, j, offset : WORD;
    temp : LeString;

BEGIN
  IF InOrder THEN EXIT;
  offset := WorkSize;
  REPEAT
    offset := (offset * 8) DIV 11;
    IF offset = 0 THEN offset := 1;
    InOrder := TRUE;
    FOR i := 1 TO WorkSize - offset DO BEGIN
      j := i + offset;
      IF DataPtr^[i] > DataPtr^[j] THEN BEGIN
        InOrder := FALSE;
        temp := DataPtr^[i];
        DataPtr^[i] := DataPtr^[j];
        DataPtr^[j] := temp;
      END;
    END;
  UNTIL InOrder AND (offset = 1);
END;

{-------------------------------------------- Init -----------}

CONSTRUCTOR TNocaseSortArray.Init(ArraySize : WORD { input });
{ construct instance of TNocaseSortArray }
```

continues

Listing 5.3. continued

```pascal
VAR temp : BYTE;

BEGIN
  TArray.Init(ArraySize);
  InOrder := FALSE;
END;

{------------------------------------------- Done -----------}

DESTRUCTOR TNocaseSortArray.Done;
{ remove instance of TNocaseSortArray }
BEGIN
  IF DataPtr <> NIL THEN
    FreeMem(DataPtr, MaxSize * SizeOf(LeString))
END;

{------------------------------------------- Search -----------}

FUNCTION TNocaseSortArray.Search(Key : LeString { input }) : WORD;

VAR lo, hi, median : WORD;
    i : WORD;

BEGIN
  IF NOT InOrder THEN
    Sort;
  lo := 1;
  hi := WorkSize;
  Key := UpCaseStr(Key);
  REPEAT
    median := (lo + hi) DIV 2;
    IF Key > UpCaseStr(DataPtr^[median]) THEN
      lo := median + 1
    ELSE
      hi := median - 1;
  UNTIL (lo > hi) OR (Key = UpCaseStr(DataPtr^[median]));

  IF Key = UpCaseStr(DataPtr^[median]) THEN
    Search := median
  ELSE
    Search := NOT_FOUND;
END;

{------------------------------------------- Sort -----------}

PROCEDURE TNocaseSortArray.Sort;
{ sort the array using the entire string }
```

Abstract Object Types

```
    VAR i, j, offset : WORD;
        temp : LeString;

BEGIN
  IF InOrder THEN EXIT;
  offset := WorkSize;
  REPEAT
    offset := (offset * 8) DIV 11;
    IF offset = 0 THEN offset := 1;
    InOrder := TRUE;
    FOR i := 1 TO WorkSize - offset DO BEGIN
      j := i + offset;
      IF UpCaseStr(DataPtr^[i]) > UpCaseStr(DataPtr^[j]) THEN BEGIN
        InOrder := FALSE;
        temp := DataPtr^[i];
        DataPtr^[i] := DataPtr^[j];
        DataPtr^[j] := temp;
      END;
    END;
  UNTIL InOrder AND (offset = 1);
END;

BEGIN
    HeapError := @HeapErrorHandler
END.
```

The TArray Object Type

After introducing the object types in the hierarchy of dynamic string arrays, let us explore each object type in more detail. The TArray object type has a constructor, a destructor, a set of data fields, and a group of methods.

The TArray object type declares the following data fields:

- The DataPtr data field is the pointer to the dynamic array of strings.

- The MaxSize data field stores the number of elements in the dynamic array.

- The WorkSize data field contains the number of elements with meaningful information. Values for the WorkSize range from 0 to MaxSize.

- The Boolean data field AllocateError stores the dynamic allocation error status.

The constructor `Init` allocates the dynamic space specified by the parameter `ArraySize`. The constructor assigns the argument for this parameter to the `MaxSize` data field, sets the `WorkSize` field to zero, and assigns empty strings to the elements of the dynamic array. The destructor `Done` recuperates the dynamic memory allocated to the array.

The `TArray` object type declares the following methods:

- The function `GetMaxSize` returns the value in the data field `MaxSize`.
- The function `GetWorkSize` returns the value in the data field `WorkSize`.
- The Boolean function `GetAllocateError` returns the value in the data field `AllocateError`. Use this function to determine whether an instance was successfully created.
- The virtual Boolean function `Store` saves the string X in the array element number `Index`. The function returns True if the argument for `Index` is valid (that is, in the range of 1 to `MaxSize`). Otherwise, the function returns False.
- The virtual Boolean function `Recall` retrieves the string from array element number `Index`. The function returns True if the argument for `Index` is valid (that is, in the range of 1 to `WorkSize`). Otherwise, the function returns False. The reference parameter X passes the retrieved string when the argument for parameter `Index` is valid.
- The virtual function `Search` returns the index of the array element that matches the search string `Key`. If there is no match, the function yields the constant `NOT_FOUND` (that is, 0). Because the object type `TArray` models an unordered array of strings, the `Search` method performs a linear search.

The TAbsSortArray Object Type

The `TAbsSortArray` object type, a descendant of `TArray`, models an abstract object type for sorted arrays. The object type declares its data field (`InOrder`), constructor, destructor, and methods as private. The `InOrder` data field stores the sort order status of an instance. The object type declares the following methods:

- The virtual Boolean function `Store` invokes the inherited `Store` method and assigns False to the data field `InOrder` if the inherited method returns True.

- The virtual function Search is an empty shell that specifies the declaration of Search methods in descendant object types. These methods conduct binary searches on the ordered array.

- The virtual procedure Sort is an empty shell that specifies the declaration of Sort methods in the descendant object types.

The TSortArray Object Type

The TSortArray object type is a descendant of TAbsSortArray. The TSortArray object type inherits the following from the parent and ancestor object types:

- The data fields from the TArray and TAbsSortArray object types
- The Recall method from object type TArray
- The Store method from object type TAbsSortArray

The TSortArray declares the constructor Init, destructor Done, method Search, and method Sort. All of these methods are fully functioning. The Search method performs case-sensitive binary search for the parameter Key in the dynamic array. The method first examines the data field InOrder to determine whether the array needs to be sorted before performing the binary search. The Sort method performs case-sensitive sorting using the Comb sort method.

The TNocaseSortArray Object Type

The TNocaseSortArray object type is another descendant of TAbsSortArray. The object type inherits the same items from its parent and ancestor object type as TSortArray. The TNocaseSortArray declares the constructor Init, destructor Done, method Search, and method Sort. All of these methods are fully functioning. The Search method performs case-insensitive binary search for the parameter Key in the dynamic array. The method first examines the data field InOrder to determine whether the array needs to be sorted before proceeding with the binary search. The Sort method carries out case-insensitive sorting using the Comb sort method.

Let's look at a program that tests the AbsArray library unit. Listing 5.4 contains the program ARRAY6.PAS, which tests the preceding unit as follows:

1. Declares Ar1 and Ar2 as instances of object types TSortArray and TNocaseSortArray, respectively.

2. Instantiates the instance Ar1. The call to constructor Init specifies that the instance has ARRAY_SIZE elements.

3. Uses a FOR loop to store the elements of the string array constant dB in the instance Ar1. The loop statement sends the Store message to instance Ar1 to store each element of array dB.

4. Sorts the instance Ar1 by sending it the Sort message. This message results in a case-sensitive ordering of the strings in instance Ar1.

5. Uses a FOR loop to display the elements in instance Ar1. The loop statements send the Recall message to the instance Ar1 to retrieve the individual array elements.

6. Searches for the elements of array dB in the instance Ar1. This task uses a FOR loop to search instance Ar1 by sending it a Search message to conduct a case-sensitive search. The program assigns the value returned by that message to the variable J. If the variable J does not contain NOT_FOUND, the program displays an array near the matching element on the screen.

7. Removes the instance Ar1 using the destructor Done.

8. Repeats steps 2 to 7 with the instance Ar2. The difference here is that the Search and Sort messages sent to instance Ar2 conduct case-insensitive operations.

Listing 5.4. The program ARRAY6.PAS, which tests the AbsArray library unit.

```
Program Array6;

{$X+,R-}
{$M 8192, 0, 655350}

Uses Crt, AbsArray;

CONST   ARRAY_SIZE = 10;
        LONG_WAIT = 2000;
        SHORT_WAIT = 1000;
        dB : ARRAY[1..ARRAY_SIZE] OF LeString =
            ( 'California', 'MICHIGAN', 'Virginia', 'Alabama',
              'ALASKA', 'Maine', 'NEW YORK', 'Texas',
              'Florida', 'Nevada');

VAR Ar1 : TSortArray;
    Ar2 : TNocaseSortArray;
    I, J : WORD;
    S : LeString;
```

Abstract Object Types 5

```
BEGIN
  ClrScr;
  Ar1.Init(ARRAY_SIZE);
  FOR I := 1 TO ARRAY_SIZE DO
    IF NOT Ar1.Store(dB[I], I) THEN
      WRITELN('Failed to store ', dB[I], ' in element ', I);
  Ar1.Sort; { sort array }
  WRITELN('Elements of array Ar1 are:');
  { display array }
  FOR I := 1 TO Ar1.GetWorkSize DO BEGIN
    Ar1.Recall(S, I);
    WRITELN(I:2, ' ', S);
  END;
  { search for array elements }
  FOR I := 1 TO ARRAY_SIZE DO BEGIN
    GotoXY(1, 24);
    ClrEol;
    WRITE('Searching for ', dB[I]);
    Delay(SHORT_WAIT);
    J := Ar1.Search(dB[I]);
    IF J <> NOT_FOUND THEN BEGIN
        GotoXY(MAX_CHARS + 5, J + 1);
        WRITE('<--- found here');
        Delay(LONG_WAIT);
        GotoXY(MAX_CHARS + 5, J + 1);
        ClrEol;
    END
    ELSE BEGIN
      GotoXY(1, 22);
      ClrEol;
      WRITE(dB[I], ' was not found');
      Delay(LONG_WAIT);
      GotoXY(1, 22);
      ClrEol;
    END;
    GotoXY(1, 24);
    ClrEol;
  END;
  Ar1.Done;
  GotoXY(1, 24);
  ClrEol;
  WRITE('Press any key to test array Ar2...');
  ReadKey;

  ClrScr;
  WRITELN('Elements of array Ar2 are:');
  Ar2.Init(ARRAY_SIZE);
  FOR I := 1 TO ARRAY_SIZE DO
    IF NOT Ar2.Store(dB[I], I) THEN
      WRITELN('Failed to store ', dB[I], ' in element ', I);
```

continues

Listing 5.4. continued

```
  Ar2.Sort; { sort array }
  { display array }
  FOR I := 1 TO Ar2.GetWorkSize DO BEGIN
    Ar2.Recall(S, I);
    WRITELN(I:2, ' ', S);
  END;
  { search for array elements }
  FOR I := 1 TO ARRAY_SIZE DO BEGIN
    GotoXY(1, 24);
    ClrEol;
    WRITE('Searching for ', dB[I]);
    Delay(SHORT_WAIT);
    J := Ar2.Search(dB[I]);
    IF J <> NOT_FOUND THEN BEGIN
        GotoXY(MAX_CHARS + 5, J + 1);
        WRITE('<--- found here');
        Delay(LONG_WAIT);
        GotoXY(MAX_CHARS + 5, J + 1);
        ClrEol;
    END
    ELSE BEGIN
      GotoXY(1, 22);
      ClrEol;
      WRITE(dB[I], ' was not found');
      Delay(LONG_WAIT);
      GotoXY(1, 22);
      ClrEol;
    END;
    GotoXY(1, 24);
    ClrEol;
  END;
  Ar2.Done;
  GotoXY(1, 24);
  ClrEol;
  WRITE('Press any key to end the program...');
  ReadKey;
END.
```

Here's a sample output for the instance Ar1 in the program of Listing 5.4:

```
[BEGIN OUTPUT]
Elements of array Ar1 are:
 1 ALASKA
 2 Alabama
 3 California
 4 Florida
 5 MICHIGAN
```

Abstract Object Types 5

```
 6 Maine              <--- found here
 7 NEW YORK
 8 Nevada
 9 Texas
10 Virginia
```

```
Searching for Maine
[END OUTPUT]
```

Here is a sample output for the instance `Ar2` in the program of Listing 5.4:

```
[BEGIN OUTPUT]
Elements of array Ar2 are:
 1 Alabama
 2 ALASKA
 3 California
 4 Florida
 5 Maine
 6 MICHIGAN           <--- found here
 7 Nevada
 8 NEW YORK
 9 Texas
10 Virginia
```

```
Searching for MICHIGAN
[END OUTPUT]
```

Summary

This chapter presented the aspects in object-oriented design that involve abstract object types. You learned about the following topics:

- Abstract object types specify *what happens* to the instance if left to the descendant object types themselves. Abstract object types either are *purely abstract* or *partially functioning*. A purely abstract object type declares no data fields and has minimal statements in its methods. A partially functioning abstract object type may declare data fields and offer at least a single functioning method.

- Abstract object types can be used as base types in hierarchies. These object types set the stage for main operations supported by various descendants in the object-type hierarchy. This kind of abstract type may be either purely abstract or partially functioning.

- Abstract object types can be used as base types in subhierarchies. These partially functioning object types define data fields and methods common to nonabstract descendant object types.

Chapter 6

Generic Object Types

This chapter looks at a level of abstraction that primarily involves object types modeling data structures using generic programming. The last chapter presented an abstract object type for stacks that store strings. The abstraction of such stacks deals with data storage. Generic programming involves a higher level of abstraction that does away with the concern for the data type of the stack elements. This chapter introduces the basics of generic programming and how you can apply it to object-oriented programming to create generic object types. You'll learn about the following topics:

- Overview of generic programming
- The elements of generic programming
- Building generic routines

- The generic linear-search function
- The generic stack object type

Overview of Generic Programming

Software reusability, maintenance, and updating are among the issues that programmers encounter. Structured programming encourages the reusability of routines in multiple programs. The ideal scheme is to reutilize code without alteration. However, such code often undergoes some update or customization in order to function in a new application. For example, routines that manipulate an array of integers in one program must be edited to work with an array of strings in another program. The result is multiple copies of similar code.

This situation applies equally to other data structures, such as lists, stacks, queues, and trees. Frequently, the programmer takes an existing instance of a data structure and customizes its code to fit a new application. The outcome is a clutter of space-wasting routines that are difficult to update and maintain.

The first step in resolving this problem is to employ *generic data structures*. The various instances of generic data structures differ from one another in basic data type, and often by other parameters pertinent to the structure itself. However, like generic arrays, they enjoy a common functionality (for example, as sorting and searching). The advantage is that all the different instances of the same structure employ the same code. This greatly simplifies maintenance and updating because the programmer is dealing with a single version of code. The changes are available to all existing client applications pending recompilation. Thus, the centralized-code scheme used by generic programming is effective in controlling application development.

Some languages, such as Ada, formally support generic programming. By contrast, other languages such as C, Pascal, and Modula-2 offer implicit support of generic programming through basic language features.

The programmer achieves additional reductions in the coding of generic data structures using object-oriented programming. Classes of similar data structures (such as ordered and unordered lists) employ inheritance to share the code of routines that implement a common functionality. For example, clearing ordered and unordered lists employs the same process. Consequently, related classes inherit such operations, further reducing the amount of coding.

6
Generic Object Types

You can combine the advantages of sound structured-programming techniques, generic programming, and OOP in shaping generic classes for popular data structures. These structures include dynamic arrays, stacks, queues, lists, hash tables, trees, and graphs. The generic classes for these structures offer quite powerful and time-saving libraries that effectively reduce the coding they require. Employing OOP classes delivers the code in an attractive form that conforms to the latest development in software engineering.

The Elements of Generic Programming

Consider the Borland Pascal function SearchString shown in Listing 6.1. It uses a linear-search algorithm to locate a string in an array of strings. The function returns the index of the matching string, or zero if no match is found. This function has two restrictions.

- First, it works with strings in general.

- Second, it works with string arrays that are of the StringArray type. This means that the basic type and size of the array are fixed.

Listing 6.1. A Borland Pascal function that implements linear search for an array of strings.

```
FUNCTION SearchString(A   : StringArray; { input }
                      Key : STRING;      { input }
                      N   : WORD         { input }) : WORD;

VAR i : WORD;
    notfound : BOOLEAN;

BEGIN
    notfound := TRUE;
    i := 1;
    WHILE notfound AND (i <= N) DO
        IF A[i] = Key THEN
            notfound := FALSE
        ELSE
            INC(i);
```

continues

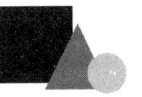

Listing 6.1. continued

```
    IF notfound THEN
        SearchString := 0
    ELSE
        SearchString := i;
END;
```

You can easily adapt the code in Listing 6.1 to work with integer arrays. Simply edit the SearchString function to yield the function SearchInteger, shown in Listing 6.2. There are now two similar versions of the linear-search function: one for string, and the other for integers.

Listing 6.2. A Borland Pascal function that implements linear search for an array of integers.

```
FUNCTION SearchInteger(A   : IntegerArray; { input }
                       Key : INTEGER;      { input }
                       N   : WORD          { input }) : WORD;

VAR i : WORD;
    notfound : BOOLEAN;

BEGIN
    notfound := TRUE;
    i := 1;
    WHILE notfound AND (i <= N) DO
        IF A[i] = Key THEN
            notfound := FALSE
        ELSE
            INC(i);

    IF notfound THEN
        SearchInteger := 0
    ELSE
        SearchInteger := i;
END;
```

Let's say that an application maintains an array of DOS files. The SearchRec record type, imported from the Dos library unit, is used. You can use either the SearchString or SearchInteger function to spawn another version for the SearchRec-typed data. In addition to changes in the function name and parameter data types, the IF statement requires minor changes to accommodate the comparison of the Name fields of the SearchRec. Listing 6.3 contains yet another version of the linear-search function.

Listing 6.3. A Borland Pascal function that implements linear search for an array of SearchRec-typed elements.

```
FUNCTION SearchDosFileName(A   : SearchRecArray; { input }
                          Key : SearchRec;      { input }
                          N   : WORD            { input }) : WORD;

VAR i : WORD;
    notfound : BOOLEAN;

BEGIN
    notfound := TRUE;
    i := 1;
    WHILE notfound AND (i <= N) DO
        IF A[i].Name = Key.Name THEN
            notfound := FALSE
        ELSE
            INC(i);

    IF notfound THEN
        SearchDosFileName := 0
    ELSE
        SearchDosFileName := i;
END;
```

We could go on and on creating more versions of the linear-search function. These versions would accommodate other predefined or user-defined types and array types of different sizes. We can create an astronomical number of versions—and, consequently, suffer the headache of maintaining them! Is there a way out? Read on.

Building Generic Routines

The process of maintaining multiple versions of similar routines is costly and error-prone. However, the previous three versions of the linear-search function can be replaced by a single generic version that accommodates arrays of varying sizes and basic data types!

The basic ingredients for building generic routines that work with arrays and other data structures are as follows:

- A pointer to the base address of the array or other data structure. The pointer is either the general-purpose `Pointer` type or a user-defined pointer type. The choice is influenced by the data-access scheme. Some data structures work with either a `Pointer` or a user-defined pointer type.
- The size of the basic element. This is a vital piece of information because you're coding generic routines to handle variable data sizes.
- Comparison functions. Generic routines that compare data elements require such functions.
- The size of the structure. This information depends on the type of data structure. Structures such as arrays, matrices, and graphs need this information. By contrast, structures such as stacks, queues, lists, and trees do not require this type of information.
- Assignment of data in generic routines is carried out using the `Move` intrinsic (predefined or built-in routine). The general syntax is:

    ```
    Move(SourcePointer^, TargetPointer^, ElementSize)
    ```

The Generic Linear-Search Function

Listing 6.4 shows a generic function that performs linear searches on arrays of any type or size. Let's first examine the parameter list:

```
FUNCTION GenSearch(A        : Pointer;    { input }
                   Key      : Pointer;    { input }
                   ElemSize,              { input }
                   N        : WORD        { input }
                   CmpFunc  : CompareFunc { input }) : WORD;
```

Parameter `A` is the pointer to the base address of the client array instead of to an array type. The parameter `Key` is the pointer to the key data used in the search, and also is declared a `Pointer`. The type associated with parameters `A` and `Key` ensures that they're not linked to any specific data type. The `ElemSize` parameter represents the byte size of each array element. It's also the size of the key data. The function retains parameter `N` from the nongeneric versions of the search function. `CmpFunc` is a procedural parameter pointing to a comparison function. Let's focus on that function.

Generic Object Types 6

A comparison function must be able to compare two variables and report the finding. If we call these two variables E1 and E2, the comparison function should return values for E1 > E2, E1 = E2, and E1 < E2. You can employ an enumerated type or the simple INTEGER type as the return type.

Having defined the return type of a comparison function, let's look at the data type associated with the parameters of the compared elements. If we're comparing, say, BYTEs, the first hunch for the parameter list of the function and its body might be this:

```
FUNCTION CompareBytes(I, J : BYTE) : INTEGER;

BEGIN
    IF I > J THEN
        CompareBytes := 1
    ELSE IF I < J THEN
        CompareBytes := -1
    ELSE
        CompareBytes := 0;
END;
```

Because we need to define a procedural type, we declare the following, based on the CompareBytes function:

```
TYPE CompareFunc = FUNCTION(I, J : BYTE) : INTEGER;
```

Let's write a comparison function for another type, such as strings. Proceeding in the same manner as with CompareBytes, we write the following function:

```
FUNCTION CompareStrings(I, J : STRING): INTEGER;

BEGIN
    IF I > J THEN
        CompareStrings := 1
    ELSE IF I < J THEN
        CompareStrings := -1
    ELSE
        CompareStrings := 0;
END;
```

At this stage, it becomes clear that the CompareStrings function (with its STRING-typed parameters) does not correspond to the CompareFunc procedural type (with its BYTE-type parameters). Back to the drawing board!

The parameters of the CompareFunc procedural type must therefore be declared as Pointer to work with comparison functions that handle any type. Thus, the correct declaration of CompareFunc type is

```
TYPE CompareFunc = FUNCTION(I, J : Pointer) : INTEGER;
```

141

Based on the preceding declaration, the `CompareBytes` function is rewritten with `Pointer`-typed parameters:

```
FUNCTION CompareBytes(I, J : Pointer): INTEGER;

BEGIN
    IF BYTE(I^) > BYTE(J^) THEN
        CompareBytes := 1
    ELSE IF BYTE(I^) < BYTE(J^) THEN
        CompareBytes := -1
    ELSE
        CompareBytes := 0;
END;
```

Because parameters I and J are pointers, type-casting must be used to coerce the data accessed by I and J into BYTEs. Similarly, the string comparison function is rewritten as follows:

```
FUNCTION CompareStrings(I, J : Pointer): INTEGER;

BEGIN
    IF STRING(I^) > STRING(J^) THEN
        CompareStrings := 1
    ELSE IF STRING(I^) < STRING(J^) THEN
        CompareStrings := -1
    ELSE
        CompareStrings := 0;
END;
```

Listing 6.4. A generic function that implements linear search for arrays of different sizes and types.

```
FUNCTION GenSearch(A        : Pointer;    { input }
                   Key      : Pointer;    { input }
                   ElemSize,              { input }
                   N        : WORD        { input }
                   CmpFunc  : CompareFunc { input }) : WORD;

TYPE PtrRec = RECORD
                seg,
                ofs : WORD;
              END;

VAR i : WORD;
    notfound : BOOLEAN;
    p : Pointer
```

```
BEGIN
    notfound := TRUE;
    i := 1;
    p := A;
    WHILE notfound AND (i <= N) DO
        IF CmpFunc(p, Key) = 0 THEN
            notfound := FALSE
        ELSE
            INC(PtrRec(p).Ofs, ElemSize);
    IF notfound THEN
        GenSearch := 0
    ELSE
        GenSearch := i;
END;
```

Let's go back to Listing 6.4 and look at how the program accesses the array elements. The address of parameter A is assigned to the local pointer p. This is not mandatory, but it's good practice to work with a copy. Initially, the pointer p has the address of the first array element. The routine compares that element with the key data using CmpFunc(p, Key). Both of the arguments to CmpFunc are pointers. The INC statement accesses the next array element. Pointer p is type-cast into the local type PtrRec, which represents the full address of any pointer. The INC statement increments the offset part by ElemSize, the size of each element. This makes pointer p access the next array element.

The Generic Stack Object Type

Armed with the knowledge of creating generic routines, let's look at an object type that models generic stacks. Listing 6.5 contains the GenStack library unit, which implements heap-based and disk-based generic stack object types.

The library unit declares three object types: TAbsStack, TGenStack, and TGenVMstack. TAbsStack is an abstract object type that declares all of its data fields and methods as private. The TAbsStack object type is a partially functioning abstract type that declares data fields and contains a few functioning methods. The data fields Height and AllocateError maintain the stack height and data allocation status, respectively. The object type declares the following methods:

- The dummy constructor and destructor. I included these special methods because of the of virtual methods Push, Pop, and Clear.

- The Boolean function GetAllocateError returns the value in the AllocateError data field.
- The Boolean function IsEmpty returns True when the Height data field is 0. Otherwise, the function returns False.
- The virtual procedure Push pushes a data item onto the stack. This method has no statements in this object type.
- The virtual Boolean function Pop pops a data item off the stack. This method has no statements in this object type.
- The virtual procedure Clear clears the stack. This method has no statements in this object type.

The library unit also declares the object type TGenStack as a descendant of TAbsStack. The descendant object type models a heap-based generic stack. The actual implementation uses the types GenStackRec and GenStackPtr to implement the supporting dynamic linked lists. The TGenStack object type declares the pointer Top to access the supporting dynamic linked list. The TGenStack object type declares a functioning constructor, a virtual destructor, and the virtual methods Push, Pop, and Clear. The statements in these methods specify how the stack operations are implemented. The constructor initializes the stack by initializing the supporting dynamic linked list. The destructor clears the supporting linked list. Notice that the parameters for the Push and Pop methods are pointers. These pointers access the data transferred between the stack and its owner. The Push and Pop methods use the Move intrinsic to transfer the data to and from the memory location accessed by the pointer parameter X.

The library unit also declares the object type TGenVMstack as another descendant of TAbsStack. This descendant object type models a disk-based generic stack. The actual implementation uses a random-access file. The TGenVMstack object type declares the DataBuffer, ErrorMessage, and VFile data fields. The TGenVMstack object type declares a functioning constructor, virtual destructor, and the virtual methods Push, Pop, and Clear. The statements in these methods specify how stack operations are implemented—with the help of the supporting file. The constructor opens the supporting random-access data file. The destructor first closes the file and then deletes it. The Push and Pop methods use pointers in a manner very similar to the TGenStack object type.

Generic Object Types

Listing 6.5. The `GenStack` library unit, which implements heap-based and disk-based generic stack object types.

```
UNIT GenStack;

{ This program implements classes of generic stacks with the following
set of operations:

   + Push
   + Pop
   + Clear
}

{*******************************************************************}
{*************************} INTERFACE {*****************************}
{*******************************************************************}

TYPE
    { ********************* Abstract Stack *************** }
    TAbsStack = OBJECT
      PRIVATE
        ElemSize,                      { byte size of data         }
        Height        : WORD;          { height of stack           }
        AllocateError : BOOLEAN;       { dynamic allocation error  }
        { ************* State Manipulation Methods ************* }
        CONSTRUCTOR Init(ElementSize : WORD { input });
        DESTRUCTOR Done; VIRTUAL;

        { ***************** State Query Methods **************** }
        FUNCTION GetAllocateError : BOOLEAN;
        FUNCTION IsEmpty : BOOLEAN;

        { ************* Object Manipulation Methods ************ }
        PROCEDURE Push(X : Pointer { input }); VIRTUAL;
        FUNCTION Pop(X : Pointer { input }) : BOOLEAN; VIRTUAL;
        PROCEDURE Clear; VIRTUAL;
    END;

    GenStackPtr = ^GenStackRec;
    GenStackRec = RECORD
        DataPtr : Pointer;
        NextLink : GenStackPtr
    END;

    TGenStack = OBJECT(TAbsStack)
        { ************* State Manipulation Methods ************* }
        CONSTRUCTOR Init(ElementSize : WORD { input });
        DESTRUCTOR Done; VIRTUAL;
```

continues

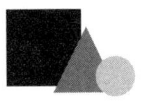

Listing 6.5. continued

```pascal
    { ************** Object Manipulation Methods ************* }
    PROCEDURE Push(X : Pointer { input  }); VIRTUAL;
    FUNCTION Pop(X : Pointer { input  }) : BOOLEAN; VIRTUAL;
    PROCEDURE Clear; VIRTUAL;
  PRIVATE
    Top : GenStackPtr; { pointer to the top of the stack }
  END;

  TGenVMstack = OBJECT(TAbsStack)
    { ************** State Manipulation Methods ************* }
    CONSTRUCTOR Init(ElementSize : WORD;   { input  }
                     Filename    : STRING { input  });
    DESTRUCTOR Done; VIRTUAL;

    { ***************** State Query Methods **************** }
    FUNCTION GetErrorMessage : STRING;

    { ************** Object Manipulation Methods ************* }
    PROCEDURE Push(X : Pointer { input  }); VIRTUAL;
    FUNCTION Pop(X : Pointer { input  }) : BOOLEAN; VIRTUAL;
    PROCEDURE Clear; VIRTUAL;
  PRIVATE
    DataBuffer   : Pointer; { pointer to data buffer }
    ErrorMessage : STRING;  { error message }
    VMfile       : FILE;    { virtual file handle }
  END;
{*******************************************************************}
{***********************} IMPLEMENTATION {*************************}
{*******************************************************************}

{---------------------------------------- HeapErrorHandler ---------}

FUNCTION HeapErrorHandler(Size : WORD { input  }) : INTEGER; FAR;

BEGIN
    HeapErrorHandler := 1
END;

{------------------------------------------------ Init -----------}

CONSTRUCTOR TAbsStack.Init(ElementSize : WORD { input  });

BEGIN
    { do nothing }
END;

{------------------------------------------------ Done -----------}
```

Generic Object Types   6

```
DESTRUCTOR TAbsStack.Done;
{ destructor used to clear the stack. }
BEGIN
    { do nothing }
END;

{---------------------------------------------- IsEmpty -----------}

FUNCTION TAbsStack.IsEmpty : BOOLEAN;
{ logical function that queries the empty-state of the stack. }
BEGIN
    IsEmpty := Height = 0
END;

{---------------------------------------------- Push -----------}

PROCEDURE TAbsStack.Push(X : Pointer { input  });
BEGIN
END;

{---------------------------------------------- Pop -----------}

FUNCTION TAbsStack.Pop(X : Pointer { output  }) : BOOLEAN;
BEGIN
  Pop := FALSE;
END;

{-------------------------------------- GetAllocateError -----------}

FUNCTION TAbsStack.GetAllocateError : BOOLEAN;
{ returns the status of dynamic allocation for the last Pop
message sent to the object. Function returns TRUE if the dynamic
allocation failed, otherwise, returns FALSE. }
BEGIN
    GetAllocateError := AllocateError
END;

{---------------------------------------------- Clear -----------}

PROCEDURE TAbsStack.Clear;
BEGIN
  { do nothing }
END;

{---------------------------------------------- Init -----------}

CONSTRUCTOR TGenStack.Init(ElementSize : WORD { input  });
{ constructor to initialize generic stack. }
```

continues

147

Listing 6.5. continued

```
BEGIN
    ElemSize := ElementSize;
    IF ElemSize = 0 THEN
        ElemSize := 1;
    Height := 0;
    AllocateError := FALSE;
    Top := NIL
END;

{------------------------------------------------ Done ------------}

DESTRUCTOR TGenStack.Done;
{ destructor used to clear the stack. }
BEGIN
    Clear
END;

{------------------------------------------------ Push ------------}

PROCEDURE TGenStack.Push(X : Pointer { input });
{ pushes the data accessed by pointer X onto the stack.}

VAR p : GenStackPtr;

BEGIN
    AllocateError := FALSE;
    IF Top <> NIL THEN BEGIN
        New(p); { allocate new stack element }
        IF p = NIL THEN BEGIN
            AllocateError := TRUE;
            Exit;
        END;
        GetMem(p^.DataPtr, ElemSize);
        IF p^.DataPtr = NIL THEN BEGIN
            AllocateError := TRUE;
            Exit;
        END;
        Move(X^, p^.DataPtr^, ElemSize);
        p^.NextLink := Top;
        Top := p
    END
    ELSE BEGIN
        New(Top);
        IF Top = NIL THEN BEGIN
            AllocateError := TRUE;
            Exit;
        END;
```

```
            GetMem(Top^.DataPtr, ElemSize);
            IF Top^.DataPtr = NIL THEN BEGIN
                AllocateError := TRUE;
                Exit;
            END;
            Move(X^, Top^.DataPtr^, ElemSize);
            Top^.NextLink := NIL
        END;
        INC(Height)
END;

{-------------------------------------------------- Pop -----------}

FUNCTION TGenStack.Pop(X : Pointer { input   }) : BOOLEAN;
{ pops the top element off the stack and returns a Boolean value.
  Function returns TRUE if the operation was successful. A
  FALSE value is returned if the Pop message is sent to an empty
  stack. }

VAR p : GenStackPtr;

BEGIN
    IF Height > 0 THEN BEGIN
        Move(Top^.DataPtr^, X^, ElemSize);
        FreeMem(Top^.DataPtr, ElemSize); { deallocate data }
        p := Top;
        Top := Top^.NextLink;
        Dispose(p); { deallocate stack node }
        DEC(Height);
        Pop := TRUE { return function value }
    END
    ELSE
        Pop := FALSE { return function value }
END;

{-------------------------------------------------- Clear -----------}

PROCEDURE TGenStack.Clear;
{ clears the generic stack object. }

VAR x : Pointer;

BEGIN
    GetMem(x, ElemSize);
    WHILE Pop(x) DO
        { do nothing };
    FreeMem(x, ElemSize);
END;
```

continues

Listing 6.5. continued

```
{------------------------------------------------ Init -----------}

CONSTRUCTOR TGenVMstack.Init(ElementSize : WORD;   { input  }
                             Filename    : STRING { input  });

{ constructor to initialize generic stack. }
BEGIN
    IF ElementSize = 0 THEN
        ElementSize := 1;
    ElemSize := ElementSize;
    Height := 0;
    Assign(VMfile, Filename);
    {$I-} Rewrite(VMfile, ElemSize); {$I+}
    IF IOresult <> 0 THEN BEGIN
        ErrorMessage := 'Cannot open file ' + Filename;
        Exit
    END;
    GetMem(DataBuffer, ElemSize);
    IF DataBuffer = NIL THEN BEGIN
        AllocateError := TRUE;
        ErrorMessage := 'Dynamic allocation error'
    END
    ELSE BEGIN
        AllocateError := FALSE;
        ErrorMessage := ''
    END;
END;

{------------------------------------------------ Done -----------}

DESTRUCTOR TGenVMstack.Done;
{ destructor used to clear the stack. }
BEGIN
    Clear;
    FreeMem(DataBuffer, ElemSize);
END;

{--------------------------------------- GetErrorMessage -----------}

FUNCTION TGenVMstack.GetErrorMessage : STRING;
{ returns the error message }
BEGIN
    GetErrorMessage := ErrorMessage
END;

{------------------------------------------------ Push -----------}

PROCEDURE TGenVMstack.Push(X : Pointer { input  });
{ pushes the data accessed by pointer X onto the stack. }
```

Generic Object Types

```
BEGIN
    INC(Height);
    Seek(VMfile, Height-1);
    BlockWrite(VMfile, X^, 1);
END;

{---------------------------------------------- Pop -----------}

FUNCTION TGenVMstack.Pop(X : Pointer { input  }) : BOOLEAN;
{ pops the top of the stack and returns a Boolean value. }
BEGIN
    IF Height > 0 THEN BEGIN
        DEC(Height);
        Seek(VMfile, Height);
        BlockRead(VMfile, X^, 1);
        Pop := TRUE
    END
    ELSE
        Pop := FALSE;
END;

{---------------------------------------------- Clear -----------}

PROCEDURE TGenVMstack.Clear;
{ clears the generic stack object. }
BEGIN
    Height := 0;
    {$I-}
    Close(VMfile);
    Erase(VMfile);
    {$I+}
END;

BEGIN
    HeapError := @HeapErrorHandler
END.
```

You easily can use the object types TGenStack and TGenVMstack in the GenStack library unit in your own program. Let's add to that library unit another one that builds on it to support screen-stack object types. Listing 6.6 contains the ScrnStak library unit, which exports the TScreenStack and TVMscreenStack object types. The TScreenStack object type pushes and pops screens using a heap-based stack. By contrast, the TVMscreenStack object type works with files. Use this disk-based object type if your application has a lot of screens to push onto a stack.

Each of the two object types declares the `PushScreen` and `PopScreen` method. The latter method is a Boolean function that enables you to detect when the screen-stack is empty. The initialization section of the `ScrnStak` library unit sets the screen pointer to the correct address, depending on whether you have a color- or monochrome-display adapter.

Listing 6.6. The `ScrnStak` library unit, which implements screen-stack object types.

```
UNIT ScrnStak;

{ This library implements a class of screen stacks. }

{*******************************************************************}
{************************} INTERFACE {*****************************}
{*******************************************************************}

Uses GenStack;

CONST SCREEN_BYTES = 4000;

TYPE
    TScreenStack = OBJECT(TGenStack)
        { ************* Object Manipulation Methods ************ }
        PROCEDURE PushScreen;
        FUNCTION PopScreen : BOOLEAN;
    END;

    TVMscreenStack = OBJECT(TGenVMstack)
        { ************* Object Manipulation Methods ************ }
        PROCEDURE PushScreen;
        FUNCTION PopScreen : BOOLEAN;
    END;

{*******************************************************************}
{************************} IMPLEMENTATION {************************}
{*******************************************************************}

VAR VideoMode : BYTE Absolute $0040:$0049;
    VideoAddress : WORD;
    VideoPtr : Pointer;

{-------------------------------------- PushScreen -----------}

PROCEDURE TScreenStack.PushScreen;
{ pushes the visible screen onto the screen stack. }
```

Generic Object Types

```
BEGIN
    Push(VideoPtr)
END;

{---------------------------------------- PopScreen -----------}

FUNCTION TScreenStack.PopScreen : BOOLEAN;
{ pops a screen from the screen stack. The popped screen
  becomes the visible screen. }
BEGIN
    PopScreen := Pop(VideoPtr);
END;

{---------------------------------------- PushScreen -----------}

PROCEDURE TVMscreenStack.PushScreen;
{ pushes the visible screen onto the screen stack. }
BEGIN
    Push(VideoPtr)
END;

{---------------------------------------- PopScreen -----------}

FUNCTION TVMscreenStack.PopScreen : BOOLEAN;
{ pops a screen from the screen stack. The popped screen
  becomes the visible screen. }
BEGIN
    PopScreen := Pop(VideoPtr);
END;

BEGIN
    IF VideoMode = 7 THEN
        VideoAddress := $B000
    ELSE
        VideoAddress := $B800;
    VideoPtr := Ptr(VideoAddress, 0);
END.
```

Let's look at a program to test the GenStack and ScrnStak library units. Listing 6.7 presents the test program that performs the following tasks:

1. Declares the S and VS as instances of TScreenStack and TVMscreenStack, respectively.

2. Instantiates the instance S using the TGenStack.Init constructor. This step passes the constant SCREEN_BYTES (imported from the ScrnStak unit) to the constructor.

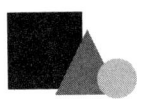

3. Assigns 0 to the screen counter variable ScreenNumber.

4. Uses a FOR loop to fill up three screens with a character and then pushes each screen onto the heap-based stack S. The loop calls the procedure FillScreen to fill in the screen and increment the screen counter variable. The loop then sends the PushScreen message to the instance S to push the screen into the stack. The loop uses the Delay procedure (exported by unit Dos) to pause for a few seconds after creating and pushing screens onto the instance S.

5. Clears the screen to display a message. The program uses the Delay procedure to pause for a few seconds.

6. Pops the screens off instance S using a WHILE loop. The condition of the loop sends a PopScreen message to instance S. The loop statement calls Delay to pause for a few seconds before popping off the next screen.

7. Removes the instance S using the destructor TGenStack.Done.

8. Repeats steps 2 to 7 with the instance VS. The program creates this instance using the file VS.DAT.

Listing 6.7. The program STACK3.PAS, which tests the GenStack and ScrnStak library units.

```
Program Stack3;

{
    This program tests the screen stack.
}
{$M 8192, 0, 655350}

Uses Crt, ScrnStak;

CONST SHORT_DELAY = 2000;
      LONG_DELAY = 3000;
      MAX_SCREENS = 3;

VAR S : TScreenStack;
    VS : TVMscreenStack;
    I, ScreenNumber : BYTE;

PROCEDURE FillScreen(VAR ScrnNum : BYTE { in/out });
```

Generic Object Types

```
    VAR row : BYTE;
        c : CHAR;
        astring : STRING;

BEGIN
    INC(ScrnNum);
    ClrScr;
    c := CHR(64 + ScrnNum);
    FillChar(astring[1], 80, c);
    astring[0] := CHR(80);
    WRITELN('Screen number ', ScrnNum);
    FOR row := 2 TO 24 DO
        WRITE(astring);
END;

BEGIN
    ClrScr;
    S.Init(SCREEN_BYTES);
    ScreenNumber := 0;
    FOR I := 1 TO MAX_SCREENS DO BEGIN
        FillScreen(ScreenNumber);
        S.PushScreen;
        Delay(SHORT_DELAY);
    END;
    ClrScr;
    WRITE('Please wait to continue...');
    Delay(SHORT_DELAY);

    WHILE S.PopScreen DO
        Delay(LONG_DELAY);

    GotoXY(1, 25);
    ClrEol;
    WRITE('Press any key to continue... ');
    ReadKey;
    S.Done;

    ClrScr;
    WRITELN('Testing virtual stacks objects');
    Delay(SHORT_DELAY);
    VS.Init(SCREEN_BYTES, 'VS.DAT');
    ScreenNumber := 0;
    FOR I := 1 TO MAX_SCREENS DO BEGIN
        FillScreen(ScreenNumber);
        VS.PushScreen;
        Delay(SHORT_DELAY);
    END;
    ClrScr;
    WRITE('Please wait...');
    Delay(SHORT_DELAY);
```

continues

Listing 6.7. continued

```
    WHILE VS.PopScreen DO
        Delay(LONG_DELAY);

    GotoXY(1, 25);
    ClrEol;
    WRITE('Press any key to end the program...');
    ReadKey;
    VS.Done;
END.
```

Here's a sample of the screen output from listing 6.1:

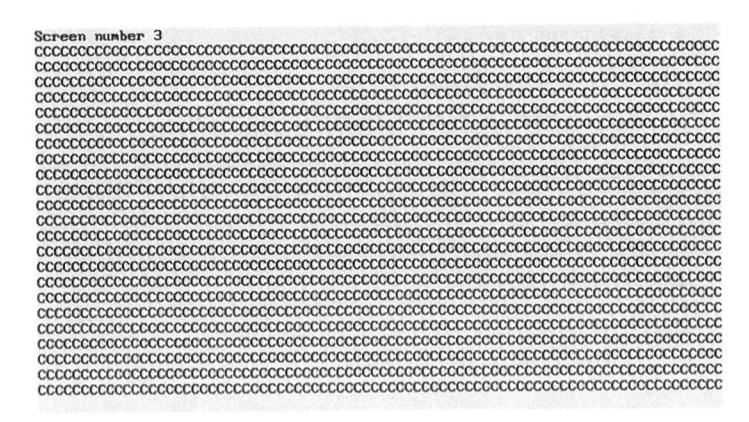

Figure 6.1. A sample screen generated by the program STACK3.PAS.

Summary

This chapter introduced you to the principles of generic programming and illustrated how you can create highly reusable generic object types by combining generic programming and OOP principles. You learned the following:

Generic Object Types

- Generic programming enables you to create reusable procedures and functions that work with a wide variety of data types. Using generic routines eliminates multiple versions of similar routines and significantly consolidates your code. Consequently, generic routines are easier to maintain than are nongeneric ones.

- You can create several versions of a linear-search function—each version for a different data type. This ability makes the case for generic programming.

- Building generic routines requires the following components:

  A pointer to the base address of the array or other data structure

  The size of the basic element

  A comparison function

  The size of the structure

- The generic linear-search function `GenSearch` performs a linear search on unordered arrays. This function shows how generic and structured programming methods work together.

- The library unit `GenStack` contains an object-type hierarchy that supports generic heap-based and disk-based stacks. The generic stack object types illustrate how generic programming and OOP work together.

Chapter 7

Metamorphic Object Types

The descendant object types in a hierarchy offer specialized instances. Typically, the base object type is an abstract or general object type, while the lower-level descendant object types are highly specialized. This chapter presents the case in which descendant object types offer functionality that is significantly different from that of the parent object type. This programming feature involves *metamorphic object types*. In this chapter you'll learn about the following topics:

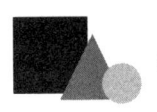

- The basics of metamorphic object types.
- An example showing an object type hierarchy that includes an array, a fixed queue, and a fixed stack.
- A test program to test object types in the `MetaMorf` library unit.

Metamorphic Object Types

Chapters 5 and 6 presented object types that implement abstract and generic stacks. These dynamic stacks are implemented using dynamic linked lists. In other words, the object types modeling the stacks actually are using linked lists in a special way to support typical stack operations.

The design of the stack object types in Chapters 5 and 6 use embedded linked-list structures. You can implement these stack object types by using a hierarchy that contains a separate object type for linked lists. You then declare the stack object type as a descendant of the list object type. Of course you should hide the inherited operations that are specific to linked lists; their use by instances of the stack object type would be inappropriate.

This scenario contains general guidelines that enable you to design an object type hierarchy that includes metamorphic object types. These guidelines are as follows:

- The descendant uses some of the inherited methods. The context of these methods may change slightly, depending on what the descendant object type is modeling.
- The descendant declares a new set of methods to support their operations. Such operations may use the inherited method, or may repackage them in a manner more suitable for the object modeled by the descendants.
- The descendants override those inherited methods that should not be used by the instances. The overriding methods must be declared private and may simply call the inherited methods, or be dummy shells.

An Array-Queue-Stack Example

With the guidelines for metamorphic object types in place, let's go on to an example. This example deals with a simple object-type hierarchy that includes object types modeling an array of strings, a fixed queue of strings, and a fixed stack of strings. Table 7.1 shows the metamorphic object-type hierarchy (however, it does not show the constructors, destructors, and private methods for the various classes). The `TStrArray` object type models a dynamic array of strings with a minimal set of operations, including storing and recalling strings from the object-type instances. Other `TStrArray` operations include the query of the maximum array size, the working array size, and the status of dynamic allocation error.

The `TStrFixedQue` object type, a descendant of `TStrArray`, models a fixed queue—once you specify the maximum size of the queue, you cannot change it. The object type has the ability to enqueue and dequeue data from either end of the queue. The operations of the modeled fixed queue include enqueuing and dequeuing strings from either end, clearing the queue, and returning the status (empty or full) of the queue.

The `TStrFixedStack` object type, a descendant of `TStrFixedQue`, models a fixed stack—once you specify the maximum size of the stack, you cannot change it. The operations supported by this object type include pushing data onto the stack, popping data off the stack, clearing the stack, and returning the empty-status or full-status of the stack.

Table 7.1. The metamorphic object-type hierarchy.

TStrArray
FUNCTION GetMaxSize
FUNCTION GetWorkSize
FUNCTION GetAllocateError
FUNCTION Store
FUNCTION Recall

continues

Table 7.1. continued

	TStrFixedQue
	FUNCTION IsEmpty
	FUNCTION IsFull
	FUNCTION PushFront
	FUNCTION PushTail
	FUNCTION PopFront
	FUNCTION PopTail
	PROCEDURE Clear

	TStrFixedStack
	FUNCTION IsEmpty (inherited)
	FUNCTION IsFull (inherited)
	FUNCTION Push
	FUNCTION Pop
	PROCEDURE Clear (inherited)

Listing 7.1 shows how the MetaMorf library unit implements the object-type hierarchy in Table 7.1.

The TStrArray Object Type

The MetaMorf library unit declares the object type TStrArray as the base of the object-type hierarchy. This object type has a constructor, a destructor, a set of public methods, and a group of private data fields. The object type declares the following data fields:

- The DataPtr data field is the pointer that accesses and manages the dynamic space of the array elements.
- The MaxSize data field stores the maximum size of the dynamic array.

- The `WorkSize` data field contains the number of array elements that store meaningful data. The constructor assigns zero to this data field.

- The `AllocateError` data field stores the status of the dynamic allocation.

The constructor `Init` creates the instance of `TStrArray` and allocates the number of dynamic elements specified by parameter `ArraySize`. The constructor assigns empty strings to the elements of the dynamic array. The destructor `Done` removes the dynamic space of the instances. The object type also declares the following methods:

- The function `GetMaxSize` returns the maximum number of array elements.

- The function `GetWorkSize` returns the number of array elements that contain meaningful data. The indices of these elements are in the range of 1 to `WorkSize`.

- The Boolean function `GetAllocateError` returns the status of the dynamic allocation.

- The Boolean function `Store` writes a string in array element number `Index`. The valid range of arguments for parameter Index is 1 to `MaxSize`. If the argument for `Index` is greater than the current value in data field `WorkSize`, the `Store` method assigns `Index` to `WorkSize`. The function returns True if the argument for Index is valid. Otherwise, the function returns False.

- The Boolean function `Recall` retrieves a string from array element number `Index`. The valid range of arguments for parameter `Index` is 1 to `WorkSize`. The function returns True if the argument for `Index` is valid. Otherwise, the function returns False.

The TStrFixedQue Object Type

The `MetaMorf` library unit also declares the `TStrFixedQue` object type. This type inherits the constructor and destructor from the parent object type. The object type contains two sets of public and private methods. The public methods support the operations of a fixed queue. Many of these methods use the methods inherited from the object type `TStrArray`. The public methods of `TStrFixedQue` are as follows:

- The Boolean function `IsEmpty` returns True if the queue is empty or False if the queue is not empty. The `IsEmpty` function basically returns the Boolean expression `WorkSize = 0`.

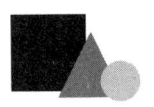

- The Boolean function `IsFull` returns True if the queue is full or False if the queue is not full. The function basically returns the Boolean expression `MaxSize = WorkSize`.

- The Boolean function `PushFront` enqueues a string at the front end of the queue. The function returns True if the string was inserted or False if the queue already was full.

- The Boolean function `PushTail` enqueues a string at the tail end of the queue. The function returns True if the string was inserted or False if the queue already was full.

- The Boolean function `PopFront` dequeues a string from the front end of the queue. The function returns True if the queue was not already empty. The reference parameter `X` passes the dequeued string.

- The Boolean function `PopTail` dequeues a string from the tail end of the queue. The function returns True if the queue was not already empty. The reference parameter `X` passes the dequeued string.

- The procedure `Clear` clears the queue by simply assigning 0 to the data field `WorkSize`.

The `TStrFixedQue` object type also declares four private methods. Two of these methods support the operations of the fixed queue. The other two override inherited methods. The four private methods are:

- The procedure `MoveUp` moves up some of the array elements by one element (while supporting the fixed queue). The parameter `Index` specifies the index of the first array element to be moved up. This procedure shifts the location of the elements in the range of `Index` to `WorkSize`.

- The procedure `MoveDn` moves down some of the array elements by one queue (while supporting the fixed queue). The parameter `Index` specifies the index of the last array element to be moved down. This procedure shifts the location of the elements in the range of 1 to `Index`.

- The Boolean function `Store` implements a private version of the inherited method `TStrArray.Store`. This kind of declaration prevents the instances of `TStrFixedQue` from sending `Store` messages because such messages are inappropriate for queues.

- The Boolean function `Recall` implements a private version of the inherited method `TStrArray.Recall`. This kind of declaration prevents client programs from sending `Recall` messages to the instances of `TStrFixedQue`; such messages are inappropriate for queues.

The TStrFixedStack Object Type

The `TStrFixedStack` object type, a descendant of `TStrFixedQue`, models a fixed stack. The `TStrFixedStack` object type inherits the constructor and destructor and declares two sets of public and private methods. The public methods, which support the operations of a fixed stack, are as follows:

- The Boolean function `Push` pushes a string onto the stack. The function returns True if the stack was not already full. Otherwise, the function returns False.

- The Boolean function `Pop` pops a string off the stack. The function returns True if the stack was not already empty. Otherwise, the function returns False.

The methods inherited by `TStrFixedQue` are `IsFull`, `IsEmpty`, and `Clear`. These methods provide operations that are common to both fixed queues and fixed stacks.

The `TStrFixedStack` object type also declares the private methods `PushFront`, `PushTail`, `PopFront`, and `PopTail`. These methods hide the inherited methods and prevent instances of `TStrFixedStack` from using them.

Listing 7.1. The `MetaMorf` library unit, which supports arrays, queues, and stacks of strings in the same object-type hierarchy.

```
Unit MetaMorf;

{ This library implements metamorphic object types }

{*****************************************************************}
{************************} INTERFACE {****************************}
{*****************************************************************}

{$V-,R-,X+}

CONST DEFAULT_SIZE = 10;
      MAX_CHARS = 20;

TYPE
    LeString = STRING[MAX_CHARS];
    OneArray = ARRAY[1..1] OF LeString;
    ArrayPtr = ^OneArray;
```

continues

Listing 7.1. continued

```pascal
  TStrArray = OBJECT
    CONSTRUCTOR Init(ArraySize : WORD);
    DESTRUCTOR Done; VIRTUAL;
    FUNCTION GetMaxSize : WORD;
    FUNCTION GetWorkSize : WORD;
    FUNCTION GetAllocateError : BOOLEAN;

    FUNCTION Store(X     : LeString; { input }
                   Index : WORD      { input })
                         : BOOLEAN; VIRTUAL;
    FUNCTION Recall(VAR X     : LeString; { output }
                        Index : WORD      { output })
                              : BOOLEAN; VIRTUAL;
  PRIVATE
    DataPtr : ArrayPtr;
    MaxSize,
    WorkSize : WORD;
    AllocateError : BOOLEAN;
  END;

  TStrFixedQue = OBJECT(TStrArray)
    FUNCTION IsEmpty : BOOLEAN;
    FUNCTION IsFull : BOOLEAN;
    FUNCTION PushFront(X : LeString { input }) : BOOLEAN;
    FUNCTION PushTail(X : LeString { input }) : BOOLEAN;
    FUNCTION PopFront(VAR X : LeString { input }) : BOOLEAN;
    FUNCTION PopTail(VAR X : LeString { input }) : BOOLEAN;
    PROCEDURE Clear;
  PRIVATE
    PROCEDURE MoveUp(Index : WORD { input } );
    PROCEDURE MoveDn(Index : WORD { input } );
    FUNCTION Store(X     : LeString; { input }
                   Index : WORD      { input })
                         : BOOLEAN; VIRTUAL;
    FUNCTION Recall(VAR X     : LeString; { output }
                        Index : WORD      { output })
                              : BOOLEAN; VIRTUAL;
  END;

  TStrFixedStack = OBJECT(TStrFixedQue)
    FUNCTION Push(X : LeString { input }) : BOOLEAN;
    FUNCTION Pop(VAR X : LeString { input }) : BOOLEAN;
   PRIVATE
    FUNCTION PushFront(X : LeString { input }) : BOOLEAN;
    FUNCTION PushTail(X : LeString { input }) : BOOLEAN;
    FUNCTION PopFront(VAR X : LeString { input }) : BOOLEAN;
    FUNCTION PopTail(VAR X : LeString { input }) : BOOLEAN;
  END;
```

Metamorphic Object Types 7

```
{*********************************************************************}
{***********************} IMPLEMENTATION {***************************}
{*********************************************************************}

{-------------------------------------------- HeapErrorHandler ---------}

FUNCTION HeapErrorHandler(Size : WORD { input  }) : INTEGER; FAR;

BEGIN
    HeapErrorHandler := 1
END;

{---------------------------------------------------- Init -----------}

CONSTRUCTOR TStrArray.Init(ArraySize : WORD { input });
{ construct instance of TStrArray }

VAR i : WORD;

BEGIN
  MaxSize := ArraySize;
  IF MaxSize = 0 THEN
    MaxSize := DEFAULT_SIZE;
  WorkSize := 0;
  GetMem(DataPtr, MaxSize * SizeOf(LeString));
  AllocateError := DataPtr = NIL;
  IF NOT AllocateError THEN
    FOR i := 1 TO MaxSize DO
      DataPtr^[i] := '';
END;

{---------------------------------------------------- Done -----------}

DESTRUCTOR TStrArray.Done;
{ remove instance of TStrArray }
BEGIN
  IF DataPtr <> NIL THEN
    FreeMem(DataPtr, MaxSize * SizeOf(LeString))
END;

{------------------------------------------------- GetMaxSize -----------}

FUNCTION TStrArray.GetMaxSize : WORD;
{ return the maximum size of the array }
BEGIN
  GetMaxSize := MaxSize
END;
```

continues

Listing 7.1. continued

```pascal
{---------------------------------------- GetWorkSize -----------}

FUNCTION TStrArray.GetWorkSize : WORD;
{ return the working size of the array }
BEGIN
  GetWorkSize := WorkSize
END;

{---------------------------------------- GetAllocateError -----------}

FUNCTION TStrArray.GetAllocateError : BOOLEAN;
{ get the allocation error status }
BEGIN
  GetAllocateError := AllocateError
END;

{---------------------------------------- Store -----------}

FUNCTION TStrArray.Store(X     : LeString; { input }
                        Index : WORD       { input }) : BOOLEAN;
{ store an array element }
BEGIN
  IF (Index > 0) AND (Index <= MaxSize) THEN BEGIN
    IF Index > WorkSize THEN
      WorkSize := Index;
    DataPtr^[Index] := X;
    Store := TRUE;
  END
  ELSE
    Store := FALSE;
END;

{---------------------------------------- Recall -----------}

FUNCTION TStrArray.Recall(VAR X     : LeString; { output }
                              Index : WORD      { input })
                              : BOOLEAN;
{ recall the contents of an array element }
BEGIN
  IF (Index > 0) AND (Index <= WorkSize) THEN BEGIN
    X := DataPtr^[Index];
    Recall := TRUE;
  END
  ELSE
    Recall := FALSE;
END;
```

Metamorphic Object Types

```
{------------------------------------------ IsEmpty -----------}

FUNCTION TStrFixedQue.IsEmpty : BOOLEAN;
{ returns TRUE if queue is empty }
BEGIN
  IsEmpty := WorkSize = 0;
END;

{------------------------------------------ IsFull -----------}

FUNCTION TStrFixedQue.IsFull : BOOLEAN;
{ returns TRUE if queue is full }
BEGIN
  IsFull := MaxSize = WorkSize;
END;

{------------------------------------------ PushFront -----------}

FUNCTION TStrFixedQue.PushFront(X : LeString { input }) : BOOLEAN;
{ inserts a string at the front end of the queue. Returns
  TRUE if the queue was not already full. Otherwise, returns FALSE. }
BEGIN
  IF WorkSize < MaxSize THEN BEGIN
    INC(WorkSize);
    MoveUp(1);
    INHERITED Store(X, 1);
    PushFront := TRUE;
  END
  ELSE
    PushFront := FALSE;
END;

{------------------------------------------ PushTail -----------}

FUNCTION TStrFixedQue.PushTail(X : LeString { input }) : BOOLEAN;
{ inserts a string at the tail end of the queue. Returns TRUE
  if the queue was not already full. Otherwise, returns FALSE. }
BEGIN
  IF WorkSize < MaxSize THEN BEGIN
    INC(WorkSize);
    INHERITED Store(X, WorkSize);
    PushTail := TRUE;
  END
  ELSE
    PushTail := FALSE;
END;
```

continues

Listing 7.1. continued

```
{---------------------------------------- PopFront ------------}

FUNCTION TStrFixedQue.PopFront(VAR X : LeString { input }) : BOOLEAN;
{ pops a string off the front end of the queue and moves all of the
  other queue elements down. Returns TRUE if the queue was not already
  empty. Otherwise, returns FALSE }
BEGIN
  IF WorkSize > 0 THEN BEGIN
    Recall(X, 1);
    MoveDn(1);
    DEC(WorkSize);
    PopFront := TRUE;
  END
  ELSE
    PopFront := FALSE;
END;

{---------------------------------------- PopTail ------------}

FUNCTION TStrFixedQue.PopTail(VAR X : LeString { input }) : BOOLEAN;
{ pops a string off the tail end of the queue and moves all of the
  other queue elements down. Returns TRUE if the queue was not already
  empty. Otherwise, returns FALSE }
BEGIN
  IF WorkSize > 0 THEN BEGIN
    Recall(X, WorkSize);
    DEC(WorkSize);
    PopTail := TRUE;
  END
  ELSE
    PopTail := FALSE;
END;

{---------------------------------------- Clear ------------}

PROCEDURE TStrFixedQue.Clear;
{ clears the queue by assigning 0 to the WorkSize
  data field }
BEGIN
  WorkSize := 0
END;

{---------------------------------------- MoveUp ------------}

PROCEDURE TStrFixedQue.MoveUp(Index : WORD { input } );

{ moves up the queue elements Index and on by one element }

VAR i : WORD;
```

Metamorphic Object Types

```
BEGIN
  FOR i := WorkSize DOWNTO Index DO
    DataPtr^[i + 1] := DataPtr^[i];
END;

{----------------------------------------- MoveDn -----------}

PROCEDURE TStrFixedQue.MoveDn(Index : WORD { input } );

{ moves down the queue elements Index and on by one element }

VAR i : WORD;

BEGIN
  FOR i := Index TO WorkSize DO
    DataPtr^[i] := DataPtr^[i + 1];
END;

{----------------------------------------- Store -----------}

FUNCTION TStrFixedQue.Store(X     : LeString; { input }
                            Index : WORD      { input }) : BOOLEAN;
{ store an array element }
BEGIN
    Store := INHERITED Store(X, Index);
END;

{----------------------------------------- Recall -----------}

FUNCTION TStrFixedQue.Recall(VAR X : LeString; { output }
                             Index : WORD      { input })
                                   : BOOLEAN;
{ recall the contents of an array element }
BEGIN
    Recall := INHERITED Recall(X, Index);
END;

{----------------------------------------- PushFront -----------}

FUNCTION TStrFixedStack.PushFront(X : LeString { input }) : BOOLEAN;
BEGIN
  PushFront := INHERITED PushFront(X)
END;

{----------------------------------------- PushTail -----------}

FUNCTION TStrFixedStack.PushTail(X : LeString { input }) : BOOLEAN;
BEGIN
  PushTail := INHERITED PushTail(X);
END;
```

continues

Listing 7.1. continued

```pascal
{---------------------------------------- PopFront -----------}

FUNCTION TStrFixedStack.PopFront(VAR X : LeString { input }) : BOOLEAN;
BEGIN
  PopFront := INHERITED PopFront(X);
END;

{---------------------------------------- PopTail ------------}

FUNCTION TStrFixedStack.PopTail(VAR X : LeString { input }) : BOOLEAN;
BEGIN
  PopTail := INHERITED PopTail(X);
END;

{---------------------------------------- Push ------------}

FUNCTION TStrFixedStack.Push(X : LeString { input }) : BOOLEAN;
{ pushes a string into the stack. Returns TRUE if the stack was
  not already full. Otherwise, returns FALSE. }
BEGIN
  Push := PushTail(X);
END;

{---------------------------------------- Pop ------------}

FUNCTION TStrFixedStack.Pop(VAR X : LeString { input }) : BOOLEAN;
{ pops a string off the stack. Returns TRUE if the stack was
  not already empty. Otherwise, returns FALSE. }
BEGIN
  Pop := PopTail(X);
END;

BEGIN
    HeapError := @HeapErrorHandler
END.
```

Test Program to Test Object Types in the Metamorf Library Unit

Let's look at a program that tests the object types in library unit MetaMorf. Listing 7.2 contains the TSMTMRF.PAS program. This program declares anArray, aQueue,

Metamorphic Object Types

and aStack as instances of object types TStrArray, TStrFixedQue, and TStrFixedStack, respectively.

The TSMTMRF.PAS program tests an instance of TStrArray as follows:

1. Creates the instance by allocating it MAX_STRINGS elements.

2. Uses a FOR loop to store the elements of the typed-constant array StringArray in the elements of instance anArray. The loop statement displays the string to be stored and then writes it to the instance anArray by sending it the message Store. The loop statement includes a call to the procedure Delay to pause at the end of each loop iteration.

3. Uses a FOR loop to recall the elements in instance anArray. The loop statement sends a message Recall to the instance anArray and stores the retrieved string in variable AString. The loop then displays the recalled string and pauses at the end of each iteration.

4. Removes the instance anArray by using the destructor Done.

The TSMTMRF.PAS program tests instances of TStrFixedQue as follows:

1. Creates the instance by allocating it MAX_STRINGS elements.

2. Uses a FOR loop to enqueue the elements of the typed constant array StringArray in the instance aQueue. The loop statement displays the string to be stored and then enqueues it in the instance aQueue by sending it the message PushTail. The loop statement includes a call to the procedure Delay to pause at the end of each loop iteration.

3. Uses a FOR loop to dequeue the elements in instance aQueue. The loop statement sends a message PopFront to the instance aQueue and stores the retrieved string in variable AString. The loop then displays the recalled string and pauses at the end of each iteration.

4. Removes the instance aQueue by using the destructor Done.

The TSMTMRF.PAS program tests instances of TStrFixedStack as follows:

1. Creates the instance by allocating it MAX_STRINGS elements.

2. Uses a FOR loop to push the elements of the typed constant array StringArray onto the instance aStack. The loop statement displays the string to be stored and then pushes it onto the instance aStack by sending it the message Push. The loop statement includes a call to the procedure Delay to pause at the end of each loop iteration.

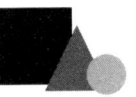

3. Uses a FOR loop to pop elements out of instance aStack. The loop statement sends a message Pop to the instance aStack and stores the retrieved string in variable AString. The loop then displays the recalled string and pauses at the end of each iteration.

4. Removes the instance aStack by using the destructor Done.

Listing 7.2. The program TSMTMRF.PAS, which tests the MetaMorf library unit.

```
Program TsMetmrf;

{
   This program tests the metamorphic object types in the MetaMorf
   library unit
}
{$X+,R-}
{$M 8192, 0, 655350}

Uses Crt, MetaMorf;

CONST WAIT = 1000;
      MAX_STRINGS = 10;

CONST StringArray : ARRAY [1..MAX_STRINGS] OF LeString =
                    ('California', 'Virginia', 'Michigan',
                     'New York', 'Washington', 'Nevada',
                     'Alabama', 'Alaska', 'Florida', 'Maine');

VAR anArray : TStrArray;
    aQueue : TStrFixedQue;
    aStack : TStrFixedStack;
    AString : LeString;
    I : BYTE;

BEGIN
    ClrScr;
    WRITELN('Testing array objects');
    anArray.Init(MAX_STRINGS);
    FOR I := 1 TO MAX_STRINGS DO BEGIN
        WRITE('Writing ', StringArray[I]:12);
        WRITELN(' to array element # ', I:2);
        anArray.Store(StringArray[I], I);
        Delay(WAIT);
    END;
    WRITE('Press any key to continue... ');
    ReadKey;
    WRITELN;
    FOR I := MAX_STRINGS DOWNTO 1 DO BEGIN
        anArray.Recall(AString, I);
```

Metamorphic Object Types

```
            WRITELN('Array(', I:2, ') = ', AString);
            Delay(WAIT);
        END;
        WRITELN;
        WRITE('Press any key to continue... ');
        ReadKey;
        anArray.Done;

        ClrScr;
        WRITELN('Testing fixed-queue objects');
        aQueue.Init(MAX_STRINGS);
        FOR I := 1 TO MAX_STRINGS DO BEGIN
            WRITELN('Pushing ', StringArray[I]:12, ' into the queue');
            aQueue.PushTail(StringArray[I]);
            Delay(WAIT);
        END;
        WRITE('Press any key to continue... ');
        ReadKey;
        WRITELN;

        WHILE aQueue.PopFront(AString) DO BEGIN
            WRITELN('Popping off ', AString:12, ' from the queue');
            Delay(WAIT);
        END;
        WRITELN;
        WRITE('Press any key to continue... ');
        ReadKey;
        aQueue.Done;

        ClrScr;
        WRITELN('Testing fixed-stack objects');
        aStack.Init(MAX_STRINGS);
        FOR I := 1 TO MAX_STRINGS DO BEGIN
            WRITELN('Pushing ', StringArray[I]:12, ' into the stack');
            aStack.Push(StringArray[I]);
            Delay(WAIT);
        END;
        WRITE('Press any key to continue... ');
        ReadKey;
        WRITELN;

        WHILE aStack.Pop(AString) DO BEGIN
            WRITELN('Popping off ', AString:12, ' from the stack');
            Delay(WAIT);
        END;
        WRITELN;
        WRITE('Press any key to end the program... ');
        ReadKey;
        aStack.Done;
END.
```

Here's a sample output for the program in Listing 7.2:

```
[BEGIN OUTPUT]
Testing array objects
Writing   California to array element #  1
Writing     Virginia to array element #  2
Writing     Michigan to array element #  3
Writing     New York to array element #  4
Writing   Washington to array element #  5
Writing       Nevada to array element #  6
Writing      Alabama to array element #  7
Writing       Alaska to array element #  8
Writing      Florida to array element #  9
Writing        Maine to array element # 10
Press any key to continue...
Array(10) = Maine
Array( 9) = Florida
Array( 8) = Alaska
Array( 7) = Alabama
Array( 6) = Nevada
Array( 5) = Washington
Array( 4) = New York
Array( 3) = Michigan
Array( 2) = Virginia
Array( 1) = California

Press any key to continue...
```

The screen clears

```
Testing fixed-queue objects
Pushing   California into the queue
Pushing     Virginia into the queue
Pushing     Michigan into the queue
Pushing     New York into the queue
Pushing   Washington into the queue
Pushing       Nevada into the queue
Pushing      Alabama into the queue
Pushing       Alaska into the queue
Pushing      Florida into the queue
Pushing        Maine into the queue
Press any key to continue...
Popping off   California from the queue
Popping off     Virginia from the queue
Popping off     Michigan from the queue
Popping off     New York from the queue
Popping off   Washington from the queue
Popping off       Nevada from the queue
Popping off      Alabama from the queue
Popping off       Alaska from the queue
Popping off      Florida from the queue
```

Metamorphic Object Types

```
Popping off       Maine from the queue

Press any key to continue...
```

The screen clears

```
Testing fixed-stack objects
Pushing    California into the stack
Pushing      Virginia into the stack
Pushing      Michigan into the stack
Pushing      New York into the stack
Pushing    Washington into the stack
Pushing        Nevada into the stack
Pushing       Alabama into the stack
Pushing        Alaska into the stack
Pushing       Florida into the stack
Pushing         Maine into the stack
Press any key to continue...
Popping off         Maine from the stack
Popping off       Florida from the stack
Popping off        Alaska from the stack
Popping off       Alabama from the stack
Popping off        Nevada from the stack
Popping off    Washington from the stack
Popping off      New York from the stack
Popping off      Michigan from the stack
Popping off      Virginia from the stack
Popping off    California from the stack

Press any key to end the program...
[END OUTPUT]
```

Summary

In this chapter you learned about descendant object types that offer functionality that is significantly different from that of the parent object type. This programming feature involves metamorphic object types. In this chapter you learned about the following topics:

- These three basic guidelines for the descendant metamorphic object types:

    The descendants use some of the inherited methods. The context of these methods may change, depending on what the descendant object type is modeling.

The descendants declare a new set of methods to support their operations. Such operations may use the inherited methods, or may repackage them in a manner more suitable for the object modeled by the descendants.

The descendants override those inherited methods that should be used by the instances. The overriding methods must be declared private and may simply call the inherited methods, or be dummy shells.

- Each object type in an object-type hierarchy can offer different operations. Consequently, each descendant object type supports a new set of methods and hides some of the inherited methods when necessary. (Listing 7.1 showed an object-type hierarchy that includes an array, a fixed queue, and a fixed stack.)

Chapter 8

Containment

Inheritance allows you to define descendant object types so that they offer new features and operations that are more specialized than those of the parent object types. Conceptually, inheritance represents the *"is a"* relationship between an object type and its descendant. Another link used in modeling real-world objects is the *"has a"* relationship. This kind of link is called, in OOP terminology, *containment*. This chapter examines containment and presents the following topics:

- The basics of containment.
- Containment and extendible records.
- Containment in an object-type hierarchy.
- Modular objects.

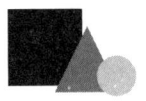

- Direct access to components of modular objects.
- Multiple inheritance.

The Basics of Containment

Containment is a method of modeling objects by defining object types that contain data fields that are themselves instances, or pointers to instances, of other object types. The object types associated with these data fields may be either members of the same object-type hierarchy or members of another hierarchy.

Figure 8.1 shows a simple object-type hierarchy that models vehicles. Each descendant object type is a special form of its parent. For example, a car *is a* vehicle, a sedan *is a* car, and so on. However, when you examine an object like a car, you realize that it's made up of several components, each being a distinct object. These components object types have their own attributes and support operations. Thus, the car object type *contains* other object types. In OOP terms, a car *has an* engine, *has a* body, and so on. You cannot say that a car *is an* engine, or *is a* body. Figure 8.2 shows the hasA relationship among a few components of a car.

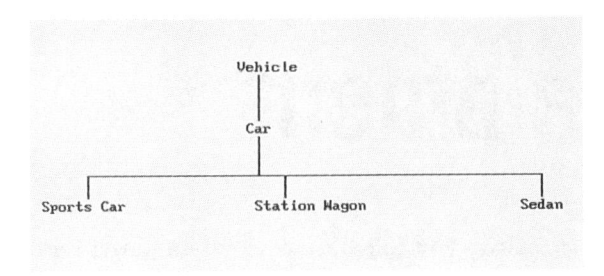

Figure 8.1. The isA *link between descendant object types.*

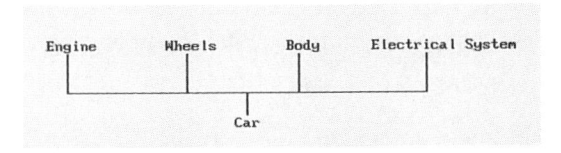

Figure 8.2. The hasA *link between an object type and its components.*

Containment 8

> Containment is a powerful method that enables software developers to link object types in different hierarchies. This programming feature becomes more relevant when the development programming language does not support multiple inheritance, as is the case with Borland Pascal. (More about multiple inheritance in the last section of this chapter.)

The next sections demonstrate how containment works with extendible records (object types with only public data fields) and with typical object types. In the latter case, I present an example in which the contained object types are transparent to the client program and another example where the components are modular—that is, opaque to the client program.

Containment and Extendible Records

In Chapter 4, I presented extendible records. The examples in that chapter used only inheritance to model extendible records using object types. It also is possible to use containment to build extendible records. However, the price to pay for this feature is the need for additional access operators to manipulate the nested data fields.

Let's look at an example. Listing 8.1 shows the program CONTAIN1.PAS, which illustrates using containment with extendible records. The program, which manages tasks, declares three object types: DateRec, TimeRec, and TaskRec:

- The object type DateRec declares three public data fields: Year, Month, and Day. These fields have the type WORD.

- The object type TimeRec declares three public data fields: Hour, Minute, and Second. These fields have the type WORD.

- The object type TaskRec also declares three data fields: Action, fDate, and fTime. The Action field is a string, whereas the fDate and fTime fields are instances of the object types DateRec and TimeRec, respectively. Thus, the TaskRec object type contains two nested object types.

Conceptually, a task *has a* time and *has a* date. This way of viewing a task is reflected by using containment to model the extendible record TaskRec. The program also declares the type TaskArray to represent an array of TaskRec.

181

The program CONTAIN1.PAS declares the following relevant routines:

- The Boolean function `IsGreater` compares the date and time of two tasks, accessed by parameters `Task1` and `Task2`. The function returns True if `Task1` occurs before `Task2`. Otherwise, the function returns False. Note that the parameters `Task1` and `Task2` require two access operators to tap into the nested data fields `Year`, `Month`, `Day`, `Hour`, `Minute`, and `Second`.

- The procedure `InitializeTasks` initializes the members of the `TaskArray`-typed reference parameter `TaskArr`. The routine uses a `FOR` loop to copy the strings from the typed constant `dB` to the `Action` data fields of the `TaskArr` elements. The procedure assigns random numbers to data fields `Year`, `Month`, `Day`, `Hour`, and `Minute`. The routine assigns 0 to the `Second` data field.

- The procedure `DisplayTasks` displays the tasks in the `TaskArray`-typed parameter `TaskArr`. The routine first clears the screen, then displays the contents of the string-typed parameter `Message`, and then displays the tasks. Each line shows the task with its date and time.

- The procedure `SortTasks` sorts the array of tasks. The `TaskArray`-typed reference parameter `TaskArr` passes the array of the task to be sorted. The routine implements the `Comb` sort method and uses the function `IsGreater` in comparing the date and time of any two tasks.

The main program section performs the following tasks:

1. Initializes the array of tasks by calling the procedure `InitializeTasks`.

2. Displays the unordered tasks in array `Tasks` by invoking the procedure `DisplayTasks`.

3. Sorts the elements of array `Tasks` by calling the procedure `SortTasks`.

4. Displays the sorted tasks in array `Tasks` by invoking the procedure `DisplayTasks`.

Listing 8.1. The program CONTAIN1.PAS, which illustrates using containment with extendible records.

```
Program Contain1;

{
  This program demonstrates the containment of extendible records.
}
```

Containment 8

```pascal
{$X+}

Uses Crt, Dos;

CONST MAX_TASKS = 10;

TYPE
  STRING80 = STRING[80];

  DateRec = OBJECT
    Year  : WORD;
    Month : WORD;
    Day   : WORD;
  END;

  TimeRec = OBJECT
    Hour   : WORD;
    Minute : WORD;
    Second : WORD;
  END;

  TaskRec = OBJECT
    Action : STRING80;
    fDate  : DateRec;
    fTime  : TimeRec;
  END;

  TaskArray = ARRAY [1..MAX_TASKS] OF TaskRec;

CONST db : ARRAY[1..MAX_TASKS] OF STRING80
        = ('Meeting with publisher', 'Trip to COMDEX',
           'C++ Workshop', 'OOP-Pascal Workshop',
           'Visual Basic conference', 'QBasic radio promotion',
           'Ada conference', 'Deadline for C++ book',
           'FORTRAN-90 workshop', 'OOP Design workshop');

VAR Tasks : TaskArray;


FUNCTION IsGreater(VAR Task1,          { input }
                       Task2 : TaskRec { input }) : BOOLEAN;

VAR totalSec1, totalSec2 : LONGINT;

BEGIN
  IF Task1.fDate.Year > Task2.fDate.Year THEN
    IsGreater := TRUE
  ELSE IF Task1.fDate.Year < Task2.fDate.Year THEN
    IsGreater := FALSE
```

continues

Listing 8.1. continued

```
    ELSE BEGIN
      IF Task1.fDate.Month > Task2.fDate.Month THEN
        IsGreater := TRUE
      ELSE IF Task1.fDate.Month < Task2.fDate.Month THEN
        IsGreater := FALSE
      ELSE BEGIN
        IF Task1.fDate.Day > Task2.fDate.Day THEN
          IsGreater := TRUE
        ELSE IF Task1.fDate.Day < Task2.fDate.Day THEN
          IsGreater := FALSE
        ELSE BEGIN
          { dates are the same! }
          WITH Task1.fTime DO
            totalSec1 := (Hour * 60 + Minute) * 60 + Second;
          WITH Task2.fTime DO
            totalSec2 := (Hour * 60 + Minute) * 60 + Second;
          IsGreater := totalSec1 > totalSec2;
        END;
      END
    END;
END;

PROCEDURE Display(I : WORD; { input }
                  C : CHAR  { input });

BEGIN
    IF I < 10 THEN
        WRITE('0',I:1)
    ELSE
        WRITE(I:2);
    WRITE(C);
END;

PROCEDURE InitializeTasks(VAR TaskArr : TaskArray { output });

VAR i : WORD;

BEGIN
  Randomize;
  { initialize array }
  FOR i := 1 TO MAX_TASKS DO BEGIN
    { assign tasks to the Action field of array TaskArr }
    TaskArr[i].Action := dB[i];
```

```
      WITH TaskArr[i].fDate DO BEGIN
        Year := 1993 + Random(3);
        Month := 1 + Random(12);
        Day := 1 + Random(28);
      END;
      WITH TaskArr[i].fTime DO BEGIN
        Hour := 9 + Random(3);
        Minute := 15 * Random(4);
        Second := 0;
      END;
   END;
END;

PROCEDURE DisplayTasks(VAR TaskArr : TaskArray; { input }
                          Message : STRING80   { input });

VAR i : WORD;

BEGIN
   ClrScr;
   WRITELN(Message);
   WRITELN;
   FOR i := 1 TO MAX_TASKS DO BEGIN
      WRITE(TaskArr[i].Action, '    ');
      GotoXY(30, WhereY);
      WITH TaskArr[i].fDate DO BEGIN
        Display(Month, '/');
        Display(Day, '/');
        Display(Year, ' ');
        WRITE('    ');
      END;
      WITH TaskArr[i].fTime DO BEGIN
        Display(Hour, ':');
        Display(Minute, ':');
        Display(Second, #0);
        WRITELN;
      END;
   END;
END;

PROCEDURE SortTasks(VAR TaskArr : TaskArray { in/out });

VAR i, j, offset : WORD;
    inOrder : BOOLEAN;
    temp : TaskRec;
```

continues

Listing 8.1. continued

```
BEGIN
  offset := MAX_TASKS;
  REPEAT
    offset := offset DIV 2;
    IF offset < 1 THEN offset := 1;
    inOrder := TRUE;
    FOR i := 1 TO MAX_TASKS - offset DO BEGIN
      j := i + offset;
      IF IsGreater(TaskArr[i], TaskArr[j]) THEN BEGIN
        inOrder := FALSE;
        temp := TaskArr[i];
        TaskArr[i] := TaskArr[j];
        TaskArr[j] := temp;
      END;
    END;
  UNTIL (offset = 1) AND inOrder;
END;

BEGIN
  InitializeTasks(Tasks);
  DisplayTasks(Tasks, 'Unordered list of tasks:');
  GotoXY(1, 24);
  WRITE('Press any key to continue...');
  ReadKey;
  SortTasks(Tasks);
  DisplayTasks(Tasks, 'Ordered list of tasks:');
  GotoXY(1, 24);
  WRITE('Press any key to end the program...');
  ReadKey;
END.
```

Here's a sample output for the program in Listing 8.1. (Remember that you're likely to get output with different dates and times because the program uses random numbers to internally assign these dates and times.)

```
[BEGIN OUTPUT]
Unordered list of tasks:

Meeting with publisher      07/26/1995    09:45:00
Trip to COMDEX              08/15/1993    11:30:00
C++ Workshop                12/08/1995    11:45:00
OOP-Pascal Workshop         05/16/1993    10:30:00
Visual Basic conference     07/19/1993    11:30:00
QBasic radio promotion      05/14/1995    09:45:00
```

Containment   8

```
Ada conference            11/20/1995    11:00:00
Deadline for C++ book     02/12/1994    11:15:00
FORTRAN-90 workshop       09/18/1994    11:15:00
OOP Design workshop       07/08/1994    10:30:00




Press any key to continue...
```

The screen clears

```
Ordered list of tasks:

OOP-Pascal Workshop       05/16/1993    10:30:00
Visual Basic conference   07/19/1993    11:30:00
Trip to COMDEX            08/15/1993    11:30:00
Deadline for C++ book     02/12/1994    11:15:00
OOP Design workshop       07/08/1994    10:30:00
FORTRAN-90 workshop       09/18/1994    11:15:00
QBasic radio promotion    05/14/1995    09:45:00
Meeting with publisher    07/26/1995    09:45:00
Ada conference            11/20/1995    11:00:00
C++ Workshop              12/08/1995    11:45:00




Press any key to end the program...
[END OUTPUT]
```

Containment in Object-Type Hierarchies

This section presents a more typical use of containment in creating object types. The program CONTAIN2.PAS, shown in Listing 8.2, uses contained object types in a manner that is transparent to the client programs. The example models a *hybrid dynamic array* of strings: the array stores part of its elements in dynamic memory and the remaining part on disk. Such an array represents a compromise solution that stores the most important (or most frequently accessed) elements in memory and the unimportant (or least frequently accessed) elements in a random-access data file.

The program declares the THybStrArray object type to model the hybrid dynamic array of strings. The object type declares a set of data fields, a constructor, a destructor, and a group of methods.

> The THybStrArray object type declares the following data fields:
>
> - The data field MemArr is an instance of object type TStrArray, declared in the PolyMorf library unit listed in Chapter 3. The MemArr data field models the component that stores strings in dynamic memory.
>
> - The data field VMArr is an instance of object type TVirtStrArray, declared in the PolyMorf library unit. This data field models the components that store strings in a random-access data file.
>
> - The data field MaxRamIndex contains the highest index of an array element that resides in dynamic memory.
>
> - The data field MaxIndex stores the highest array index.

The constructor Init creates the hybrid array instance using the three parameters InMemArraySize, InFileArraySize, and Filename. The parameter InMemArraySize specifies the number of memory-based array elements. The parameter InFileArraySize specifies the number of file-based array elements. The parameter Filename indicates the name of the supporting data file. The constructor performs the following tasks:

- Invokes the TStrArray.Init constructor, using the data field MemArr, to create the portion of the hybrid array stored in dynamic memory.

- Invokes the `TVirtStrArray.Init` constructor, using the data field `VMArr`, to create the portion of the hybrid array stored in a data file.

- Stores the highest in-memory index in the `MaxRamIndex` field. This task sends the message `GetMaxSize` to the data field `MemArr`. The value returned by the message is the highest in-memory index.

- Calculates the value for highest index of the hybrid array. This task involves sending the message `GetMaxSize` to the data field `VMArr`. The constructor stores the calculated value in the `MaxIndex` data field.

The constructor `Done` removes the instance of `THybStrArray` by invoking the destructors `TStrArray.Done` and `TVirtStrArray.Done` using the `MemArr` and `VMArr` data fields, respectively. By using the destructors of the contained object types, the `THybStrArray` object type deallocates the dynamic memory resources and deletes the supporting file with little overhead.

The `THybStrArray` object type declares the following methods:

- The Boolean function `Store` saves a string in the array element number `Index`. The function returns True if the argument for parameter `Index` is in the range of 1 to `MaxIndex`. Otherwise, the function returns False. If the argument of `Index` is less than or equal to the value in field `MaxRamIndex`, the method sends a `Store` message to the `MemArr` data field. The arguments of that message are `aStr` and `Index`. Otherwise, the method sends a `Store` message to data field `VMArr`, with the arguments `aStr` and `Index` - `MaxRamIndex`.

- The Boolean function `Recall` retrieves a string from the array element number `Index`. The function returns True if the argument for parameter `Index` is in the range of 1 to `GetWorkSize`. Otherwise, the function returns False. If the argument of `Index` is less than or equal to the value in field `MaxRamIndex`, the method sends a `Recall` message to the `MemArr` data field. The arguments of that message are `aStr` and `Index`. Otherwise, the method sends a `Recall` message to data field `VMArr`, with the arguments `aStr` and `Index` - `MaxRamIndex`.

- The function `GetWorkSize` returns the working size of a hybrid array. The function returns the sum of the values returned by the `GetWorkSize` messages sent to the `MemArr` and `VMArr` data fields.

- The function `GetMaxSize` returns the size of the hybrid array.

The CONTAIN2.PAS program contains the following miscellaneous routines that assist in testing an instance of `THybStrArray`:

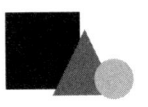

- The procedure InitArray initializes an instance of THybStrArray, accessed by the reference parameter anArray. The routine sends a set of Store messages to the parameter AnArray to write a group of names in that array.

- The procedure DisplayArray displays the elements in a THybStrArray instance, accessed by the reference parameter anArray. The routine performs the following tasks:

    1. Clears the screen.

    2. Displays the string in the parameter Message.

    3. Uses a FOR loop to send Recall messages to the parameter anArray. The loop then displays the string obtained from the Recall message if that message returns True.

- The procedure SortArray sorts the elements in a THybStrArray instance, accessed by the reference parameter anArray. The routine implements the Comb sort method and accesses the elements of parameter anArray by sending it Store and Recall messages.

The main program section declares Arr as the instance of object type THybStrArray. The program performs the following tasks:

1. Instantiates the Arr instance by using the constructor Init.

2. Initializes the instance Arr by calling the procedure InitArray.

3. Displays the unordered elements in instance Arr by calling the DisplayArray procedure.

4. Sorts the elements in instance Arr by invoking the SortArray procedure.

5. Displays the sorted elements in instance Arr by calling the DisplayArray procedure.

6. Removes the instance Arr by using the constructor Done.

Listing 8.2. The program CONTAIN2.PAS, which uses contained object types in a transparent way.

```
Program Contain2;

{
  This program demonstrates the containment of object types.
}

{$X+}
```

Containment

```
    Uses Crt, PolyMorf;

CONST MAX_IN_RAM = 5;
      MAX_IN_FILE = 5;
      MAX_ELEMS = MAX_IN_RAM + MAX_IN_FILE;
      FILENAME = 'ARR.DAT';

TYPE
   THybStrArray = OBJECT
     CONSTRUCTOR Init(InMemArraySize,         { input }
                      InFileArraySize : WORD; { input }
                      Filename        : STRING { input });
     DESTRUCTOR Done;
     FUNCTION Store(aStr  : LSTRING; { input }
                    Index : WORD     { input })
                          : BOOLEAN; VIRTUAL;
     FUNCTION Recall(VAR aStr  : LSTRING; { output }
                         Index : WORD     { input })
                               : BOOLEAN; VIRTUAL;
     FUNCTION GetWorkSize : WORD;
     FUNCTION GetMaxSize : WORD;
    PRIVATE
     MemArr : TStrArray;
     VMArr : TVirtStrArray;
     MaxRamIndex : WORD;
     MaxIndex : WORD;
   END;


{------------------------------------------------ Init -----------}

CONSTRUCTOR THybStrArray.Init(
                    InMemArraySize,         { input }
                    InFileArraySize : WORD; { input }
                    Filename        : STRING { input });
BEGIN
  MemArr.Init(InMemArraySize);
  VMArr.Init(InFileArraySize, Filename);
  MaxRamIndex := MemArr.GetMaxSize;
  MaxIndex := MaxRamIndex + VMArr.GetMaxSize;
END;

{------------------------------------------------ Done -----------}

DESTRUCTOR THybStrArray.Done;
BEGIN
  MemArr.Done;
  VMArr.Done;
END;

{------------------------------------------------ Store -----------}
```

continues

Listing 8.2. continued

```
FUNCTION THybStrArray.Store(aStr  : LSTRING; { input  }
                            Index : WORD     { input })
                                  : BOOLEAN;
BEGIN
  IF (Index > 0) AND (Index <= MaxIndex) THEN BEGIN
    IF Index <= MaxRamIndex THEN
      Store := MemArr.Store(aStr, Index)
    ELSE
      Store := VMArr.Store(aStr, Index - MaxRamIndex);
  END
  ELSE
    Store := FALSE;
END;

{------------------------------------------ Recall -----------}

FUNCTION THybStrArray.Recall(VAR aStr  : LSTRING; { output }
                                Index : WORD     { input })
                                      : BOOLEAN;
BEGIN
  IF (Index > 0) AND (Index <= GetWorkSize) THEN BEGIN
    IF Index <= MaxRamIndex THEN
      Recall := MemArr.Recall(aStr, Index)
    ELSE
      Recall := VMArr.Recall(aStr, Index - MaxRamIndex);
  END
  ELSE
    Recall := FALSE;

END;

{------------------------------------- GetWorkSize -----------}

FUNCTION THybStrArray.GetWorkSize : WORD;
BEGIN
  GetWorkSize := MemArr.GetWorkSize + VMArr.GetWorkSize;
END;


{-------------------------------------- GetMaxSize -----------}

FUNCTION THybStrArray.GetMaxSize : WORD;
BEGIN
  GetMaxSize := MaxIndex;
END;

{-------------------- miscellaneous procedures -------------------}

PROCEDURE InitArray(VAR anArray : THybStrArray { output });
```

Containment 8

```
  BEGIN
    anArray.Store('California', 1);
    anArray.Store('Virginia', 2);
    anArray.Store('Michigan', 3);
    anArray.Store('New York', 4);
    anArray.Store('Nevada', 5);
    anArray.Store('Alabama', 6);
    anArray.Store('Alaska', 7);
    anArray.Store('Ohio', 8);
    anArray.Store('Indiana', 9);
    anArray.Store('Colorado', 10);
  END;

PROCEDURE DisplayArray(VAR anArray : THybStrArray; { input }
                          Message : STRING       { input });

VAR i : WORD;
    s : LSTRING;

BEGIN
  ClrScr;
  WRITELN(Message);
  WRITELN;
  FOR i := 1 TO anArray.GetWorkSize DO
    IF anArray.Recall(s, i) THEN
      WRITELN(s);
END;

PROCEDURE SortArray(VAR anArray : THybStrArray { in/out });

VAR i, j, offset : WORD;
    inOrder : BOOLEAN;
    sI, sJ : LSTRING;

BEGIN
  offset := anArray.GetWorkSize;
  REPEAT
    offset := offset DIV 2;
    IF offset < 1 THEN offset := 1;
    inOrder := TRUE;
    FOR i := 1 TO anArray.GetWorkSize - offset DO BEGIN
      j := i + offset;
      anArray.Recall(sI, i);
      anArray.Recall(sJ, j);
      IF sI > sJ THEN BEGIN
        inOrder := FALSE;
        anArray.Store(sI, j);
        anArray.Store(sJ, i);
      END;
    END;
  UNTIL (offset = 1) AND inOrder;
END;
```

continues

Listing 8.2. continued

```
VAR Arr : THybStrArray;

BEGIN
  ClrScr;
  Arr.Init(MAX_IN_RAM, MAX_IN_FILE, FILENAME);
  InitArray(Arr);
  DisplayArray(Arr, 'Unordered hybrid array is:');
  GotoXY(1, 24);
  WRITE('Press any key to continue...');
  ReadKey;
  SortArray(Arr);
  DisplayArray(Arr, 'Ordered hybrid array is:');
  GotoXY(1, 24);
  WRITE('Press any key to end the program...');
  ReadKey;
  Arr.Done;
END.
```

Here's a sample output for the program in Listing 8.2:

```
[BEGIN OUTPUT]
Unordered hybrid array is:

California
Virginia
Michigan
New York
Nevada
Alabama
Alaska
Ohio
Indiana
Colorado




            Press any key to continue...
```

Containment 8

The screen clears

```
Ordered hybrid array is:

Alabama
Alaska
California
Colorado
Indiana
Michigan
Nevada
New York
Ohio
Virginia




Press any key to end the program...
[END OUTPUT]
```

Modular Objects

The contained object types in the example of the last section are transparent and inaccessible to the client program. The example presents the type of containment that hides the contained object-type instances. Thus, you may alter the implementation of methods in THybStrArray without affecting the program itself. This section presents another kind of containment: one that supports accessible modular components.

Listing 8.3 contains the next example, program CONTAIN3.PAS. This program models the most common modular object we share: the PC itself.

A PC is an object that contains modular objects. Many of these contained objects are accessible. For example, you frequently access the keyboard, disk drive, and video monitor as modular components of your PC. You may even open up a PC for inspection or to upgrade its memory, hard disk, and CPU. In other words, the components of the PC are visible and accessible.

The program declares the enumerated data type `Processor`. This type represents the family of Intel 80x86 processors. The program also declares the object type `TMemory`, `THardDisk`, `TCPU`, and `TPC` to model the memory, hard disk, CPU and PC, respectively.

The `TMemory` object type has a single data field, `kRam`, in which to store the amount of memory (in kilobytes). The object type declares three methods: `SetRam`, `GetRam`, and `Show`. These methods set and query the value in data field `kRam` and display the amount of memory.

The `THardDisk` object type has a single data field, `megStorage`, in which to store the amount of mass storage (in megabytes). The object type declares three methods: `SetStorage`, `GetStorage`, and `Show`. These methods set and query the value in data field `megStorage` and display the amount of storage.

The `TCPU` object type has a single data field, `CPUtype`, in which to store the type of CPU. The object type declares three methods: `SetCPU`, `GetCPU`, and `Show`. These methods set and query the value in data field `CPUtype` and display the CPU type, respectively.

The `TPC` object type has three data fields: `Memory`, `HardDisk`, and `CPU`. These fields are instances of the object types `TMemory`, `THardDisk`, and `TCPU`. The object type declares the methods `SetRam`, `GetRam`, `SetStorage`, `GetStorage`, `SetCPU`, and `GetCPU` to set and query the contained instances `Memory`, `HardDisk`, and `CPU`.

The main program section declares `PC` as an instance of object type `TPC`. The program performs the following tasks:

1. Sends a `SetRam` message to the instance `PC` to set the amount of memory.

2. Sends a `SetStorage` message to the instance `PC` to set the amount of hard disk storage.

3. Sends a `SetCPU` message to the instance `PC` to set the CPU type.

4. Sends a `Show` message to the instance `PC` to display the current state of the instance.

5. Repeats steps 1 to 3 with a new set of messages that assign a different set of values to the instance `PC`.

Containment 8

> This example shows how the host object type must provide the methods to allow you to communicate with the contained instances. As the example shows, these methods seem redundant when you wish to individually manipulate a contained instance.

Listing 8.3. The program CONTAIN3.PAS, which uses contained object types to represent modular objects.

```
Program Contain3;

{
  This program illustrates modular objects.
}

{$X+}

Uses Crt;

TYPE
    Processor = (Intel8088, Intel80286, Intel80386SX,
                 Intel80386DX, Intel80486SX,
                 Intel80486DX, Intel80586SX,
                 Intel80586DX);

    TMemory = OBJECT
      PROCEDURE SetRam(newRam : WORD { input });
      FUNCTION GetRam : WORD;
      PROCEDURE Show;
     PRIVATE
      kRam : WORD;
    END;

    THardDisk = OBJECT
      PROCEDURE SetStorage(newStorage : WORD { input });
      FUNCTION GetStorage : WORD;
      PROCEDURE Show;
     PRIVATE
       megStorage : WORD;
    END;

    TCPU = OBJECT
      PROCEDURE SetCPU(newCPU : Processor { input });
      FUNCTION GetCPU : Processor;
      PROCEDURE Show;
```

continues

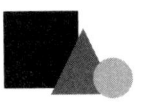

Listing 8.3. continued

```
    PRIVATE
      CPUtype : Processor;
    END;

    TPC = OBJECT
      PROCEDURE SetRam(newRam : WORD { input });
      FUNCTION GetRam : WORD;
      PROCEDURE SetStorage(newStorage : WORD { input });
      FUNCTION GetStorage : WORD;
      PROCEDURE SetCPU(newCPU : Processor { input });
      FUNCTION GetCPU : Processor;
      PROCEDURE Show;
     PRIVATE
       Memory : TMemory;
       HardDisk : THardDisk;
       CPU : TCPU;
    END;

{---------------------------------------- SetRam --------------}

PROCEDURE TMemory.SetRam(newRam : WORD { input });
BEGIN
  kRam := newRam;
END;

{---------------------------------------- GetRam --------------}

FUNCTION TMemory.GetRam : WORD;
BEGIN
  GetRam := kRam;
END;

{---------------------------------------- Show --------------}

PROCEDURE TMemory.Show;
BEGIN
  WRITE('Memory: ', kRam, ' Kbytes');
END;

{---------------------------------------- SetStorage --------------}

PROCEDURE THardDisk.SetStorage(newStorage : WORD { input });
BEGIN
  megStorage := newStorage;
END;

{---------------------------------------- GetStorage --------------}

FUNCTION THardDisk.GetStorage : WORD;
```

Containment 8

```
  BEGIN
    GetStorage := megStorage;
  END;

  {---------------------------------------------- Show -------------}

  PROCEDURE THardDisk.Show;
  BEGIN
    WRITE('Hard disk: ', megStorage, ' Mbytes storage');
  END;

  {---------------------------------------------- SetCPU -------------}

  PROCEDURE TCPU.SetCPU(newCPU : Processor { input });
  BEGIN
    CPUtype := newCPU;
  END;

  {---------------------------------------------- GetCPU -------------}

  FUNCTION TCPU.GetCPU : Processor;
  BEGIN
    GetCPU := CPUtype;
  END;

  {---------------------------------------------- Show -------------}

  PROCEDURE TCPU.Show;
  BEGIN
    WRITE('CPU: ');
    CASE CPUtype OF
      Intel8088     : WRITE('8088');
      Intel80286    : WRITE('80286');
      Intel80386SX  : WRITE('80386SX');
      Intel80386DX  : WRITE('80386DX');
      Intel80486SX  : WRITE('80486SX');
      Intel80486DX  : WRITE('80486DX');
      Intel80586SX  : WRITE('80586SX');
      Intel80586DX  : WRITE('80586DX');
    END;
  END;

  {---------------------------------------------- SetRam -------------}

  PROCEDURE TPC.SetRam(newRam : WORD { input });
  BEGIN
    Memory.SetRam(newRam);
  END;
```

continues

Listing 8.3. continued

```
{------------------------------------------ GetRam --------------}

FUNCTION TPC.GetRam : WORD;
BEGIN
  GetRam := Memory.GetRam;
END;

{------------------------------------------ SetStorage --------------}

PROCEDURE TPC.SetStorage(newStorage : WORD { input });
BEGIN
  HardDisk.SetStorage(newStorage);
END;

{------------------------------------------ GetStorage --------------}

FUNCTION TPC.GetStorage : WORD;
BEGIN
  GetStorage := HardDisk.GetStorage;
END;

{------------------------------------------ SetCPU --------------}

PROCEDURE TPC.SetCPU(newCPU : Processor { input });
BEGIN
  CPU.SetCPU(newCPU);
END;

{------------------------------------------ GetCPU --------------}

FUNCTION TPC.GetCPU : Processor;
BEGIN
  GetCPU := CPU.GetCPU;
END;

{------------------------------------------ Show --------------}

PROCEDURE TPC.Show;
BEGIN
  Memory.Show; WRITELN;
  HardDisk.Show; WRITELN;
  CPU.Show; WRITELN;
END;

{-------------------------- MAIN --------------------------}

VAR PC : TPC;
```

Containment 8

```
BEGIN
  ClrScr;
  WRITELN('System configuration:');
  PC.SetRam(16000);
  PC.SetStorage(340);
  PC.SetCPU(Intel80486DX);
  PC.Show;
  WRITELN;
  WRITELN('New system configuration:');
  PC.SetRam(32000);
  PC.SetStorage(600);
  PC.SetCPU(Intel80586SX);
  PC.Show;
  WRITELN;
  WRITE('Press any key to end the program...');
  ReadKey;
END.
```

Here's a sample output for the program in Listing 8.3:

```
[BEGIN OUTPUT]
System configuration:
Memory: 16000 Kbytes
Hard disk: 340 Mbytes storage
CPU: 80486DX

New system configuration:
Memory: 32000 Kbytes
Hard disk: 600 Mbytes storage
CPU: 80586SX

Press any key to end the program...
[END OUTPUT]
```

Direct Access to Components of Modular Objects

The example in the last section declared the TPC object type in such a way that you could not access the contained instances. The simplicity of the example tends to hide complications that arise in more evolved modular objects. If the contained object types contain more methods with longer parameter lists, the host object type needs to match these methods and parameter lists. This redundancy is contrary to the software reusability preached by OOP!

You can simplify the design of the host object type by using pointers to the contained instances. All you need then are methods that access these pointers. This approach enables you to manipulate the contained instances using other, ordinary instances. These instances receive the message defined in the object type of the contained instances.

Let's put the above programming method to work. Listing 8.4 shows the program CONTAIN4.PAS, which offers more direct access to the modular components. The program declares the same object types as does the program in Listing 8.3 and also adds three pointer types (PMemory, PHardDisk, and PCPU) to the contained object types. The object types TMemory, THardDisk, and TCPU are the same in both Listings 8.3 and 8.4.

The TPC object type has a new character in Listing 8.4. It declares the methods SetComponents and GetComponents to set and query the contained instances Memory, HardDisk, and CPU. The methods pass pointers to the contained object types. The SetComponents method copies the data from the pointers to the data fields. The GetComponents method performs the reverse action. If the nested object types have pointers that access dynamic data, you must use special copy methods.

The main program declares PC, aMemory, aHardDisk, and aCPU as instances of the object types TPC, TMemory, THardDisk, and TCPU, respectively. The program performs the following tasks:

1. Sends the messages SetRam, SetStorage, and SetCPU to the instances aMemory, aHardDisk, and aCPU, respectively. These messages set the data fields in these instances.

2. Sends a SetComponents message to the instance PC. The message passes the addresses of the instances aMemory, aHardDisk, and aCPU.

3. Sends the message Show to instance PC to display the hardware components of that instance.

4. Sends the message GetComponents to instance PC to obtain a copy of its contained instances.

5. Sends the GetRam message to the instance aMemory. The program stores the result of this message in variable X.

6. Doubles the value in variable X.

7. Sends the SetRam message to instance aMemory and supplies message with the argument X.

8. Sends the GetStorage message to the instance aHardDisk. The program stores the result of this message in variable X.

Containment 8

9. Increases the value in variable x by 300.
10. Sends the `SetStorage` message to instance aMemory and supplies the message with argument X.
11. Sends the message `GetCPU` to instance aCPU. The program takes the successful result of the message and assigns it the enumerated variable CPUvar.
12. Sends the message `SetCPU` to instance aCPU and supplies the message with argument CPUvar.
13. Sends the message `SetComponents` to the instance PC. This message assigns the new values in instance aMemory, aHardDisk, and aCPU to the contained instances of PC.
14. Sends the message `Show` to instance PC to display the new hardware components of that instance.

Listing 8.4. The program CONTAIN4.PAS, which offers more direct access to the modular components.

```
Program Contain4;

{
  This program illustrates modular objects using pointers.
}

{$X+}

Uses Crt;

TYPE
    Processor = (Intel8088, Intel80286, Intel80386SX,
                 Intel80386DX, Intel80486SX,
                 Intel80486DX, Intel80586SX,
                 Intel80586DX);

    PMemory = ^TMemory;
    TMemory = OBJECT
      PROCEDURE SetRam(newRam : LONGINT { input });
      FUNCTION GetRam : LONGINT;
      PROCEDURE Show;
    PRIVATE
      kRam : LONGINT;
    END;
```

continues

203

Listing 8.4. continued

```pascal
    PHardDisk = ^THardDisk;
    THardDisk = OBJECT
      PROCEDURE SetStorage(newStorage : LONGINT { input });
      FUNCTION GetStorage : LONGINT;
      PROCEDURE Show;
     PRIVATE
       megStorage : LONGINT;
    END;

    PCPU = ^TCPU;
    TCPU = OBJECT
      PROCEDURE SetCPU(newCPU : Processor { input });
      FUNCTION GetCPU : Processor;
      PROCEDURE Show;
     PRIVATE
      CPUtype : Processor;
    END;

    TPC = OBJECT
      PROCEDURE SetComponents(pMemoryObj   : PMemory;    { input }
                              pHardDiskObj : PHardDisk;  { input }
                              pCPUObj      : PCPU        { input });
      PROCEDURE GetComponents(pMemoryObj   : PMemory;    { in/out }
                              pHardDiskObj : PHardDisk;  { in/out }
                              pCPUObj      : PCPU        { in/out });
      PROCEDURE Show;
     PRIVATE
       Memory : TMemory;
       HardDisk : THardDisk;
       CPU : TCPU;
    END;

{-------------------------------------------- SetRam --------------}

PROCEDURE TMemory.SetRam(newRam : LONGINT { input });
BEGIN
  kRam := newRam;
END;

{-------------------------------------------- GetRam --------------}

FUNCTION TMemory.GetRam : LONGINT;
BEGIN
  GetRam := kRam;
END;

{-------------------------------------------- Show ----------------}

PROCEDURE TMemory.Show;
```

Containment 8

```
BEGIN
  WRITE('Memory: ', kRam, ' Kbytes');
END;

{------------------------------------ SetStorage -------------}

PROCEDURE THardDisk.SetStorage(newStorage : LONGINT { input });
BEGIN
  megStorage := newStorage;
END;

{------------------------------------ GetStorage -------------}

FUNCTION THardDisk.GetStorage : LONGINT;
BEGIN
  GetStorage := megStorage;
END;

{--------------------------------------- Show -------------}

PROCEDURE THardDisk.Show;
BEGIN
  WRITE('Hard disk: ', megStorage, ' Mbytes storage');
END;

{--------------------------------------- SetCPU -------------}

PROCEDURE TCPU.SetCPU(newCPU : Processor { input });
BEGIN
  CPUtype := newCPU;
END;

{--------------------------------------- GetCPU -------------}

FUNCTION TCPU.GetCPU : Processor;
BEGIN
  GetCPU := CPUtype;
END;

{--------------------------------------- Show -------------}

PROCEDURE TCPU.Show;
BEGIN
  WRITE('CPU: ');
  CASE CPUtype OF
    Intel8088     : WRITE('8088');
    Intel80286    : WRITE('80286');
    Intel80386SX  : WRITE('80386SX');
    Intel80386DX  : WRITE('80386DX');
    Intel80486SX  : WRITE('80486SX');
```

continues

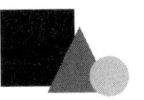

Listing 8.4. continued

```pascal
    Intel80486DX : WRITE('80486DX');
    Intel80586SX : WRITE('80586SX');
    Intel80586DX : WRITE('80586DX');
  END;
END;

{--------------------------------- SetComponents -------------}

PROCEDURE TPC.SetComponents(pMemoryObj   : PMemory;  { input }
                            pHardDiskObj : PHardDisk; { input }
                            pCPUObj      : PCPU      { input });

BEGIN
  Memory := pMemoryObj^;
  HardDisk := pHardDiskObj^;
  CPU := pCPUObj^;
END;


{--------------------------------- GetComponents -------------}

PROCEDURE TPC.GetComponents(pMemoryObj   : PMemory;  { in/out }
                            pHardDiskObj : PHardDisk; { in/out }
                            pCPUObj      : PCPU      { in/out });

BEGIN
  pMemoryObj^ := Memory;
  pHardDiskObj^ := HardDisk;
  pCPUObj^ := CPU;
END;

{------------------------------------------ Show -------------}

PROCEDURE TPC.Show;
BEGIN
  Memory.Show; WRITELN;
  HardDisk.Show; WRITELN;
  CPU.Show; WRITELN;
END;

{--------------------------- MAIN ---------------------------}

VAR PC : TPC;
    aMemory : TMemory;
    aHardDisk : THardDisk;
    aCPU : TCPU;
    X : LONGINT;
    CPUvar : Processor;
```

Containment 8

```
BEGIN
  ClrScr;
  WRITELN('System configuration:');
  aMemory.SetRam(16000);
  aHardDisk.SetStorage(340);
  aCPU.SetCPU(Intel80486DX);
  PC.SetComponents(@aMemory, @aHardDisk, @aCPU);
  PC.Show;
  WRITELN;
  WRITELN('New system configuration:');
  PC.SetComponents(@aMemory, @aHardDisk, @aCPU);
  { double the memory }
  X := aMemory.GetRam;
  X := 2 * X;
  aMemory.SetRam(X);

  { add 300 MBytes disk storage }
  X := aHardDisk.GetStorage;
  INC(X, 300);
  aHardDisk.SetStorage(X);
  { upgrade to the next CPU }
  CPUvar := Succ(aCPU.GetCPU);
  aCPU.SetCPU(CPUvar);

  { update system configuration }
  PC.SetComponents(@aMemory, @aHardDisk, @aCPU);
  PC.Show;
  WRITELN;
  WRITE('Press any key to end the program...');
  ReadKey;
END.
```

Here's a sample output for the program in Listing 8.4:

```
[BEGIN OUTPUT]
System configuration:
Memory: 16000 Kbytes
Hard disk: 340 Mbytes storage
CPU: 80486DX

New system configuration:
Memory: 32000 Kbytes
Hard disk: 640 Mbytes storage
CPU: 80586SX

Press any key to end the program...
[END OUTPUT]
```

Multiple Inheritance: What If?

There are two general OOP lineage schemes for defining descendant object types: *single inheritance* and *multiple inheritance*. Borland Pascal supports only single inheritance, where each descendant object type has one and only one parent object type. By contrast, multiple inheritance allows a descendant object type to have multiple parent object types. The conceptual links between object types in multiple inheritance use the hasA relationship, just as in containment.

Many OOP programmers have criticized multiple inheritance as the object-oriented design version of Russian Roulette. These programmers much prefer using containment over multiple inheritance. For now, you need not worry about multiple inheritance in Borland Pascal. While it's true that Object Pascal (the inspiration of Borland's OOP extensions to Turbo Pascal and Borland Pascal) doesn't support multiple inheritance, that doesn't mean we might never *see* multiple inheritance in Borland Pascal. In fact, TopSpeed Pascal (a Pascal compiler sold by Clarion) does support multiple inheritance.

When I wrote the CONTAIN2.PAS program shown in Listing 8.2, I couldn't help but ask myself, "What would the program look like if Borland Pascal supported multiple inheritance?" The answer is Listing 8.5. Keep in mind that the program in Listing 8.5 *will not* run.

I wrote the first line in the declaration of object type THybStrArray as follows:

```
THybStrArray = OBJECT(VIRTUAL TStrArray, VIRTUAL TVirtStrArray)
```

Notice two things about the above declaration fragment:

- The OBJECT clause contains a comma-delimited list of two object types. These types are the parents of THybStrArray.

- The keyword VIRTUAL is used in the OBJECT clause. I included the VIRTUAL keyword twice because both parent object types have a common base object type. This declaration, used in C++, tells the (would-be) compiler that the parent object types have a common ancestor object type. Otherwise, the compiler might get confused about redundant base object types!

The declaration of the THybStrArray object type involves two data fields, neither of which is an instance of an object type. Under multiple inheritance, there's no need to declare data fields that are instances of object types TStrArray and TVirtStrArray.

The rest of the code in Listing 8.5 resembles that of Listing 8.2. The main differences are:

- References to the data field MemArr in Listing 8.2 are replaced with the TStrArray object type in Listing 8.5.

- References to the data field VMArr in Listing 8.2 are replaced with the TVirtStrArray object type in Listing 8.5.

By specifying parent object types with the methods, you can invoke particular inherited methods in implementing the descendant's method. This kind of reference is needed when the parent object types are members of the same object-type hierarchy.

The functions, procedures, and main program sections are not affected by the use of multiple inheritance in the THybStrArray. This is because multiple inheritance affects the design of the object type, and not its interface.

Listing 8.5. The uncompilable program CONTAIN5.PAS, which illustrates what program CONTAIN2.PAS would look like if Borland Pascal supported multiple inheritance.

```
Program Contain5;

{
  ***************************************************************
  ************************* WARNING!! ********************
  ***************************************************************

  This program WILL NOT compile. It serves to illustrate
  how program CONTAIN2 would look if Borland Pascal were
  to support multiple inheritance.
}

{$X+}

Uses Crt, PolyMorf;

CONST MAX_IN_RAM = 5;
      MAX_IN_FILE = 5;
      MAX_ELEMS = MAX_IN_RAM + MAX_IN_FILE;
      FILENAME = 'ARR.DAT';
```

continues

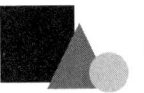

Listing 8.5. continued

```
TYPE
   { declare object type as a descendant of two parents }
   THybStrArray = OBJECT(VIRTUAL TStrArray, VIRTUAL TVirtStrArray)
     CONSTRUCTOR Init(InMemArraySize,             { input }
                     InFileArraySize : WORD;     { input }
                     Filename        : STRING { input });
     DESTRUCTOR Done;
     FUNCTION Store(aStr  : LSTRING; { input  }
                    Index : WORD     { input })
                          : BOOLEAN; VIRTUAL;
     FUNCTION Recall(VAR aStr  : LSTRING; { output }
                         Index : WORD     { input })
                               : BOOLEAN; VIRTUAL;
     FUNCTION GetWorkSize : WORD;
     FUNCTION GetMaxSize : WORD;
   PRIVATE
     MaxRamIndex : WORD;
     MaxIndex : WORD;
   END;

{------------------------------------------- Init -----------}

CONSTRUCTOR THybStrArray.Init(
                   InMemArraySize,             { input }
                   InFileArraySize : WORD;     { input }
                   Filename        : STRING { input });
BEGIN
  TStrArray.Init(InMemArraySize);
  TVirtStrArray.Init(InFileArraySize, Filename);
  MaxRamIndex := TStrArray.GetMaxSize;
  MaxIndex := MaxRamIndex + TVirtStrArray.GetMaxSize;
END;

{------------------------------------------- Done -----------}

DESTRUCTOR THybStrArray.Done;
BEGIN
  TStrArray.Done;
  TVirtStrArray.Done;
END;

{------------------------------------------- Store ----------}

FUNCTION THybStrArray.Store(aStr  : LSTRING; { input }
                            Index : WORD     { input })
                                  : BOOLEAN;
```

Containment 8

```
BEGIN
  IF Index <= MaxIndex THEN BEGIN
    IF Index <= MaxRamIndex THEN
      Store := TStrArray.Store(aStr, Index)
    ELSE
      Store := TVirtStrArray.Store(aStr, Index - MaxRamIndex);
  END
  ELSE
    Store := FALSE;
END;

{-------------------------------------------- Recall -----------}

FUNCTION THybStrArray.Recall(VAR aStr  : LSTRING; { output }
                              Index : WORD    { input })
                                   : BOOLEAN;
BEGIN
  IF Index <= MaxIndex THEN BEGIN
    IF Index <= MaxRamIndex THEN
      Recall := TStrArray.Recall(aStr, Index)
    ELSE
      Recall := TVirtStrArray.Recall(aStr, Index - MaxRamIndex);
  END
  ELSE
    Recall := FALSE;
END;

{-------------------------------------------- GetWorkSize -----------}

FUNCTION THybStrArray.GetWorkSize : WORD;
BEGIN
  GetWorkSize := TStrArray.GetWorkSize + TVirtStrArray.GetWorkSize;
END;

{-------------------------------------------- GetMaxSize -----------}

FUNCTION THybStrArray.GetMaxSize : WORD;
BEGIN
  GetMaxSize := MaxIndex;
END;

{--------------------- miscellaneous procedures ------------------}

PROCEDURE InitArray(VAR anArray : THybStrArray { output });

BEGIN
  anArray.Store('California', 1);
  anArray.Store('Virginia', 2);
```

continues

Listing 8.5. continued

```pascal
  anArray.Store('Michigan', 3);
  anArray.Store('New York', 4);
  anArray.Store('Nevada', 5);
  anArray.Store('Alabama', 6);
  anArray.Store('Alaska', 7);
  anArray.Store('Ohio', 8);
  anArray.Store('Indiana', 9);
  anArray.Store('Colorado', 10);
END;

PROCEDURE DisplayArray(VAR anArray : THybStrArray; { input }
                          Message : STRING      { input });

VAR i : WORD;
    s : LSTRING;

BEGIN
  ClrScr;
  WRITELN(Message);
  WRITELN;
  FOR i := 1 TO anArray.GetWorkSize DO
    IF anArray.Recall(s, i) THEN
      WRITELN(s);
END;

PROCEDURE SortArray(VAR anArray : THybStrArray { in/out });

VAR i, j, offset : WORD;
    inOrder : BOOLEAN;
    sI, sJ : LSTRING;

BEGIN
  offset := anArray.GetWorkSize;
  REPEAT
    offset := offset DIV 2;
    IF offset < 1 THEN offset := 1;
    inOrder := TRUE;
    FOR i := 1 TO anArray.GetWorkSize - offset DO BEGIN
      j := i + offset;
      anArray.Recall(sI, i);
      anArray.Recall(sJ, j);
      IF sI > sJ THEN BEGIN
        inOrder := FALSE;
        anArray.Store(sI, j);
        anArray.Store(sJ, i);
      END;
    END;
  UNTIL (offset = 1) AND inOrder;
END;
```

Containment   8

```
{--------------------------- MAIN --------------------------}
VAR I : WORD;
    Arr : THybStrArray;

BEGIN
  ClrScr;
  Arr.Init(MAX_IN_RAM, MAX_IN_FILE, FILENAME);
  InitArray(Arr);
  DisplayArray(Arr, 'Unordered hybrid array is:');
  GotoXY(1, 24);
  WRITE('Press any key to continue...');
  ReadKey;
  SortArray(Arr);
  DisplayArray(Arr, 'Ordered hybrid array is:');
  GotoXY(1, 24);
  WRITE('Press any key to end the program...');
  ReadKey;
  Arr.Done;
END.
```

Summary

This chapter presented containment, a method for designing object types. You learned about the following topics:

- Containment is a method of modeling real-world objects by defining object types that contain data fields that are themselves instances, or pointers to instances, of other object types. The object types associated with these data fields may be either members of the same object-type hierarchy or members of another hierarchy. Containment builds on the hasA conceptual link between object types.

- Containment enables extendible records to contain other extendible records that are declared in a separate object-type hierarchy.

- Typical containment in an object-type hierarchy uses contained instances in a transparent manner. The program client is unaware of the contained instances.

- Modular objects support data fields that are instances of highly developed object types. One approach to design makes the contained instances transparent to the client of the host object type. Consequently, the host object type must declare all of the methods that manage contained instances. Some of these methods are duplicates of the methods declared in the object types of the contained instances.

- Direct access to components of modular objects is another approach to managing the contained instances of a modular object. Using pointers, host object types eliminate redundant methods and allow client programs to exchange data with the contained instances using separately declared instances of the same object types (that is, each contained instance has an uncontained sister instance).

- Multiple inheritance is a scheme of inheritance that allows you to declare a descendant object type from multiple parent object types. Like containment, multiple inheritance uses the conceptual link hasA in declaring object types.

Chapter 9

Privileged Instances and Pseudo-Private Methods

Borland Pascal supports object types with private and public components. Instances of an object type can access neither private data fields nor private methods; attempting to call private components results in a compile-time error. The same restriction applies to object types declared in another program module. This chapter looks at a way to *pseudo-hide* the methods of an object type. The basic technique revolves around making a method pseudo-private by preventing it from offering a typical response. You'll learn about the following topics:

- Privileged instances of an object type
- Pseudo-private methods using pseudo-hiding techniques

Privileged Instances

Consider the example of employees in one company who use computer terminals to perform various tasks. These employees usually have different access privileges. Some can use only applications, others can invoke programming tools (at various levels), and still others have the privilege of low-level access. Figure 9.1 shows the hierarchy of the company's employees based on their access levels. To model this hierarchy, declare an object-type hierarchy in which each object type supports its own operations.

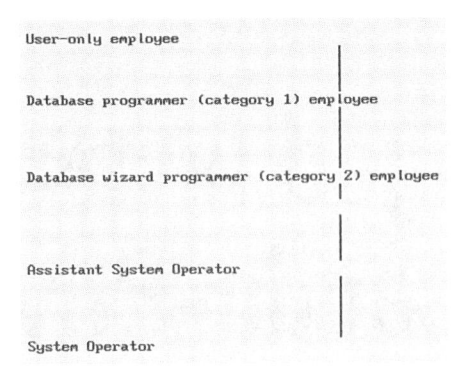

```
User-only employee
         |
Database programmer (category 1) employee
         |
Database wizard programmer (category 2) employee
         |
Assistant System Operator
         |
System Operator
```

Figure 9.1. The hierarchy of employee classes based on access levels and privileges.

Modeling the employees in Figure 9.1 with an object-type hierarchy is suitable because the hierarchy is linear, eliminating potential redundant operations in the hierarchy. Now let's consider another example modeling a more complicated case. Suppose a client asks you to model an object-type hierarchy for dynamic arrays that have the combination of features shown in Table 9.1. The three features are `order`, `expendability`, and `file I/O support`. These three features require eight (that is, 2 to the power of 3, the number of features) object types. Figure 9.2 shows the corresponding object-type hierarchy.

Privileged Instances and Pseudo-Private Methods

Table 9.1. The combination of features for the hierarchy of dynamic-array object types.

Sorted	Expandable	Enable file I/O	Object Type
No	No	No	TUArray
No	No	Yes	TUArray_IO
No	Yes	No	TFlexUArray
No	Yes	Yes	TFlexUArray_IO
Yes	No	No	TOArray
Yes	No	Yes	TOArray_IO
Yes	Yes	No	TFlexOArray
Yes	Yes	Yes	TFlexOArray_IO

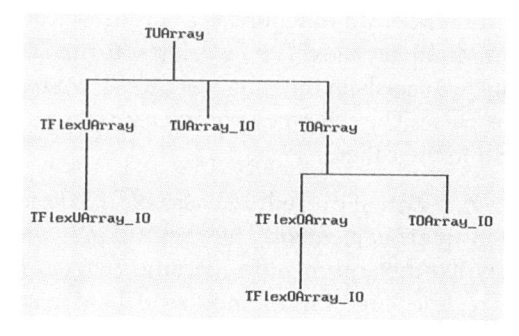

Figure 9.2. The TUArray object-type hierarchy.

Let's look at the implementation of the object-type hierarchy in Figure 9.2. Listing 9.1 shows the source code for the Polymrf2 library unit, which declares and implements the eight object types in Figure 9.2. First, we'll go over the object types in Listing 9.1.

The TUArray Object Type

The TUArray object type models unordered dynamic arrays of strings. The object type declares the following data fields:

- The MaxSize data field specifies the total number of array elements.

217

- The WorkSize data field contains the number of elements that store meaningful data. The constructor assigns 0 to the WorkSize field of a new instance.

- The DataPtr data field is the pointer to the dynamic array.

The constructor Init creates an instance with a number of elements specified by parameter ArraySize. The constructor fills the array elements with empty strings. The destructor Done recuperates the dynamic memory allocated for the array.

The TUArray object type declares the following methods:

- The virtual Boolean function Store writes a string at a specified array index. The function returns True if the argument for parameter Index is in the range of 1 to MaxSize. Otherwise, the function returns False. If the valid argument of Index is greater than the data field WorkSize, the function updates WorkSize with the value of Index.

- The virtual Boolean function Recall retrieves a string from the array element number Index. The function returns True when the argument of parameter Index is in the range of 1 to WorkSize. Otherwise, the function returns False. The reference parameter X passes the accessed array element to the caller.

- The private virtual procedure UnSafeStore performs a quick storage of a string in an array element. This method is a version of function Store that *assumes* that the argument for parameter Index is in the range of 1 to WorkSize. I declared this method as private to speed up the operations of the methods Sort while denying it access to the instances of TUArray.

- The private virtual procedure UnSafeRecall performs a quick retrieval of a string from an array element. This method is a version of function Recall that *assumes* that the argument for parameter Index is in the range of 1 to WorkSize. I declared this method as private to speed up the operations of the methods Sort and Search while denying it access to the instances of TUArray.

- The function GetWorkSize returns the value in the WorkSize data field. This result tells you how many meaningful strings there are in an instance of TUArray.

- The function GetMaxSize returns the value in the MaxSize data field.

- The function LinSearch performs a linear search for a string in the array. The function returns the index of the matching element, or returns the constant NOT_FOUND (which is 0) when no match is found. The Search method uses the UnSafeRecall method to quickly retrieve data from the array elements. Because the method UnSafeRecall is virtual, the descendant object types can inherit the Search method and use it with their own versions of UnSafeRecall. Thus, the Search method supports polymorphic behavior.

The TFlexUArray Object Type

The TFlexUArray object type, a descendant of TUArray, models expandable unordered string arrays. The object type inherits the constructor Init, the destructor Done, the data fields, and the methods from its parent. The TFlexUArray object type only declares the Expand method, which supports expanding the instances at runtime. The parameter NewMaxSize specifies the new expanded size of the array. The function Expand returns True if the array was expanded, or False in the following cases:

- The argument for NewMaxSize is equal to or less than the value in data filed MaxSize
- The dynamic allocation fails

The TUArray_IO Object Type

The TUArray_IO object type, a descendant of TUArray, models unordered string arrays that can read and write strings in text files. The object type inherits the constructor Init, destructor Done, the data fields, and the methods from its parent. The TUArray_IO object type declares the following methods:

- The Boolean function WriteArr writes the first WorkSize strings in an instance to the file specified by the parameter Filename. The function returns True if the Filename is valid. Otherwise, the function performs no file output and returns False.
- The Boolean function ReadArr reads the up to MaxSize strings from the file specified by the parameter Filename. The function returns True if the Filename is valid. Otherwise, the function performs no file input and returns False.

The TFlexUArray_IO Object Type

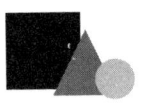

The `TFlexUArray_IO` object type, a descendant of `TFlexUArray`, models expandable unordered string arrays with text file I/O capabilities. The object type inherits the constructor, destructor, data fields, and methods from its parent. The `TFlexUArray_IO` object type declares the `WriteArr` and `ReadArr` methods to support the text file I/O capabilities. These methods are identical to the ones in the `TUArray_IO` object type and are therefore redundant in the object-type hierarchy.

The `TFlexUArray_IO` object type, a descendant of `TFlexUArray`, models expandable unordered string arrays with text file I/O capabilities. The `TFlexUArray_IO` object type inherits its constructor, destructor, data fields, and methods from its parent. The `TFlexUArray_IO` object type declares the `WriteArr` and `ReadArr` methods to support the text file I/O capabilities. These methods are identical to those in the `TUArray_IO` object type and are therefore redundant in the object-type hierarchy.

The TOArray Object Type

The `TOArray` object type, a descendant of `TUArray`, models ordered dynamic arrays of strings. The object type declares the `InOrder` Boolean data field to be a flag that monitors the order of the array.

The constructor `Init` creates an instance with a number of elements specified by parameter `ArraySize`. The statement in the constructor first calls the constructor `TUArray.Init` and sets the `InOrder` data field to False.

The `TOArray` object type declares the following methods:

- The Boolean function `Store` stores a string in array element number `Index`. The function calls the inherited method `Store`. If the inherited method returns True, the function `TOArray.Store` assigns False to the data field `InOrder`, because storing a string in the array most likely will corrupt any existing sort order.

- The procedure `Sort` sorts the first `WorkSize` array elements in ascending order. The procedure uses the Shell-Metzner algorithm and sends `UnSafeRecall` and `UnSafeStore` messages to read and write the array elements. Because the methods `UnSafeStore` and `UnSafeRecall` are virtual, descendant object types can inherit the `Sort` method and use it with their own versions of `UnSafeStore` and `UnSafeRecall`. Thus, the `Sort` method supports polymorphic behavior.

- The function BinSearch performs a binary search for a string in the array. The method sorts the array by sending a Sort message when the InOrder data field is False. The function returns the index of the matching element, or returns the constant NOT_FOUND (which is 0) when no match is found. The BinSearch method uses the UnSafeRecall method to quickly retrieve data from the array elements. Because the method UnSafeRecall is virtual, descendant object types can inherit the BinSearch method and use it with their own versions of UnSafeRecall. Thus, the BinSearch method supports polymorphic behavior.

The TFlexOArray Object Type

The TFlexOArray, a descendant of TOArray, models expandable ordered string arrays. The object type inherits the constructor Init, the destructor Done, the data fields, and the methods from its parent. The TFlexOArray object type declares only the Expand method, which supports expanding the instances at runtime. This method is identical to the method TFlexUArray.Expand and therefore is redundant in the object-type hierarchy.

The TOArray_IO Object Type

The TOArray_IO, a descendant of TOArray, models ordered string arrays that can read and write strings in text files. The object type inherits the constructor Init, the destructor Done, the data fields, and the methods from its parent. The TOArray_IO object type declares the WriteArr and ReadArr methods. These methods perform operations identical to TUArray_IO.WriteArr and TUArray_IO.ReadArr.

The TFlexOArray_IO Object Type

The TFlexOArray_IO object type, a descendant of TFlexOArray, models expandable ordered string arrays with text file I/O capabilities. The TFlexOArray_IO object type inherits its constructor, destructor, data fields, and methods from its parent. The TFlexOArray_IO object type declares the WriteArr and ReadArr methods to support the text file I/O capabilities. These methods are identical to the ones in the TOArray_IO object type.

> This object-type hierarchy contains redundant Expand, WriteArr, and ReadArr methods. The nonlinear branching of object types in the hierarchy dictates these redundant methods. If you look at the implementation section in Listing 9.1, you see that these methods call the local functions ExpandArray, WriteArray, and ReadArray. These local functions are inaccessible outside their method and serve the different versions of Expand, WriteArr, and ReadArr. Using these local functions shortens the code but does not eliminate the redundant methods. If you declare the object-type hierarchy in multiple modules, you must use one of the following design methods:
>
> - Export the functions ExpandArray, WriteArray, and ReadArray. This approach enables other library units to use these functions—at the cost of making them visible to client programs.
>
> - Reimplement the functions ExpandArray, WriteArray, and ReadArray as local to the library unit. This solution is redundant, but succeeds in hiding these functions.

Listing 9.1. The source code for the `Polymrf2` library unit.

```
UNIT Polymrf2;

{ This library implements polymorphic arrays. }

{***************************************************************}
{********************} INTERFACE {********************}
{***************************************************************}

{$X+}

CONST STRING_SIZE = 80;
      NOT_FOUND = 0;

TYPE
  LSTRING = STRING[STRING_SIZE];
  OneString = ARRAY [1..1] OF LSTRING;
  OneStringPtr = ^OneString;

  TUArray = OBJECT
      CONSTRUCTOR Init(ArraySize : WORD { input });
      DESTRUCTOR Done; VIRTUAL;
```

Privileged Instances and Pseudo-Private Methods

```
      FUNCTION Store(aStr  : LSTRING; { input  }
                     Index : WORD     { input  })
                           : BOOLEAN; VIRTUAL;
      FUNCTION Recall(VAR aStr  : LSTRING; { output }
                          Index : WORD     { input  })
                           : BOOLEAN; VIRTUAL;
      FUNCTION GetWorkSize : WORD;
      FUNCTION GetMaxSize : WORD;
      FUNCTION LinSearch(SearchStr : LSTRING { input  }) : WORD;
    PRIVATE
      MaxSize,
      WorkSize { current size } : WORD;
      DataPtr : OneStringPtr;
      PROCEDURE UnSafeStore(aStr  : LSTRING; { input  }
                            Index : WORD     { input  });
                             VIRTUAL;
      PROCEDURE UnSafeRecall(VAR aStr  : LSTRING; { output }
                                 Index : WORD     { input  });
                             VIRTUAL;
END;

TFlexUArray = OBJECT(TUArray)
  FUNCTION Expand(NewMaxSize : WORD { input }) : BOOLEAN;
END;

TUArray_IO = OBJECT(TUArray)
  FUNCTION WriteArr(Filename : LSTRING { input }) : BOOLEAN;
  FUNCTION ReadArr(Filename : LSTRING { input }) : BOOLEAN;
END;

TFlexUArray_IO = OBJECT(TFlexUArray)
  FUNCTION WriteArr(Filename : LSTRING { input }) : BOOLEAN;
  FUNCTION ReadArr(Filename : LSTRING { input }) : BOOLEAN;
END;

TOArray = OBJECT(TUArray)
    CONSTRUCTOR Init(ArraySize : WORD { input  });
    FUNCTION Store(aStr  : LSTRING; { input  }
                   Index : WORD     { input  })
                         : BOOLEAN; VIRTUAL;
    PROCEDURE Sort;
    FUNCTION BinSearch(SearchStr : LSTRING { input  }) : WORD;
  PRIVATE
    InOrder : BOOLEAN;
END;

TFlexOArray = OBJECT(TOArray)
  FUNCTION Expand(NewMaxSize : WORD { input }) : BOOLEAN;
END;
```

continues

Listing 9.1. continued

```
  TOArray_IO = OBJECT(TOArray)
    FUNCTION WriteArr(Filename : LSTRING { input }) : BOOLEAN;
    FUNCTION ReadArr(Filename : LSTRING { input }) : BOOLEAN;
  END;

  TFlexOArray_IO = OBJECT(TFlexOArray)
    FUNCTION WriteArr(Filename : LSTRING { input }) : BOOLEAN;
    FUNCTION ReadArr(Filename : LSTRING { input }) : BOOLEAN;
  END;

{************************************************************}
{*******************} IMPLEMENTATION {*******************}
{************************************************************}

{$R-}

{---------------------------------------- HeapErrorHandler ----------}

FUNCTION HeapErrorHandler(Size : WORD { input }) : INTEGER; FAR;

BEGIN
    HeapErrorHandler := 1
END;

{---------------------------------------- ExpandArray ------------}

FUNCTION ExpandArray(VAR pArr       : OneStringPtr; { in/out }
                    VAR maxElems    : WORD;         { input  }
                        newMaxElems,                { input  }
                        numElems    : WORD          { input  })
                                    : BOOLEAN;

VAR p : OneStringPtr;
    i : WORD;

BEGIN
  IF newMaxElems <= maxElems THEN BEGIN
    ExpandArray := FALSE;
    EXIT
  END;
  { create new array }
  GetMem(p, newMaxElems * STRING_SIZE);
  IF p <> NIL THEN BEGIN
    FOR i := 1 TO numElems DO
      p^[i] := pArr^[i];
    FOR i := numElems + 1 TO newMaxElems DO
      p^[i] := '';
    FreeMem(pArr, maxElems * STRING_SIZE);
    pArr := p;
```

Privileged Instances and Pseudo-Private Methods

```
      maxElems := newMaxElems;
      ExpandArray := TRUE;
    END
    ELSE
      ExpandArray := FALSE;
END;


{---------------------------------------- WriteArray -----------}

FUNCTION WriteArray(pArr     : OneStringPtr; { input }
                    numElems : WORD;         { input }
                    Filename : LSTRING       { input }) : BOOLEAN;

VAR f : TEXT;
    i : WORD;

BEGIN
  {$I-}
  Assign(f, Filename);
  Rewrite(f);
  {$I+}
  IF IOResult = 0 THEN BEGIN
    FOR i := 1 TO numElems DO
      WRITELN(f, pArr^[i]);
    Close(f);
    WriteArray := TRUE;
  END
  ELSE
    WriteArray := FALSE;
END;

{---------------------------------------- ReadArray -----------}

FUNCTION ReadArray(     pArr     : OneStringPtr; { in/out }
                        maxElems : WORD;         { input }
                    VAR numElems : WORD;         { output }
                        Filename : LSTRING       { input }) : BOOLEAN;

VAR f : TEXT;
    i : WORD;

BEGIN
  {$I-}
  Assign(f, Filename);
  Reset(f);
  {$I+}
  IF IOResult = 0 THEN BEGIN
    numElems := 0;
```

continues

Listing 9.1. continued

```
    WHILE (NOT Eof(f)) AND (numElems < maxElems) DO BEGIN
      INC(numElems);
      READLN(f, pArr^[numElems]);
    END;
    Close(f);
    ReadArray := TRUE;
  END
  ELSE
    ReadArray := FALSE;
END;

{------------------------------------------------ Init ------------}

CONSTRUCTOR TUArray.Init(ArraySize : WORD { input  });
{ create instance of TUArray }
BEGIN
  { allocate dynamic memory }
  GetMem(DataPtr, ArraySize * STRING_SIZE);
  IF DataPtr = NIL THEN BEGIN
    Fail;
    EXIT;
  END;
  MaxSize := ArraySize;
  WorkSize := 0;
  { assign null strings to dynamic array }
  WHILE ArraySize > 0 DO BEGIN
      Store('', ArraySize);
      DEC(ArraySize)
  END;
END;

{------------------------------------------------ Done ------------}

DESTRUCTOR TUArray.Done;
{ remove instance of TUArray }
BEGIN
  IF DataPtr <> NIL THEN
    FreeMem(DataPtr, MaxSize * STRING_SIZE);
END;

{------------------------------------------------ Store -----------}

FUNCTION TUArray.Store(aStr  : LSTRING; { input  }
                       Index : WORD     { input  })
                             : BOOLEAN;
{ store string aStr at element number Index }
BEGIN
  IF Index <= MaxSize THEN BEGIN
```

Privileged Instances and Pseudo-Private Methods

```
      IF Index > WorkSize THEN
        WorkSize := Index;
      DataPtr^[Index] := aStr;
      Store := TRUE
    END
    ELSE
      Store := FALSE
END;

{---------------------------------------------- Recall -----------}

FUNCTION TUArray.Recall(VAR aStr  : LSTRING; { output }
                            Index : WORD    { output })
                                  : BOOLEAN;
{ recall string from element number Index }
BEGIN
  IF Index <= WorkSize THEN BEGIN
    aStr := DataPtr^[Index];
    Recall := TRUE
  END
  ELSE
    Recall := FALSE
END;

{---------------------------------------------- LinSearch -----------}

FUNCTION TUArray.LinSearch(SearchStr : LSTRING { input  }) : WORD;
{ perform linear search for SearchStr in array }
VAR i : WORD;
    notFound : BOOLEAN;
    s : LSTRING;

BEGIN
  i := 1;
  notFound := TRUE;
  WHILE (i <= WorkSize) AND notFound DO BEGIN
    UnSafeRecall(s, i);
    If s <> SearchStr THEN
      INC(i)
    ELSE
      notFound := FALSE;
  END;
  { search for data }
  { found a match? }
  IF NotFound THEN
    LinSearch := NOT_FOUND
  ELSE
    LinSearch := i;
END;
```

continues

Listing 9.1. continued

```
{------------------------------------ UnSafeStore -----------}

PROCEDURE TUArray.UnSafeStore(aStr  : LSTRING; { input  }
                              Index : WORD     { input  });
{ store string aStr at element number Index }
BEGIN
  DataPtr^[Index] := aStr;
END;

{------------------------------------ UnSafeRecall -----------}

PROCEDURE TUArray.UnSafeRecall(VAR aStr  : LSTRING; { output }
                                   Index : WORD     { input  });
{ recall string from element number Index }
BEGIN
    aStr := DataPtr^[Index];
END;

{------------------------------------ GetWorkSize -----------}

FUNCTION TUArray.GetWorkSize : WORD;
{ return working size of array }
BEGIN
  GetWorkSize := WorkSize;
END;

{------------------------------------ GetMaxSize -----------}

FUNCTION TUArray.GetMaxSize : WORD;
{ return maximum size of array }
BEGIN
  GetMaxSize := MaxSize;
END;

{-------------------------------------------- Init -----------}

CONSTRUCTOR TOArray.Init(ArraySize : WORD { input  });
{ create instance of TOArray }
BEGIN
  { allocate dynamic memory }
  TUArray.Init(ArraySize);
  InOrder := FALSE;
END;

{-------------------------------------------- Store -----------}

FUNCTION TOArray.Store(aStr  : LSTRING; { input  }
                       Index : WORD     { input  })
                     : BOOLEAN;
```

Privileged Instances and Pseudo-Private Methods

```
    { store string aStr at element number Index }

    VAR ok : BOOLEAN;

    BEGIN
      ok := INHERITED Store(aStr, Index);
      IF ok THEN InOrder := FALSE;
      Store := ok;
    END;


    {------------------------------------------------ Sort -----------}

    PROCEDURE TOArray.Sort;
    { sort array using Shell-Metzner method }
    VAR offset, i, j : WORD;
        strI, strJ : LSTRING;

    BEGIN
      IF WorkSize < 2 THEN EXIT;
      offset := WorkSize;
      WHILE offset > 1 DO BEGIN
        offset := offset div 2;
        REPEAT
          InOrder := TRUE;
          FOR j := 1 TO WorkSize - offset DO BEGIN
            i := j + offset;
            UnSafeRecall(strJ, j);
            UnSafeRecall(strI, i);
            IF strI < strJ THEN BEGIN
              UnSafeStore(strI, j);
              UnSafeStore(strJ, i);
              InOrder := FALSE
            END; { IF }
          END; { FOR }
        UNTIL InOrder;
      END; { WHILE }
    END;


    {------------------------------------------------ BinSearch -----------}

    FUNCTION TOArray.BinSearch(SearchStr : LSTRING { input  }) : WORD;
    { perform binary search for SearchStr in array }
    VAR low, high, median : WORD;
        strMedian : LSTRING;

    BEGIN
      { array needs to be sorted? }
      IF NOT InOrder THEN
        Sort;
```

continues

Listing 9.1. continued

```pascal
  { set initial search limits }
  low := 1;
  high := WorkSize;
  { search for data }
  REPEAT
    median := (low + high) div 2;
    UnSafeRecall(strMedian, median);
    IF SearchStr < strMedian THEN
      high := median - 1
    ELSE
      low := median + 1;
  UNTIL (SearchStr = strMedian) OR (low > high);
  { found a match? }
  IF SearchStr = strMedian THEN
    BinSearch := median
  ELSE
    BinSearch := NOT_FOUND;
END;

{---------------------------------------- Expand -----------}

FUNCTION TFlexUArray.Expand(NewMaxSize : WORD { input }) : BOOLEAN;
{ expand unordered array }
BEGIN
  Expand := ExpandArray(DataPtr, MaxSize, NewMaxSize, WorkSize);
END;

{---------------------------------------- WriteArr -----------}

FUNCTION TUArray_IO.WriteArr(Filename : LSTRING { input }) : BOOLEAN;
{ write unordered array }
BEGIN
  WriteArr := WriteArray(DataPtr, WorkSize, Filename);
END;

{---------------------------------------- ReadArr -----------}

FUNCTION TUArray_IO.ReadArr(Filename : LSTRING { input }) : BOOLEAN;
{ read unordered array }
BEGIN
  ReadArr := ReadArray(DataPtr, MaxSize, WorkSize, Filename);
END;

{---------------------------------------- WriteArr -----------}

FUNCTION TFlexUArray_IO.WriteArr(Filename : LSTRING { input })
                                          : BOOLEAN;
{ write expandable unordered array }
BEGIN
```

```
    WriteArr := WriteArray(DataPtr, WorkSize, Filename);
END;

{---------------------------------------------- ReadArr -----------}

FUNCTION TFlexUArray_IO.ReadArr(Filename : LSTRING { input })
                                         : BOOLEAN;
{ read expandable unordered array }
BEGIN
  ReadArr := ReadArray(DataPtr, MaxSize, WorkSize, Filename);
END;

{---------------------------------------------- Expand ------------}

FUNCTION TFlexOArray.Expand(NewMaxSize : WORD { input }) : BOOLEAN;
{ expand ordered array }
BEGIN
  Expand := ExpandArray(DataPtr, MaxSize, NewMaxSize, WorkSize);
END;

{---------------------------------------------- WriteArr ----------}

FUNCTION TOArray_IO.WriteArr(Filename : LSTRING { input }) : BOOLEAN;
{ write ordered array }
BEGIN
  WriteArr := WriteArray(DataPtr, WorkSize, Filename);
END;

{---------------------------------------------- ReadArr -----------}

FUNCTION TOArray_IO.ReadArr(Filename : LSTRING { input }) : BOOLEAN;
{ read ordered array }
BEGIN
  ReadArr := ReadArray(DataPtr, MaxSize, WorkSize, Filename);
END;

{---------------------------------------------- WriteArr ----------}

FUNCTION TFlexOArray_IO.WriteArr(Filename : LSTRING { input })
                                          : BOOLEAN;
{ write expandable ordered array }
BEGIN
  WriteArr := WriteArray(DataPtr, WorkSize, Filename);
END;

{---------------------------------------------- ReadArr -----------}

FUNCTION TFlexOArray_IO.ReadArr(Filename : LSTRING { input })
                                         : BOOLEAN;
```

continues

Listing 9.1. continued

```
{ read expandable ordered array }
BEGIN
  ReadArr := ReadArray(DataPtr, MaxSize, WorkSize, Filename);
END;

BEGIN
  HeapError := @HeapErrorHandler;
END.
```

Testing Privileged Instances

Let's look at a sample program that tests the various object types declared in the Polymrf2 library unit. Listing 9.2 shows the test program ARRAY7.PAS. This program declares instances for the eight object types in unit Polymrf2 and tests these instances. The ARRAY7.PAS program allows you to proceed through the different test phases either by using a timed pause or by pressing keys.

The ARRAY7.PAS program tests the instances of TOArray, TOArray_IO, TFlexOArray, and TFlexOArray_IO in much the same way it tests the corresponding object types that model unordered arrays. The difference in this part of the program is that the program systematically sends a Sort message, after assigning strings to the array elements, to sort these elements. The remaining tasks are the same as those in the group of unordered-array object types.

Testing Object Type TUArray

The ARRAY7.PAS program performs the following tasks to test UArray, the instance of TUArray:

1. Instantiates the instance UArray to have 10 elements.

2. Uses a FOR loop to store the elements of the typed constant dB1 in the instance UArray. The loop statement sends the message Store to the instance UArray to perform this task.

3. Displays the elements in instance UArray by calling the procedure ShowArray.

4. Removes the instance UArray by using the destructor Done.

Privileged Instances and Pseudo-Private Methods

Testing Object Type TUArray_IO

The ARRAY7.PAS program performs the following tasks to test UArray_IO, the instance of TUArray_IO:

1. Instantiates the instance UArray_IO to have 10 elements.

2. Uses a FOR loop to store the elements of the typed constant dB1 in the instance UArray_IO. The loop statement sends the message Store to the instance UArray_IO to perform this task.

3. Displays the elements in instance UArray_IO by calling the procedure ShowArray.

4. Writes the elements in instance UArray_IO to the text file ARR.DAT. The program performs this task by sending the message WriteArr to the instance UArray_IO.

5. Uses a FOR loop to write empty strings to the instance UArray_IO.

6. Displays the current contents of instance UArray_IO by calling the procedure ShowArray.

7. Reads the strings from the text file ARR.DAT by sending the ReadArr message to the instance UArray_IO.

8. Displays the new contents of instance UArray_IO by calling the procedure ShowArray.

9. Removes the instance UArray_IO by using the destructor Done.

Testing Object Type TFlexUArray

The ARRAY7.PAS program performs the following tasks to test FlexUArray, the instance of TFlexUArray:

1. Instantiates the instance FlexUArray to have 10 elements.

2. Uses a FOR loop to store the elements of the typed constant dB1 in the instance FlexUArray. The loop statement sends the message Store to the instance FlexUArray to perform this task.

3. Displays the elements in instance FlexUArray by calling the procedure ShowArray.

4. Doubles the size of the instance FlexUArray by sending it the message Expand. If the Expand message returns True, the program executes steps 5 and 6. Otherwise, the program displays an error message and resumes at step 7.

5. Uses a FOR loop to store the elements of the typed constant dB2 in the added elements of instance FlexUArray. The loop statement sends the message Store to the instance FlexUArray to perform this task.

6. Displays the elements in the expanded instance FlexUArray by calling the procedure ShowArray.

7. Removes the instance FlexUArray by using the destructor Done.

Testing Object Type TFlexUArray_IO

The ARRAY7.PAS program performs the following tasks to test FlexUArray_IO, the instance of TFlexUArray_IO:

1. Instantiates the instance FlexUArray_IO to have 10 elements.

2. Uses a FOR loop to store the elements of the typed constant dB1 in the instance FlexUArray_IO. The loop statement sends the message Store to the instance FlexUArray_IO to perform this task.

3. Displays the elements in instance FlexUArray_IO by calling the procedure ShowArray.

4. Doubles the size of the instance FlexUArray_IO by sending it the message Expand. If the Expand message returns True, the program executes steps 5 and 6. Otherwise, the program displays an error message and resumes at step 7.

5. Uses a FOR loop to store the elements of the typed constant dB2 in the added elements of instance FlexUArray_IO. The loop statement sends the message Store to the instance FlexUArray_IO to perform this task.

6. Displays the elements in the expanded instance FlexUArray_IO by calling the procedure ShowArray.

7. Writes the elements in instance FlexUArray_IO to the text file ARR.DAT. The program performs this task by sending the message WriteArr to the instance FlexUArray_IO.

8. Uses a FOR loop to write empty strings to the instance FlexUArray_IO.

9. Displays the current contents of instance FlexUArray_IO by calling the procedure ShowArray.

10. Reads the strings from the text file ARR.DAT by sending the ReadArr message to the instance FlexUArray_IO.

11. Displays the new contents of instance FlexUArray_IO by calling the procedure ShowArray.

12. Removes the instance FlexUArray_IO by using the destructor Done.

Listing 9.2. The program ARRAY7.PAS, which tests the object types declared in the Polymrf2 library unit.

```
Program Array7;

{
  This program tests various arrays in library Polymrf2.
}

{$X+,R-}
{$M 8192, 0, 655350}

Uses Crt, Polymrf2;

CONST MAX_STRINGS = 10;
      FILENAME = 'ARR.DAT';
      dB1 : ARRAY[1..MAX_STRINGS] OF LSTRING =
                ('Michigan', 'California', 'Montana', 'Nevada',
                 'New Mexico', 'New York', 'West Virginia', 'Maine',
                 'Virginia', 'Florida');
      dB2 : ARRAY[1..MAX_STRINGS] OF LSTRING =
                ('Illinois', 'Texas', 'Alabama', 'Alaska',
                 'Louisiana', 'Georgia', 'Maryland', 'Vermont',
                 'North Carolina', 'South Carolina');

VAR UArray : TUArray;
    UArray_IO : TUArray_IO;
    FlexUArray : TFlexUArray;
    FlexUArray_IO : TFlexUArray_IO;
    OArray : TOArray;
    OArray_IO : TOArray_IO;
    FlexOArray : TFlexOArray;
    FlexOArray_IO : TFlexOArray_IO;
    I : WORD;
    Pause : BOOLEAN;
    Wait : WORD;
    C : CHAR;
```

continues

Listing 9.2. continued

```pascal
PROCEDURE ShowArray(    Msg     : STRING;    { input }
                    VAR A       : TUArray   { input });

VAR i : WORD;
    s : LSTRING;

BEGIN
  ClrScr;
  WRITELN(Msg); WRITELN;
  FOR i := 1 TO A.GetWorkSize DO
    IF A.Recall(s, i) THEN
      WRITELN(s)
    ELSE
      WRITELN('Index ', i, ' is out of range');
END;

PROCEDURE PressKey;
BEGIN
   IF Pause THEN
     Delay(Wait)
   ELSE BEGIN
     WRITELN;
     WRITE('Press any key...');
     ReadKey;
   END;
END;

BEGIN
   REPEAT
     ClrScr;
     WRITE('Want to use pause feature? (Y/N) ');
     C := UpCase(ReadKey);
     WRITELN(C);
     WRITELN;
   UNTIL C IN ['Y', 'N'];
   Pause := C = 'Y';
   IF Pause THEN BEGIN
     WRITE('Enter the delay (milliseconds) : ');
     READLN(Wait);
     IF Wait = 0 THEN Wait := 1000;
   END;
   { test instance UArray }
   UArray.Init(10);
   FOR I := 1 TO MAX_STRINGS DO
     UArray.Store(dB1[I], i);
   ShowArray('Array UArray contains the following data:',
             UArray);
   PressKey;
   UArray.Done;
```

Privileged Instances and Pseudo-Private Methods

```
{ test instance UArray_IO }
UArray_IO.Init(10);
FOR I := 1 TO MAX_STRINGS DO
  UArray_IO.Store(dB1[I], i);
ShowArray('Array UArray_IO contains the following data:',
          UArray_IO);
PressKey;
UArray_IO.WriteArr(FILENAME);
FOR I := 1 TO UArray_IO.GetWorkSize DO
  UArray_IO.Store('', i);
ShowArray('After clearing array UArray_IO ' +
                    'it contains the following data:',
          UArray_IO);
PressKey;
UArray_IO.ReadArr(FILENAME);
ShowArray('After reading array UArray_IO from file ' +
                    FILENAME +
                    ', it contains:',
          UArray_IO);
UArray_IO.Done;
PressKey;

{ test instance FlexUArray }
FlexUArray.Init(10);
FOR I := 1 TO MAX_STRINGS DO
  FlexUArray.Store(dB1[I], i);
ShowArray('Array FlexUArray contains the following data:',
          FlexUArray);
PressKey;
IF FlexUArray.Expand(2 * MAX_STRINGS) THEN BEGIN
  FOR I := 1 TO MAX_STRINGS DO
    FlexUArray.Store(dB2[I], MAX_STRINGS + i);
  ShowArray('The expanded array FlexUArray ' +
                      'contains the following data:',
            FlexUArray);
  PressKey;
END
ELSE BEGIN
  WRITELN('Failed to expand array FlexUArray');
  PressKey;
END;
FlexUArray.Done;

{ test instance FlexUArray_IO }
FlexUArray_IO.Init(10);
FOR I := 1 TO MAX_STRINGS DO
  FlexUArray_IO.Store(dB1[I], i);
ShowArray('Array FlexUArray_IO contains the following data:',
          FlexUArray_IO);
PressKey;
```

continues

Listing 9.2. continued

```
IF FlexUArray_IO.Expand(2 * MAX_STRINGS) THEN BEGIN
  FOR I := 1 TO MAX_STRINGS DO
    FlexUArray_IO.Store(dB2[I], MAX_STRINGS + i);
  ShowArray('The expanded array FlexUArray_IO ' +
                  'contains the following data:',
         FlexUArray_IO);
  PressKey;
END
ELSE BEGIN
  WRITELN('Failed to expand array FlexUArray_IO');
  PressKey;
END;
FlexUArray_IO.WriteArr(FILENAME);
FOR I := 1 TO FlexUArray_IO.GetWorkSize DO
  FlexUArray_IO.Store('', i);
ShowArray('After clearing array FlexUArray_IO ' +
                 'it contains the following data:',
         FlexUArray_IO);
PressKey;
FlexUArray_IO.ReadArr(FILENAME);
ShowArray('After reading array FlexUArray_IO from file ' +
                FILENAME +
                ', it contains:',
         FlexUArray_IO);
PressKey;
FlexUArray_IO.Done;

{ test instance OArray }
OArray.Init(10);
FOR I := 1 TO MAX_STRINGS DO
  OArray.Store(dB1[I], i);
ShowArray('Array OArray contains the following data:',
        OArray);
PressKey;
OArray.Sort;
ShowArray('Sorted array OArray contains ' +
                'the following data:',
        OArray);
PressKey;
OArray.Done;

{ test instance OArray_IO }
OArray_IO.Init(10);
FOR I := 1 TO MAX_STRINGS DO
  OArray_IO.Store(dB1[I], i);
OArray_IO.Sort;
ShowArray('Array OArray_IO contains the following data:',
        OArray_IO);
```

Privileged Instances and Pseudo-Private Methods

```
    PressKey;
    OArray_IO.WriteArr(FILENAME);
    FOR I := 1 TO OArray_IO.GetWorkSize DO
      OArray_IO.Store('', i);
    ShowArray('After clearing array OArray_IO ' +
                'it contains the following data:',
            OArray_IO);
    PressKey;
    OArray_IO.ReadArr(FILENAME);
    ShowArray('After reading array OArray_IO from file ' +
                FILENAME +
                ', it contains:',
            OArray_IO);
    OArray_IO.Done;
    PressKey;

    { test instance FlexOArray }
    FlexOArray.Init(10);
    FOR I := 1 TO MAX_STRINGS DO
      FlexOArray.Store(dB1[I], i);
    FlexOArray.Sort;
    ShowArray('Array FlexOArray contains the following data:',
            FlexOArray);
    PressKey;
    IF FlexOArray.Expand(2 * MAX_STRINGS) THEN BEGIN
      FOR I := 1 TO MAX_STRINGS DO
        FlexOArray.Store(dB2[I], MAX_STRINGS + i);
      FlexOArray.Sort;
      ShowArray('The expanded array FlexOArray ' +
                  'contains the following data:',
            FlexOArray);
      PressKey;
    END
    ELSE BEGIN
      WRITELN('Failed to expand array FlexOArray');
      PressKey;
    END;
    FlexOArray.Done;

    { test instance FlexOArray_IO }
    FlexOArray_IO.Init(10);
    FOR I := 1 TO MAX_STRINGS DO
      FlexOArray_IO.Store(dB1[I], i);
    FlexOArray_IO.Sort;
    ShowArray('Array FlexOArray_IO contains the following data:',
            FlexOArray_IO);
    PressKey;
    IF FlexOArray_IO.Expand(2 * MAX_STRINGS) THEN BEGIN
      FOR I := 1 TO MAX_STRINGS DO
```

continues

Listing 9.2. continued

```
      FlexOArray_IO.Store(dB2[I], MAX_STRINGS + i);
    FlexOArray_IO.Sort;
    ShowArray('The expanded array FlexOArray_IO ' +
                  'contains the following data:',
           FlexOArray_IO);
    PressKey;
  END
  ELSE BEGIN
    WRITELN('Failed to expand array FlexOArray_IO');
    PressKey;
  END;
  FlexOArray_IO.WriteArr(FILENAME);
  FOR I := 1 TO FlexOArray_IO.GetWorkSize DO
    FlexOArray_IO.Store('', i);
  ShowArray('After clearing array FlexOArray_IO ' +
                 'it contains the following data:',
           FlexOArray_IO);
  PressKey;
  FlexOArray_IO.ReadArr(FILENAME);
  ShowArray('After reading array FlexOArray_IO from file ' +
                 FILENAME +
                 ', it contains:',
           FlexOArray_IO);
  PressKey;
  FlexOArray_IO.Done;

END.
```

Here's a sample output for the program in Listing 9.2, showing the elements of instance UArray:

```
[BEGIN OUTPUT]
Array UArray contains the following data:

Michigan
California
Montana
Nevada
New Mexico
New York
West Virginia
Maine
Virginia
Florida

Press any key...
[END OUTPUT]
```

Privileged Instances and Pseudo-Private Methods

Here's another sample output for the program in Listing 9.2, this time showing the elements of instance `FlexOArray`:

```
[BEGIN OUTPUT]
The expanded array FlexOArray contains the following data:

Alabama
Alaska
California
Florida
Georgia
Illinois
Louisiana
Maine
Maryland
Michigan
Montana
Nevada
New Mexico
New York
North Carolina
South Carolina
Texas
Vermont
Virginia
West Virginia

Press any key...
[END OUTPUT]
```

Using Privileged Instances

We can replace the set of eight object types exported by the `Polymrf3` unit by a single object type. The design of the new object type follows these guidelines:

- The object type has all of the possible operations.
- Instances of the object type have access to all of the methods.
- The methods may not respond properly to all these instances, depending on the access levels (or privileges, if you prefer) of the instances.

Does the preceding approach violate OOP principles? The zealous OOP purist certainly will consider this approach to be heresy (and probably recommend that I be replaced with another, more professional programmer!). More reasonable practicing OOP programmers will consider the following factors:

- The need to reduce complexity. This certainly is the main reason for using such an approach. This reduction not only benefits the consolidated object types but also simplifies the process of adding descendant object types.

- Whether or not the original object-type hierarchy is based on a subjective analysis of operations. One could argue that the creation of the object-type hierarchy in unit `Polymrf2` is based on arbitrary choices.

Listing 9.3 shows the source code for the `Polymrf3` library unit, which declares the single object type `TArray`. This object type replaces the eight object types in unit `Polymrf2`. Notice the following aspects in the interface part of the `Polymrf3` library unit:

- The declaration of the enumerated data type `ArrayModeEnum`. This data type lists the eight possible modes of operating the instances of object type `TArray`.

- The declaration of object type `TArray` contains all of the operations found in the object types of unit `Polymrf2`.

- The `TArray` object type has an additional data field, namely, `ArrayMode`. This data field saves the `ArrayModeEnum` enumerated value for the instances of `TArray`.

- The constructor `Init` has a second parameter of type `ArrayModeEnum`. The arguments for this parameter specify the access privilege of an instance.

The methods `Sort`, `BinSearch`, `Expand`, `WriteArr`, and `ReadArr` do not perform their normal tasks unless the enumerated value in data field `ArrayMode` is appropriate. For example, if you create an instance of `TArray` with the `UArray` access mode and send the `Sort` message, the `Sort` method will exit without actually sorting the element of the targeted instance. Thus, while you technically still have access to the method, you cannot use it to perform its duties.

Listing 9.3. The source code for the `Polymrf3` library unit.

```
UNIT Polymrf3;

{ This library implements polymorphic arrays. }

{***************************************************************}
{*********************} INTERFACE {*********************}
{***************************************************************}

{$X+}
```

Privileged Instances and Pseudo-Private Methods

```
CONST STRING_SIZE = 80;
      NOT_FOUND = 0;

TYPE
  LSTRING = STRING[STRING_SIZE];
  OneString = ARRAY [1..1] OF LSTRING;
  OneStringPtr = ^OneString;
  ArrayModeEnum = (UArray, UArray_IO, FlexUArray, FlexUArray_IO,
                   OArray, OArray_IO, FlexOArray, FlexOArray_IO);

  TArray = OBJECT
      CONSTRUCTOR Init(ArraySize    : WORD;            { input }
                       theArrayMode : ArrayModeEnum { input });
      DESTRUCTOR Done; VIRTUAL;
      FUNCTION Store(aStr  : LSTRING; { input }
                     Index : WORD    { input })
                           : BOOLEAN; VIRTUAL;
      FUNCTION Recall(VAR aStr : LSTRING; { output }
                          Index : WORD    { input })
                           : BOOLEAN; VIRTUAL;
      FUNCTION GetWorkSize : WORD;
      FUNCTION GetMaxSize : WORD;
      FUNCTION LinSearch(SearchStr : LSTRING { input }) : WORD;
      PROCEDURE Sort;
      FUNCTION BinSearch(SearchStr : LSTRING { input }) : WORD;
      FUNCTION Expand(NewMaxSize : WORD { input }) : BOOLEAN;
      FUNCTION WriteArr(Filename : LSTRING { input }) : BOOLEAN;
      FUNCTION ReadArr(Filename : LSTRING { input }) : BOOLEAN;
    PRIVATE
      MaxSize,
      WorkSize { current size } : WORD;
      DataPtr : OneStringPtr;
      InOrder : BOOLEAN;
      ArrayMode : ArrayModeEnum;
      PROCEDURE UnSafeStore(aStr  : LSTRING; { input }
                            Index : WORD    { input });
                            VIRTUAL;
      PROCEDURE UnSafeRecall(VAR aStr  : LSTRING; { output }
                                 Index : WORD    { input });
                                 VIRTUAL;
  END;

{************************************************************}
{******************} IMPLEMENTATION {******************}
{************************************************************}

{$R-}

{---------------------------------------- HeapErrorHandler ----------}
```

continues

Listing 9.3. continued

```
FUNCTION HeapErrorHandler(Size : WORD { input  }) : INTEGER; FAR;

BEGIN
    HeapErrorHandler := 1
END;

{----------------------------------------- ExpandArray ------------}

FUNCTION ExpandArray(VAR pArr        : OneStringPtr; { in/out }
                    VAR maxElems     : WORD;         { input   }
                        newMaxElems,                 { input   }
                        numElems     : WORD          { input   })
                                     : BOOLEAN;

VAR p : OneStringPtr;
    i : WORD;

BEGIN
  IF newMaxElems <= maxElems THEN BEGIN
    ExpandArray := FALSE;
    EXIT
  END;
  { create new array }
  GetMem(p, newMaxElems * STRING_SIZE);
  IF p <> NIL THEN BEGIN
    FOR i := 1 TO numElems DO
      p^[i] := pArr^[i];
    FOR i := numElems + 1 TO newMaxElems DO
      p^[i] := '';
    FreeMem(pArr, maxElems * STRING_SIZE);
    pArr := p;
    maxElems := newMaxElems;
    ExpandArray := TRUE;
  END
  ELSE
    ExpandArray := FALSE;
END;

{----------------------------------------- WriteArray ------------}

FUNCTION WriteArray(pArr     : OneStringPtr; { input }
                    numElems : WORD;         { input }
                    Filename : LSTRING       { input }) : BOOLEAN;

VAR f : TEXT;
    i : WORD;

BEGIN
  {$I-}
```

Privileged Instances and Pseudo-Private Methods

```
    Assign(f, Filename);
    Rewrite(f);
    {$I+}
    IF IOResult = 0 THEN BEGIN
      FOR i := 1 TO numElems DO
        WRITELN(f, pArr^[i]);
      Close(f);
      WriteArray := TRUE;
    END
    ELSE
      WriteArray := FALSE;
END;

{------------------------------------------- ReadArray ------------}

FUNCTION ReadArray(     pArr      : OneStringPtr; { in/out }
                        maxElems  : WORD;         { input  }
                    VAR numElems  : WORD;         { output }
                        Filename  : LSTRING       { input  }) : BOOLEAN;

VAR f : TEXT;
    i : WORD;

BEGIN
  {$I-}
  Assign(f, Filename);
  Reset(f);
  {$I+}
  IF IOResult = 0 THEN BEGIN
    numElems := 0;
    WHILE (NOT Eof(f)) AND (numElems < maxElems) DO BEGIN
      INC(numElems);
      READLN(f, pArr^[numElems]);
    END;
    Close(f);
    ReadArray := TRUE;
  END
  ELSE
    ReadArray := FALSE;
END;

{---------------------------------------------- Init ------------}

CONSTRUCTOR TArray.Init(ArraySize    : WORD;            { input }
                        theArrayMode : ArrayModeEnum    { input });
{ create instance of TArray }
BEGIN
  { allocate dynamic memory }
  GetMem(DataPtr, ArraySize * STRING_SIZE);
```

continues

Listing 9.3. continued

```
  IF DataPtr = NIL THEN BEGIN
    Fail;
    EXIT;
  END;
  MaxSize := ArraySize;
  WorkSize := 0;
  InOrder := FALSE;
  ArrayMode := theArrayMode;
  { assign null strings to dynamic array }
  WHILE ArraySize > 0 DO BEGIN
      Store('', ArraySize);
      DEC(ArraySize)
  END;
END;

{---------------------------------------------- Done -----------}

DESTRUCTOR TArray.Done;
{ remove instance of TArray }
BEGIN
  IF DataPtr <> NIL THEN
    FreeMem(DataPtr, MaxSize * STRING_SIZE);
END;

{---------------------------------------------- Store ----------}

FUNCTION TArray.Store(aStr  : LSTRING; { input }
                     Index : WORD    { input })
                           : BOOLEAN;
{ store string aStr at element number Index }
BEGIN
  IF Index <= MaxSize THEN BEGIN
    IF Index > WorkSize THEN
      WorkSize := Index;
    DataPtr^[Index] := aStr;
    InOrder := FALSE;
    Store := TRUE
  END
  ELSE
    Store := FALSE
END;

{---------------------------------------------- Recall ---------}

FUNCTION TArray.Recall(VAR aStr  : LSTRING; { output }
                           Index : WORD    { output })
                                 : BOOLEAN;
{ recall string from element number Index }
BEGIN
```

Privileged Instances and Pseudo-Private Methods

```
    IF Index <= WorkSize THEN BEGIN
      aStr := DataPtr^[Index];
      Recall := TRUE
    END
    ELSE
      Recall := FALSE
END;

{--------------------------------------------- LinSearch -----------}

FUNCTION TArray.LinSearch(SearchStr : LSTRING { input  }) : WORD;
{ perform linear search for SearchStr in array }
VAR i : WORD;
    notFound : BOOLEAN;
    s : LSTRING;

BEGIN
  i := 1;
  notFound := TRUE;
  WHILE (i <= WorkSize) AND notFound DO BEGIN
    UnSafeRecall(s, i);
    If s <> SearchStr THEN
      INC(i)
    ELSE
      notFound := FALSE;
  END;
  { search for data }
  { found a match? }
  IF NotFound THEN
    LinSearch := NOT_FOUND
  ELSE
    LinSearch := i;
END;

{--------------------------------------------- UnSafeStore -----------}

PROCEDURE TArray.UnSafeStore(aStr  : LSTRING; { input  }
                             Index : WORD     { input  });
{ store string aStr at element number Index }
BEGIN
  DataPtr^[Index] := aStr;
END;

{--------------------------------------------- UnSafeRecall -----------}

PROCEDURE TArray.UnSafeRecall(VAR aStr  : LSTRING; { output }
                                  Index : WORD     { input  });
{ recall string from element number Index }
BEGIN
    aStr := DataPtr^[Index];
END;
```

continues

Listing 9.3. continued

```pascal
{----------------------------------------- GetWorkSize ------------}

FUNCTION TArray.GetWorkSize : WORD;
{ return working size of array }
BEGIN
  GetWorkSize := WorkSize;
END;

{----------------------------------------- GetMaxSize ------------}

FUNCTION TArray.GetMaxSize : WORD;
{ return maximum size of array }
BEGIN
  GetMaxSize := MaxSize;
END;

{----------------------------------------- Sort ------------}

PROCEDURE TArray.Sort;
{ sort array using Shell-Metzner method }
VAR offset, i, j : WORD;
    strI, strJ : LSTRING;

BEGIN
  { incorrect array mode? }
  IF (ArrayMode <> OArray)      AND
     (ArrayMode <> OArray_IO)   AND
     (ArrayMode <> FlexOArray)  AND
     (ArrayMode <> FlexOArray_IO) THEN
     EXIT;
  IF WorkSize < 2 THEN EXIT;
  offset := WorkSize;
  WHILE offset > 1 DO BEGIN
    offset := offset div 2;
    REPEAT
      InOrder := TRUE;
      FOR j := 1 TO WorkSize - offset DO BEGIN
        i := j + offset;
        UnSafeRecall(strJ, j);
        UnSafeRecall(strI, i);
        IF strI < strJ THEN BEGIN
          UnSafeStore(strI, j);
          UnSafeStore(strJ, i);
          InOrder := FALSE
        END; { IF }
      END; { FOR }
    UNTIL InOrder;
  END; { WHILE }
END;
```

Privileged Instances and Pseudo-Private Methods

```
{------------------------------------------------- BinSearch -----------}

FUNCTION TArray.BinSearch(SearchStr : LSTRING { input  }) : WORD;
{ perform binary search for SearchStr in array }
VAR low, high, median : WORD;
    strMedian : LSTRING;

BEGIN
  { incorrect array mode? }
  IF (ArrayMode <> OArray)        AND
     (ArrayMode <> OArray_IO)     AND
     (ArrayMode <> FlexOArray)    AND
     (ArrayMode <> FlexOArray_IO) THEN BEGIN
    BinSearch := NOT_FOUND;
    EXIT;
  END;
  { array needs to be sorted? }
  IF NOT InOrder THEN
    Sort;
  { set initial search limits }
  low := 1;
  high := WorkSize;
  { search for data }
  REPEAT
    median := (low + high) div 2;
    UnSafeRecall(strMedian, median);
    IF SearchStr < strMedian THEN
      high := median - 1
    ELSE
      low := median + 1;
  UNTIL (SearchStr = strMedian) OR (low > high);
  { found a match? }
  IF SearchStr = strMedian THEN
    BinSearch := median
  ELSE
    BinSearch := NOT_FOUND;
END;

{------------------------------------------------- Expand -----------}

FUNCTION TArray.Expand(NewMaxSize : WORD { input }) : BOOLEAN;
{ expand unordered array }
BEGIN
  { incorrect array mode? }
  IF (ArrayMode = FlexUArray)     OR
     (ArrayMode = FlexUArray_IO)  OR
     (ArrayMode = FlexOArray)     OR
     (ArrayMode = FlexOArray_IO)  THEN
    Expand := ExpandArray(DataPtr, MaxSize, NewMaxSize, WorkSize)
  ELSE
```

continues

Listing 9.3. continued

```pascal
    Expand := FALSE;
END;

{--------------------------------------------- WriteArr -----------}

FUNCTION TArray.WriteArr(Filename : LSTRING { input }) : BOOLEAN;
{ write unordered array }
BEGIN
  { incorrect array mode? }
  IF (ArrayMode = UArray_IO)       OR
     (ArrayMode = FlexUArray_IO) OR
     (ArrayMode = OArray_IO)       OR
     (ArrayMode = FlexOArray_IO) THEN
    WriteArr := WriteArray(DataPtr, WorkSize, Filename)
  ELSE
    WriteArr := FALSE;
END;

{--------------------------------------------- ReadArr -----------}

FUNCTION TArray.ReadArr(Filename : LSTRING { input }) : BOOLEAN;
{ read unordered array }
BEGIN
  { incorrect array mode? }
  IF (ArrayMode = UArray_IO)       OR
     (ArrayMode = FlexUArray_IO) OR
     (ArrayMode = OArray_IO)       OR
     (ArrayMode = FlexOArray_IO) THEN
    ReadArr := ReadArray(DataPtr, MaxSize, WorkSize, Filename)
  ELSE
    ReadArr := FALSE;
END;

BEGIN
  HeapError := @HeapErrorHandler;
END.
```

Listing 9.4 shows the program ARRAY8.PAS, which tests the TArray object type exported by the Polymrf3 library unit. I created this test program by editing the one in Listing 9.2. Notice the following differences:

- Program ARRAY8.PAS declares only one instance of object type TArray.

- The program instantiates the instance anArray with different access mode values. Once the program ends the testing for that access mode, it uses the destructor Done to remove the instance.

Listing 9.4. The program ARRAY8.PAS, which tests the `TArray` object type exported by the `Polymrf3` library unit.

```pascal
Program Array8;

{
  This program tests various arrays in library Polymrf3.
}

{$X+,R-}
{$M 8192, 0, 655350}

Uses Crt, Polymrf3;

CONST MAX_STRINGS = 10;
      FILENAME = 'ARR.DAT';
      dB1 : ARRAY[1..MAX_STRINGS] OF LSTRING =
                ('Michigan', 'California', 'Montana', 'Nevada',
                 'New Mexico', 'New York', 'West Virginia', 'Maine',
                 'Virginia', 'Florida');
      dB2 : ARRAY[1..MAX_STRINGS] OF LSTRING =
                ('Illinois', 'Texas', 'Alabama', 'Alaska',
                 'Louisiana', 'Georgia', 'Maryland', 'Vermont',
                 'North Carolina', 'South Carolina');

VAR anArray : TArray;
    I : WORD;
    Pause : BOOLEAN;
    Wait : WORD;
    C : CHAR;

PROCEDURE ShowArray(   Msg : STRING;    { input }
                   VAR A   : TArray     { input });

VAR i : WORD;
    s : LSTRING;

BEGIN
  ClrScr;
  WRITELN(Msg); WRITELN;
  FOR i := 1 TO A.GetWorkSize DO
    IF A.Recall(s, i) THEN
      WRITELN(s)
    ELSE
      WRITELN('Index ', i, ' is out of range');
END;

PROCEDURE PressKey;
BEGIN
```

continues

Listing 9.4. continued

```pascal
    IF Pause THEN
      Delay(Wait)
    ELSE BEGIN
      WRITELN;
      WRITE('Press any key...');
      ReadKey;
    END;
  END;
END;

BEGIN
  REPEAT
    ClrScr;
    WRITE('Want to use pause feature? (Y/N) ');
    C := UpCase(ReadKey);
    WRITELN(C);
    WRITELN;
  UNTIL C IN ['Y', 'N'];
  Pause := C = 'Y';
  IF Pause THEN BEGIN
    WRITE('Enter the delay (milliseconds) : ');
    READLN(Wait);
    IF Wait = 0 THEN Wait := 1000;
  END;
  { test instance anArray }
  anArray.Init(10, UArray);
  FOR I := 1 TO MAX_STRINGS DO
    anArray.Store(dB1[I], i);
  ShowArray('UArray-mode array contains the following data:',
            anArray);
  PressKey;
  anArray.Done;

  { test instance anArray }
  anArray.Init(10, UArray_IO);
  FOR I := 1 TO MAX_STRINGS DO
    anArray.Store(dB1[I], i);
  ShowArray('UArray_IO array contains the following data:',
            anArray);
  PressKey;
  anArray.WriteArr(FILENAME);
  FOR I := 1 TO anArray.GetWorkSize DO
    anArray.Store('', i);
  ShowArray('After clearing array it contains the following data:',
            anArray);
  PressKey;
  anArray.ReadArr(FILENAME);
  ShowArray('After reading array from file ' + FILENAME +
            ', it contains:', anArray);
  anArray.Done;
  PressKey;
```

Privileged Instances and Pseudo-Private Methods

```
{ test instance anArray }
anArray.Init(10, FlexUArray);
FOR I := 1 TO MAX_STRINGS DO
  anArray.Store(dB1[I], i);
ShowArray('FlexUArray-mode array contains the following data:',
          anArray);
PressKey;
IF anArray.Expand(2 * MAX_STRINGS) THEN BEGIN
  FOR I := 1 TO MAX_STRINGS DO
    anArray.Store(dB2[I], MAX_STRINGS + i);
  ShowArray('The expanded array contains the following data:',
            anArray);
  PressKey;
END
ELSE BEGIN
  WRITELN('Failed to expand array anArray');
  PressKey;
END;
anArray.Done;

{ test instance anArray }
anArray.Init(10, FlexUArray_IO);
FOR I := 1 TO MAX_STRINGS DO
  anArray.Store(dB1[I], i);
ShowArray('FlexUArray_IO-mode array contains the following data:',
          anArray);
PressKey;
IF anArray.Expand(2 * MAX_STRINGS) THEN BEGIN
  FOR I := 1 TO MAX_STRINGS DO
    anArray.Store(dB2[I], MAX_STRINGS + i);
  ShowArray('The expanded array contains the following data:',
            anArray);
  PressKey;
END
ELSE BEGIN
  WRITELN('Failed to expand array anArray');
  PressKey;
END;
anArray.WriteArr(FILENAME);
FOR I := 1 TO anArray.GetWorkSize DO
  anArray.Store('', i);
ShowArray('After clearing array, it contains the following data:',
          anArray);
PressKey;
anArray.ReadArr(FILENAME);
ShowArray('After reading array from file ' + FILENAME +
          ', it contains:', anArray);
PressKey;
anArray.Done;
```

continues

Listing 9.4. continued

```pascal
{ test instance anArray }
anArray.Init(10, OArray);
FOR I := 1 TO MAX_STRINGS DO
  anArray.Store(dB1[I], i);
ShowArray('OArray-mode array contains the following data:',
          anArray);
PressKey;
anArray.Sort;
ShowArray('Sorted array contains the following data:',
          anArray);
PressKey;
anArray.Done;

{ test instance anArray }
anArray.Init(10, OArray_IO);
FOR I := 1 TO MAX_STRINGS DO
  anArray.Store(dB1[I], i);
anArray.Sort;
ShowArray('OArray_IO-mode array contains the following data:',
          anArray);
PressKey;
anArray.WriteArr(FILENAME);
FOR I := 1 TO anArray.GetWorkSize DO
  anArray.Store('', i);
ShowArray('After clearing array, it contains the following data:',
          anArray);
PressKey;
anArray.ReadArr(FILENAME);
ShowArray('After reading array from file ' + FILENAME +
          ', it contains:', anArray);
anArray.Done;
PressKey;

{ test instance anArray }
anArray.Init(10, FlexOArray);
FOR I := 1 TO MAX_STRINGS DO
  anArray.Store(dB1[I], i);
anArray.Sort;
ShowArray('FlexOArray-mode array contains the following data:',
          anArray);
PressKey;
IF anArray.Expand(2 * MAX_STRINGS) THEN BEGIN
  FOR I := 1 TO MAX_STRINGS DO
    anArray.Store(dB2[I], MAX_STRINGS + i);
  anArray.Sort;
  ShowArray('The expanded array contains the following data:',
            anArray);
  PressKey;
END
ELSE BEGIN
```

Privileged Instances and Pseudo-Private Methods

```
      WRITELN('Failed to expand array anArray');
      PressKey;
    END;
    anArray.Done;

    { test instance anArray }
    anArray.Init(10, FlexOArray_IO);
    FOR I := 1 TO MAX_STRINGS DO
      anArray.Store(dB1[I], i);
    anArray.Sort;
    ShowArray('FlexOArray_IO-mode anArray contains the ' +
              'following data:', anArray);
    PressKey;
    IF anArray.Expand(2 * MAX_STRINGS) THEN BEGIN
      FOR I := 1 TO MAX_STRINGS DO
        anArray.Store(dB2[I], MAX_STRINGS + i);
      anArray.Sort;
      ShowArray('The expanded array contains the following data:',
                anArray);
      PressKey;
    END
    ELSE BEGIN
      WRITELN('Failed to expand array anArray');
      PressKey;
    END;
    anArray.WriteArr(FILENAME);
    FOR I := 1 TO anArray.GetWorkSize DO
      anArray.Store('', i);
    ShowArray('After clearing array, it contains the following data:',
              anArray);
    PressKey;
    anArray.ReadArr(FILENAME);
    ShowArray('After reading array from file ' + FILENAME +
              ', it contains:', anArray);
    PressKey;
    anArray.Done;

END.
```

Here's a sample output for the program in Listing 9.4, showing the elements of instance `FlexUArray`:

```
[BEGIN OUTPUT]
The expanded array contains the following data:

Michigan
California
Montana
Nevada
```

```
New Mexico
New York
West Virginia
Maine
Virginia
Florida
Illinois
Texas
Alabama
Alaska
Louisiana
Georgia
Maryland
Vermont
North Carolina
South Carolina

Press any key...
[END OUTPUT]
```

Here is a sample output for the program in Listing 9.4, showing the elements of instance OArray:

```
[BEGIN OUTPUT]
OArray-mode array contains the following data:

Michigan
California
Montana
Nevada
New Mexico
New York
West Virginia
Maine
Virginia
Florida

Press any key...
[END OUTPUT]
```

Pseudo-Private Methods

The last section showed how to pseudo-hide methods from instances of an object type. You can apply a similar principle to pseudo-hide methods in descendant object types. Moreover, you can "unhide" the same methods in grandchild descendants. The techniques require the following components and approach:

Privileged Instances and Pseudo-Private Methods

- The first declaration of a pseudo-hidden method in an object type requires the declaration of an accompanying *enablement* Boolean data field. This data field acts as an enable/disable flag used to disable or enable normal operations of the method with descendant object types.

- The constructors of the descendant object types are responsible for setting the proper Boolean value to the various (inherited and newly declared) enablement flags.

Let's put the preceding method to work by applying it to the object-type hierarchy in Figure 9.1. By using pseudo-private methods, I can create a linear object-type hierarchy, as shown in Table 9.2. The figure indicates where in the hierarchy the pseudo-private methods are declared, disabled, and enabled.

Table 9.2. Using pseudo-private methods to create a linear object-type hierarchy to model the dynamic string arrays.

Descendant object types	*Pseudo-private methods*
TUArray	
TFlexUArray	Expand (declared)
TUArray_IO	Expand (disabled)
	WriteArr (declared)
	ReadArr (declared)
TFlexUArray_IO	Expand (enabled)
	WriteArr (declared)
	ReadArr (declared)
TOArray	Expand (disabled)
	WriteArr (disabled)
	ReadArr (disabled)
TFlexOArray	Expand (enabled)
	WriteArr (disabled)
	ReadArr (disabled)

continues

Table 9.2. continued

Descendant object types	Pseudo-private methods
TOArray_IO	Expand (disabled)
	WriteArr (enabled)
	ReadArr (enabled)
TFlexOArray_IO	Expand (enabled)
	WriteArr (enabled)
	ReadArr (enabled)

Listing 9.5 shows the source code for the Polymrf4 library unit. This unit declares the linear object-type hierarchy shown in Figure 9.3.

First, we'll discuss the object types in Listing 9.3.

The TUArray Object Type

The TUArray object type in unit Polymrf4 is the same as object type TUArray in unit Polymrf2.

The TFlexUArray Object Type

The TFlexUArray object type, a descendant of TUArray, declares a constructor, the pseudo-private method Expand and the data field EnableExpand. This data field is the enablement flag for the method Expand. The constructor Init sets the EnableExpand data field to True.

The TUArray_IO Object Type

The TUArray_IO object type, a descendant of TFlexArray, declares a constructor, the pseudo-private methods WriteArr and ReadArr, and the data field EnableIO. This data field is the enablement flag for the methods WriteArr and ReadArr. The constructor Init sets the EnableIO data field to True and also sets the inherited data field EnableExpand to False. The latter assignment prevents the instances of object type TUArray_IO from actually expanding the number of array elements.

The TFlexUArray_IO Object Type

The TFlexUArray_IO object type, a descendant of TUArray_IO, only declares the constructor Init. This constructor sets the inherited data fields EnableExpand and EnableIO to True.

The TOArray Object Type

The TOArray object type, a descendant of TFlexUArray_IO, declares a constructor; the methods Store, Sort, and BinSearch; and the data field InOrder. The constructor Init performs the same tasks as the version of TOArray in unit Polymrf2. In addition, the constructor sets the inherited data fields EnableExpand and EnableIO to False. These assignments prevent instances of TOArray from expanding the number of array elements and from performing text file I/O.

The TFlexOArray Object Type

The TFlexOArray object type, a descendant of TOArray, declares the constructor Init. This constructor sets the inherited data fields EnableExpand and EnableIO to True and False, respectively. These assignments allow the instance of TFlexOArray to expand the number of array elements but not to perform text file I/O.

The TFlexOArray_IO Object Type

The TFlexOArray_IO object type, a descendant of TFLexOArray, declares the constructor Init. This constructor sets the inherited data fields EnableExpand and EnableIO to True. These assignments allow the instance of TFlexOArray_IO to expand the number of array elements and perform text file I/O.

Listing 9.5. The source code for the `Polymrf4` library unit.

```
UNIT Polymrf4;

{ This library implements polymorphic arrays }

{**************************************************************}
{**********************} INTERFACE {***********************}
{**************************************************************}

{$X+}

CONST STRING_SIZE = 80;
      NOT_FOUND = 0;

TYPE
  LSTRING = STRING[STRING_SIZE];
  OneString = ARRAY [1..1] OF LSTRING;
  OneStringPtr = ^OneString;

  TUArray = OBJECT
      CONSTRUCTOR Init(ArraySize : WORD { input  });
      DESTRUCTOR Done; VIRTUAL;
      FUNCTION Store(aStr  : LSTRING; { input  }
                     Index : WORD     { input  })
                           : BOOLEAN; VIRTUAL;
      FUNCTION Recall(VAR aStr  : LSTRING; { output }
                          Index : WORD     { input  })
                                : BOOLEAN; VIRTUAL;
      FUNCTION GetWorkSize : WORD;
      FUNCTION GetMaxSize : WORD;
      FUNCTION LinSearch(SearchStr : LSTRING { input  }) : WORD;
    PRIVATE
      MaxSize,
      WorkSize { current size } : WORD;
      DataPtr : OneStringPtr;
      PROCEDURE UnSafeStore(aStr  : LSTRING; { input  }
                            Index : WORD     { input  });
                                   VIRTUAL;
      PROCEDURE UnSafeRecall(VAR aStr  : LSTRING; { output }
                                 Index : WORD     { input  });
                                        VIRTUAL;
  END;

  TFlexUArray = OBJECT(TUArray)
      CONSTRUCTOR Init(ArraySize : WORD { input  });
      FUNCTION Expand(NewMaxSize : WORD { input  }) : BOOLEAN;
    PRIVATE
      EnableExpand : BOOLEAN;
  END;
```

Privileged Instances and Pseudo-Private Methods   9

```
  TUArray_IO = OBJECT(TFlexUArray)
    CONSTRUCTOR Init(ArraySize : WORD { input });
    FUNCTION WriteArr(Filename : LSTRING { input }) : BOOLEAN;
    FUNCTION ReadArr(Filename : LSTRING { input }) : BOOLEAN;
   PRIVATE
    EnableIO : BOOLEAN;
  END;

  TFlexUArray_IO = OBJECT(TUArray_IO)
    CONSTRUCTOR Init(ArraySize : WORD { input });
  END;

  TOArray = OBJECT(TFlexUArray_IO)
     CONSTRUCTOR Init(ArraySize : WORD { input });
     FUNCTION Store(aStr  : LSTRING; { input }
                    Index : WORD     { input })
                                     : BOOLEAN; VIRTUAL;
     PROCEDURE Sort;
     FUNCTION BinSearch(SearchStr : LSTRING { input }) : WORD;
    PRIVATE
     InOrder : BOOLEAN;
  END;

  TFlexOArray = OBJECT(TOArray)
    CONSTRUCTOR Init(ArraySize : WORD { input });
  END;

  TOArray_IO = OBJECT(TFlexOArray)
    CONSTRUCTOR Init(ArraySize : WORD { input });
  END;

  TFlexOArray_IO = OBJECT(TOArray_IO)
    CONSTRUCTOR Init(ArraySize : WORD { input });
  END;
{************************************************************}
{*******************} IMPLEMENTATION {*******************}
{************************************************************}

{$R-}

{---------------------------------------- HeapErrorHandler ----------}

FUNCTION HeapErrorHandler(Size : WORD { input }) : INTEGER; FAR;

BEGIN
    HeapErrorHandler := 1
END;

{---------------------------------------- ExpandArray -----------}
```

continues

Listing 9.5. continued

```pascal
FUNCTION ExpandArray(VAR pArr       : OneStringPtr; { in/out }
                    VAR maxElems    : WORD;         { input  }
                        newMaxElems,                { input  }
                        numElems    : WORD          { input  })
                                    : BOOLEAN;

VAR p : OneStringPtr;
    i : WORD;

BEGIN
  IF newMaxElems <= maxElems THEN BEGIN
    ExpandArray := FALSE;
    EXIT
  END;
  { create new array }
  GetMem(p, newMaxElems * STRING_SIZE);
  IF p <> NIL THEN BEGIN
    FOR i := 1 TO numElems DO
      p^[i] := pArr^[i];
    FOR i := numElems + 1 TO newMaxElems DO
      p^[i] := '';
    FreeMem(pArr, maxElems * STRING_SIZE);
    pArr := p;
    maxElems := newMaxElems;
    ExpandArray := TRUE;
  END
  ELSE
    ExpandArray := FALSE;
END;


{----------------------------------------- WriteArray ------------}

FUNCTION WriteArray(pArr     : OneStringPtr; { input }
                    numElems : WORD;         { input }
                    Filename : LSTRING       { input }) : BOOLEAN;

VAR f : TEXT;
    i : WORD;

BEGIN
  {$I-}
  Assign(f, Filename);
  Rewrite(f);
  {$I+}
  IF IOResult = 0 THEN BEGIN
    FOR i := 1 TO numElems DO
      WRITELN(f, pArr^[i]);
    Close(f);
```

Privileged Instances and Pseudo-Private Methods 9

```
      WriteArray := TRUE;
    END
    ELSE
      WriteArray := FALSE;
END;

{---------------------------------------------- ReadArray -----------}
FUNCTION ReadArray(      pArr      : OneStringPtr; { in/out }
                         maxElems  : WORD;         { input  }
                     VAR numElems  : WORD;         { output }
                         Filename  : LSTRING       { input  }) : BOOLEAN;
VAR f : TEXT;
    i : WORD;

BEGIN
  {$I-}
  Assign(f, Filename);
  Reset(f);
  {$I+}
  IF IOResult = 0 THEN BEGIN
    numElems := 0;
    WHILE (NOT Eof(f)) AND (numElems < maxElems) DO BEGIN
      INC(numElems);
      READLN(f, pArr^[numElems]);
    END;
    Close(f);
    ReadArray := TRUE;
  END
  ELSE
    ReadArray := FALSE;
END;

{---------------------------------------------- Init -----------}
CONSTRUCTOR TUArray.Init(ArraySize : WORD { input   });
{ create instance of TUArray }
BEGIN
  { allocate dynamic memory }
  GetMem(DataPtr, ArraySize * STRING_SIZE);
  IF DataPtr = NIL THEN BEGIN
    Fail;
    EXIT;
  END;
  MaxSize := ArraySize;
  WorkSize := 0;
  { assign null strings to dynamic array }
  WHILE ArraySize > 0 DO BEGIN
```

continues

Listing 9.5. continued

```pascal
      Store('', ArraySize);
      DEC(ArraySize)
  END;
END;

{------------------------------------------------ Done ------------}

DESTRUCTOR TUArray.Done;
{ remove instance of TUArray }
BEGIN
  IF DataPtr <> NIL THEN
    FreeMem(DataPtr, MaxSize * STRING_SIZE);
END;

{------------------------------------------------ Store -----------}

FUNCTION TUArray.Store(aStr  : LSTRING; { input }
                      Index : WORD    { input })
                            : BOOLEAN;
{ store string aStr at element number Index }
BEGIN
  IF Index <= MaxSize THEN BEGIN
    IF Index > WorkSize THEN
      WorkSize := Index;
    DataPtr^[Index] := aStr;
    Store := TRUE
  END
  ELSE
    Store := FALSE
END;

{------------------------------------------------ Recall ----------}

FUNCTION TUArray.Recall(VAR aStr  : LSTRING; { output }
                           Index : WORD    { output })
                                 : BOOLEAN;
{ recall string from element number Index }
BEGIN
  IF Index <= WorkSize THEN BEGIN
    aStr := DataPtr^[Index];
    Recall := TRUE
  END
  ELSE
    Recall := FALSE
END;

{------------------------------------------------ LinSearch -------}
```

Privileged Instances and Pseudo-Private Methods

```
FUNCTION TUArray.LinSearch(SearchStr : LSTRING { input }) : WORD;
{ perform linear search for SearchStr in array }
VAR i : WORD;
    notFound : BOOLEAN;
    s : LSTRING;

BEGIN
  i := 1;
  notFound := TRUE;
  WHILE (i <= WorkSize) AND notFound DO BEGIN
    UnSafeRecall(s, i);
    If s <> SearchStr THEN
      INC(i)
    ELSE
      notFound := FALSE;
  END;
  { search for data }
  { found a match? }
  IF NotFound THEN
    LinSearch := NOT_FOUND
  ELSE
    LinSearch := i;
END;

{------------------------------------ UnSafeStore -----------}

PROCEDURE TUArray.UnSafeStore(aStr  : LSTRING; { input }
                              Index : WORD     { input });
{ store string aStr at element number Index }
BEGIN
  DataPtr^[Index] := aStr;
END;

{------------------------------------ UnSafeRecall -----------}

PROCEDURE TUArray.UnSafeRecall(VAR aStr  : LSTRING; { output }
                                   Index : WORD     { input });
{ recall string from element number Index }
BEGIN
    aStr := DataPtr^[Index];
END;

{------------------------------------ GetWorkSize -----------}

FUNCTION TUArray.GetWorkSize : WORD;
{ return working size of array }
BEGIN
  GetWorkSize := WorkSize;
END;
```

continues

Listing 9.5. continued

```pascal
{------------------------------------ GetMaxSize -----------}

FUNCTION TUArray.GetMaxSize : WORD;
{ return maximum size of array }
BEGIN
  GetMaxSize := MaxSize;
END;

{------------------------------------------- Init -----------}

CONSTRUCTOR TFlexUArray.Init(ArraySize : WORD { input  });
{ create instance of TUArray }
BEGIN
  TUArray.Init(ArraySize);
  EnableExpand := TRUE;
END;

{--------------------------------------- Expand -----------}

FUNCTION TFlexUArray.Expand(NewMaxSize : WORD { input }) : BOOLEAN;
{ expand unordered array }
BEGIN
  IF EnableExpand THEN
    Expand := ExpandArray(DataPtr, MaxSize, NewMaxSize, WorkSize)
  ELSE
    Expand := FALSE;
END;

{------------------------------------------- Init -----------}

CONSTRUCTOR TUArray_IO.Init(ArraySize : WORD { input  });
{ create instance of TUArray_IO }
BEGIN
  TUArray.Init(ArraySize);
  EnableExpand := FALSE;
  EnableIO := TRUE;
END;

{--------------------------------------- WriteArr -----------}

FUNCTION TUArray_IO.WriteArr(Filename : LSTRING { input }) : BOOLEAN;
{ write unordered array }
BEGIN
  IF EnableIO THEN
    WriteArr := WriteArray(DataPtr, WorkSize, Filename)
  ELSE
    WriteArr := FALSE;
END;
```

Privileged Instances and Pseudo-Private Methods

```
{---------------------------------------------- Init -----------}

CONSTRUCTOR TFlexUArray_IO.Init(ArraySize : WORD { input });
{ create instance of TFlexUArray_IO }
BEGIN
  TUArray.Init(ArraySize);
  EnableExpand := TRUE;
  EnableIO := TRUE;
END;

{---------------------------------------------- ReadArr -----------}

FUNCTION TUArray_IO.ReadArr(Filename : LSTRING { input }) : BOOLEAN;
{ read unordered array }
BEGIN
  IF EnableIO THEN
    ReadArr := ReadArray(DataPtr, MaxSize, WorkSize, Filename)
  ELSE
    ReadArr := FALSE;
END;


{---------------------------------------------- Init -----------}

CONSTRUCTOR TOArray.Init(ArraySize : WORD { input });
{ create instance of TOArray }
BEGIN
  { allocate dynamic memory }
  TUArray.Init(ArraySize);
  InOrder := FALSE;
  EnableExpand := FALSE;
  EnableIO := FALSE;
END;

{---------------------------------------------- Store -----------}

FUNCTION TOArray.Store(aStr  : LSTRING; { input }
                       Index : WORD     { input })
                             : BOOLEAN;
{ store string aStr at element number Index }

VAR ok : BOOLEAN;

BEGIN
  ok := INHERITED Store(aStr, Index);
  IF ok THEN InOrder := FALSE;
  Store := ok;
END;

{---------------------------------------------- Sort -----------}
```

continues

Listing 9.5. continued

```pascal
PROCEDURE TOArray.Sort;
{ sort array using Shell-Metzner method }
VAR offset, i, j : WORD;
    strI, strJ : LSTRING;

BEGIN
  IF WorkSize < 2 THEN EXIT;
  offset := WorkSize;
  WHILE offset > 1 DO BEGIN
    offset := offset div 2;
    REPEAT
      InOrder := TRUE;
      FOR j := 1 TO WorkSize - offset DO BEGIN
        i := j + offset;
        UnSafeRecall(strJ, j);
        UnSafeRecall(strI, i);
        IF strI < strJ THEN BEGIN
          UnSafeStore(strI, j);
          UnSafeStore(strJ, i);
          InOrder := FALSE
        END; { IF }
      END; { FOR }
    UNTIL InOrder;
  END; { WHILE }
END;

{----------------------------------------------- BinSearch ------------}

FUNCTION TOArray.BinSearch(SearchStr : LSTRING { input }) : WORD;
{ perform binary search for SearchStr in array }
VAR low, high, median : WORD;
    strMedian : LSTRING;

BEGIN
  { array needs to be sorted? }
  IF NOT InOrder THEN
    Sort;
  { set initial search limits }
  low := 1;
  high := WorkSize;
  { search for data }
  REPEAT
    median := (low + high) div 2;
    UnSafeRecall(strMedian, median);
    IF SearchStr < strMedian THEN
      high := median - 1
```

Privileged Instances and Pseudo-Private Methods

```
    ELSE
      low := median + 1;
  UNTIL (SearchStr = strMedian) OR (low > high);
  { found a match? }
  IF SearchStr = strMedian THEN
    BinSearch := median
  ELSE
    BinSearch := NOT_FOUND;
END;

{-------------------------------------------- Init -----------}

CONSTRUCTOR TFlexOArray.Init(ArraySize : WORD { input });
{ create instance of TFlexOArray }
BEGIN
  TOArray.Init(ArraySize);
  EnableExpand := TRUE;
  EnableIO := FALSE;
END;

{-------------------------------------------- Init -----------}

CONSTRUCTOR TOArray_IO.Init(ArraySize : WORD { input });
{ create instance of TOArray_IO }
BEGIN
  TOArray.Init(ArraySize);
  EnableExpand := FALSE;
  EnableIO := TRUE;
END;

{-------------------------------------------- Init -----------}

CONSTRUCTOR TFlexOArray_IO.Init(ArraySize : WORD { input });
{ create instance of TFlexOArray_IO }
BEGIN
  TOArray.Init(ArraySize);
  EnableExpand := TRUE;
  EnableIO := TRUE;
END;

BEGIN
  HeapError := @HeapErrorHandler;
END.
```

Testing the Polymrf4 Library Unit

Listing 9.6 shows the program ARRAY9.PAS, which tests the object-type hierarchy exported by the `Polymrf4` library unit. The program is similar to ARRAY7.PAS (in Listing 9.2), except in that it attempts to expand instance OArray by sending it the message Expand. The sample output shows the error message displayed by the program when the Expand message returns False.

Listing 9.6. The program ARRAY9.PAS, which tests the object-type hierarchy exported by the `Polymrf4` library unit.

```
Program Array9;

{
  This program tests various arrays in library Polymrf4.
}

{$X+,R-}
{$M 8192, 0, 655350}

Uses Crt, Polymrf4;

CONST MAX_STRINGS = 10;
      FILENAME = 'ARR.DAT';
      dB1 : ARRAY[1..MAX_STRINGS] OF LSTRING =
              ('Michigan', 'California', 'Montana', 'Nevada',
               'New Mexico', 'New York', 'West Virginia', 'Maine',
               'Virginia', 'Florida');
      dB2 : ARRAY[1..MAX_STRINGS] OF LSTRING =
              ('Illinois', 'Texas', 'Alabama', 'Alaska',
               'Louisiana', 'Georgia', 'Maryland', 'Vermont',
               'North Carolina', 'South Carolina');

VAR UArray : TUArray;
    UArray_IO : TUArray_IO;
    FlexUArray : TFlexUArray;
    FlexUArray_IO : TFlexUArray_IO;
    OArray : TOArray;
    OArray_IO : TOArray_IO;
    FlexOArray : TFlexOArray;
    FlexOArray_IO : TFlexOArray_IO;
    I : WORD;
    Pause : BOOLEAN;
    Wait : WORD;
    C : CHAR;
```

Privileged Instances and Pseudo-Private Methods

```
PROCEDURE ShowArray(    Msg     : STRING;    { input }
                    VAR A       : TUArray    { input });
VAR i : WORD;
    s : LSTRING;

BEGIN
  ClrScr;
  WRITELN(Msg); WRITELN;
  FOR i := 1 TO A.GetWorkSize DO
    IF A.Recall(s, i) THEN
      WRITELN(s)
    ELSE
      WRITELN('Index ', i, ' is out of range');
END;

PROCEDURE PressKey;
BEGIN
   IF Pause THEN
     Delay(Wait)
   ELSE BEGIN
     WRITELN;
     WRITE('Press any key...');
     ReadKey;
   END;
END;

BEGIN
   REPEAT
     ClrScr;
     WRITE('Want to use pause feature? (Y/N) ');
     C := UpCase(ReadKey);
     WRITELN(C);
     WRITELN;
   UNTIL C IN ['Y', 'N'];
   Pause := C = 'Y';
   IF Pause THEN BEGIN
     WRITE('Enter the delay (milliseconds) : ');
     READLN(Wait);
     IF Wait = 0 THEN Wait := 1000;
   END;
   { test instance UArray }
   UArray.Init(10);
   FOR I := 1 TO MAX_STRINGS DO
     UArray.Store(dB1[I], i);
   ShowArray('Array UArray contains the following data:',
             UArray);
   PressKey;
   UArray.Done;
```

continues

Listing 9.6. continued

```pascal
{ test instance UArray_IO }
UArray_IO.Init(10);
FOR I := 1 TO MAX_STRINGS DO
  UArray_IO.Store(dB1[I], i);
ShowArray('Array UArray_IO contains the following data:',
          UArray_IO);
PressKey;
UArray_IO.WriteArr(FILENAME);
FOR I := 1 TO UArray_IO.GetWorkSize DO
  UArray_IO.Store('', i);
ShowArray('After clearing array UArray_IO ' +
                   'it contains the following data:',
          UArray_IO);
PressKey;
UArray_IO.ReadArr(FILENAME);
ShowArray('After reading array UArray_IO from file ' +
                   FILENAME +
                   ', it contains:',
          UArray_IO);
UArray_IO.Done;
PressKey;

{ test instance FlexUArray }
FlexUArray.Init(10);
FOR I := 1 TO MAX_STRINGS DO
  FlexUArray.Store(dB1[I], i);
ShowArray('Array FlexUArray contains the following data:',
          FlexUArray);
PressKey;
IF FlexUArray.Expand(2 * MAX_STRINGS) THEN BEGIN
  FOR I := 1 TO MAX_STRINGS DO
    FlexUArray.Store(dB2[I], MAX_STRINGS + i);
  ShowArray('The expanded array FlexUArray ' +
                     'contains the following data:',
            FlexUArray);
  PressKey;
END
ELSE BEGIN
  WRITELN('Failed to expand array FlexUArray');
  PressKey;
END;
FlexUArray.Done;

{ test instance FlexUArray_IO }
FlexUArray_IO.Init(10);
FOR I := 1 TO MAX_STRINGS DO
  FlexUArray_IO.Store(dB1[I], i);
ShowArray('Array FlexUArray_IO contains the following data:',
          FlexUArray_IO);
```

Privileged Instances and Pseudo-Private Methods

```
  PressKey;
  IF FlexUArray_IO.Expand(2 * MAX_STRINGS) THEN BEGIN
    FOR I := 1 TO MAX_STRINGS DO
      FlexUArray_IO.Store(dB2[I], MAX_STRINGS + i);
    ShowArray('The expanded array FlexUArray_IO ' +
                    'contains the following data:',
            FlexUArray_IO);
    PressKey;
  END
  ELSE BEGIN
    WRITELN('Failed to expand array FlexUArray_IO');
    PressKey;
  END;
  FlexUArray_IO.WriteArr(FILENAME);
  FOR I := 1 TO FlexUArray_IO.GetWorkSize DO
    FlexUArray_IO.Store('', i);
  ShowArray('After clearing array FlexUArray_IO ' +
                   'it contains the following data:',
          FlexUArray_IO);
  PressKey;
  FlexUArray_IO.ReadArr(FILENAME);
  ShowArray('After reading array FlexUArray_IO from file ' +
                  FILENAME +
                  ', it contains:',
          FlexUArray_IO);
  PressKey;
  FlexUArray_IO.Done;

  { test instance OArray }
  OArray.Init(10);
  FOR I := 1 TO MAX_STRINGS DO
    OArray.Store(dB1[I], i);
  ShowArray('Array OArray contains the following data:',
          OArray);
  PressKey;
  OArray.Sort;
  ShowArray('Sorted array OArray contains ' +
                  'the following data:',
          OArray);
  PressKey;
  IF OArray.Expand(2 * MAX_STRINGS) THEN BEGIN
    FOR I := 1 TO MAX_STRINGS DO
      OArray.Store(dB2[I], MAX_STRINGS + i);
    ShowArray('The expanded array FlexUArray_IO ' +
                    'contains the following data:', OArray);
    PressKey;
  END
  ELSE BEGIN
    WRITELN;
```

continues

Listing 9.6. continued

```pascal
      WRITELN;
      WRITELN('Cannot expand the elements in instance OArray');
      WRITELN;
      PressKey;
  END;
  OArray.Done;

  { test instance OArray_IO }
  OArray_IO.Init(10);
  FOR I := 1 TO MAX_STRINGS DO
    OArray_IO.Store(dB1[I], i);
  OArray_IO.Sort;
  ShowArray('Array OArray_IO contains the following data:',
            OArray_IO);
  PressKey;
  OArray_IO.WriteArr(FILENAME);
  FOR I := 1 TO OArray_IO.GetWorkSize DO
    OArray_IO.Store('', i);
  ShowArray('After clearing array OArray_IO ' +
              'it contains the following data:',
            OArray_IO);
  PressKey;
  OArray_IO.ReadArr(FILENAME);
  ShowArray('After reading array OArray_IO from file ' +
              FILENAME +
              ', it contains:',
            OArray_IO);
  OArray_IO.Done;
  PressKey;

  { test instance FlexOArray }
  FlexOArray.Init(10);
  FOR I := 1 TO MAX_STRINGS DO
    FlexOArray.Store(dB1[I], i);
  FlexOArray.Sort;
  ShowArray('Array FlexOArray contains the following data:',
            FlexOArray);
  PressKey;
  IF FlexOArray.Expand(2 * MAX_STRINGS) THEN BEGIN
    FOR I := 1 TO MAX_STRINGS DO
      FlexOArray.Store(dB2[I], MAX_STRINGS + i);
    FlexOArray.Sort;
    ShowArray('The expanded array FlexOArray ' +
                'contains the following data:',
              FlexOArray);
    PressKey;
  END
  ELSE BEGIN
```

```
      WRITELN('Failed to expand array FlexOArray');
      PressKey;
    END;
    FlexOArray.Done;

    { test instance FlexOArray_IO }
    FlexOArray_IO.Init(10);
    FOR I := 1 TO MAX_STRINGS DO
      FlexOArray_IO.Store(dB1[I], i);
    FlexOArray_IO.Sort;
    ShowArray('Array FlexOArray_IO contains the following data:',
              FlexOArray_IO);
    PressKey;
    IF FlexOArray_IO.Expand(2 * MAX_STRINGS) THEN BEGIN
      FOR I := 1 TO MAX_STRINGS DO
        FlexOArray_IO.Store(dB2[I], MAX_STRINGS + i);
      FlexOArray_IO.Sort;
      ShowArray('The expanded array FlexOArray_IO ' +
                'contains the following data:',
                FlexOArray_IO);
      PressKey;
    END
    ELSE BEGIN
      WRITELN('Failed to expand array FlexOArray_IO');
      PressKey;
    END;
    FlexOArray_IO.WriteArr(FILENAME);
    FOR I := 1 TO FlexOArray_IO.GetWorkSize DO
      FlexOArray_IO.Store('', i);
    ShowArray('After clearing array FlexOArray_IO ' +
              'it contains the following data:',
              FlexOArray_IO);
    PressKey;
    FlexOArray_IO.ReadArr(FILENAME);
    ShowArray('After reading array FlexOArray_IO from file ' +
              FILENAME +
              ', it contains:',
              FlexOArray_IO);
    PressKey;
    FlexOArray_IO.Done;

END.
```

Here's a sample output for the program in Listing 9.6:

[BEGIN OUTPUT]
Sorted array OArray contains the following data:

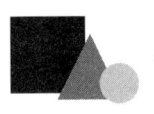

```
California
Florida
Maine
Michigan
Montana
Nevada
New Mexico
New York
Virginia
West Virginia

Press any key...

Cannot expand the elements in instance OArray

Press any key...
[END OUTPUT]
```

Summary

This chapter presented programming tricks that allow you to manipulate the effective execution of specific methods. You learned about the following topics:

- Creating privileged instances of an object type by specifying the privilege level (typically using an enumerated type). The privileged level specifies which methods offer a normal response. This technique enables a single object type to replace a hierarchy of object types.

- Creating pseudo-private methods in an object-type hierarchy. These methods can be enabled and disabled in descendant object types. Implementing this feature involves the use of an *enablement data field* that is assigned the appropriate value by the constructors of the object types.

Chapter 10

Disabled Instances

A discussion of the modeling of real-world objects would be incomplete if we left out cases in which objects malfunction; objects, like people, can "get sick" and even become disabled. This chapter deals with malfunctioning instances of object types and looks at how to deal with both individual instances and contained instances. The topics covered by this chapter are:

- The basics of disabled instances
- Disabling instances of an object type
- Disabling contained instances

Basics of Disabled Instances

Modeling the malfunction or impairment of an instance must take the consequence and nature of the malfunction into account. There are three general outcomes for malfunctioning instances:

- Fatal: the malfunctioning instance is so critical to the program that it halts the program. A real-world example of a fatal malfunction is a dead battery in a car.

- Conditional: the malfunction is temporary and is the result of specific conditions. Once the program rectifies the offending condition, the instance once again is operational. A real-world example of this condition is when your car requires several attempts to start it.

- Partial: the malfunction affects one or more components that make up the instance. This kind of malfunction may lead to a complete shutdown if the impaired component is critical. On the other hand, if the impaired component is not critical, the system continues to operate—without the support of the malfunctioning component. A real-world example of this is the malfunctioning gas gauge in a car. The gauge does not prevent you from operating the car.

Disabled Single Instances

This section looks at the conditional malfunction of single instances. You need the following components to implement an object type that supports this kind of malfunction:

- An enablement flag that indicates whether or not the instance is operational.

- A Boolean function that queries the enablement flag.

- The inclusion of IF statements in the various methods so that program execution quickly exits these methods when the instance is disabled.

- The declaration of at least one method that allows the instance to be re-enabled, under the right conditions.

Let's look at an example. Listing 10.1 shows the program ARRAY10.PAS, which illustrates the conditional malfunction of an instance. The program declares the object type `TVirtStrArray`, which models a disk-based dynamic array of strings. Instances of `TVirtStrArray` are enabled when they're either instantiated or re-initialized with a valid random-access data file. Otherwise, these instances are disabled and do not respond properly (from the operating aspect) to the messages they receive.

The `TVirtStrArray` object type declares the following data fields:

- The `MaxSize` data field specifies the total number of array elements.

- The `WorkSize` data field contains the number of elements that store meaningful data. The constructor assigns 0 to the `WorkSize` field of a new instance.

- The `InOrder` data field maintains the sort-order status of the array.

- The `Enabled` data field is the enablement flag.

The constructor `Init` creates the Boolean method `SelectNewFile` to initialize the instance. If the method returns False, the constructor invokes the special procedure `Fail`. The destructor `Done` closes the supporting data file and then deletes it.

The `TVirtStrArray` object type declares the following methods:

- The Boolean function `SelectNewFile` initializes an instance with a number of elements specified by parameter `ArraySize` and stored in the data file `aStr`. The function opens the data file and writes `ArraySize` number of empty strings.

- The virtual Boolean function `Store` writes a string at a specified array index. The function returns True if the argument for parameter Index is in the range of 1 to `MaxSize`. Otherwise, the function returns False. If the valid argument of `Index` is greater than the data field `WorkSize`, the function updates `WorkSize` with the value of `Index`.

- The virtual Boolean function `Recall` retrieves a string from the array element number `Index`. The function returns True when the argument of parameter `Index` is in the range of 1 to `WorkSize`. Otherwise, the function returns False. The reference parameter `X` passes the accessed array element to the caller.

- The private virtual procedure `UnSafeStore` performs a quick storage of a string in an array element. This method is a version of function `Store` that *assumes* that the argument for parameter `Index` is in the range of 1 to `WorkSize`. I declared this method as private to speed up the operations of the methods `Sort` while denying it access to the instances of `TVirtStrArray`.

- The private virtual procedure UnSafeRecall performs a quick retrieval of a string from an array element. This method is a version of function Recall that *assumes* that the argument for parameter Index is in the range of 1 to WorkSize. I declared this method as private to speed up the operations of the methods Sort and Search while denying it access to the instances of TVirtStrArray.

- The function GetWorkSize returns the value in the WorkSize data field. This result tells you how many meaningful strings there are in an instance of TVirtStrArray.

- The function GetMaxSize returns the value in the MaxSize data field.

- The Boolean function IsEnabled returns the enablement state of an instance.

- The procedure Sort sorts the first WorkSize array elements in ascending order. The procedure uses the Shell-Metzner algorithm and sends UnSafeRecall and UnSafeStore messages to read and write the array elements.

- The function Search performs a binary search for a string in the array. The method sorts the array by sending a Sort message when the InOrder data field is False. The function returns the index of the matching element, or returns the constant NOT_FOUND (which is 0) when no match is found. The Search method uses the UnSafeRecall method to quickly retrieve data from the array elements.

The ARRAY10.PAS program contains the procedures ShowArray and TestInstance to display and test an instance of TVirtStrArray, respectively. The main program section declares the instance of TVirtStrArray, anArr, and performs the following tests:

1. Instantiates the instance anArr using the constant VALID_FILENAME (which is the string ARR.DAT).

2. Calls the procedure TestInstance to test the instance anArr. This procedure assigns unordered strings to the elements of the tested instance, displays these elements, sorts them, and then displays them again in their new order.

3. Reinitializes the instance anArr with the filename INVALID_FILENAME (which is the string <>.DAT) by sending the message SelectNewFile to the instance. The invalid filename ends up disabling the instance anArr.

Disabled Instances 10

4. Calls the procedure TestInstance. This routine displays an error message indicating that the instance anArr is disabled.

5. Reinitializes the instance anArr with the filename VALID_FILENAME by sending the message SelectNewFile to the instance. The valid filename rehabilitates the instance anArr.

6. Calls the procedure TestInstance, which assigns unordered strings to the element of the tested instance, displays these elements, sorts them, and then displays them again in their new order.

Listing 10.1. The program ARRAY10.PAS, which illustrates the conditional malfunction of an instance.

```
Program Array10;

{
  This program illustrates an object type that can disable
  its instances in the case of operational errors.
}

{$X+}

Uses Crt;

CONST STRING_SIZE = 80;
      NOT_FOUND = 0;

TYPE
  LSTRING = STRING[STRING_SIZE];
  TFILE = FILE OF LSTRING;

  TVirtStrArray = OBJECT
      CONSTRUCTOR Init(ArraySize : WORD;   { input }
                       aStrFile  : LSTRING { input });
      DESTRUCTOR Done;
      FUNCTION SelectNewFile(ArraySize : WORD;   { input }
                             aStrFile  : LSTRING { input })
                            : BOOLEAN;
      FUNCTION Store(aStr  : LSTRING; { input }
                     Index : WORD     { input })
                    : BOOLEAN; VIRTUAL;
      FUNCTION Recall(VAR aStr : LSTRING; { output }
                          Index : WORD    { output })
                    : BOOLEAN; VIRTUAL;
      FUNCTION GetWorkSize : WORD;
```

continues

Listing 10.1. continued

```
      FUNCTION GetMaxSize : WORD;
      FUNCTION IsEnabled : BOOLEAN;
      PROCEDURE Sort;
      FUNCTION Search(SearchStr : LSTRING { input  }) : WORD;
    PRIVATE
      MaxSize,
      WorkSize : WORD;
      InOrder,
      Enabled : BOOLEAN;
      FileVar : TFILE;
      PROCEDURE UnSafeStore(aStr  : LSTRING; { input  }
                            Index : WORD     { input  });
                                  VIRTUAL;
      PROCEDURE UnSafeRecall(VAR aStr  : LSTRING; { output }
                                 Index : WORD    { input });
                                  VIRTUAL;
  END;

{------------------------------------------------- Init ------------}

CONSTRUCTOR TVirtStrArray.Init(ArraySize : WORD;    { input  }
                               aStrFile  : LSTRING { input });
{ create an instance of TVirtStrArray }
BEGIN
  IF NOT SelectNewFile(ArraySize, aStrFile) THEN
    Fail;
END;

{------------------------------------------------- Done ------------}

DESTRUCTOR TVirtStrArray.Done;
{ remove instance of TVirtStrArray by closing
  and deleting the supporting data file }
BEGIN
  IF Enabled THEN BEGIN
    Close(FileVar);
    {$I+} Erase(FileVar); {$I-}
  END;
END;

{---------------------------------------------- SelectNewFile ------------}

FUNCTION TVirtStrArray.SelectNewFile(
                       ArraySize : WORD;    { input  }
                       aStrFile  : LSTRING { input })
                                 : BOOLEAN;
{ create an instance of TVirtStrArray }
BEGIN
  WorkSize := 0;
```

Disabled Instances

```
    InOrder := FALSE;
    Assign(FileVar, aStrFile);
    {$I-} Rewrite(FileVar); {$I+}
    IF IOResult <> 0 THEN BEGIN
      MaxSize := 0;
      Enabled := FALSE;
      SelectNewFile := FALSE;
      Exit;
    END;
    Enabled := TRUE;
    MaxSize := ArraySize;
    { assign null strings to dynamic array }
    Seek(FileVar, 0);
    aStrFile := '';
    WHILE ArraySize > 0 DO BEGIN
      WRITE(FileVar, aStrFile);
      DEC(ArraySize)
    END;
    SelectNewFile := TRUE;
END;


{---------------------------------------------- Store -----------}

FUNCTION TVirtStrArray.Store(aStr  : LSTRING; { input  }
                             Index : WORD    { input  })
                                   : BOOLEAN;
{ store string aStr at element number Index }
BEGIN
  IF Enabled AND (Index > 0) AND (Index <= MaxSize) THEN BEGIN
    IF Index > WorkSize THEN
      WorkSize := Index;
    Seek(FileVar, Index-1);
    WRITE(FileVar, aStr);
    InOrder := FALSE;
    Store := TRUE
  END
  ELSE
    Store := FALSE
END;


{---------------------------------------------- Recall -----------}

FUNCTION TVirtStrArray.Recall(VAR aStr  : LSTRING; { output }
                                  Index : WORD    { input  })
                                        : BOOLEAN;
{ recall string from element number Index }
BEGIN
  IF Enabled AND (Index > 0) AND (Index <= WorkSize) THEN BEGIN
    Seek(FileVar, Index - 1);
```

continues

Listing 10.1. continued

```
    READ(FileVar, aStr);
    Recall := TRUE
  END
  ELSE
    Recall := FALSE
END;

{-------------------------------------- UnSafeStore ------------}

PROCEDURE TVirtStrArray.UnSafeStore(aStr  : LSTRING; { input  }
                                    Index : WORD     { input  });
{ store string aStr at element number Index }
BEGIN
  IF Enabled THEN BEGIN
    Seek(FileVar, Index-1);
    WRITE(FileVar, aStr);
  END;
END;

{-------------------------------------- UnSafeRecall ------------}

PROCEDURE TVirtStrArray.UnSafeRecall(VAR aStr  : LSTRING; { output }
                                         Index : WORD     { input  });
{ recall string from element number Index }
BEGIN
  IF Enabled THEN BEGIN
    Seek(FileVar, Index - 1);
    READ(FileVar, aStr);
  END;
END;

{--------------------------------------- GetWorkSize ------------}

FUNCTION TVirtStrArray.GetWorkSize : WORD;
{ return working size of array }
BEGIN
  GetWorkSize := WorkSize;
END;

{--------------------------------------- GetMaxSize ------------}

FUNCTION TVirtStrArray.GetMaxSize : WORD;
{ return maximum size of array }
BEGIN
  GetMaxSize := MaxSize;
END;

{--------------------------------------- IsEnabled ------------}
```

Disabled Instances

```
FUNCTION TVirtStrArray.IsEnabled : BOOLEAN;
{ return enabled status of instance }
BEGIN
  IsEnabled := Enabled;
END;


{---------------------------------------------- Sort -----------}

PROCEDURE TVirtStrArray.Sort;
{ sort array using Shell-Metzner method }
VAR offset, i, j : WORD;
    strI, strJ : LSTRING;

BEGIN
  IF (NOT Enabled) OR (WorkSize < 2) THEN
    EXIT;
  offset := WorkSize;
  WHILE offset > 1 DO BEGIN
    offset := offset div 2;
    REPEAT
      InOrder := TRUE;
      FOR j := 1 TO WorkSize - offset DO BEGIN
        i := j + offset;
        UnSafeRecall(strJ, j);
        UnSafeRecall(strI, i);
        IF strI < strJ THEN BEGIN
          UnSafeStore(strI, j);
          UnSafeStore(strJ, i);
          InOrder := FALSE
        END; { IF }
      END; { FOR }
    UNTIL InOrder;
  END; { WHILE }
END;

{---------------------------------------------- Search -----------}

FUNCTION TVirtStrArray.Search(SearchStr : LSTRING { input  }) : WORD;
{ perform binary search for SearchStr in array }
VAR low, high, median : WORD;
    strMedian : LSTRING;

BEGIN
  IF NOT Enabled THEN BEGIN
    Search := NOT_FOUND;
    EXIT;
  END;
  { array needs to be sorted? }
  IF NOT InOrder THEN
    Sort;
```

continues

Listing 10.1. continued

```pascal
  { set initial search limits }
  low := 1;
  high := WorkSize;
  { search for data }
  REPEAT
    median := (low + high) div 2;
    UnSafeRecall(strMedian, median);
    IF SearchStr < strMedian THEN
      high := median - 1
    ELSE
      low := median + 1;
  UNTIL (SearchStr = strMedian) OR (low > high);
  { found a match? }
  IF SearchStr = strMedian THEN
    Search := median
  ELSE
    Search := NOT_FOUND;
END;

CONST MAX_STRINGS = 10;
      VALID_FILENAME = 'ARR.DAT';
      INVALID_FILENAME = '<>.DAT';
      dB : ARRAY [1..MAX_STRINGS] OF LSTRING =
          ('France', 'England', 'Germany', 'Ireland',
           'Spain', 'Italy', 'Greece', 'Sweden' ,
           'Norway', 'Portugal');

PROCEDURE ShowArray(VAR Arr : TVirtStrArray; { input }
                    Msg : STRING      { input });

VAR i : WORD;
    s : LSTRING;

BEGIN
  ClrScr;
  WRITELN(Msg);
  WRITELN;
  FOR i := 1 TO Arr.GetWorkSize DO BEGIN
    Arr.Recall(s, i);
    WRITELN(s);
  END;
  WRITELN;
  WRITE('Press any key to continue...');
  ReadKey;
END;

PROCEDURE TestInstance(VAR Arr : TVirtStrArray { input });

VAR ok : BOOLEAN;
    i : WORD;
```

Disabled Instances

```
BEGIN
  IF Arr.IsEnabled THEN BEGIN
    FOR i := 1 TO MAX_STRINGS DO
      Arr.Store(db[i], i);
    ShowArray(Arr, 'Unsorted Array is:');
    Arr.Sort;
    ShowArray(Arr, 'Sorted Array is:');
  END
  ELSE BEGIN
    ClrScr;
    WRITELN('Instance anArr is disabled!');
    WRITELN;
    WRITE('Press any key to continue...');
    ReadKey;
  END;
END;

VAR anArr : TVirtStrArray;

BEGIN
  { instantiate the instance anArr with a valid filename }
  anArr.Init(MAX_STRINGS, VALID_FILENAME);
  TestInstance(anArr);
  { re-instantiate the instance anArr with an invalid filename }
  anArr.SelectNewFile(MAX_STRINGS, INVALID_FILENAME);
  TestInstance(anArr);
  { re-instantiate the instance anArr with a valid filename }
  anArr.SelectNewFile(MAX_STRINGS, VALID_FILENAME);
  TestInstance(anArr);
  anArr.Done;
END.
```

Here's part of the output for the program in Listing 10.1:

```
[BEGIN OUTPUT]
Unsorted Array is:

France
England
Germany
Ireland
Spain
Italy
Greece
Sweden
Norway
Portugal

Press any key to continue...
```

The screen clears

```
Sorted Array is:

England
France
Germany
Greece
Ireland
Italy
Norway
Portugal
Spain
Sweden

Press any key to continue...
```

The screen clears

```
Instance anArr is disabled!

Press any key to continue...
```

The screen clears

```
[END OUTPUT]
```

The remaining two screens are identical to the first two.

Disabling Contained Instances

This section looks at the case in which it's possible to shut down the offending contained instance and yet maintain a level of functionality in the host instance. The best example that comes to mind is an airplane with four engines: should one engine malfunction, the pilot shuts it down and keeps flying with the other three engines. It doesn't make sense to crash the airplane just because one engine fails!

To implement shutting down a contained object type, a special shutdown data field is used to monitor the status of the contained object type. As long as the shutdown field is False, the contained object type responds normally to the messages it receives. The shutdown field is set to True when the state of the contained object type indicates damage. Beyond this point, the methods of the malfunctioning object type give minimal or no response.

Listing 10.2 shows a program that simulates the above airplane example. The TEngine object type models an airplane engine. The Fuel data field keeps track of the remaining fuel used by the engine. The FuelRate is the current rate of burning fuel. The ShutDown data field is used to keep track of engine malfunctions. The method Start supplies the initial values for the Fuel and FuelRate data fields, and sets the ShutDown data field to False. The amount of remaining fuel is queried by the GetFuel method. The rate of burning fuel is set and queried by the SetFuelRate and GetFuelRate methods, respectively. The method UpdateFuel updates the value of the Fuel data field based on the given BurnTime. This method is used to decrement the amount of remaining fuel. Finally, the ShutDown method irreversibly shuts down the engine. When ShutDown is set to True, the methods SetFuelrate, GetFuelRate, and UpdateFuel cease to respond in the normal fashion. Consequently, the instance of TEngine stops functioning.

The object type TFly contains a four-member array of type TEngine. The WillCrash method is used to check whether or not all four engines have stopped, leading to an imminent crash.

The program uses a REPEAT-UNTIL loop to simulate the passing of time. Each engine is supplied initially with 1,000 pounds of fuel and set to burn at 100 pounds per hour. The updated amount of fuel and fuel-burn rate are displayed for all four engines. A small menu below the engine data reminds you that you can type L to land the airplane, or press S to reset the fuel burn rate of a functioning engine.

To add some excitement to the simulation, the program provides two sources of trouble that lead to an engine shutdown:

- The first results from setting the fuel-burn rate below a critical value (assigned to the constant CRITICAL_FUEL_RATE).

- The second simulates random causes. A random number between 0 and 1 is generated. If the number exceeds 0.95 (less than a 5 percent chance), the engine is shutdown.

You certainly are welcome to expand on the simulation to make it more interesting. The main point made by the program is to show how to deal with malfunctioning object variables.

Listing 10.2. The program FLY.PAS, which illustrates disabling contained instances.

```pascal
Program Fly;

{ Program illustrates disabling contained instances }

{$X+}

Uses Crt, Dos;

CONST CRITICAL_FUEL_RATE = 10; { lb/hr }

TYPE
    TEngine = OBJECT
        PROCEDURE Start(FuelAdded,          { input }
                        TheFuelRate : REAL { input });
        FUNCTION GetFuel : REAL;
        PROCEDURE SetFuelRate(TheFuelRate : REAL { input });
        FUNCTION GetFuelRate : REAL;
        PROCEDURE UpdateFuel(BurnTime : REAL { input });
        PROCEDURE ShutEngine;
      PRIVATE
        Fuel : REAL;
        FuelRate : REAL;
        ShutDown : BOOLEAN;
      END;

    TFly = OBJECT
       Engine : ARRAY [1..4] OF TEngine;
       FUNCTION WillCrash : BOOLEAN;
    END;

PROCEDURE TEngine.Start(FuelAdded,          { input }
                        TheFuelRate : REAL { input });
BEGIN
    Fuel := FuelAdded;
    FuelRate := TheFuelRate;
    ShutDown := FALSE;
END;

FUNCTION TEngine.GetFuel : REAL;
BEGIN
    GetFuel := Fuel
END;

PROCEDURE TEngine.SetFuelRate(TheFuelRate : REAL { input });
BEGIN
    IF ShutDown THEN Exit;
    FuelRate := TheFuelRate;
END;
```

Disabled Instances   10

```
FUNCTION TEngine.GetFuelRate : REAL;
BEGIN
    IF ShutDown THEN GetFuelRate := 0
                ELSE GetFuelRate := FuelRate;
END;


PROCEDURE TEngine.UpdateFuel(BurnTime : REAL { input  });
BEGIN
    IF ShutDown THEN Exit;
    Fuel := Fuel - BurnTime * FuelRate;
    IF (FuelRate < CRITICAL_FUEL_RATE) OR
       (Fuel <= 0) THEN ShutEngine;
END;

PROCEDURE TEngine.ShutEngine;
BEGIN
    ShutDown := TRUE
END;

FUNCTION TFly.WillCrash;
BEGIN
    WillCrash := Engine[1].ShutDown AND Engine[2].ShutDown AND
                 Engine[3].ShutDown AND Engine[4].ShutDown
END;

CONST DeltaTime = 1; { hour }

VAR Airplane : TFly;
    I, J : WORD;
    FlightTime, X : REAL;
    AKey : CHAR;

PROCEDURE ShowData;
BEGIN
    ClrScr;
    WRITELN('Time : ', FlightTime:2:0, ' hours');
    FOR I := 1 TO 4 DO BEGIN
        X := Random(10000) / 10000;
        IF X > 0.95 THEN { trouble }
            Airplane.Engine[I].ShutEngine;
        WRITELN('Engine ', I:1,
                ' Fuel = ', AirPlane.Engine[I].GetFuel:3:0, ' lbs ',
                ' Burn Rate = ', AirPlane.Engine[I].GetFuelRate:3:0,
                ' lb/hr');
        Airplane.Engine[I].UpdateFuel(DeltaTime);
    END;

END;
```

continues

Listing 10.2. continued

```
BEGIN
    FOR I := 1 TO 4 DO
        AirPlane.Engine[I].Start(1000, 100);
    FlightTime := 0;
    REPEAT
        FlightTime := FlightTime + DeltaTime;
        ShowData;
        WRITELN;
        WRITELN(
        'Your choices are: Keep flying, Land now, Set fuel rate');
        WRITELN; WRITE('> ');
        AKey := UpCase(ReadKey); ; WRITELN(AKey);
        IF AKey = 'S' THEN BEGIN
            WRITELN;
            REPEAT
              WRITE('Enter engine and new fuel rate : ');
              READLN(J, X);
            UNTIL J IN [1..4];
            Airplane.Engine[J].SetFuelRate(X);
        END;
    UNTIL AirPlane.WillCrash OR (AKey = 'L');
    ShowData;
    IF Airplane.WillCrash THEN BEGIN
        WRITELN;
        WRITELN('You crashed!');
    END
    ELSE BEGIN
        WRITELN;
        WRITELN('You landed after flying ', FlightTime:2:0, ' hours');
    END;
    WRITELN; WRITE('Press any key to end the program...');
    ReadKey;
END.
```

Here's a sample output for the program in Listing 10.2:

```
[BEGIN OUTPUT]
Time :  4 hours
Engine 1 Fuel = 834 lbs   Burn Rate =  33 lb/hr
Engine 2 Fuel = 700 lbs   Burn Rate = 100 lb/hr
Engine 3 Fuel = 700 lbs   Burn Rate = 100 lb/hr
Engine 4 Fuel = 700 lbs   Burn Rate = 100 lb/hr

Your choices are: Keep flying, Land now, Set fuel rate

> S

Enter engine and new fuel rate : 2 80
[END OUTPUT]
```

Disabled Instances

Summary

This chapter presented cases in which objects malfunction. You learned about the following topics:

- There are three basic kinds of instance malfunctions: fatal, conditional, and partial. Fatal malfunction halts the program. Conditional malfunction is temporary and is the result of specific conditions. Once the program rectifies the offending condition, the instance once again is operational. Partial malfunction affects one or more components that make up the instance. When the impaired component is not critical, the system continues to operate, but without the support of the malfunctioning component.

- Disabling instances of an object type requires a Boolean data field that acts as an enablement flag. The methods affected by the disablement must exit if the enablement flag is False. The object type should declare at least one method that, under the right conditions, allows the instance to be reenabled.

- Disabling contained instances in a host object requires an approach similar to that used with single disabled instances. In the case of an object type with a contained instance, the object has an enablement flag for each contained instance.

Chapter 11

Disciplined Instances

Most instances of an object type require some form of initialization before they're used. For object types that declare virtual methods, sending the constructor message before any other message is in order. The same object types require that destructors be invoked as part of disposing of the object variables in procedures, functions, or programs. Object types that do not declare virtual methods frequently must be initialized by sending the proper messages. The general rule is that once an object variable is initialized, you can send it messages in any order. There are applications in which the object variables must receive messages in a certain order. Such cases deal with object types that model state engines. This chapter discusses:

- The basics of disciplined instances
- An example that illustrates a disciplined instance

The Basics of Disciplined Instances

Disciplined instances are the product of object types that model *state engines*. Throughout the lifetime of an instance, that instance has a state. A mathematical graph (which is a data structure with multiple and custom links between its nodes) usually is used in modeling a state-engine object. For example, Figure 11.1 shows the states of a stick-shift gear of a car. The arrows indicate unidirectional and bi-directional shifts between various states.

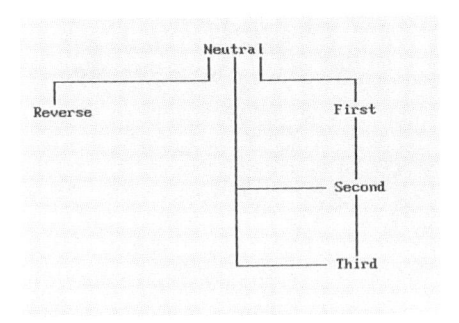

```
                       Neutral
        ┌─────────────────┬─────────────┐
    Reverse                           First
                          ├─────────── Second
                          └─────────── Third
```

Figure 11.1. The states of the stick-shift gear of a car.

Implementing disciplined object types depends on the exact object being modeled. The following general guidelines assist in designing the disciplined object types:

- Declare, when appropriate, an enumerated data type that lists the various states.
- Include, in the object type declaration, a state data field to monitor the current state of the instances.
- Where applicable, insert a decision-making statement in methods to determine whether or not the instance is at the proper level (or levels) to offer the normal response.
- Insert the statements in the appropriate methods that alter the state of the instance.
- Optionally, define a method that returns the current state of the instance.

Disciplined Instances **11**

How does a method react to the improper state of an instance? There are two possible cases:

- The method exits without performing its normal task. The method may set certain values to data fields, reference parameters, and function results to indicate that it did not perform its normal task. Apply this approach in the following cases:

  The shift in state requires external input (from the user, a communication port, a timer action, and so on).

  The current state of the instance prevents the method from automatically updating the state by sending messages.

- The method may—depending on the application and the particular value of the current state—be able to automatically shift the state to the appropriate value by sending messages. These messages update the state to the sought value, which then allows the method to perform its normal task.

The difference between the first and second approach here is analogous to the difference between automatic and standard transmissions in cars.

A Basic Statistics Example

Let's look at an example. The next library unit, `LinReg`, shown in Listing 11.1, exports the disciplined object type `TLinReg`. This object type models a linear-regression object using a state engine. The object type performs linear regression between two observed variables: X (the independent variable) and Y (the dependent variable). The object type also provides projections of X on Y. As a state engine, the linear regression has three states:

1. Initialization of statistical summations (`initSum`). This state indicates that the statistical summations have fewer than three observations.

2. Preparation for linear regression (`readyForLinReg`). This state is attained when the statistical summations have more than two observations.

3. Preparation for projections (`readyForProject`). This state is reached when the instances calculate linear regression statistics. These statistics include the slope, intercept, correlation coefficient, mean values, and standard deviation for observed variables. Once the regression slope and intercept are available, the instances can estimate the values of variable Y for various values of variable X.

Figure 11.2 shows the states of linear regression and how various messages shift these states.

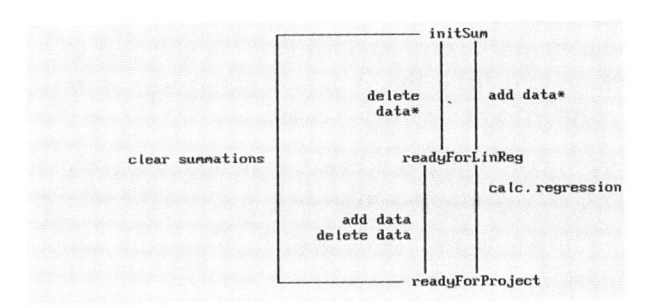

```
                         ┌──── initSum ────┐
                         │                 │
                      delete      .     add data*
                      data*                │
                         │                 │
         clear summations        readyForLinReg
                                           │
                                           │  calc. regression
                                           │
                         add data          │
                         delete data       │
                         │                 │
                         └── readyForProject┘
```

Figure 11.2. The states of linear regression. The * indicates multiple messages are needed to perform the shift in state.

The `LinReg` library unit declares the enumerated data type `LinRegState`, the record `LinRegRec`, and the object type `TLinReg`. The `LinRegState` defines the three states of the linear regression state engine. The `LinRegRec` defines a record that contains the following data fields:

- `NumObs`, the number of observations
- `Slope`, the regression slope
- `Intercept`, the regression intercept
- `R2`, the correlation coefficient
- `MeanX`, the mean value for the X observations
- `MeanY`, the mean value for the Y observations
- `SdevX`, the standard deviation value for the X observations
- `SdevY`, the standard deviation value for the Y observations

The `TLinReg` object type declares a number of data fields and a collection of methods. The data fields can be categorized into the following groups:

- Data fields for the statistical summations: `Sum`, `SumX`, `SumXX`, `SumY`, `SumYY`, and `SumXY`.
- Regression data fields: `fSlope`, `fIntercept`, `fR2`, `fMeanX`, `fMeanY`, `fSdevX`, and `fSDevY`.
- The data field `State`, which maintains the state of the instances of `TLinReg`.

Disciplined Instances   11

The `TLinReg` object type declares the following methods:

- The procedure `ClearSums` initializes the summation data fields and sets the `State` field to `initSum`. The client programs need to send the `ClearSums` messages to properly initialize the instances of `TLinReg`. Client programs also can send the `ClearSums` message to reset the instances of `TLinReg` and prepare them to process another set of observations.

- The procedure `AddData` adds a pair of X and Y observations to the statistical summations. The method sets the state to `readyForLinReg` if there are more than two observations. Otherwise, the procedure sets the state to `initSum`. This procedure may promote or demote the state of an instance, depending on the current state.

- The procedure `DelData` deletes a pair of X and Y observations from the statistical summations. The procedure sets the state to `readyForLinReg` if there are more than two observations. Otherwise, the procedure sets the state to `initSum`. This procedure may promote or demote the state of an instance, depending on the current state.

- The Boolean function `CalcLinReg` calculates the linear regression (if the state of the instance is not `initSum`) and returns True. Otherwise, the function returns False. The reference parameter `LinRegVar` (which has the `LinRegRec` type) passes the regression results to the caller. The procedure performs the following tasks for different state values:

    When the state is `initSum`, the method assigns the constant `BAD_RESULT` (a very large negative number) to the data fields of the `LinRegVar` parameter. The function returns False in this case.

    When the state is `readyForLinReg`, the method calculates the regression statistics, saves them in the data fields, copies these data fields into the fields of parameter `LinRegVar` (by calling the nested procedure `copyResults`), sets the state `readyForProject`, and returns True.

    When the state is `readyForProject`, the method simply copies the data fields into the fields of parameter `LinRegVar` (by calling the nested procedure `copyResults`) and returns True.

    Notice that the method `CalcLinReg` does not send messages to shift the state of an instance.

- The Boolean function `ProjectXonY` calculates the estimated value of Y for a given value of X. The function returns True if it is able to calculate the value for Y. Otherwise, the function returns False. The function performs the following tasks:

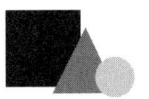

Sends the `CalcLinReg` message if the State field has the value `readyForLinReg`. This task illustrates the ability of a disciplined instance to automatically shift its state.

Calculates the value for Y and returns True when the State field has the value `readyForProject`. If the State field is not `readyForProject`, the function assigns BAD_VALUE to the parameter Y and returns False.

Listing 11.1. The source code of the `LinReg` library unit, which exports a disciplined object type.

```
Unit LinReg;

{
  This library implements a disciplined object type
  that performs statistical linear regression
}
{***************************************************************}
{*********************} INTERFACE {*****************************}
{***************************************************************}

CONST BAD_RESULT = -1.0E+30;

TYPE
    LinRegState = (initSum, readyForLinReg, readyForProject);
    LinRegRec = RECORD
      NumObs,
      Slope,
      Intercept,
      R2,
      MeanX,
      MeanY,
      SdevX,
      SdevY : REAL;
    END;

    TLinReg = OBJECT
      PROCEDURE ClearSums;
      PROCEDURE AddData(X,         { input }
                        Y : REAL { input });
      PROCEDURE DelData(X,         { input }
                        Y : REAL { input });
      FUNCTION CalcLinReg(VAR LinRegVar : LinRegRec { output })
                                       : BOOLEAN;
      FUNCTION ProjectXonY(    X : REAL; { input }
                           VAR Y : REAL  { output }) : BOOLEAN;
      PRIVATE
```

Disciplined Instances 11

```
        Sum,
        SumX,
        SumXX,
        SumY,
        SumYY,
        SumXY,
        fMeanX,
        fMeanY,
        fSdevX,
        fSdevY,
        fSlope,
        fIntercept,
        fR2        : REAL;
        State : LinRegState;
      END;

{**************************************************}
{*******************} IMPLEMENTATION {*******************}
{**************************************************}

PROCEDURE incr(VAR X     : REAL; { in/out }
                   Delta : REAL  { input  });
BEGIN
  X := X + Delta
END;

{-------------------------------------------- ClearSums ---------}

PROCEDURE TLinReg.ClearSums;
BEGIN
  Sum := 0;
  SumX := 0;
  SumXX := 0;
  SumY := 0;
  SumYY := 0;
  SumXY := 0;
  State := initSum;
END;

{-------------------------------------------- AddData ---------}

PROCEDURE TLinReg.AddData(X,        { input  }
                          Y : REAL  { input  });
BEGIN
  incr(Sum, 1);
  incr(SumX, X);
  incr(SumXX, SQR(X));
  incr(SumY, Y);
  incr(SumYY, SQR(Y));
```

continues

Listing 11.1. continued

```pascal
  incr(SumXY, X * Y);
  IF Sum > 2 THEN
    State := readyForLinReg
  ELSE
    State := initSum;
END;

{---------------------------------------------- DelData ---------}

PROCEDURE TLinReg.DelData(X,        { input  }
                          Y : REAL  { input  });
BEGIN
  IF Sum > 0 THEN BEGIN
    incr(Sum, -1);
    incr(SumX, -X);
    incr(SumXX, -SQR(X));
    incr(SumY, -Y);
    incr(SumYY, -SQR(Y));
    incr(SumXY, -X * Y);
    IF Sum < 3 THEN
      State := initSum
    ELSE
      State := readyForLinReg;

    IF Sum <= 0 THEN
      ClearSums;
  END;
END;

{---------------------------------------------- CalcLinReg ---------}

FUNCTION TLinReg.CalcLinReg(VAR LinRegVar : LinRegRec { output })
                                         : BOOLEAN;

  PROCEDURE copyResults;
  BEGIN
    WITH LinRegVar DO BEGIN
      NumObs := Sum;
      MeanX := fMeanX;
      MeanY := fMeanY;
      SdevX := fSdevX;
      SdevY := fSdevY;
      Slope :=  fSlope;
      Intercept := fIntercept;
      R2 := fR2;
    END;
  END;
```

```
BEGIN
  CASE State OF
    initSum:
    BEGIN
      WITH LinRegVar DO BEGIN
        NumObs := BAD_RESULT;
        Slope := BAD_RESULT;
        Intercept := BAD_RESULT;
        R2 := BAD_RESULT;
        MeanX := BAD_RESULT;
        MeanY := BAD_RESULT;
        SdevX := BAD_RESULT;
        SdevY := BAD_RESULT;
      END;
      CalcLinReg := FALSE;
    END;

    readyForLinReg :
    BEGIN
      fMeanX := SumX / Sum;
      fMeanY := SumY / Sum;
      fSdevX := SQRT((SumXX - SQR(SumX) / Sum) / (Sum - 1));
      fSdevY := SQRT((SumYY - SQR(SumY) / Sum) / (Sum - 1));
      fSlope :=  (SumXY - fMeanX * fMeanY * Sum) /
                 (SQR(fSdevX) * (Sum - 1));
      fIntercept := fMeanY - fSlope * fMeanX;
      fR2 := SQR(fSdevX / fSdevY * fSlope);
      copyResults;
      State := readyForProject;
      CalcLinReg := TRUE;
    END;

    readyForProject:
    BEGIN
      copyResults;
      CalcLinReg := TRUE;
    END;
  END;
END;

{--------------------------------------------- ProjectXonY ---------}

FUNCTION TLinReg.ProjectXonY(    X : REAL; { input }
                             VAR Y : REAL  { output }) : BOOLEAN;

    { dummy local variable }
VAR dummy : LinRegRec;
```

continues

Listing 11.1. continued

```
BEGIN
  { can the instance obtain the regression results? }
  IF State = readyForLinReg THEN
    { note the parameters in the CalcLinReg message are
      not used in the method ProjectXonY }
    CalcLinReg(dummy);

  IF State = readyForProject THEN BEGIN
    Y := fIntercept + fSlope * X;
    ProjectXonY := TRUE;
  END
  ELSE BEGIN
    Y := BAD_RESULT;
    ProjectXonY := FALSE;
  END;
END;

END.
```

Let's look at a test program that uses the TLinReg object type, exported by the LinReg library unit. Listing 11.2 contains the TSSTAT.PAS test program, which declares LR, the instance of TLinReg, and the following procedures:

- The procedure CalcReg sends the message CalcLinReg to the instance LR and supplies it with the local variable LRrec (which has the LinRegRec data type). If the message returns True, the routine displays the data fields of the local variable LRrec. These fields contain the statistics for the linear regression. If the CalcLinReg message returns False, the routine displays an error message.

- The procedure Project handles projecting the values of X and Y. The procedure prompts you for a value of X and then sends a ProjectXonY message to the instance LR. If the message returns True, the routine displays the values of Y and X. Otherwise, the procedure displays an error message. If the ProjectXonY message returns True, the routine Project asks if you wish to project another value. The routine loops until you either respond negatively to the above request or until the ProjectXonY message returns False.

The main program section performs the following tasks:

1. Sends a ClearSums message to the instance LR to initialize its data fields.

2. Calls the procedure CalcReg to display the regression results. Because the instance LR was just initialized in the previous statement, the procedure

Disciplined Instances 11

CalcReg ends up displaying an error message stating that the instance has insufficient data.

3. Reseeds the random-number generator.

4. Uses a FOR loop to assign pairs of X and Y values. The values of X range from 0 to 99. The values of Y are calculated based on the equation 32 + 1.8 * X, with an added random-error term. The last statement in the loop sends an AddData message to the instance LR.

5. Calls the procedure Project to project values of X on Y. The procedure Project sends the ProjectXonY to the instance LR. Because state of instance LR is readyForLinReg, the method ProjectXonY is able to shift that state to readyForProject by sending the message CalcLinReg. Consequently, the procedure Project is able to calculate the projected values of Y.

6. Calls the procedure CalcReg. This routine sends the CalcLinReg message to the instance LR. Because the state of instance LR is readyForProject, the method CalcLinReg simply copies the data fields of instance LR to the reference parameter LRrec. The routine CalcReg provides and displays the sought regression statistics. The values for the slope, intercept, and correlation coefficient should be close to 1.8, 32, and 1.

7. Calls the procedure Project again to project more values of X on Y. The procedure Project sends the ProjectXonY to the instance LR. Because the state of instance LR is readyForProject, the method ProjectXonY proceeds to calculate the projected value.

Listing 11.2. The program TSSTAT.PAS, which tests the disciplined object type, TLinReg, exported by the LinReg library unit.

```
Program TsStat;

{
  This program tests the disciplined object type in unit LinReg.
}

{$X+}

Uses Crt, LinReg;

CONST MAX = 100;

VAR X, Y, Yerror : REAL;
```

continues

305

Listing 11.2. continued

```pascal
    I : WORD;
    LR : TLinReg;

PROCEDURE CalcReg;

VAR LRrec : LinRegRec;

BEGIN
    IF LR.CalcLinReg(LRrec) THEN
      WITH LRrec DO BEGIN
        WRITELN('Number of observations = ', Trunc(NumObs));
        WRITELN('Mean of X = ', MeanX);
        WRITELN('Mean of Y = ', MeanY);
        WRITELN('Sdev of X = ', SdevX);
        WRITELN('Sdev of Y = ', SdevY);
        WRITELN('Coefficient of correlation = ', R2:7:5);
        WRITELN('Slope = ', Slope);
        WRITELN('Intercept ', Intercept);
      END
    ELSE
        WRITELN('Not enough data for regression');
END;

PROCEDURE Project;

VAR ok, goOn : BOOLEAN;
    c : CHAR;

BEGIN
  ok := TRUE;
  goOn := TRUE;
  REPEAT
    WRITELN;
    WRITE('Enter X : ');
    READLN(X);
    IF LR.ProjectXonY(X, Y) THEN BEGIN
      WRITELN('Y = ', Y, ' for X = ', X);
    END
    ELSE BEGIN
      WRITELN('Cannot project X on Y');
      ok := FALSE;
    END;

    IF ok THEN BEGIN
      WRITELN;
      WRITE('Another projection? (Y/N) ');
      c := UpCase(ReadKey); WRITELN(c);
      goOn := c = 'Y';
    END;
```

Disciplined Instances 11

```
        UNTIL NOT (ok AND goOn);
        WRITELN;

    END;

BEGIN
        ClrScr;
        WRITELN('Attempt to obtain slope and intercept');
        LR.ClearSums;
        CalcReg;
        WRITELN;
        Randomize;
        FOR I := 1 TO MAX DO BEGIN
            X := Random(100);
            Yerror := 2.0 - Random(4);
            Y := 32 + 1.8 * X + Yerror;
            LR.AddData(X, Y);
        END;
        WRITELN('Attempt to project X on Y');
        Project;
        WRITELN('Attempt to obtain slope and intercept');
        CalcReg;
        WRITELN;
        WRITELN('Attempt to project X on Y');
        Project;
        WRITELN;
        WRITE('Press any key to end the program...');
        ReadKey;
END.
```

Here's a sample output for the program in Listing 11.2. Keep in mind that your results will vary due to the use of random numbers.

```
[BEGIN OUTPUT]
Attempt to obtain slope and intercept
Not enough data for regression

Attempt to project X on Y

Enter X : 10
Y =  5.0704918342E+01 for X =  1.0000000000E+01

Another projection? (Y/N) N

Attempt to obtain slope and intercept
Number of observations = 100
Mean of X =  5.5110000000E+01
```

```
Mean of Y  =   1.3167800000E+02
Sdev of X  =   3.0135684743E+01
Sdev of Y  =   5.4103939586E+01
Coefficient of correlation = 0.99963
Slope =   1.7950140026E+00
Intercept    3.2754778316E+01

Attempt to project X on Y

Enter X : 100
Y =  2.1225617858E+02 for X  =   1.0000000000E+02

Another projection? (Y/N) N


Press any key to end the program...
[END OUTPUT]
```

Summary

This chapter presented special object types that implement state engines. This kind of object requires that you send messages to its instances in a certain sequence. The sequence is determined by the nature of the modeled objects and the actual implementation. Implementing disciplined objects requires the following general guidelines:

- The declaration of an enumerated data type that lists the various states
- The definition a state data field
- Where applicable, the use of decision-making statements in methods to determine whether or not the instance is at the proper level to require the normal response
- The inclusion of statements in the appropriate methods that alter the state of the instance
- An optional method that queries the state of an instance

The chapter also presented a linear-regression object type that implements a state engine. The implementation demonstrates that there are two general approaches to handling inadequate state values. The first approach causes the responding method to exit and not perform its intended tasks. The second approach shows how the responding method in turn sends messages to promote the state to the desired value.

Chapter 12

Emulating C++ Static Members

The OOP extensions of Borland Pascal have been influenced by both Object Pascal and C++. C++ classes permit you to define both static data members and static member functions. (A data member is the equivalent of a data field in Borland Pascal. A member function is the equivalent of a method in Borland Pascal.) In such C++ classes, there is only one copy of each static data member, regardless of the number of class instances.

Conceptually, you can say that the static data member is a property of the class itself, and not of the instances. This notion is valid when you think of a class as a special object that creates objects. In fact, pure OOP languages (such as SmallTalk) consider classes to be objects. (SmallTalk considers *every* language component an object.)

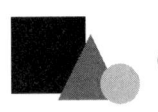

This chapter looks at how to emulate C++ static members and the benefits this emulation brings to the design of an object type. You'll learn about the following topics:

- Basics of static members
- Implementing static members
- Examples of static members

Basics of Static Members

The basic notion behind emulated static members (I'll drop the world *emulated* from now on) comes from a sense of commonality among the instances of an object type. You can regard this commonality as a property of the object type itself.

What are static members used for, you might ask? Here are a few examples that show the use and kinds of static members:

- Counting the number of current instances of an object type. This application of static members indicates that they are a property of the object type itself, and not of the instances.

- Managing common errors and error messages. Using static members to flag and manage errors and error messages enables you to consolidate memory resources. You can regard this kind of static member either as a property of the object type or as a data field commonly shared between the instances.

- Sharing common data. Static members in the form of arrays of simple types or records can consolidate the storage of data common to all of the instances. You can regard this kind of static member either as a property of the object type or as a data field commonly shared between the instances.

- Managing dynamic memory. Static members can be used to implement your own scheme for managing dynamic memory. Such a scheme would reserve a block of dynamic memory ahead of time. The instances of the object type then would receive part of that reserved dynamic memory at runtime. This approach enables you to reduce heap fragmentation and control dynamic allocation.

- Communication between instances. Using static members enables you to allow various instances of an object type to communicate with each other.

Implementing Static Members

Implementing static members is easy and requires the following components:

- The object type that supports static members *must* be declared in a library unit.

- Static members are declared as variables in the implementation section. This kind of declaration ensures that they are inaccessible to client programs.

- The object type declares methods to access the static members. In most of the cases, an object type needs methods that return the values in the static members.

- The unit initialization code is responsible for initializing static members.

Thus, static members really are not part of any object type! They simply are variables that are local to the implementation section of a unit. Fortunately, their inaccessibility outside the implementation section allows this programming trick to work.

> **WARNING**
>
> The programming trick used to implement static members may cause side effects in a hierarchy of object types that use and inherit these static members. The problem here is that the entire hierarchy will share the static members. Thus, static members become an attribute of the entire hierarchy, or one of its subhierarchies, and not just of individual object types.

An Instance-Counting Example

Let's look at the first example. Listing 12.1 shows the library unit Static1, which uses a static member to count the number of instances of the object type TStrArray. The TStrArray object type declares the following data fields:

- The MaxSize data field specifies the total number of array elements.
- The WorkSize data field contains the number of elements that store meaningful data. The constructor assigns 0 to the WorkSize field of a new instance.
- The DataPtr data field accesses the dynamic memory of the array elements.

The constructor Init allocates the dynamic memory for the array elements and assigns empty strings to these elements. The destructor Done closes the supporting data file and then deletes it.

The TStrArray object type declares the following methods:

- The virtual Boolean function Store writes a string at a specified array index. The function returns True if the argument for parameter Index is in the range of 1 to MaxSize. Otherwise, the function returns False. If the valid argument of Index is greater than the data field WorkSize, the function updates WorkSize with the value of Index.
- The virtual Boolean function Recall retrieves a string from the array element number Index. The function returns True when the argument of parameter Index is in the range of 1 to WorkSize. Otherwise, the function returns False. The reference parameter X passes the accessed array element to the caller.
- The function GetWorkSize returns the value in the WorkSize data field. This result tells you how many meaningful strings there are in an instance of TStrArray.
- The function GetMaxSize returns the value in the MaxSize data field.
- The function GetNumInstances returns the current number of instances.

The Static1 unit declares the variable NumInstances inside the implementation section. The unit initialization section assigns 0 to the variable NumInstances. The constructor Init increments the variable NumInstances, while the destructor Done decrements it. The method GetNumInstances returns the value in the variable NumInstances.

Listing 12.1. The library unit `Static1`, which uses a static member to count the number of instances of an object type.

```
UNIT Static1;

{
  This library implements arrays with a pseudo-static member
  that counts the current number of instances
}

{***************************************************************}
{*********************} INTERFACE {*********************}
{***************************************************************}

{$X+}

CONST STRING_SIZE = 80;
      NOT_FOUND   = 0;

TYPE
  LSTRING = STRING[STRING_SIZE];
  OneString = ARRAY [1..1] OF LSTRING;
  OneStringPtr = ^OneString;

  TStrArray = OBJECT
      CONSTRUCTOR Init(ArraySize : WORD { input });
      DESTRUCTOR Done;
      FUNCTION Store(aStr  : LSTRING; { input }
                     Index : WORD     { input })
                           : BOOLEAN; VIRTUAL;
      FUNCTION Recall(VAR aStr  : LSTRING; { output }
                          Index : WORD     { input })
                           : BOOLEAN; VIRTUAL;
      FUNCTION GetWorkSize : WORD;
      FUNCTION GetMaxSize : WORD;
      FUNCTION GetNumInstances : WORD;
    PRIVATE
      MaxSize,
      WorkSize : WORD;
      DataPtr  : OneStringPtr;
  END;

{***************************************************************}
{******************} IMPLEMENTATION {******************}
{***************************************************************}

{$R-}

VAR NumInstances : WORD;
```

continues

Listing 12.1. continued

```
{------------------------------------- HeapErrorHandler ----------}

FUNCTION HeapErrorHandler(Size : WORD { input  }) : INTEGER; FAR;

BEGIN
    HeapErrorHandler := 1
END;

{------------------------------------------------ Init -----------}

CONSTRUCTOR TStrArray.Init(ArraySize : WORD { input  });
{ create instance of TStrArray }
BEGIN
  { allocate dynamic memory }
  GetMem(DataPtr, ArraySize * STRING_SIZE);
  IF DataPtr = NIL THEN BEGIN
    Fail;
    EXIT;
  END;
  MaxSize := ArraySize;
  WorkSize := 0;
  INC(NumInstances);
  { assign null strings to dynamic array }
  WHILE ArraySize > 0 DO BEGIN
      Store('', ArraySize);
      DEC(ArraySize)
  END;
END;

{------------------------------------------------ Done -----------}

DESTRUCTOR TStrArray.Done;
{ remove instance of TStrArray }
BEGIN
  IF DataPtr <> NIL THEN BEGIN
    FreeMem(DataPtr, MaxSize * STRING_SIZE);
    DEC(NumInstances);
  END;
END;

{------------------------------------------------ Store ----------}

FUNCTION TStrArray.Store(aStr  : LSTRING; { input  }
                         Index : WORD    { input  })
                               : BOOLEAN;
{ store string aStr at element number Index }
BEGIN
  IF (Index > 0) AND (Index <= MaxSize) THEN BEGIN
    IF Index > WorkSize THEN
      WorkSize := Index;
```

```
      DataPtr^[Index] := aStr;
      Store := TRUE
    END
    ELSE
      Store := FALSE
END;

{--------------------------------------- Recall -----------}

FUNCTION TStrArray.Recall(VAR aStr  : LSTRING; { output }
                              Index : WORD     { output })
                                    : BOOLEAN;
{ recall string from element number Index }
BEGIN
  IF (Index > 0) AND (Index <= WorkSize) THEN BEGIN
    aStr := DataPtr^[Index];
    Recall := TRUE
  END
  ELSE
    Recall := FALSE
END;

{--------------------------------------- GetWorkSize -----------}

FUNCTION TStrArray.GetWorkSize : WORD;
{ return working size of array }
BEGIN
  GetWorkSize := WorkSize;
END;

{--------------------------------------- GetMaxSize -----------}

FUNCTION TStrArray.GetMaxSize : WORD;
{ return maximum size of array }
BEGIN
  GetMaxSize := MaxSize;
END;

{--------------------------------------- GetNumInstances -----------}

FUNCTION TStrArray.GetNumInstances : WORD;
{ return working size of array }
BEGIN
  GetNumInstances := NumInstances;
END;


BEGIN
  HeapError := @HeapErrorHandler;
  NumInstances := 0;
END.
```

Listing 12.2 shows the program ARRAY11.PAS, which tests the instance-counting object type exported by unit `Static1`. The test program declares the array of `TStrArray` object type, `Arrs`, and performs the following tasks:

1. Uses a nested FOR loop to instantiate the members of array `Arrs`. Each iteration in the outer loop instantiates a member of array `Arrs` and then displays the current number of instances. The loop obtains the latter information by sending the `GetNumInstances` message to instance `Arrs[1]`. The inner FOR loop assigns the elements of the array constant `dB`, by sending the Store message to the instance `Arrs[I]`.

2. Uses a downward-counting FOR loop to remove the instances in array `Arrs`. The loop statements invoke the destructor `Done` and then display the current number of instances. The loop obtains the latter information by sending the `GetNumInstances` message to instance `Arrs[1]`.

> I used the expression `Arrs[1].GetNumInstances` to obtain the current number of instances. You can replace index 1 with any other valid index. Apparently, sending the `GetNumInstances` message is not affected by the destructor's action. In fact, it's not affected by the constructor's action, either. If you insert the statement `WRITELN(Arrs[1].GetNumInstances)` before the nested FOR loop, you get 0, followed by the results you see in the sample output.

Listing 12.2. The program ARRAY11.PAS, which tests the instance-counting object type exported by unit `Static1`.

```
Program Array11;

{
  This program tests the static object types in unit Static1.
}

{$X+,R-}
{$M 8192, 0, 655350}

Uses Crt, Static1;

CONST MAX_ARRAYS = 10;
      MAX_STRINGS = 10;
      dB : ARRAY [1..MAX_STRINGS] OF LSTRING =
```

Emulating C++ Static Members

```
               ('Richmond', 'San Francisco', 'Seattle', 'New York',
                'Orlando', 'Detroit', 'Indianapolis', 'Phoenix',
                'Atlanta', 'Dallas');

  VAR Arrs : ARRAY [1..MAX_ARRAYS] OF TStrArray;
      I, J : WORD;

BEGIN
  ClrScr;
  WRITELN('Creating instances and assigning them strings');
  WRITELN;
  FOR I := 1 TO MAX_ARRAYS DO BEGIN
    Arrs[I].Init(MAX_STRINGS);
    WRITELN('There are ', Arrs[1].GetNumInstances:2,
            ' instance(s) of TStrArray');
    FOR J := 1 TO MAX_STRINGS DO
      Arrs[I].Store(dB[J], J);
  END;
  WRITELN;
  WRITE('Press any key to remove the instances...');
  ReadKey;
  WRITELN;
  WRITELN;
  FOR I := MAX_ARRAYS DOWNTO 1 DO BEGIN
    Arrs[I].Done;
    WRITELN('There are ', Arrs[1].GetNumInstances:2,
            ' instance(s) of TStrArray');
  END;
  WRITELN;
  WRITE('Press any key to end the program...');
  ReadKey;
  WRITELN;
END.
```

Here's a sample output for the program in Listing 12.2:

```
[BEGIN OUTPUT]
Creating instances and assigning them strings

There are  1 instance(s) of TStrArray
There are  2 instance(s) of TStrArray
There are  3 instance(s) of TStrArray
There are  4 instance(s) of TStrArray
There are  5 instance(s) of TStrArray
There are  6 instance(s) of TStrArray
There are  7 instance(s) of TStrArray
There are  8 instance(s) of TStrArray
There are  9 instance(s) of TStrArray
There are 10 instance(s) of TStrArray
```

```
Press any key to remove the instances...

There are  9 instance(s) of TStrArray
There are  8 instance(s) of TStrArray
There are  7 instance(s) of TStrArray
There are  6 instance(s) of TStrArray
There are  5 instance(s) of TStrArray
There are  4 instance(s) of TStrArray
There are  3 instance(s) of TStrArray
There are  2 instance(s) of TStrArray
There are  1 instance(s) of TStrArray
There are  0 instance(s) of TStrArray

Press any key to end the program...[END OUTPUT]
```

A Shared Data Example

This section presents a second example illustrating the use of static members to provide common data to the instances of an object type. Listing 12.3 shows the source code for the Static2 library unit, which supports a bit-set object type, TBitSet. This object type models the set of eight bits in a byte. The unit declares the BitRange type, which defines the range of valid bit indices, 0 to 7. The Static2 library unit also declares the object type TBitSet. This object type declares the following data fields:

- The SetSize data field stores the number of bits that are set in an instance of TBitSet.
- The Bits data field stores the byte that contains the set of bits.

The Static2 library unit declares the typed constant array BitVal to emulate a static member. This array contains the values of each bit in a bit set, and represents data commonly used by the instance of TBitSet.

The TBitSet object type declares the following methods:

- The procedure Init initializes an instance by assigning 0 to both the SetSize and Bits data fields.
- The function GetSetSize returns the number of bits that are set in the bit set.
- The procedure SetBit sets bit number BitNum.
- The procedure ClearBit clears bit number BitNum.

Emulating C++ Static Members

- The function `IsSet` returns True if bit number `BitNum` is set. Otherwise, the function returns False.

- The function `IsClear` returns True if bit number `BitNum` is clear. Otherwise, the function returns False.

The last four methods use the array `BitVal` to query or manipulate the bits in data field `Bits`. The `BitVal` array emulates a static member that consolidates memory resources for the instances of object type `TBitSet`. This kind of static member can be inherited without creating side effects.

Listing 12.3. The source code for the `Static2` library unit, which supports a bit set object type.

```
UNIT Static2;

{
This library implements an object type that uses a local array.
}

{**************************************************************}
{*********************} INTERFACE {*********************}
{**************************************************************}

{$X+}

CONST LOW_BIT = 0;
      HIGH_BIT = 7;

TYPE
  BitRange = LOW_BIT..HIGH_BIT;

  TBitSet = OBJECT
    PROCEDURE Init;
    FUNCTION GetSetSize : BYTE;
    PROCEDURE SetBit(BitNum : BitRange { input });
    PROCEDURE ClearBit(BitNum : BitRange { input });
    FUNCTION IsSet(BitNum : BitRange { input }) : BOOLEAN;
    FUNCTION IsClear(BitNum : BitRange { input })  : BOOLEAN;
   PRIVATE
    SetSize,
    Bits    : BYTE;
  END;

{**************************************************************}
{*******************} IMPLEMENTATION {*******************}
{**************************************************************}
```

continues

Listing 12.3. continued

```pascal
{$R-}

CONST MAX_BITS = 8;
      BitVal : ARRAY [0..MAX_BITS-1] OF BYTE =
              (1, 2, 4, 8, 16, 32, 64, 128);

{-------------------------------------------------- Init -----------}

PROCEDURE TBitSet.Init;
{ initialize bit set }
BEGIN
  Bits := 0;
  SetSize := 0
END;

{----------------------------------------- GetSetSize -----------}

FUNCTION TBitSet.GetSetSize : BYTE;
{ get the size of the bit set }
BEGIN
  GetSetSize := SetSize;
END;

{----------------------------------------- SetBit ---------------}

PROCEDURE TBitSet.SetBit(BitNum : BitRange { input });
{ set a bit }
BEGIN
  IF (Bits AND BitVal[BitNum]) = 0 THEN BEGIN
    Bits := Bits OR BitVal[BitNum];
    INC(SetSize);
  END;
END;

{----------------------------------------- ClearBit ------------}

PROCEDURE TBitSet.ClearBit(BitNum : BitRange { input });
{ clear a bit }
BEGIN
  IF (Bits AND BitVal[BitNum]) <> 0 THEN BEGIN
    Bits := Bits XOR BitVal[BitNum];
    DEC(SetSize);
  END;
END;

{----------------------------------------- IsSet ---------------}

FUNCTION TBitSet.IsSet(BitNum : BitRange { input }) : BOOLEAN;
```

```
{ query if a bit is set }
BEGIN
  IsSet := (Bits AND BitVal[BitNum]) <> 0;
END;

{---------------------------------------- IsClear ------------}

FUNCTION TBitSet.IsClear(BitNum : BitRange { input }) : BOOLEAN;
{ query if a bit is clear }
BEGIN
  IsClear := (Bits AND BitVal[BitNum]) = 0;
END;

END.
```

Let's look at a program that tests the object type exported by the Static2 library unit. Listing 12.4 shows the source code for TSBITS.PAS, the test program. This interactive program allows you to set or clear the bits in a byte. TSBITS.PAS declares the procedure ShowBits, which displays the bits of a TBitSet instance along with commenting text. The program declares the instance of TBitSet, BitSet, displays the initial bits of BitSet, and then repeatedly prompts you for the following information:

- Whether or not you wish to manipulate the bits of the bit set. If you answer with a letter other than Y or y, the program ends.

- The bit number. If you enter a bit number outside the range of 0 to 7, the program reprompts you.

- To set or clear the bit you specified. The program prompts you to enter + or – to set or clear the bit, respectively. If you enter a character other than + or –, the program reprompts you.

The program then displays the current bit set by calling the ShowBits procedure.

Listing 12.4. The source code for program TSBITS.PAS, which tests the object type exported by the Static2 unit.

```
Program TsBits;

{
  This program tests the bit set object type in unit Static2.
}
```

continues

Listing 12.4. continued

```pascal
{$X+}

Uses Crt, Static2;

PROCEDURE ShowBits(    Message : STRING; { input }
                   VAR B       : TBitSet { input });

VAR j : BitRange;

BEGIN
  WRITE(Message);
  FOR j := HIGH_BIT DOWNTO LOW_BIT DO
    IF B.IsSet(j) THEN
      WRITE(' 1')
    ELSE
      WRITE(' 0');
  WRITELN;
END;

VAR BitSet : TBitSet;
    I : BitRange;
    C, Sign : CHAR;

BEGIN
  ClrScr;
  BitSet.Init;
  ShowBits('Initial bit set is ', BitSet);
  REPEAT
    WRITE('Want to toggle a bit? (Y/N) ');
    C := UpCase(ReadKey); WRITELN(C);
    IF C = 'Y' THEN BEGIN
      WRITELN;
      REPEAT
        WRITE('Enter a bit number : ');
        READLN(I);
      UNTIL ABS(I) IN [LOW_BIT..HIGH_BIT];
      REPEAT
        WRITE('Enter + to set bit, - to clear bit ');
        Sign := ReadKey;
        WRITELN(Sign);
      UNTIL Sign IN ['+', '-'];
      IF Sign <> '-' THEN
        BitSet.SetBit(I)
      ELSE
        BitSet.ClearBit(I);
      ShowBits('Bits now are ', BitSet);
```

```
      END
   UNTIL C <> 'Y';
   WRITELN;
   WRITELN;
   WRITE('Press any key to end the program...');
   ReadKey;
   WRITELN;
END.
```

Here's a sample output for the program in Listing 12.4:

```
[BEGIN OUTPUT]
Initial bit set is  0 0 0 0 0 0 0 0
Want to toggle a bit? (Y/N) Y

Enter a bit number : 0
Enter + to set bit, - to clear bit: +
Bits now are  0 0 0 0 0 0 0 1
Want to toggle a bit? (Y/N) Y

Enter a bit number : 5
Enter + to set bit, - to clear bit: +
Bits now are  0 0 1 0 0 0 0 1
Want to toggle a bit? (Y/N) Y

Enter a bit number : 7
Enter + to set bit, - to clear bit: +
Bits now are  1 0 1 0 0 0 0 1
Want to toggle a bit? (Y/N) Y

Enter a bit number : 5
Enter + to set bit, - to clear bit: -
Bits now are  1 0 0 0 0 0 0 1
Want to toggle a bit? (Y/N) Y


Press any key to end the program...
[END OUTPUT]
```

Summary

This chapter introduced you to a programming trick that emulates the static data members in C++. Such members support information common to all instances of an object type. Conceptually, you can regard static members as attributes of the object type itself. Applications for static members include instance counting, managing error messages, consolidating common data, managing dynamic memory, and exchanging messages between instances.

The emulation of static members requires the following components:

- The object type that supports static members *must* be declared in a library unit.
- Static members are declared as variable in the implementation section. This kind of declaration ensures that they are inaccessible to client programs.
- The object type declares methods to access the static members. In most of the cases, an object type needs methods that return the values in the static members.
- The unit initialization code is responsible for initializing static members.

The chapter presented two examples. The first example showed how to use static members to count instances. The second example showed how to use static members to offer data common to all instances on an object type.

Chapter 13

The Oberon Solution

Oberon is the latest programming language invented by Nicklaus Wirth, father of Pascal and Modula-2. While Oberon is not full-fledged object-oriented programming, it supports a few elements of OOP. In this chapter, I discuss two special features of Oberon and then emulate them in Borland Pascal. You'll learn about the following topics:

- Extendible records in Oberon
- Emulating methods in Oberon
- Emulating the Oberon solution

Extendible Records in Oberon

Oberon does not support the declaration of object types that encapsulate data fields and methods. However, Oberon allows you to create a record that is a descendant of another record. Chapter 4 shows you how to implement this feature in Borland Pascal. Here's an example of a small hierarchy of Oberon records:

```
MODULE Test;

(* ********** Oberon Code ************* *)
TimeRec = RECORD
     fHour   : INTEGER;
     fMinute : INTEGER;
     fSecond : INTEGER;
END;

DateTimeRec = RECORD(TimeRec)
     fYear  : INTEGER;
     fMonth : INTEGER;
     fDay   : INTEGER;
END;

VAR DT : DateTimeRec;

BEGIN
     (* assign 12:45:00 to DT *)
     DT.fHour := 12;
     DT.fMinute := 45;
     DT.fSecond := 0;
     (* assign Feb 26, 1994 to DT *)
     DT.fYear := 1994;
     DT.fMonth := 2;
     DT.fDay := 26;
     (* other statements *)
END Test.
```

This code shows that the variable DT needs only one access operator to access any one of the fields inherited from the TimeRec record. You can emulate the above Oberon records using Borland Pascal object types with public data fields.

Emulating Methods in Oberon

Oberon does not support encapsulating functions and procedures in a record, nor does it support private components of a record. However, you can emulate object types in Oberon by declaring data fields that are procedural types. Then, when you initialize an Oberon record, you assign the actual routines to the procedural data fields. In fact, you can alter the above assignment at runtime.

This programming feature allows you to implement *late binding* (which I call *deferred binding* in order to distinguish it from the "late binding" in Borland Pascal), as well as *rebinding!* Consider the ability to perform deferred binding with a class that models an array, for example. Deferred binding allows the client program, and not the implementation unit, to select methods to sort and search. This means that client programmers can choose their favorite or proprietary routines to perform operations such as sorting and searching. Thus, deferred binding adds flexibility to the design of an object type. It also adds responsibility to the client programs.

The ability to alter the routines at runtime also can bring more flexibility. For example, we know that certain array-sorting methods are better than others, depending on the current number of array elements. QuickSort is suitable for relatively large arrays, whereas the `Comb` sort or Shell-Metzner sort methods are better for relatively smaller arrays. Therefore, you can alter the sorting methods at run time as the number of array elements changes.

Emulating the Oberon Solution

How do you implement deferred binding in Borland Pascal? This section presents the guidelines for emulating deferred binding in Borland Pascal.

The basic technique for implementing deferred binding uses procedural types. However, there's one problem with using external routines: they do not have access to the private data fields of an object type. The work-around solution is as follows:

- Declare procedural types for the late binding methods. These procedural types must declare a parameter list that supplies and returns all of the information needed.

- Declare private procedural data fields for the deferred binding methods.

- Include the required procedural parameters in the constructors. The constructor assigns these parameters to the procedural data fields to perform the deferred binding.

- Declare methods that are shells that invoke the routines accessed by procedural data fields. The parameter lists of these methods need not be detailed because they have automatic access to the data fields of the object type.

An Array Example

Let me present an example that shows the deferred binding and rebinding of methods in an object type. Listing 13.1 shows the source code for the Oberon library unit. This unit exports various data types and the object type TStrArray, which supports dynamic arrays with deferred binding and rebinding of methods. The unit exports the procedural types SortProc and SearchProc. The SortProc type is associated with procedures that take the following two parameters:

- The pointer-type OneStringPtr parameter accesses a dynamic array of LSTRINGs.
- The WORD-type parameter passes the number of array elements to sort.

The SearchProc type is associated with functions that take the following three parameters:

- The pointer-type OneStringPtr accesses a dynamic array of LSTRINGs.
- The WORD-type parameter passes the number of array elements to search.
- The LSTRING-type parameter passes the search string.

The search function returns the index of the matching string, or NOT_FOUND if no match is found.

The TStrArray object type declares the following data fields:

- The MaxSize data field specifies the total number of array elements.
- The WorkSize data field contains the number of elements that store meaningful data. The constructor assigns 0 to the WorkSize field of a new instance.
- The DataPtr data field is the pointer to the dynamic array.
- The InOrder Boolean data field is a flag that monitors the order of the array.
- The ptrSort data field is of the SortProc procedural type. This data field is used to bind an instance of TStrArray with the actual sort procedure.
- The ptrSearch data field is of the SearchProc procedural type. This data field is used to bind an instance with the actual search function.

The constructor Init creates an instance with a number of elements specified by parameter ArraySize. The constructor fills the array elements with empty strings. The arguments of the procedural parameters pSort and pSearch are assigned to the ptrSort and ptrSearch data fields, respectively. These parameters perform deferred binding of the instances of TStrArray with the sorting and searching routines. The destructor Done recuperates the dynamic memory allocated for the array.

The TStrArray object type declares the following methods:

- The virtual Boolean function Store writes a string at a specified array index. The function returns True if the argument for parameter Index is in the range of 1 to MaxSize. Otherwise, the function returns False. If the valid argument of Index is greater than the data field WorkSize, the function updates WorkSize with the value of Index. The function assigns False to the data field InOrder, because storing a string in the array most likely will corrupt any existing sort order. You can add more statements in function Store to test whether or not the stored element actually corrupts the order of the array (if the array already is sorted).

- The virtual Boolean function Recall retrieves a string from the array element number Index. The function returns True when the argument of parameter Index is in the range of 1 to WorkSize. Otherwise, the function returns False. The reference parameter X passes the accessed array element to the caller.

- The function GetWorkSize returns the value in the WorkSize data field. This result tells you how many meaningful strings there are in an instance of TStrArray.

- The function GetMaxSize returns the value in the MaxSize data field.

- The procedure Sort sorts the first WorkSize array elements in ascending order. The method invokes the procedure bound with the instance by the ptrSort data field.

- The function Search searches for a string in the array elements. The method invokes the Search function bound with the instance by the ptrSearch data field. The function returns the index of the matching element, or the constant NOT_FOUND (which is 0) when no match is found.

- The procedure SetSortMethod binds the new sort procedure accessed by the pNewSort parameter to the ptrSort data field.

- The procedure SetSearchMethod binds the new search function accessed by the pNewSearch parameter to the ptrSearch data field.

Listing 13.1. The source code for the `Oberon` library unit, which exports an object type with deferred binding and rebinding methods.

```pascal
UNIT Oberon;

{
  This library implements arrays with very deferred binding methods.
}
{*************************************************************}
{*********************} INTERFACE {***********************}
{*************************************************************}

{$X+}

CONST STRING_SIZE = 80;
      NOT_FOUND = 0;

TYPE
  LSTRING = STRING[STRING_SIZE];
  OneString = ARRAY [1..1] OF LSTRING;
  OneStringPtr = ^OneString;
  SortProc = PROCEDURE(ArrPtr : OneStringPtr; N : WORD);
  SearchProc = FUNCTION(ArrPtr : OneStringPtr;
                        N : WORD;
                        SearchStr : LSTRING) : WORD;

  TStrArray = OBJECT
      CONSTRUCTOR Init(ArraySize : WORD;     { input }
                       pSort     : SortProc; { input }
                       pSearch   : SearchProc { input });
      DESTRUCTOR Done;
      FUNCTION Store(aStr  : LSTRING; { input }
                     Index : WORD     { input })
                     : BOOLEAN; VIRTUAL;
      FUNCTION Recall(VAR aStr  : LSTRING; { output }
                          Index : WORD     { input })
                          : BOOLEAN; VIRTUAL;
      FUNCTION GetWorkSize : WORD;
      FUNCTION GetMaxSize : WORD;
      PROCEDURE Sort;
      FUNCTION Search(SearchStr : LSTRING { input }) : WORD;
      PROCEDURE SetSortMethod(pNewSort : SortProc { input });
      PROCEDURE SetSearchMethod(pNewSearch : SearchProc { input });
    PRIVATE
      MaxSize,
      WorkSize : WORD;
      DataPtr  : OneStringPtr;
      InOrder  : BOOLEAN;
      ptrSort  : SortProc;
      ptrSearch : SearchProc;
  END;
```

The Oberon Solution

```
{************************************************************}
{*******************} IMPLEMENTATION {*******************}
{************************************************************}

{$R-}

{return--------------------------------- HeapErrorHandler ---------}

FUNCTION HeapErrorHandler(Size : WORD { input  }) : INTEGER; FAR;

BEGIN
    HeapErrorHandler := 1
END;

{------------------------------------------------- Init -----------}

CONSTRUCTOR TStrArray.Init(ArraySize : WORD;        { input }
                           pSort     : SortProc;    { input }
                           pSearch   : SearchProc { input });
{ create instance of TStrArray }
BEGIN
  { allocate dynamic memory }
  GetMem(DataPtr, ArraySize * STRING_SIZE);
  IF DataPtr = NIL THEN BEGIN
    Fail;
    EXIT;
  END;
  MaxSize := ArraySize;
  WorkSize := 0;
  InOrder := FALSE;
  ptrSort := pSort;
  ptrSearch := pSearch;
  { assign null strings to dynamic array }
  WHILE ArraySize > 0 DO BEGIN
      Store('', ArraySize);
      DEC(ArraySize)
  END;
END;

{------------------------------------------------- Done -----------}

DESTRUCTOR TStrArray.Done;
{ remove instance of TStrArray }
BEGIN
  IF DataPtr <> NIL THEN
    FreeMem(DataPtr, MaxSize * STRING_SIZE);
END;
```

continues

Listing 13.1. continued

```
{------------------------------------------------ Store ------------}

FUNCTION TStrArray.Store(aStr  : LSTRING; { input  }
                        Index : WORD     { input  })
                              : BOOLEAN;
{ store string aStr at element number Index }
BEGIN
  IF (Index > 0) AND (Index <= MaxSize) THEN BEGIN
    IF Index > WorkSize THEN
      WorkSize := Index;
    DataPtr^[Index] := aStr;
    InOrder := FALSE;
    Store := TRUE
  END
  ELSE
    Store := FALSE
END;

{------------------------------------------------ Recall ------------}

FUNCTION TStrArray.Recall(VAR aStr  : LSTRING; { output }
                             Index : WORD     { output })
                                   : BOOLEAN;
{ recall string from element number Index }
BEGIN
  IF (Index > 0) AND (Index <= WorkSize) THEN BEGIN
    aStr := DataPtr^[Index];
    Recall := TRUE
  END
  ELSE
    Recall := FALSE
END;

{-------------------------------------------- GetWorkSize ------------}

FUNCTION TStrArray.GetWorkSize : WORD;
{ return working size of array }
BEGIN
  GetWorkSize := WorkSize;
END;

{-------------------------------------------- GetMaxSize ------------}

FUNCTION TStrArray.GetMaxSize : WORD;
{ return maximum size of array }
BEGIN
  GetMaxSize := MaxSize;
END;
```

The Oberon Solution

```
{------------------------------------------------- Sort -----------}

PROCEDURE TStrArray.Sort;
BEGIN
  ptrSort(DataPtr, WorkSize);
  InOrder := TRUE;
END;

{----------------------------------------------- Search -----------}

FUNCTION TStrArray.Search(SearchStr : LSTRING { input }) : WORD;
{ perform binary search for SearchStr in array }

BEGIN
  { array needs to be sorted? }
  IF NOT InOrder THEN
    Sort;
  Search := ptrSearch(DataPtr, WorkSize, SearchStr);
END;

{------------------------------------- SetSortMethod -----------}

PROCEDURE TStrArray.SetSortMethod(pNewSort : SortProc { input });
BEGIN
  ptrSort := pNewSort;
END;

{------------------------------------ SetSearchMethod -----------}

PROCEDURE TStrArray.SetSearchMethod(pNewSearch : SearchProc { input });
BEGIN
  ptrSearch := pNewSearch;
END;

BEGIN
  HeapError := @HeapErrorHandler;
END.
```

Let's put the object type TStrArray to work. Listing 13.2 shows the source code for the program TSOBERON.PAS, which tests the deferred binding object type TStrArray. The program declares the sorting procedures ShellSort and CombSort. The parameter list of these two methods conform to the procedural type SortProc. This match of parameter lists enables the program to bind the sort procedures with the instance of TStrArray. In addition, the program declares the binary search function BinSearch and the linear search function LinSearch. The parameter lists and function results of the search functions conform to the procedural type SearchProc. This match of parameter lists and function result enables the program to bind the search functions with the instance of TStrArray.

333

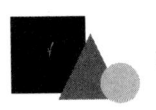

The program declares the instance anArr and performs the following relevant tasks:

1. Instantiates the instance Arr using the constructor Init. This task specifies that the array has MAX_STRINGS elements and uses the sort procedure ShellSort and the search function BinSearch. Thus, the constructor performs deferred binding with the procedure ShellSort and the function BinSearch.

2. Uses a FOR loop to store the elements of the typed constant array dB1 in the elements of instance Arr. The loop sends the Store message to the instance Arr to perform this task.

3. Displays the unordered elements of instance Arr by calling the procedure ShowArray.

4. Sorts the elements in instance Arr by sending the Sort message to the instance. If you single-step through the program execution, you'll notice that the program executes the procedure ShellSort.

5. Displays the sorted elements of instance Arr by calling the procedure ShowArray.

6. Searches for the elements of array dB1 in the instance Arr. This task involves sending the message Search to the instance Arr. If you single-step through the program execution you'll notice that the program executes the function BinSearch. If the message returns a value other than NOT_FOUND, the program displays an arrow to the left of the matching array element. The program also displays the search string at the bottom of the screen and uses the Delay statement to pause at the end of each search iteration.

7. Sends the SetSortMethod to instance Arr to rebind the procedure CombSort with the ptrSort data field.

8. Sends the SetSearchMethod to instance Arr to rebind the function LinSearch with the ptrSearch data field.

9. Repeats tasks 2 to 6, using the typed constant array dB2 instead of dB1.

10. Removes the instance Arr using the constructor Done.

The Oberon Solution   13

Listing 13.2. The source code for the program TSOBERON.PAS, which tests the deferred binding object type `TStrArray`.

```
Program TsOberon;

{
  This program tests the object types in unit Oberon.
}

{$X+,R-}
{$M 8192, 0, 655350}

Uses Crt, Oberon;

CONST MAX_STRINGS = 10;
      RIGHT_MARGIN = 20;
      BOTTOM_ROW = 24;
      ERROR_ROW = 22;
      WAIT = 3000;
      dB1 : ARRAY [1..MAX_STRINGS] OF LSTRING =
            ('Richmond', 'San Francisco', 'Seattle', 'New York',
             'Orlando', 'Detroit', 'Indianapolis', 'Phoenix',
             'Atlanta', 'Dallas');

      dB2 : ARRAY [1..MAX_STRINGS] OF LSTRING =
            ('Virginia', 'California', 'Washington', 'New York',
             'Florida', 'Michigan', 'Indiana', 'Arizona',
             'Georgia', 'Texas');

{$F+}

{------------------------------------ ShellSort -----------}

PROCEDURE ShellSort(p : OneStringPtr; { input }
                    N : WORD          { input });
{ sort array using Shell-Metzner method }
VAR offset, i, j : WORD;
    inOrder : BOOLEAN;
    temp : LSTRING;

BEGIN
  IF N < 2 THEN EXIT;
  offset := N;
  WHILE offset > 1 DO BEGIN
    offset := offset div 2;
    REPEAT
      inOrder := TRUE;
      FOR j := 1 TO N - offset DO BEGIN
        i := j + offset;
```

continues

Listing 13.2. continued

```pascal
        IF p^[i] < p^[j] THEN BEGIN
          temp := p^[j];
          p^[j] := p^[i];
          p^[i] := temp;
          inOrder := FALSE
        END; { IF }
      END; { FOR }
    UNTIL inOrder;
  END; { WHILE }
END;

{------------------------------------------ CombSort ------------}

PROCEDURE CombSort(p : OneStringPtr; { input }
                   N : WORD          { input });
{ sort array using the Comb method }
VAR offset, i, j : WORD;
    inOrder : BOOLEAN;
    temp : LSTRING;

BEGIN
  IF N < 2 THEN EXIT;
  offset := N;
  REPEAT
    offset := offset DIV 2;
    IF offset < 1 THEN offset := 1;
    inOrder := TRUE;
    FOR i := 1 TO N - offset DO BEGIN
      j := i + offset;
      IF p^[i] > p^[j] THEN BEGIN
        temp := p^[j];
        p^[j] := p^[i];
        p^[i] := temp;
        inOrder := FALSE
      END; { IF }
    END;
  UNTIL (offset = 1) AND inOrder;
END;

{------------------------------------------ BinSearch ------------}

FUNCTION BinSearch(p         : OneStringPtr; { input }
                   N         : WORD;         { input }
                   SearchStr : LSTRING       { input })
                             : WORD;
{ perform binary search }
VAR low, high, median : WORD;

BEGIN
```

The Oberon Solution

```
  { set initial search limits }
  low := 1;
  high := N;
  { search for data }
  REPEAT
    median := (low + high) div 2;
    IF SearchStr < p^[median] THEN
      high := median - 1
    ELSE
      low := median + 1;
  UNTIL (SearchStr = p^[median]) OR (low > high);
  { found a match? }
  IF SearchStr = p^[median] THEN
    BinSearch := median
  ELSE
    BinSearch := NOT_FOUND;
END;

{-------------------------------------------- LinSearch -----------}

FUNCTION LinSearch(p         : OneStringPtr; { input }
                   N         : WORD;         { input }
                   SearchStr : LSTRING       { input })
                             : WORD;
{ perform linear search }
VAR i : WORD;
    notFound : BOOLEAN;

BEGIN
  { set initial search limits }
  i := 1;
  notFound := TRUE;
  { search for data }
  WHILE (i <= N) AND notFound DO
    IF SearchStr <> p^[i] THEN
      INC(i)
    ELSE
      notFound := FALSE;

  { found a match? }
  IF notFound THEN
    LinSearch := NOT_FOUND
  ELSE
    LinSearch := i;
END;

{$F-}

PROCEDURE ShowArray(    Msg : STRING;   { input }
                    VAR A   : TStrArray { input });
```

continues

Listing 13.2. continued

```pascal
VAR i : WORD;
    x : LSTRING;

BEGIN
  ClrScr;
  WRITELN(Msg); WRITELN;
  FOR i := 1 TO A.GetWorkSize DO
    IF A.Recall(x, i) THEN
      WRITELN(x)
    ELSE
      WRITELN('Index ', i, ' is out of range');
END;

PROCEDURE PressKey;
BEGIN
   WRITELN;
   WRITE('Press any key...');
   ReadKey;
   WRITELN;
END;

VAR Arr : TStrArray;
    I, J : WORD;

BEGIN
  ClrScr;
  Arr.Init(MAX_STRINGS, ShellSort, BinSearch);
  FOR I := 1 TO MAX_STRINGS DO
    Arr.Store(dB1[I], I);
  ShowArray('Unordered array of strings is:', Arr);
  PressKey;
  Arr.Sort;
  ShowArray('Sorted array of strings is:', Arr);
  PressKey;
  GotoXY(1, WhereY - 1);
  ClrEol;
  FOR I := 1 TO MAX_STRINGS DO BEGIN
    GotoXY(1, BOTTOM_ROW);
    ClrEol;
    WRITE('Searching for ', dB1[I]);
    J := Arr.Search(dB1[I]);
    IF J <> NOT_FOUND THEN BEGIN
      GotoXY(RIGHT_MARGIN, J + 2);
      WRITE('<---- found match');
      Delay(WAIT);
      GotoXY(RIGHT_MARGIN, J + 2);
      ClrEol;
    END
    ELSE BEGIN
      GotoXY(1, ERROR_ROW);
```

The Oberon Solution

```
      WRITE('No match found');
      Delay(WAIT);
      GotoXY(1, ERROR_ROW);
      ClrEol;
    END
  END;
  GotoXY(1, BOTTOM_ROW);
  ClrEol;
  WRITE('Press any key to continue...');
  ReadKey;
  WRITELN;

  ClrScr;
  Arr.SetSortMethod(CombSort);
  Arr.SetSEarchMethod(LinSearch);
  FOR I := 1 TO MAX_STRINGS DO
    Arr.Store(dB2[I], I);
  ShowArray('Unordered array of new strings is:', Arr);
  PressKey;
  Arr.Sort;
  ShowArray('Sorted array of new strings is:', Arr);
  PressKey;
  GotoXY(1, WhereY - 1);
  ClrEol;
  FOR I := 1 TO MAX_STRINGS DO BEGIN
    GotoXY(1, BOTTOM_ROW);
    ClrEol;
    WRITE('Searching for ', dB2[I]);
    J := Arr.Search(dB2[I]);
    IF J <> NOT_FOUND THEN BEGIN
      GotoXY(RIGHT_MARGIN, J + 2);
      WRITE('<---- found match');
      Delay(WAIT);
      GotoXY(RIGHT_MARGIN, J + 2);
      ClrEol;
    END
    ELSE BEGIN
      GotoXY(1, ERROR_ROW);
      WRITE('No match found');
      Delay(WAIT);
      GotoXY(1, ERROR_ROW);
      ClrEol;
    END
  END;
  Arr.Done;
  GotoXY(1, BOTTOM_ROW);
  ClrEol;
  WRITE('Press any key to end the program...');
  ReadKey;
  WRITELN;
END.
```

Here's a sample output for the program in Listing 13.2. The output includes snapshots from the search processes.

```
[BEGIN OUTPUT]
Unordered array of strings is:

Richmond
San Francisco
Seattle
New York
Orlando
Detroit
Indianapolis
Phoenix
Atlanta
Dallas

Press any key...
```

The screen clears

```
Sorted array of strings is:

Atlanta
Dallas
Detroit
Indianapolis
New York
Orlando
Phoenix
Richmond
San Francisco
Seattle

Press any key...
```

The screen clears

```
Sorted array of strings is:

Atlanta
Dallas
Detroit              <---- found match
Indianapolis
New York
Orlando
Phoenix
Richmond
San Francisco
Seattle

Searching for Detroit
```

The Oberon Solution

The screen clears

Unordered array of new strings is:

Virginia
California
Washington
New York
Florida
Michigan
Indiana
Arizona
Georgia
Texas

Press any key...

The screen clears

Sorted array of new strings is:

Arizona
California
Florida
Georgia
Indiana
Michigan
New York
Texas
Virginia
Washington

Press any key...

The screen clears

Sorted array of new strings is:

Arizona
California
Florida
Georgia
Indiana
Michigan
New York   <---- found match
Texas
Virginia
Washington

Searching for New York
[END OUTPUT]

Summary

This chapter presented the emulation of deferred binding and rebinding of methods, as inspired by the Oberon programming language. You learned about the following topics:

- Extendible records in Oberon allow the creation of descendant records that inherit data fields from ancestor records. This feature matches the way Borland Pascal descendant object types inherit data fields from their ancestor object types.

- Emulating methods in Oberon are based on using procedural-typed data fields. This approach allows Oberon records to emulate simple forms of object types. However, these emulated object types enjoy deferred binding and rebinding.

- Emulating the Oberon solution can be done by using procedural-typed data fields that support deferred binding and rebinding of methods. The constructor must have parameters that bind these special methods. The object type may declare additional methods for rebinding. The object type invokes the procedural-typed data fields using shell methods.

Chapter 14

Turbo Vision Collections

The Turbo Vision hierarchy offers object types that are related to the user interface of DOS applications. This hierarchy also includes supporting object types—collections, which manage storing data structures. Collection object types are generic, dynamically expanding arrays that can store mixed data types. Turbo Vision offers a variety of collections: sorted, unordered, general purpose, string, and file collections (exported by the StdDlg library unit). The beauty of collections is their independence—you can also apply them to applications that are not Turbo Vision applications.

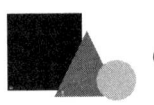

This chapter discusses using collections in non-Turbo Vision applications. You'll learn about the following:

- Unordered collections
- Sorted collections
- String collections

Unordered Collections

Turbo Vision offers the TCollection object type to manage unordered dynamic arrays. The lowest index of a collection member is 0. This object type is aimed primarily at the descendants of TObject, although you can store basic data types, records, and object types that are not related to Turbo Vision.

The TCollection object type offers a good number of methods that enable you to insert, delete, search, retrieve, and overwrite data. In Listing 14.1, I present program MKCOLCT1.PAS to illustrate the functionality of TCollection and introduce you to most of its methods. The program declares two object types: TToDo and TToDoList. The TToDo object type models the members of the collection and is a descendant of TObject. TToDo contains two PString data fields that store data for an individual to-do task. The TToDoList object type models the collection for the TToDo object type. Although not itself a child of TObject, TToDoList contains the DoList data field, a pointer to TCollection. In addition, TToDoList has a constructor, a destructor, and owns the Run method.

To make the program easier to run, I made it supply its own data. The Data typed constant supplies five RToDo records. The Data array is declared as follows:

```
RToDo = RECORD
    fToDo    : STRING40;
    fDueDate : STRING8;
END;
ToDoArray = ARRAY [0..MAX_DATA-1] OF RToDo;

CONST
    Data : ToDoArray = ( (fToDo : 'Lunch with John';
                          fDueDate : '01/23/93'),
                         (fToDo : 'Buy 486 computer';
                          fDueDate : '05/03/94'),
                         (fToDo : 'Sell 8086 computer';
                          fDueDate : '03/03/92'),
```

```
    (fToDo : 'Write Turbo Vision Book';
     fDueDate : '03/31/93'),
    (fToDo : 'Plan trip to Paris';
     fDueDate : '06/22/93'));
```

The lowest array index is 0, to match the indexing scheme of a collection.

The individual to-do datum is created and removed by using the Init constructor and Done destructor, respectively. The TToDo.Init constructor initializes the ToDoStr and DueDate data fields by using the NewStr function, causing the dynamic allocation of strings with the exact size of the Pascal-string argument of NewStr. Initializing the two data fields by using the NewStr function causes collections to use less heap memory than other object types. The TToDo.Done destructor disposes of the dynamic strings by using the DisposeStr routine. The collection is initialized by the TToDoList.Init constructor. The constructor arguments are used to set the initial collection size and the size increment. The TCollection.Init constructor is called to create the dynamic collection. The TToDoList.Done constructor removes the collection by invoking the TCollection.Done destructor in the Dispose call.

The TToDoList.Run method tests the various TCollection methods. It contains several nested routines needed for the test. The Run method examines the following TCollection methods, listed here in the order in which they are tested:

1. The Insert method inserts data in the collection and is declared as follows:

   ```
   PROCEDURE Insert(Item : POINTER) : ; VIRTUAL;
   ```

   The Item parameter is a pointer to the dynamically allocated data. In this case, the argument for Item is a PToDo pointer. The insertion is done directly, using a call to New, as follows:

   ```
   DoList^.Insert(New(PToDo, Init(fToDo, fDueDate)));
   ```

   fToDo and fDueDate are the fields of the Data[i] array member. The program displays the to-do records in the order in which they are inserted.

2. The At method retrieves data from the collection by its positional indices. At is declared as follows:

   ```
   FUNCTION At(Index : INTEGER) : POINTER;
   ```

   The valid range of indices for a collection is 0 to Count-1. (Count is a public data field that stores the number of collection members.) An out-of-range index returns a NIL pointer and invokes the TCollection.Error method.

The test program uses a FOR-DO loop with the control variable iterating from 0 to DoList^.Count-1. The individual collection member is accessed by using the PToDo-typed pointer, dataPtr. A WITH statement inside the FOR loop displays the dynamic strings pointed to by the ToDoStr and DueDate data fields. The pointer dataPtr does not need to allocate additional dynamic memory to access a member of the collection. If you need to copy the data from a collection member, you should use a second PToDo-typed pointer and have that pointer allocate the dynamic memory for the copy. The program displays the collection data as the data is accessed by dataPtr.

3. The ForEach iterator method enables you to apply a routine to each member of the collection. The ForEach method is declared as follows:

```
PROCEDURE ForEach(Action : POINTER);
```

The Action parameter is a pointer to a procedure declared with the FAR directive. The Action procedure must be local and must have one parameter: a pointer to the basic processed object type.

The MKCOLCT1.PAS program uses the local viewAll procedure to view the collection members, using the ForEach iterator. This is done by the following statement located inside routine viewAll:

```
ToDoList^.ForEach(@showElement);
```

This method causes the local procedure showElement to be applied to every collection member. The FAR local showElement procedure has one PToDo-typed parameter, which accesses and displays the fields of the TToDo object type.

4. The FirstThat method searches for the first collection member that contains specific data. The FirstThat method is declared as follows:

```
FUNCTION FirstThat(Test : POINTER) : POINTER;
```

The Test parameter is a pointer to a FAR local Boolean function. The Test function is applied to each collection member until a true result is returned by Test, or until the entire collection has been tested. If a match is found, the FirstThat method returns the pointer to the matching element. Otherwise, it returns a NIL. The Test function must have one pointer parameter to access the basic object type.

The test program uses the FirstThat method to scan for the first collection member with a due date of 1993. The local variable aDueDate is assigned the search string /93. The following statement is used to trigger the search:

```
dataPtr := DoList^.FirstThat(@scanDueDate);
```

The `scanDueDate` is the FAR local Boolean function that scans for the first occurrence of `aDueDate` substring in the `E^.DueDate^` string. The program displays the `Lunch with John` entry, because it's the first one that matches the content of `aDueDate`.

5. The `LastThat` method probes for the last collection member that matches specific search data. The method examines the collection members from last to first. The method is declared as:

    ```
    FUNCTION LastThat(Test : POINTER) : POINTER;
    ```

    The `LastThat` method complements the `FirstThat` method. Both methods use the same FAR local Boolean function in examining a collection. The test program sends a `LastThat` message to the dynamic instance `DoList^` to find that last entry with a 93 due date. The program returns the `Plan trip to Paris` entry.

    The program also shows how to use the `ForEach` method to display all the 1993 entries. The FAR local procedure `showDueDate93` is supplied as an argument to the `ForEach` method. This local procedure displays a to-do entry only if its due-date string contains the substring /93.

6. The `AtDelete` method enables you to delete a collection member by specifying its positional index. The `AtDelete` method is declared as follows:

    ```
    PROCEDURE AtDelete(Index : INTEGER);
    ```

    The collection member at `Index` is removed, and the index position of all subsequent members is decreased by 1. Out-of-range indices cause the `TCollection.Error` method to be invoked.

TIP

When deleting multiple collection members, using the `ATDelete` method, begin with members at the highest indices. This scheme will save you from having to update the indices of the other members you want to delete.

The test program deletes the elements at indices 3 and 1, then displays the updated collection.

7. The `AtInsert` method inserts new data at a specified index. The method is declared as follows:

   ```
   PROCEDURE AtInsert(Index : INTEGER; Item : POINTER);
   ```

   The argument for the `Index` parameter directs the data insertion, causing the index position of all the elements at and beyond `Index` to be moved toward the end by one position. The argument for parameter `Item` must be a pointer to the basic object type. If the argument for `Index` equals the `TCollection.Count` data field, the collection is expanded by the preset increment value before `AtInsert` is called. The `TCollection.Error` is called if the `Index` is out of range or if the collection cannot be further expanded. In either case, the data accessed by `Item` is not inserted in the collection.

   The program reinserts the data from `Data[1]` and `Data[3]`, in that order, which enables the program to restore the original sequence of the collection members. This is revealed by a call to the local procedure `viewAll`.

8. The `IndexOf` method returns the index of a given collection member. The method is declared as follows:

   ```
   FUNCTION IndexOf(Item : POINTER) : INTEGER; VIRTUAL;
   ```

   The `Item` points to the search data. The function returns the index of the matching collection member, or –1 if no match is found. The program uses a FOR-DO loop to send the `At(i)` message to `DoList^` and then assigns the obtained pointer address to `dataPtr`. The `IndexOf` message uses the `dataPtr` as its argument. An IF statement examines the result of `IndexOf` to determine whether the search data matched a collection member. It is interesting to note that replacing `dataPtr` with `@Data[i]` returns a –1 result for all values of `i`. This happens because the elements of array `Data` are not of type `TToDo`, even though they contain similar data fields. The FOR-DO loop displays the collection members, because each iteration succeeds in matching a collection member.

9. The `AtPut` method overwrites the data of an existing collection member. This method is declared as follows:

   ```
   PROCEDURE AtPut(Index : INTEGER; Item : POINTER);
   ```

   The parameter `Index` specifies the positional index of the member to be overwritten. The dynamic heap space of the older member is recovered

Turbo Vision Collections

automatically and new space is allocated for the new data accessed by pointer `Item`. If the value of `Index` is out of range, the method `TCollection.Error` is called.

Using the `AtPut` method, the program swaps the collection members at index 1 and 3. (Remember, the first member has an index of 0.) The arguments for the `AtPut` method are similar to those for `AtInsert`. A call to the local procedure `viewAll` confirms the swap.

10. The `DeleteAll` method deletes all the collection members. This method is declared as follows:

    PROCEDURE DeleteAll;

    The last test performed by the program deletes all the collection members by sending a `DeleteAll` message to `DoList^`. The last invocation of `viewAll` produces no to-do list, confirming the action of method `DeleteAll`.

Listing 14.1. Program MKCOLCT1.PAS, which tests various methods of the `TCollection` object type.

```
Program Make_Collection1;
{
 This program tests the various methods of the unsorted TCollection
 object type. The data is provided by the program itself. The
 program does not employ the Turbo Vision interface.
}
{$B-,V-,X+}

Uses Objects, Crt;

CONST MAX_DATA = 5;

TYPE
     STRING8 = STRING[8];
     STRING40 = STRING[40];

     RToDo = RECORD
        fToDo    : STRING40;
        fDueDate : STRING8;
     END;
     ToDoArray = ARRAY [0..MAX_DATA-1] OF RToDo;

CONST
     Data : ToDoArray = ( (fToDo : 'Lunch with John';
                           fDueDate : '01/23/93'),
```

continues

Listing 14.1. continued

```
                              (fToDo : 'Buy 486 computer';
                               fDueDate : '05/03/94'),
                              (fToDo : 'Sell 8086 computer';
                               fDueDate : '03/03/92'),
                              (fToDo : 'Write Turbo Vision Book';
                               fDueDate : '03/31/93'),
                              (fToDo : 'Plan trip to Paris';
                               fDueDate : '06/22/93'));

TYPE
    PToDo = ^TToDo;
    TToDo = OBJECT(TObject)
       ToDoStr,
       DueDate : PString;
       CONSTRUCTOR Init(WhatToDo,
                        TheDueDate  : STRING);
       DESTRUCTOR Done; VIRTUAL;
    END;

    TToDoList = OBJECT
       DoList : PCollection;
       CONSTRUCTOR Init(InitialSize,
                        Increment    : WORD);
       DESTRUCTOR Done;
       PROCEDURE Run;
    END;

{ ------------------- TToDo ------------------ }

CONSTRUCTOR TToDo.Init(WhatToDo,
                       TheDueDate : STRING);
BEGIN
    ToDoStr := NewStr(WhatToDo);
    DueDate := NewStr(TheDueDate);
END;

DESTRUCTOR TToDo.Done;
BEGIN
    DisposeStr(ToDoStr);
    DisposeStr(DueDate);
END;

{ ------------------- TToDoList ------------------ }
CONSTRUCTOR TToDoList.Init(InitialSize,
                           Increment    : WORD);
BEGIN
    DoList := New(PCollection, Init(InitialSize, Increment));
```

```
END;

DESTRUCTOR TToDoList.Done;
BEGIN
     Dispose(DoList, Done);
END;

PROCEDURE TToDoList.Run;

VAR i, j : INTEGER;
    aDueDate : STRING8;
    dataPtr : PToDo;

    { ------------------ local routines -------------- }

    PROCEDURE wait;

    VAR aKey : CHAR;

    BEGIN
        WRITELN;
        WRITE('Press any key to continue...');
        aKey := ReadKey;
        WHILE Keypressed DO
            aKey := ReadKey;
        WRITELN;
    END;

    PROCEDURE showElement(E : PToDo); FAR;
    BEGIN
        WITH E^ DO BEGIN
           WRITE(ToDoStr^);
           GotoXY(50, WhereY);
           WRITELN(DueDate^);
        END;
    END;

    FUNCTION scanDueDate(E : PToDo) : BOOLEAN; FAR;
    BEGIN
        scanDueDate := Pos(aDueDate, E^.DueDate^) > 0;
    END;

    PROCEDURE showDueDate93(E : PToDo); FAR;
    BEGIN
        IF Pos('/93', E^.DueDate^) > 0 THEN
            WITH E^ DO BEGIN
               WRITE(ToDoStr^);
               GotoXY(50, WhereY);
               WRITELN(DueDate^);
            END;
    END;
```

continues

Listing 14.1. continued

```pascal
    PROCEDURE viewAll(Title : STRING);
    BEGIN
        ClrScr;
            WRITELN(Title);
            WRITELN;
            WRITELN('To-Do':20, ' ':29, 'Due Date':8);
            WRITELN;
            DoList^.ForEach(@showElement);
            wait;
    END;

    PROCEDURE displayMember(E : PToDo);
    BEGIN
        IF E = NIL THEN Exit;
           WITH E^ DO BEGIN
              WRITE(ToDoStr^);
              GotoXY(50, WhereY);
              WRITELN(DueDate^);
           END;
    END;

BEGIN { -------------------- Run ---------------------- }
    TextColor(White);
    TextBackground(Blue);
    {-------------------------------------------------------
                        Insert Data
    -----------------------------------------------------}
    ClrScr;
    WRITELN('Inserting the following data in the To-Do list:');
    WRITELN;
    WRITELN('To-Do':20, ' ':29, 'Due Date':8);
    WRITELN;
    FOR i := 0 TO MAX_DATA-1 DO BEGIN
        WITH Data[i] DO BEGIN
            WRITE(fToDo);
            GotoXY(50, WhereY); WRITELN(fDueDate);
            DoList^.Insert(New(PToDo, Init(fToDo, fDueDate)));
        END;
    END;
    wait;
    {-------------------------------------------------------
       Visit and display collection members using the At method
    -----------------------------------------------------}
    ClrScr;
    WRITELN('Visit collection members using the At method');
    WRITELN;
    WRITELN(' # ','To-Do':17, ' ':29, 'Due Date':8);
    WRITELN;
```

```
      FOR i := 0 TO DoList^.Count-1 DO BEGIN
         dataPtr := DoList^.At(i);
         WITH dataPtr^ DO BEGIN
            WRITE(i:2,' : ',ToDoStr^);
            GotoXY(50, WhereY); WRITELN(DueDate^);
         END;
      END;
END;
wait;
{-------------------------------------------------------
  Display the collection members using the ForEach method
  (found in the nested viewAll procedure)
  ----------------------------------------------------}
viewAll('Display collection members using the ForEach method');
{-------------------------------------------------------
  Display first To-Do task for 1993 using the FirstThat method
  ----------------------------------------------------}
ClrScr;
WRITELN('Display first 1993 task using the FirstThat method');
WRITELN;
WRITELN('To-Do':20, ' ':29, 'Due Date':8);
WRITELN;
aDueDate := '/93';
dataPtr := DoList^.FirstThat(@scanDueDate);
displayMember(dataPtr);
wait;
{-------------------------------------------------------
   Display last To-Do task for 1993 using the LastThat method
  ----------------------------------------------------}
ClrScr;
WRITELN('Display last 1993 task using the LastThat method');
WRITELN;
WRITELN('To-Do':20, ' ':29, 'Due Date':8);
WRITELN;
aDueDate := '/93';
dataPtr := DoList^.LastThat(@scanDueDate);
displayMember(dataPtr);
wait;
{-------------------------------------------------------
  Display all To-Do tasks for 1993 using the ForEach method
  ----------------------------------------------------}
ClrScr;
WRITELN('Display all 1993 tasks using the ForEach method');
WRITELN;
WRITELN('To-Do':20, ' ':29, 'Due Date':8);
WRITELN;
DoList^.ForEach(@showDueDate93);
wait;
{-------------------------------------------------------
  Delete elements 1 and 3 using the AtDelete method
```

continues

Listing 14.1. continued

```
   ----------------------------------------------------------}
ClrScr;
WRITELN('Delete elements 1 and 3 using the AtDelete method:');
WRITELN;
WRITELN('To-Do':20, ' ':29, 'Due Date':8);
WRITELN;
WITH DoList^ DO BEGIN
   AtDelete(3);
   AtDelete(1);
   ForEach(@showElement);
END;
wait;
{---------------------------------------------------------
   Reinsert elements 1 and 3 using the AtInsert method
  ----------------------------------------------------------}
ClrScr;
WRITELN('Reinsert elements 1 and 3 using the AtInsert method:');
WRITELN;
WRITELN('To-Do':20, ' ':29, 'Due Date':8);
WRITELN;
{ reinsert elements 1 and 3 }
DoList^.AtInsert(1, New(PToDo, Init(Data[1].fToDo,
                                    Data[1].fDueDate)));
DoList^.AtInsert(3, New(PToDo, Init(Data[3].fToDo,
                                    Data[3].fDueDate)));
viewAll('After reinserting the deleted elements, this list is:');

{---------------------------------------------------------
           Obtain the indices of the collection members
           using the IndexOf and At methods
  ----------------------------------------------------------}
ClrScr;
WRITELN('Testing the IndexOf method:');
WRITELN;
WRITELN(' # ','To-Do':17, ' ':29, 'Due Date':8);
WRITELN;
FOR i := DoList^.Count-1 DOWNTO 0 DO BEGIN
    dataPtr := DoList^.At(i);
    j := DoList^.IndexOf(dataPtr);
    IF j <> -1 THEN
       WITH Data[j] DO BEGIN
          WRITE(j:2,' : ',fToDo);
          GotoXY(50, WhereY); WRITELN(fDueDate);
       END;
END;
wait;
{---------------------------------------------------------
     Swap elements 1 and 3 using the AtPut method
  ----------------------------------------------------------}
WITH DoList^ DO BEGIN
```

Turbo Vision Collections

```
            dataPtr := New(PToDo, Init(Data[1].fToDo, Data[1].fDueDate));
            AtPut(3, dataPtr);
            dataPtr := New(PToDo, Init(Data[3].fToDo, Data[3].fDueDate));
            AtPut(1, dataPtr);
        END;
        viewAll('Swapping elements 1 and 3 with the AtPut method');
        {--------------------------------------------------------
           Deleting all the collection members using the DeleteAll method
         --------------------------------------------------------}
        DoList^.DeleteAll;
        viewAll('List should be empty now, after using method DeleteAll');
    END;

VAR ToDo : TToDoList;

BEGIN
    ToDo.Init(MAX_DATA, MAX_DATA DIV 2);
    ToDo.Run;
    ToDo.Done;
END.
```

Here's the output generated by the program in Listing 14.1:

```
[BEGIN Output]
Inserting the following data in the To-Do list:

                To-Do                           Due Date

Lunch with John                                 01/23/93
Buy 486 computer                                05/03/94
Sell 8086 computer                              03/03/92
Write Turbo Vision Book                         03/31/93
Plan trip to Paris                              06/22/93

Press any key to continue...
```

The screen clears

```
Visit collection members using the At method

    #           To-Do                           Due Date

    0 : Lunch with John                         01/23/93
    1 : Buy 486 computer                        05/03/94
    2 : Sell 8086 computer                      03/03/92
    3 : Write Turbo Vision Book                 03/31/93
    4 : Plan trip to Paris                      06/22/93

Press any key to continue...
```

The screen clears

Display collection members using the ForEach method

```
         To-Do                              Due Date

Lunch with John                             01/23/93
Buy 486 computer                            05/03/94
Sell 8086 computer                          03/03/92
Write Turbo Vision Book                     03/31/93
Plan trip to Paris                          06/22/93
```

Press any key to continue...

The screen clears

Display first 1993 task using the FirstThat method

```
         To-Do                              Due Date

Lunch with John                             01/23/93
```

Press any key to continue...

The screen clears

Display last 1993 task using the LastThat method

```
         To-Do                              Due Date

Plan trip to Paris                          06/22/93
```

Press any key to continue...

The screen clears

Display all 1993 tasks using the ForEach method

```
         To-Do                              Due Date

Lunch with John                             01/23/93
Write Turbo Vision Book                     03/31/93
Plan trip to Paris                          06/22/93
```

Press any key to continue...

The screen clears

Delete elements 1 and 3 using the AtDelete method:

```
         To-Do                              Due Date

Lunch with John                             01/23/93
Sell 8086 computer                          03/03/92
Plan trip to Paris                          06/22/93
```

Turbo Vision Collections

Press any key to continue...

The screen clears

After reinserting the deleted elements, this list is:

To-Do	Due Date
Lunch with John	01/23/93
Buy 486 computer	05/03/94
Sell 8086 computer	03/03/92
Write Turbo Vision Book	03/31/93
Plan trip to Paris	06/22/93

Press any key to continue...

The screen clears

Testing the IndexOf method:

#	To-Do	Due Date
4 :	Plan trip to Paris	06/22/93
3 :	Write Turbo Vision Book	03/31/93
2 :	Sell 8086 computer	03/03/92
1 :	Buy 486 computer	05/03/94
0 :	Lunch with John	01/23/93

Press any key to continue...

The screen clears

Swapping elements 1 and 3 with the AtPut method

To-Do	Due Date
Lunch with John	01/23/93
Write Turbo Vision Book	03/31/93
Sell 8086 computer	03/03/92
Buy 486 computer	05/03/94
Plan trip to Paris	06/22/93

Press any key to continue...

The screen clears

List should be empty now, after using method DeleteAll

To-Do	Due Date

Press any key to continue...
[END Output]

Sorted Collections

The Turbo Vision hierarchy also offers sorted collections by expanding `TCollection` into the `TSortedCollection` object type. This descendant of `TCollection` really is an abstract object type that maintains nonduplicate collection members in an ordered fashion. Therefore, to use the `TSortedCollection` object type, you must expand and override one (and possibly two) of its methods:

- The first method you must override is `TSortedCollection.Compare`, a virtual method that compares key portions (possibly the entire data item) of the data types to arrange your custom-sorted collection. The `Compare` method is declared as follows:

  ```
  FUNCTION Compare(Key1, Key2 : POINTER) : INTEGER; VIRTUAL;
  ```

  The parameters `Key1` and `Key2` are declared pointers, to make the `Compare` method generic. The function `Compare` returns the following results:

  ```
  0 if Key1^ = Key2^
  1 if Key1^ > Key2^
  -1 if Key1^ < Key2^
  ```

- The second virtual function you frequently will need to override is `KeyOf`. This function returns the key portion of your data, used in sorting and searching. The `KeyOf` method is declared as follows:

  ```
  FUNCTION KeyOf(Item : POINTER) : POINTER; VIRTUAL;
  ```

  The `Item` parameter points to the single data element. The function value returns the pointer to the portion of that data element representing the key.

The `TSortedCollection` overrides the virtual methods `Insert` and `IndexOf`. A new virtual method, `Search`, is introduced to search for data in the ordered collections. (We discuss the `Compare`, `KeyOf`, and `Search` methods in more detail in the next program example—Listing 14.2.)

Listing 14.2 presents a non-Turbo Vision test program to examine the various aspects of sorted collections. The MKCOLCT2.PAS program is somewhat similar to MKCOLCT1.PAS. I have replaced the due-date fields in record `RTodo` and object type `TToDo` with the `WORD`-typed fields, `fPriority` and `Priority`, that serve as the sorting key. This change also affects the implementation of the `TToDo.Init` constructor and the `TToDo.Done` destructor. The MKCOLCT2.PAS program also declares the `TTaskCollection` object type as a descendant of `TSortedCollection`, as follows:

Turbo Vision Collections 14

```
TTaskCollection = OBJECT(TSortedCollection)
    FUNCTION Compare(Key1, Key2 : POINTER) : INTEGER; VIRTUAL;
    FUNCTION KeyOf(Item : POINTER) : POINTER; VIRTUAL;
END;
```

The `TTaskCollection` declares its own versions of methods `Compare` and `KeyOf`. The `Compare` method uses the WORD typecasts Key1^ and Key2^ in performing the sought comparison. The comparison is coded to arrange the collection members in ascending order.

The `KeyOf` function returns the pointer to the `Priority` data field by performing the following steps:

1. Typecasting the argument of `Item` into `PToDo`
2. Returning the `Priority` data field of its reference
3. Returning the address of the `Priority` data field

The test program declares the `TToDoList` object type, with the `PTaskCollection`-typed `DoList` data field. The declared methods of `TToDoList` are the same in MKCOLCT1.PAS as in MKCOLCT2.PAS. The method Run implements the following set of tests:

1. The `Insert` method inserts new collection members while maintaining them in ascending order. The `Insert` method used here is inherited from `TSortedCollection`. The program displays the data in the order in which it is inserted.

2. The `ForEach` method, inherited from `TCollection`, is used here to access the collection members in the order in which they are stored. The local procedure `viewAll` shows the collection of tasks ordered according to their priority number.

3. The `Search` method looks up sorted collection members. The method is declared as follows:

   ```
   FUNCTION Search(    Key   : POINTER;
                   VAR Index : INTEGER) : BOOLEAN; VIRTUAL;
   ```

   The `Key` parameter is the pointer to the key data needed for the search. The reference parameter, `Index`, returns the index of the matching member or, if no match is found, the index where the item would be inserted.

   The test program uses the `KeyOf` method to extract the key data accessed by pointer `dataPtr`. The index value is returned through the local variable j. The FOR-DO loop containing the `Search` method displays the sorted collection members in the order in which the information appears in the array `Data`.

Listing 14.2. Program MKCOLCT2.PAS, which tests various methods of the `TSortedCollection` object type.

```pascal
Program Make_Collection2;

{
 This program demonstrates using the TSortedCollection object type to
 order a group of records.

}

{$B-,V-,X+}

Uses Objects, Crt;

CONST MAX_DATA = 5;

TYPE
     STRING40 = STRING[40];

     RToDo = RECORD
        fToDo    : STRING40;
        fPriority : WORD;
     END;
     ToDoArray = ARRAY [0..MAX_DATA-1] OF RToDo;

CONST
     Data : ToDoArray = ( (fToDo : 'Lunch with John';
                           fPriority : 11),
                          (fToDo : 'Buy 486 computer';
                           fPriority : 91),
                          (fToDo : 'Sell 8086 computer';
                           fPriority : 71),
                          (fToDo : 'Write Turbo Vision Book';
                           fPriority : 51),
                          (fToDo : 'Plan trip to Paris';
                           fPriority : 31));

TYPE
     PToDo = ^TToDo;
     TToDo = OBJECT(TObject)
        ToDoStr : PString;
        Priority : WORD;
        CONSTRUCTOR Init(WhatToDo    : STRING;
                         ThePriority : WORD);
        DESTRUCTOR Done; VIRTUAL;
     END;

     PTaskCollection = ^TTaskCollection;
     TTaskCollection = OBJECT(TSortedCollection)
```

Turbo Vision Collections 14

```
            FUNCTION Compare(Key1, Key2 : POINTER) : INTEGER; VIRTUAL;
            FUNCTION KeyOf(Item : POINTER) : POINTER; VIRTUAL;
        END;

        TToDoList = OBJECT
          DoList : PTaskCollection;
          CONSTRUCTOR Init(InitialSize,
                           Increment    : WORD);
          DESTRUCTOR Done;
          PROCEDURE Run;
        END;

{ ------------------ TToDo ------------------ }

CONSTRUCTOR TToDo.Init(WhatToDo    : STRING;
                       ThePriority : WORD);
BEGIN
    ToDoStr := NewStr(WhatToDo);
    Priority := ThePriority;
END;

DESTRUCTOR TToDo.Done;
BEGIN
    DisposeStr(ToDoStr);
END;

{ ------------------ TTaskCollection ------------------ }

FUNCTION TTaskCollection.Compare(Key1, Key2 : POINTER) : INTEGER;
BEGIN
    IF WORD(Key1^) > WORD(Key2^) THEN
       Compare := 1
    ELSE IF WORD(Key1^) < WORD(Key2^) THEN
       Compare := -1
    ELSE
       Compare := 0;
END;

FUNCTION TTaskCollection.KeyOf(Item : POINTER) : POINTER;
BEGIN
    KeyOf := @PToDo(Item)^.Priority
END;

{ ------------------ TToDoList ------------------ }

CONSTRUCTOR TToDoList.Init(InitialSize,
                           Increment    : WORD);
BEGIN
    DoList := New(PTaskCollection, Init(InitialSize, Increment));
END;
```

continues

Listing 14.2. continued

```
DESTRUCTOR TToDoList.Done;
BEGIN
     Dispose(DoList, Done);
END;

PROCEDURE TToDoList.Run;

VAR i, j : INTEGER;
    dataPtr : PToDo;
    { ------------------ local routines --------------- }
    PROCEDURE wait;
    VAR akey : CHAR;
    BEGIN
         WRITELN;
         WRITE('Press any key to continue...');
         aKey := ReadKey;
         WHILE Keypressed DO
              aKey := ReadKey;
         WRITELN;
    END;

    PROCEDURE showelement(E : PToDo); FAR;
    BEGIN
         WITH E^ DO BEGIN
              WRITE(ToDoStr^);
              GotoXY(50, WhereY);
              WRITELN(Priority);
         END;
    END;

    PROCEDURE viewAll(Title : STRING);
    BEGIN
         ClrScr;
         WRITELN(Title);
         WRITELN;
         WRITELN('To-Do':20, ' ':25, 'Priority':8);
         WRITELN;
         DoList^.ForEach(@showelement);
         wait;
    END;
BEGIN { -------------------- Run --------------------- }
    TextColor(White);
    TextBackground(Blue);
    {------------------------------------------------------
                         Insert Data
    ------------------------------------------------------}
    ClrScr;
    WRITELN('Inserting the following data in the To-Do list:');
```

```
        WRITELN;
        WRITELN('To-Do':20, ' ':25, 'Priority':8);
        WRITELN;
        FOR i := 0 TO MAX_DATA-1 DO BEGIN
           WITH Data[i] DO BEGIN
              WRITE(fToDo);
              GotoXY(50, WhereY); WRITELN(fPriority);
              DoList^.Insert(New(PToDo, Init(fToDo, fPriority)));
           END;
        END;
        wait;
        {---------------------------------------------------------
           Display the collection members using the ForEach method
           (found in the nested viewAll procedure)
        ---------------------------------------------------------}
        viewAll('Display collection members using the ForEach method');
        {---------------------------------------------------------
              Obtain the indices of the collection members
              using the Search and At methods
        ---------------------------------------------------------}
        ClrScr;
        WRITELN('Testing the Search method to display entry order:');
        WRITELN;
        WRITELN(' # ','To-Do':17, ' ':25, 'Priority':8);
        WRITELN;
        WITH DoList^ DO
            FOR i := 0 TO MAX_DATA-1 DO BEGIN
                dataPtr := New(PToDo, Init(Data[i].fToDo,
                                           Data[i].fPriority));
                IF Search(KeyOf(dataptr), j) THEN BEGIN
                    Dispose(dataPtr, Done);
                    dataPtr := At(j);
                    WITH dataPtr^ DO BEGIN
                        WRITE(i:2,' : ',ToDoStr^);
                        GotoXY(50, WhereY); WRITELN(Priority);
                    END;
                END;
            END;
        wait;
END;

VAR ToDo : TToDoList;

BEGIN
    ToDo.Init(MAX_DATA, MAX_DATA DIV 2);
    ToDo.Run;
    ToDo.Done;
END.
```

Here's the output generated by the program in Listing 14.2:

```
[BEGIN Output]
Inserting the following data in the To-Do list:

            To-Do                            Priority

Lunch with John                                 11
Buy 486 computer                                91
Sell 8086 computer                              71
Write Turbo Vision Book                         51
Plan trip to Paris                              31

Press any key to continue...
```

The screen clears

```
Display collection members using the ForEach method

            To-Do                            Priority

Lunch with John                                 11
Plan trip to Paris                              31
Write Turbo Vision Book                         51
Sell 8086 computer                              71
Buy 486 computer                                91

Press any key to continue...
```

The screen clears

```
Testing the Search method to display entry order:

    #       To-Do                            Priority

    0 : Lunch with John                         11
    1 : Buy 486 computer                        91
    2 : Sell 8086 computer                      71
    3 : Write Turbo Vision Book                 51
    4 : Plan trip to Paris                      31

Press any key to continue...

[END Output]
```

Sorted String Collections

I mentioned earlier in this chapter that while collections were designed to work with descendants of TObject, they also can work with records or objects that are not descendants of TObject. (I refer to both of these types as *custom data types*.) The first non-object types that come to mind are strings. Turbo Vision offers the TStringCollection object type, a descendant of TSortedCollection, to maintain ordered lists of strings.

The declaration of TStringCollection, as well as that of any other sorted and unsorted collections of custom data type, must follow a set of rules. These rules dictate the way you must declare a certain group of methods if you want to use them with Turbo Vision applications. In the case of unordered collections, you must declare the following virtual methods:

```
PROCEDURE FreeItem(Item : POINTER); VIRTUAL;
FUNCTION GetItem(VAR S : Stream) : POINTER; VIRTUAL;
PROCEDURE PutItem(VAR S : Stream; Item : POINTER); VIRTUAL;
```

The FreeItem method is responsible for disposing of custom data types that are not descendants of TObject. The GetItem and PutItem methods ensure proper stream I/O for custom data types. (Streams are covered in Chapter 15.)

To declare sorted collections for custom data types, you need new versions of the preceding three methods, as well as the Compare method and possibly the KeyOf method. In fact, the declaration of TStringCollection comprises the FreeItem, GetItem, PutItem, and Compare methods. The KeyOf method is not needed, because the entire string also is the key for sorting and searching.

If you're using collections of custom data types in applications that are not Turbo Vision applications, you can leave out the GetItem and PutItem methods.

Listing 14.3. shows the MKCOLCT3.PAS program that uses the TStringCollection. This program is adapted from MKCOLCT2.PAS, and performs the same kinds of tests. The TToDo object type no longer is needed because the Borland Pascal string is the basic type.

Listing 14.3. Program MKCOLCT3.PAS, which tests the different methods of the TStringCollection object type.

```
Program Make_Collection3;

{
  This program demonstrates using the TStringCollection object type to
```

continues

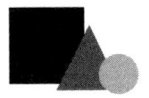

```pascal
 maintain a sorted group of strings.
}
{$B-,V-,X+}

Uses Objects, Crt;

CONST MAX_DATA = 5;

TYPE
    STRING40 = STRING[40];
    ToDoArray = ARRAY [0..MAX_DATA-1] OF STRING40;

CONST
    Data : ToDoArray = ('Lunch with John',
                       'Buy 486 computer',
                       'Sell 8086 computer',
                       'Write Turbo Vision Book',
                       'Plan trip to Paris');

TYPE
    TToDoList = OBJECT
        DoList : PStringCollection;
        CONSTRUCTOR Init(InitialSize,
                         Increment   : WORD);
        DESTRUCTOR Done;
        PROCEDURE Run;
    END;

{ -------------------- TToDoList ------------------ }

CONSTRUCTOR TToDoList.Init(InitialSize,
                           Increment   : WORD);
BEGIN
    DoList := New(PStringCollection, Init(InitialSize, Increment));
END;

DESTRUCTOR TToDoList.Done;
BEGIN
    Dispose(DoList, Done);
END;

PROCEDURE TToDoList.Run;

VAR i, j : INTEGER;
    dataPtr : PString;
    { ----------------- local routines -------------- }

    PROCEDURE wait;

    VAR aKey : CHAR;
```

Turbo Vision Collections

```pascal
    BEGIN
        WRITELN;
        WRITE('Press any key to continue...');
        aKey := ReadKey;
        WHILE Keypressed DO
            aKey := ReadKey;
        WRITELN;
    END;

    PROCEDURE showElement(E : PString); FAR;
    BEGIN
        WRITELN(E^);
    END;

    PROCEDURE viewAll(Title : STRING);
    BEGIN
        ClrScr;
        WRITELN(Title);
        WRITELN;
        WRITELN('To-Do':15);
        WRITELN;
        DoList^.ForEach(@showElement);
        wait;
    END;

BEGIN { -------------------- Run --------------------- }
    TextColor(White);
    TextBackground(Blue);
    ClrScr;
    {---------------------------------------------------
                     Insert Data
    ---------------------------------------------------}
    WRITELN('Inserting the following data in the To-Do list:');
    WRITELN;
    WRITELN('To-Do':15);
    WRITELN;
    FOR i := 0 TO MAX_DATA-1 DO BEGIN
        WRITELN(Data[i]);
        dataPtr := NewStr(Data[i]);
        DoList^.Insert(dataPtr);
    END;
    wait;
    {---------------------------------------------------
       Display the collection members using the ForEach method
       (found in the nested viewAll procedure)
    ---------------------------------------------------}
    viewAll('Display collection members using the ForEach method');
    {---------------------------------------------------
        Obtain the indices of the collection members
        using the Search and At methods
```

continues

367

Listing 14.3. continued

```
               -----------------------------------------------------------}
        ClrScr;
        WRITELN('Testing the Search method to display entry order:');
        WRITELN;
        WRITELN(' # ','To-Do':17);
        WRITELN;
        WITH DoList^ DO
            FOR i := 0 TO MAX_DATA-1 DO BEGIN
                 dataPtr := NewStr(Data[i]);
                 IF Search(KeyOf(dataptr), j) THEN BEGIN
                     DisposeStr(dataPtr);
                     dataPtr := At(j);
                     WRITELN(i:2,' : ',dataPtr^);
                 END;
            END;
       wait;
END;

VAR ToDo : TToDoList;

BEGIN
    ToDo.Init(MAX_DATA, MAX_DATA DIV 2);
    ToDo.Run;
    ToDo.Done;
END.
```

Here's the output generated by the program in Listing 14.3:

```
[BEGIN Output]
Inserting the following data in the To-Do list:

        To-Do

Lunch with John
Buy 486 computer
Sell 8086 computer
Write Turbo Vision Book
Plan trip to Paris

Press any key to continue...
```

The screen clears

```
Display collection members using the ForEach method

        To-Do
```

Turbo Vision Collections 14

```
Buy 486 computer
Lunch with John
Plan trip to Paris
Sell 8086 computer
Write Turbo Vision Book

Press any key to continue...
```

The screen clears

```
Testing the Search method to display entry order:

#              To-Do

0 : Lunch with John
1 : Buy 486 computer
2 : Sell 8086 computer
3 : Write Turbo Vision Book
4 : Plan trip to Paris

Press any key to continue...

[END Output]
```

Unsorted String Collections

Using sorted collections of strings has the advantage of fast searches. In many applications, however, the strings must be stored in the order in which they're inserted, and must not be sorted. One example of an application in which sorting the lines of text is simply out of the question is a file viewer. In Listing 14.4, I present MKCOLCT4.PAS, a program to declare and test TUnorderedStringCollection, the following unordered collection of Borland Pascal strings:

```
PUnorderedStringCollection = ^TUnorderedStringCollection;
TUnorderedStringCollection = OBJECT(TCollection)
  PROCEDURE FreeItem(P : POINTER); VIRTUAL;
END;
```

Because MKCOLCT4.PAS isn't a Turbo Vision program, I need to declare only the FreeItem method in TUnorderedStringCollection. The body of the FreeItem method contains a single statement that disposes of the object pointed to by the argument for P.

The code of the MKCOLCT4.PAS program is similar to that of MKCOLCT3.PAS in Listing 14.3—the TSortedCollection identifier has been replaced with the identifier TUnorderedStringCollection. The functionality of each program is different despite the similarity of the code.

Listing 14.4. The MKCOLCT4.PAS program, which demonstrates managing an unordered string collection.

```
Program Make_Collection4;

{
 This program demonstrates using a descendant of the TCollection
 object type to maintain a group of unordered strings.
}

{$B-,V-,X+}

Uses Objects, Crt;

CONST MAX_DATA = 5;

TYPE
     STRING40 = STRING[40];
     ToDoArray = ARRAY [0..MAX_DATA-1] OF STRING40;

CONST
     Data : ToDoArray = ('Lunch with John',
                        'Buy 486 computer',
                        'Sell 8086 computer',
                        'Write Turbo Vision Book',
                        'Plan trip to Paris');

TYPE
     PUnorderedStringCollection = ^TUnorderedStringCollection;
     TUnorderedStringCollection = OBJECT(TCollection)
         PROCEDURE FreeItem(P : POINTER); VIRTUAL;
     END;

     TToDoList = OBJECT
         DoList : PUnorderedStringCollection;
         CONSTRUCTOR Init(InitialSize,
                          Increment     : WORD);
         DESTRUCTOR Done;
         PROCEDURE Run;
     END;

{ ---------------- TUnorderedStringCollection ------------ }

PROCEDURE TUnorderedStringCollection.FreeItem(P : POINTER);
BEGIN
```

```pascal
     DisposeStr(P);
END;

{ ------------------- TToDoList ----------------- }

CONSTRUCTOR TToDoList.Init(InitialSize,
                           Increment   : WORD);
BEGIN
     DoList := New(PUnorderedStringCollection,
                   Init(InitialSize, Increment));
END;

DESTRUCTOR TToDoList.Done;
BEGIN
     Dispose(DoList, Done);
END;

PROCEDURE TToDoList.Run;

VAR i, j : INTEGER;
    dataPtr : PString;

    { ----------------- local routines -------------- }

    PROCEDURE wait;

    VAR aKey : CHAR;

    BEGIN
         WRITELN;
         WRITE('Press any key to continue...');
         aKey := ReadKey;
         WHILE Keypressed DO
              aKey := ReadKey;
         WRITELN;
    END;

    PROCEDURE showElement(E : PString); FAR;
    BEGIN
         WRITELN(E^);
    END;

    PROCEDURE viewAll(Title : STRING);
    BEGIN
         ClrScr;
         WRITELN(Title);
         WRITELN;
         WRITELN('To-Do':15);
         WRITELN;
```

continues

Listing 14.4. continued

```
            DoList^.ForEach(@showElement);
            wait;
        END;

BEGIN { -------------------- Run ---------------------- }
    TextColor(White);
    TextBackground(Blue);
    ClrScr;
    {------------------------------------------------------
                        Insert Data
     ----------------------------------------------------}
    WRITELN('Inserting the following data in the To-Do list:');
    WRITELN;
    WRITELN('To-Do':15);
    WRITELN;
    FOR i := 0 TO MAX_DATA-1 DO BEGIN
        WRITELN(Data[i]);
        dataPtr := NewStr(Data[i]);
        DoList^.Insert(dataPtr);
    END;
    wait;
    {------------------------------------------------------
      Visit and display collection members using the At method
     ----------------------------------------------------}
    ClrScr;
    WRITELN('Visit collection members using the At method');
    WRITELN;
    WRITELN(' # ','To-Do':17);
    WRITELN;
    FOR i := 0 TO DoList^.Count-1 DO BEGIN
        dataPtr := DoList^.At(i);
        WRITELN(i:2,' : ',dataPtr^);
    END;
    wait;
    {------------------------------------------------------
      Display the collection members using the ForEach method
      (found in the nested viewAll procedure)
     ----------------------------------------------------}
    viewAll('Display collection members using the ForEach method');
    {------------------------------------------------------
            Obtain the indices of the collection members
            using the IndexOf and At methods
     ----------------------------------------------------}
    ClrScr;
    WRITELN('Testing the IndexOf method to display entry order:');
    WRITELN;
    WRITELN(' # ','To-Do':17);
    WRITELN;
```

```
        WITH DoList^ DO
            FOR i := DoList^.Count-1 DOWNTO 0 DO BEGIN
                dataPtr := DoList^.At(i);
                j := DoList^.IndexOf(dataptr);
                IF j > -1 THEN BEGIN
                    WRITELN(j:2,' : ',Data[j]);
                END;
            END;
        wait;
END;
VAR ToDo : TToDoList;

BEGIN
    ToDo.Init(MAX_DATA, MAX_DATA DIV 2);
    ToDo.Run;
    ToDo.Done;
END.
```

Here's the output generated by the program in Listing 14.4:

```
[BEGIN Output]
Inserting the following data in the To-Do list:

         To-Do

Lunch with John
Buy 486 computer
Sell 8086 computer
Write Turbo Vision Book
Plan trip to Paris

Press any key to continue...
```

The screen clears

```
Visit collection members using the At method

  #            To-Do

 0 : Lunch with John
 1 : Buy 486 computer
 2 : Sell 8086 computer
 3 : Write Turbo Vision Book
 4 : Plan trip to Paris

Press any key to continue...
```

The screen clears

```
Display collection members using the ForEach method

        To-Do

Lunch with John
Buy 486 computer
Sell 8086 computer
Write Turbo Vision Book
Plan trip to Paris

Press any key to continue...
```

The screen clears

```
Testing the IndexOf method to display entry order:

  #             To-Do

  4 : Plan trip to Paris
  3 : Write Turbo Vision Book
  2 : Sell 8086 computer
  1 : Buy 486 computer
  0 : Lunch with John

Press any key to continue...
[END Output]
```

Summary

This chapter presented the collection as a versatile data structure, an indexible list structure. You learned about the following topics:

- Turbo Vision presents the object type TCollection to models unordered collections. These collections store data items of the same or of different types. The data items are stored in no particular order.

- Turbo Vision offers the object type TSortedCollection, which represents sorted collections. These collections store data items in an ordered fashion. To enforce this order, the data types of the inserted items must have sort-key fields.

- Turbo Vision offers the TStringCollection object type as a descendant of TSortedCollection, to maintain ordered lists of strings. You also can create an object type to store unordered strings.

Chapter 15

Persistent Objects and Streams

File input and output is vital to storing a wide variety of data. When I began to learn programming in Pascal, I used the TEXT-based file I/O with the WRITE, WRITELN, READ, and READLN intrinsics. I later mastered the use of FILE OF <type> files to store and access records in random-access binary files. As I got more comfortable with programming in Turbo Pascal, I began to use the BlockWrite and BlockRead procedures to save mixed data types in the same binary file. You can use the intrinsics BlockRead and BlockWrite to store and recall the objects that model classes. This approach works fine when the object variables belong to a simple hierarchy. Performing file I/O with a complex object-type hierarchy like that of Turbo Vision requires a radically different solution. Fortunately, part of the Turbo Vision hierarchy—streams—provides this solution.

Streams enable you to store and recall various instances of object types (also called *persistent objects*), taking into account the Virtual Method Table (VMT) information. (Chapter 1 has more information about VMT.) Without using streams, writing VMT data to a file is meaningless—and reading it back is, in the words of a famous science fiction character, illogical!

This chapter explores the following aspects of streams:

- The features of streams
- The TStream subhierarchy
- The Load and Store methods
- Object-type registration
- The StrmErr library unit
- Sequential stream I/O
- Random-access stream I/O
- Polymorphic streams
- Streams and collections

The Features of Streams

The concept of object-oriented streams is borrowed from the C++ language to implement file I/O for C++ classes. Turbo Vision streams offer polymorphic file I/O to the descendants of TObject, giving you the best of both untyped and typed file I/O. Type checking occurs at run time to accommodate the dynamic nature of object-type instances. Because VMT data properly is stored and retrieved from a stream, streams can store not only Turbo Vision object types, but also their user-defined descendants, which are not yet declared! This is made possible by a simple task called *registration*, which we discuss later in this chapter.

The TStream Subhierarchy

The Turbo Vision hierarchy contains the `TStream` subhierarchy, shown here:

```
TStream --------------- TDosStream ------------- TBufStream
        |
        |-------- TEmsStream
        |
        |-------- TMemoryStream
```

The declaration for the `TStream` object type and its descendants are shown Listing 15.1. (This listing also includes the declaration of the special `TStreamRec` record type used in object-type registration, described later.)

Listing 15.1. The declaration of the `TStream` subhierarchy.

```
PStreamRec = ^TStreamRec;
TStreamRec = record
  ObjType: Word;
  VmtLink: Word;
  Load: Pointer;
  Store: Pointer;
  Next: Word;
end;

PStream = ^TStream;
TStream = object(TObject)
  Status: Integer;
  ErrorInfo: Integer;
  constructor Init;
  procedure CopyFrom(var S: TStream; Count: Longint);
  procedure Error(Code, Info: Integer); virtual;
  procedure Flush; virtual;
  function Get: PObject;
  function GetPos: Longint; virtual;
  function GetSize: Longint; virtual;
  procedure Put(P: PObject);
  procedure Read(var Buf; Count: Word); virtual;
  function ReadStr: PString;
  procedure Reset;
  procedure Seek(Pos: Longint); virtual;
  function StrRead: PChar;
  procedure StrWrite(P: PChar);
  procedure Truncate; virtual;
```

continues

Listing 15.1. continued

```pascal
    procedure Write(var Buf; Count: Word); virtual;
    procedure WriteStr(P: PString);
  end;

{ DOS file name string }
{$IFDEF Windows}
  FNameStr = PChar;
{$ELSE}
  FNameStr = string[79];
{$ENDIF}

  PDosStream = ^TDosStream;
  TDosStream = object(TStream)
    Handle: Word;
    constructor Init(FileName: FNameStr; Mode: Word);
    destructor Done; virtual;
    function GetPos: Longint; virtual;
    function GetSize: Longint; virtual;
    procedure Read(var Buf; Count: Word); virtual;
    procedure Seek(Pos: Longint); virtual;
    procedure Truncate; virtual;
    procedure Write(var Buf; Count: Word); virtual;
  end;

  PBufStream = ^TBufStream;
  TBufStream = object(TDosStream)
    Buffer: Pointer;
    BufSize: Word;
    BufPtr: Word;
    BufEnd: Word;
    constructor Init(FileName: FNameStr; Mode, Size: Word);
    destructor Done; virtual;
    procedure Flush; virtual;
    function GetPos: Longint; virtual;
    function GetSize: Longint; virtual;
    procedure Read(var Buf; Count: Word); virtual;
    procedure Seek(Pos: Longint); virtual;
    procedure Truncate; virtual;
    procedure Write(var Buf; Count: Word); virtual;
  end;

  PEmsStream = ^TEmsStream;
  TEmsStream = object(TStream)
    Handle: Word;
    PageCount: Word;
    Size: Longint;
    Position: Longint;
```

```
  constructor Init(MinSize, MaxSize: Longint);
  destructor Done; virtual;
  function GetPos: Longint; virtual;
  function GetSize: Longint; virtual;
  procedure Read(var Buf; Count: Word); virtual;
  procedure Seek(Pos: Longint); virtual;
  procedure Truncate; virtual;
  procedure Write(var Buf; Count: Word); virtual;
end;

PMemoryStream = ^TMemoryStream;
TMemoryStream = object(TStream)
  SegCount: Integer;
  SegList: PWordArray;
  CurSeg: Integer;
  BlockSize: Integer;
  Size: Longint;
  Position: Longint;
  constructor Init(ALimit: Longint; ABlockSize: Word);
  destructor Done; virtual;
  function GetPos: Longint; virtual;
  function GetSize: Longint; virtual;
  procedure Read(var Buf; Count: Word); virtual;
  procedure Seek(Pos: Longint); virtual;
  procedure Truncate; virtual;
  procedure Write(var Buf; Count: Word); virtual;
private
  function ChangeListSize(ALimit: Word): Boolean;
end;
```

TStream itself is an abstract object type and possesses no constructor or destructor. It declares two data fields: Status and ErrorInfo. The Status field stores the error status of the stream. Turbo Vision predefines the following stXXXX constants as stream error codes:

Error Code	Value	Meaning
stOK	0	No stream error
stError	−1	Stream-access error
stInitError	−2	Cannot initialize stream
stReadError	−3	Read beyond end of the stream
stWriteError	−4	Failed to expand stream
stGetError	−5	Get an unregistered object type
stPutError	−6	Put an unregistered object type

Turbo Vision also predefines the following stXXXX constants that specify the stream access modes:

Access Mode	Value	Meaning
stCreate	$3C00	Create a new file
stOpenRead	$3D00	Open existing file for read-only
stOpenWrite	$3D01	Open existing file for write-only
stOpen	$3D02	Open existing file to read and write

The value of the Status field should be examined after each stream I/O operation vulnerable to error. The ErrorInfo data field offers DOS or EMS error codes when the Status field is stError, stInitError, stReadError, or stWriteError. When the Status field is stGetError, the ErrorInfo stores the object type ID (the value of the ObjType data field in record TStreamRec) of the offending unregistered object type. When Status is stPutError, ErrorInfo stores the VMT data-segment offset (the VmtLink field of the TStreamRec record) of the offending unregistered object type. Listing 15.2 shows the StrmErr library unit that exports the following routines:

1. The GetStreamError function returns a string that describes the current error status of stream S. If the S.Status is stOK, a null string is returned.

2. The Boolean SayStreamError function displays the result of function GetStreamError in a message box with an OK button. The SayStreamError returns true if S.Status is not stOK, and returns false otherwise.

3. The Boolean TellStreamError function, an advanced version of function SayStreamError, allows you to include text before and after the result of the GetStreamError function (to enhance the wording of the error-message box).

Listing 15.2. The STRMERR.PAS library unit.

```
UNIT StrmErr;

{======================================================================
          Copyright (c) 1989, 1990    Namir Clement Shammas

     LIBRARY NAME: StrmErr

     VERSION:  1.0.0                                      DATE 4/8/1991

     PURPOSE: Exports functions that translate stream errors
              into text (in optional dialog boxes).


=======================================================================}
```

```
{$X+}
{*********************************************************************}
{*************************} INTERFACE {******************************}
{*********************************************************************}

Uses Objects;

    FUNCTION GetStreamErrorString(VAR S : TStream) : STRING;
    FUNCTION SayStreamError(VAR S : TStream) : BOOLEAN;
    FUNCTION TellStreamError(VAR S         : TStream;
                                 PreMessage,
                                 PostMessage : STRING) : BOOLEAN;

{*********************************************************************}
{***********************} IMPLEMENTATION {***************************}
{*********************************************************************}

Uses MsgBox;

FUNCTION GetStreamErrorString(VAR S : TStream) : STRING;

VAR errStr : STRING;

BEGIN
    CASE S.Status OF
        stError     :
                errStr := 'Access error';
        stInitError :
                errStr := 'Cannot initialize stream';
        stReadError :
                errStr := 'Cannot read beyond end of stream';
        stWriteError :
                errStr := 'Cannot expand stream';
        stGetError  :
                errStr := 'Get of unregistered object type';
        stPutError  :
                errStr := 'Put of unregistered object type';
        ELSE
                errStr := '';
    END;
        GetStreamErrorstring := errStr;
END;

FUNCTION SayStreamError(VAR S : TStream) : BOOLEAN;

VAR message : STRING;
```

continues

Listing 15.2. continued

```
BEGIN
    message := GetStreamErrorString(S);
    IF message <> '' THEN
        MessageBox(message, NIL, mfError + mfOKButton);
    SayStreamError := S.Status <> stOK;
END;

FUNCTION TellStreamError(VAR S                      : TStream;
                            PreMessage,
                            PostMessage : STRING) : BOOLEAN;

VAR message : STRING;

BEGIN
    message := GetStreamErrorString(S);
    IF message <> '' THEN
        MessageBox(PreMessage + message + PostMessage,
                   NIL, mfError + mfOKButton);
    TellStreamError := S.Status <> stOK;
END;

END.
```

TStream methods fall into the following categories:

- Object type I/O provided by the Put and Get methods
- Data field I/O implemented by the Write and Read methods
- Special string I/O offered by the WriteStr and ReadStr methods
- Random-access I/O provided by the GetPos, GetSize, and Seek methods
- Stream copying with the CopyFrom method
- Error handling with the Error and Reset methods
- Other miscellaneous methods, such as Truncate and Flush

The TStream object type is used in the Load constructor and Store method declared in the majority of Turbo Vision object types. The Load constructor enables you to create an object type instance that previously was saved to a stream, using the Store method.

Persistent Objects and Streams 15

> ☞ If a stream error occurs, all further stream operations are suspended. Your application must send a Reset message to clear the stream-error condition.

The TDosStream object type implements an unbuffered stream for DOS files. This object type is adequate if you're sending data to a stream in big chunks. By contrast, sending a great deal of data in small chunks benefits more from the buffered DOS-file stream object type, TBufStream. The TDosStream object type declares a file-handle data field, Handle, and overrides some of the TStream methods. The TBufStream object type declares additional data fields to manage the buffer allocated at run time.

The TEmsStream object type is another descendant of TStream that stores data in the EMS memory. This object type enables you to perform a fast stream I/O with EMS memory. You can use the CopyFrom method to copy a stream from a DOS file to EMS memory for faster access. The following code fragment shows how easy it is to copy a DOS stream to an EMS stream:

```
TheEmsStream := New(TEmsStream, Init(TheDosStream^.GetSize));
TheDosStream^.Seek(0);
TheEmsStream.CopyFrom(TheDosStream, TheDosStream^.GetSize);
```

Copying to a buffered stream is no more difficult than from a TDosStream.

The Load and Store Methods

Each user-defined descendant of TObject can be made streamable. This involves declaring the constructor Load and method Store. The general syntax for the Load constructor is

```
CONSTRUCTOR <DescendantOfTObject>.Load(VAR S : TStream);
BEGIN

  [<parentObjectType>.Load(S);]
  S.Read(<data_field_1>, SizeOf(<data_field_1>)
  S.Read(<data_field_2>, SizeOf(<data_field_2>)
     .....
  S.Read(<data_field_n>, SizeOf(<data_field_n>)
END;
```

Invoking the parent's Load constructor usually is required, except for TObject. The Read messages are sent to the stream S to read the various data fields declared in the user-defined object type. Each Read message has two arguments: the input value for a data field and the corresponding byte size. The general syntax for the Store method is

```
PROCEDURE <DescendantOfTObject>.Store(VAR S : TStream);
BEGIN

   [<parentObjectType>.Store(S);]
   S.Write(<data_field_1>, SizeOf(<data_field_1>)
   S.Write(<data_field_2>, SizeOf(<data_field_2>)
     .....
   S.Write(<data_field_n>, SizeOf(<data_field_n>)
END;
```

The Write messages are sent to the stream S to write the data fields to the streams. The arguments for the Write method resemble those of the Read method.

As an example, consider the following simple object type, TComplex:

```
PComplex = ^TComplex;
TComplex = OBJECT(TObject)
    Xreal,
    Yimag : REAL;
    CONSTRUCTOR Init(X, Y : REAL);
    CONSTRUCTOR Load(VAR S : TStream);
    PROCEDURE Show;
    PROCEDURE Store(VAR S : TStream); VIRTUAL;
END;
```

To make TComplex streamable, the object type is declared as a descendant of TObject. The user-defined object type defines the Load constructor and the Store method, as follows:

```
CONSTRUCTOR TComplex.Load(VAR S : TStream);
BEGIN
   S.Read(Xreal, SizeOf(Xreal));
   S.Read(Yimag, SizeOf(Yimag));
END;

PROCEDURE TComplex.Store(VAR S : TStream);
BEGIN
   S.Write(Xreal, SizeOf(Xreal));
   S.Write(Yimag, SizeOf(Yimag));
END;
```

The TComplex object type is used in the demonstration program MKSTRM1.PAS, shown in Listing 15.3.

PROGRAMMING TIP:

A user-defined object type that uses data fields to store dynamic arrays (except strings) should have additional data fields that store the actual—and possibly the maximum—sizes of the dynamic arrays. These size-data fields should be read before the dynamic array is read. For example, consider the following object type that models a dynamic array of REALs:

```
TRealArray = OBJECT(TObject)
  MaxSize  : WORD;
  WorkSize : WORD;
  DataPtr  : Pointer;
  CONSTRUCTOR Init(TheMaxSize : WORD);
  CONSTRUCTOR Load(VAR S : TStream);
  { other methods }
  PROCEDURE Store(VAR S : TStream);
END;

CONSTRUCTOR TRealArray.Load(VAR S : TStream);
BEGIN
  S.Read(MaxSize, SizeOf(MaxSize));
  S.Read(WorkSize, SizeOf(WorkSize));
  GetMem(DataPtr, MaxSize * SizeOf(REAL));
  S.Read(DataPtr^, WorkSize * SizeOf(REAL));
END;
    PROCEDURE TRealArray.Store(VAR S : TStream);
    BEGIN
      S.Write(MaxSize, SizeOf(MaxSize));
      S.Write(WorkSize, SizeOf(WorkSize));
      S.Write(DataPtr^, WorkSize * SizeOf(REAL));
    END;
```

The Store method first writes the MaxSize and WorkSize data fields to the stream and then sends WorkSize elements of the dynamic array. The constructor Load reads the MaxSize and WorkSize data fields. It uses the obtained value of MaxSize to allocate the space for the entire dynamic array. The value of the WorkSize field is used to read the elements of the dynamic array from the stream.

Object-Type Registration

Object-type registration—a two-step process for user-defined object types—is essential for any stream I/O. In the first step, you declare a TStreamRec-typed constant for the descendant of Turbo Vision object types you create. These typed constants assign values to the first four TStreamRec data fields. The ObjType field is assigned a unique ID for the object type. The VmtLink is assigned the VMT offset segment to the object type. The Load and Store fields are pointers to the methods that load and store the stream (typically, Load and Store). In the case of TComplex, the corresponding TStreamRec-typed constant is declared as follows:

```
RComplex : TStreamRec = (
    ObjType : 150;
    VmtLink : Ofs(TypeOf(TComplex)^);
    Load : @TComplex.Load ;
    Store: @TComplex.Store);
```

The TypeOf function is a special function used in obtaining the VMT address of an object type.

You need not declare the StreamRec-typed constants for the Turbo Vision object types. This already is done in the various Turbo Vision library units. The second step in stream registration, however, is required by all descendants of TObject that are involved in stream I/O. This step involves calling the RegisterType procedure to register the various TStreamRec-type records. In the case of TComplex, the following call is needed:

```
RegisterType(RComplex);
```

To make the registration of its object types a bit easier, Turbo Vision provides a number of RegisterXXXX procedures to register the various groups of object types. Table 15.1 lists the RegisterXXXX procedures for Turbo Vision object types and their standard extensions.

Table 15.1. The **RegisterXXXX** procedures for the Turbo Vision object types and their standard extensions.

RegisterXXXX Procedure	Object Type	Object ID
RegisterApp	TBackground	30
	TDeskTop	31
RegisterColorSel	TColorSelector	21
	TMonoSelector	22

Persistent Objects and Streams — 15

RegisterXXXX Procedure	Object Type	Object ID
	TColorDisplay	23
	TColorGroupList	24
	TColorItemList	25
	TColorDialog	26
RegisterDialogs	TDialog	10
	TInputLine	11
	TButton	12
	TCluster	13
	TRadioButtons	14
	TCheckBoxes	15
	TListBox	16
	TStaticText	17
	TLabel	18
	THistory	19
	TParamText	20
RegisterEditors	TEditor	70
	TMemo	71
	TFileEditor	72
	TIndicator	73
	TFileWindow	74
RegisterMenus	TMenuBar	40
	TMenuBox	41
	TStatusLine	42
RegisterObjects	TCollection	50
	TStringCollection	51
RegisterStdDlg	TFileInputLine	60
	TFileCollection	61
	TFileList	62
	TFileInfoPane	63
	TFileDialog	64
	TDirCollection	65
	TDirListBox	66
	TChDirDialog	67
RegisterViews	TView	1
	TFrame	2

continues

387

Table 15.1. continued

RegisterXXXX Procedure	Object Type	Object ID
RegisterViews	TScrollBar	3
	TScroller	4
	TListViewer	5
	TGroup	6
	TWindow	7

I recommend that you register the different object types at the beginning of the main program section or within the constructor of the application object type, if one is declared to accommodate other purposes. Either approach permits you to use the Load constructors to instantiate various object types.

Sequential Stream I/O

Having covered the different aspects of preparing an object type for stream I/O, let's look into the actual process of stream I/O, beginning with sequential input and output.

First come the general steps for sequentially writing object instances to a stream. After registering the object types involved, open the stream. (This step is similar to opening a file.) The following is the general form for the TDosStream and TBufStream object types:

```
<aStream>.Init(<filename>, stCreate);                    { TDosStream }
<aStream>.Init(<filename>, stCreate, <buffer_size>);     { TBufStream }
```

The stCreate mode creates a new file if one does not exist. If the file exists, it is first deleted and then created.

Next, to verify that the stream is properly opened, check the Status field or use the SayStreamError function exported by the StrmErr library unit, as follows:

```
IF <aStream>.Status <> stOK THEN <handle_error>
IF GetStreamError(<aStream>) THEN <handle_error>
```

Then, put the object instances in the stream, using a battery of Put messages:

```
<aStream>.Put(<PointerToObjectTypeInstance>);
```

Persistent Objects and Streams 15

This message writes the object instances sequentially to a stream. Checking the Status field of the stream is recommended, at least during the development phase of your Turbo Vision applications. When you've finished writing to the stream, close it, as follows:

```
Dispose(<aStream>, Done);
```

The sequence of steps for reading from a stream is similar to the sequence of steps for writing to it. After registering the object types involved, open the stream. The following is the general form for opening the TDosStream and TBufStream object types:

```
<aStream>.Init(<filename>, stOpenRead);{ TDosStream }
<aStream>.Init(<filename>, stOpenRead, <buffer_size>);{ TBufStream }
```

The stOpenRead mode ensures that the stream is read-only.

Next, to verify that the stream is properly opened, check the Status field or use the SayStreamError function exported by the StrmErr library unit, as follows:

```
IF <aStream>.Status <> stOK THEN <handle_error>
IF SayStreamError(<aStream>) THEN <handle_error>
```

Read the object instances from the stream, using a battery of Get messages:

```
<PointerToObjectTypeInstance>:=<ObjectPointerType>(<aStream>.Get);
```

This reads the object instances sequentially from a stream. As with stream output, it's a good step to check the Status field of the stream. Finally, close the stream when you've finished writing to it, as follows:

```
Dispose(<aStream>, Done);
```

You may be wondering about the connection between the Load and Store methods and the Put and Get methods. After all, the Load constructor and Store method are needed to make an object streamable. However, when the time comes to perform stream I/O, the Get and Put methods are used. The following pseudocode explains what happens when a stream receives a Put message, and how the Store method is involved. Similarly, this pseudocode explains what happens when a stream receives a Get message.

```
Obtain the ID from the stream

Search the list of registered object types for a matching ID
If no match is found then raise the stGetError condition and stop
Get the VMT data and Load methods from the registration record
Use the Load method to read the instance from the stream
```

Obtain the VMT pointer from offset 0 of the object type Search for a match in the list of registered types. If no match is found, raise the stPutError condition and stop Get the ID of the matching object type. Write the ID to the stream. Invoke the Store method to write the instance of the object type.

> **PROGRAMMING TIP**
>
> You can place NIL objects in a stream. Such objects can be used as an end-of-objects marker when reading the stream. NIL objects have a 0 ID.

Listing 15.3 shows MKSTRM1.PAS, a non-Turbo Vision program that demonstrates both sequential and random-access stream I/O with instances of the same object type. Let's focus on the sequential I/O for now. The program declares the TComplex object type as a descendant of TObject. The TComplex object type (which I presented earlier in this chapter) declares the Init and Load constructors, a Show method, and a Store method. You can assign values to the data fields of TComplex by using either of the constructors. The Show method displays the value of the Xreal and Yimag data fields.

Listing 15.3. Program MKSTRM1.PAS, which demonstrates both sequential and random-access stream I/O for instances of the same object type.

```
Program Make_Stream1;

{
 This program illustrates sequential and random access streams of
 a small object type based on TObject.
}

{$B-,V-,X+}

Uses Objects, StrmErr, Crt;

CONST BUFFER_SIZE = 1024;
      FILENAME    = 'MKSTRM1.STM';

TYPE
     ComplexRec = RECORD
             Reel : REAL;
             Imag : REAL;
     END;
```

Persistent Objects and Streams

```
    PComplex = ^TComplex;
    TComplex = OBJECT(TObject)
        Xreal,
        Yimag : REAL;
        CONSTRUCTOR Init(X, Y : REAL);
        CONSTRUCTOR Load(VAR S : TStream);
        PROCEDURE Show;
        PROCEDURE Store(VAR S : TStream); VIRTUAL;
    END;

CONST
    RComplex : TStreamRec = (
        ObjType : 150;
        VmtLink : Ofs(TypeOf(TComplex)^);
        Load    : @TComplex.Load;
        Store   : @TComplex.Store
    );

    MAX = 5;
    { array that internally provides data }
    Data : ARRAY [1..MAX] OF ComplexRec =
        ( (Reel : 1.0; Imag : 1.0),
          (Reel : 2.0; Imag : 2.0),
          (Reel : 3.0; Imag : 3.0),
          (Reel : 4.0; Imag : 4.0),
          (Reel : 5.0; Imag : 5.0) );

{ ----------------------- TComplex ---------------------- }

CONSTRUCTOR TComplex.Init(X, Y : REAL);
BEGIN
    Xreal := X;
    Yimag := Y;
END;

CONSTRUCTOR TComplex.Load(VAR S : TStream);
BEGIN
    S.Read(Xreal, SizeOf(Xreal));
    S.Read(Yimag, SizeOf(Yimag));
END;

PROCEDURE TComplex.Show;
BEGIN
    IF Xreal > 0 THEN
        WRITE(Xreal:1:0,' + i')
    ELSE
        WRITE('(', Xreal:1:0,') + i');
    IF Yimag > 0 THEN
        WRITELN(YImag:1:0)
    ELSE
```

continues

Listing 15.3. continued

```
        WRITELN('(', Yimag:1:0,')');
END;

PROCEDURE TComplex.Store(VAR S : TStream);
BEGIN
    S.Write(Xreal, SizeOf(Xreal));
    S.Write(Yimag, SizeOf(Yimag));
END;

PROCEDURE Run;

VAR aKey : CHAR;
    i : BYTE;
    p : ARRAY [1..MAX] OF PComplex;
    posIndex : ARRAY [1..MAX] OF LONGINT;
    appStream : TBufStream;

    PROCEDURE initObjects;
    VAR i : BYTE;
    BEGIN
        FOR i := 1 TO MAX DO
            p[i] := New(PComplex, Init(Data[i].Reel,
                                       Data[i].Imag));
    END;

    PROCEDURE disposeObjects;
    VAR i : BYTE;
    BEGIN
        FOR i := 1 TO MAX DO BEGIN
            Dispose(p[i]);
            p[i] := NIL;
        END;
    END;

    PROCEDURE showObjects;
    VAR i : BYTE;
    BEGIN
        WRITELN('Data is: ');
        FOR i := 1 TO MAX DO
            p[i]^.Show;
        WRITELN;
    END;

    PROCEDURE putObjects;
    VAR i : BYTE;
    BEGIN
        FOR i := 1 TO MAX DO
            appStream.Put(p[i]);
    END;
```

Persistent Objects and Streams 15

```
    PROCEDURE getObjects;
    VAR i : BYTE;
    BEGIN
        FOR i := 1 TO MAX DO
            p[i] := PComplex(appStream.Get);
    END;

BEGIN
    ClrScr;
    initObjects; { create dynamic array of TComplex instances }
    WRITELN('Storing data sequentially to the stream');
    showObjects;
    { open file to write data }
    appStream.Init(FILENAME, stCreate, BUFFER_SIZE);
    IF SayStreamError(appStream) THEN BEGIN
        disposeObjects;
        Halt(1);
    END;
    putObjects;
    disposeObjects;
    appStream.Done;
    { open stream for sequential input }
    appStream.Init(FILENAME, stOpenRead, BUFFER_SIZE);
    IF SayStreamError(appStream) THEN
        Halt(1);
    WRITELN('Reading data sequentially from the stream');
    getObjects;
    showObjects;
    disposeObjects;
    appStream.Done;
    WRITE('Press any key...');
    aKey := ReadKey; WRITELN; WRITELN;
    { open stream to random-access read and write }
    appStream.Init(FILENAME, stOpen, BUFFER_SIZE);
    IF SayStreamError(appStream) THEN
        Halt(1);
    { mark the position of each object in the stream }
    FOR i := 1 TO MAX DO BEGIN
        posIndex[i] := appStream.GetPos;
        p[i] := PComplex(appStream.Get);
    END;
    WRITELN('Reading 2nd and 4th members');
    appStream.Seek(posIndex[2]);
    Dispose(p[2]);
    p[2] := NIL;
    p[2] := PComplex(appStream.Get);
    appStream.Seek(posIndex[4]);
    Dispose(p[4]);
    p[4] := NIL;
```

continues

Listing 15.3. continued

```
    p[4] := PComplex(appStream.Get);
    p[2]^.Show;
    p[4]^.Show;
    WRITELN;
    WRITELN('Writing 2nd and 4th members to 3rd and 5th members');
    appStream.Seek(posIndex[3]);
    appStream.Put(p[2]);
    appStream.Seek(posIndex[5]);
    appStream.Put(p[4]);
    disposeObjects;
    appStream.Seek(0); { go back to the beginning of the stream }
    getObjects; { re-read the objects }
    showObjects;
    disposeObjects;
    appStream.Done;
    WRITELN;
    WRITE('Press any key...');
    aKey := ReadKey; WRITELN;
END;

BEGIN
    RegisterType(RComplex);
    Run;
END.
```

The program also declares the TStreamRec-typed constant RComplex, to register TComplex for stream I/O. The stream registration is performed by the first statement in the main program section. The program also declares the ComplexRec record to supply demonstration data internally. The typed constant array Data contains five ComplexRec elements.

The Run procedure demonstrates the various stream I/O operations. It declares an array of MAX pointers (p) to TComplex, and a buffered stream (appStream). The Run procedure also contains a number of nested routines that are used repeatedly to initialize, display, and dispose of the dynamic instances of TComplex.

The program performs the following tasks to demonstrate sequential stream I/O:

1. Calls the nested procedure initObjects to create the MAX instances of TComplex, and initializes them with the Reel and Imag fields of Data[i]

2. Invokes the showObjects to display the contents of the dynamic instances of TComplex

3. Opens a 1K buffered stream and creates a new file, MKSTRM1.STM

4. Examines the error status of the stream with a call to function SayStreamError, exported by the StrmErr unit. If the function result is true, the nested procedure disposeObjects is called and the program then is halted.

5. Invokes the nested procedure putObjects to store the TComplex instances by sending a Put message to stream appStream, as follows:

```
PROCEDURE putObjects;
VAR i : BYTE;
BEGIN
    FOR i := 1 TO MAX DO
        appStream.Put(p[i]);
END;
```

6. Calls the nested disposeObjects procedure to eliminate the dynamic instances of TComplex and assign NILs to the elements of array p.

7. Closes the stream AppStream by sending it a Done message.

8. Reopens the buffered stream in the stOpenRead access mode:

```
appStream.Init(FILENAME, stOpenRead, BUFFER_SIZE);
```

9. Examines the error status of the stream by using function SayStreamError; if the result is True, the program halts

10. Uses the nested procedure getObjects to read the instances of TComplex from the stream. The Get messages are sent to the stream appStream to obtain the sought instances. The result of Get is typecast with PComplex, as follows:

```
PROCEDURE getObjects;
VAR i : BYTE;
BEGIN
    FOR i := 1 TO MAX DO
        p[i] := PComplex(appStream.Get);
END;
```

11. Invokes the nested showObject procedure to display the TComplex instances by sending them TComplex.Show messages. The displayed values should match those shown earlier. Both sets of data appear on the same screen for comparison.

12. Calls the nested procedure disposeObjects to dispose of the TComplex instances.

13. Closes the stream by sending a Done message to appStream.

Here's the output generated by the program in Listing 15.3:

```
[BEGIN Output]
Storing data sequentially to the stream
Data is:
1 + i1
2 + i2
3 + i3
4 + i4
5 + i5

Reading data sequentially from the stream
Data is:
1 + i1
2 + i2
3 + i3
4 + i4
5 + i5

Press any key...

Reading 2nd and 4th members
2 + i2
4 + i4

Writing 2nd and 4th members to 3rd and 5th members
Data is:
1 + i1
2 + i2
2 + i2
4 + i4
4 + i4


Press any key...
[END Output]
```

Random-Access Stream I/O

The TStream subhierarchy supports random-access stream I/O. The general steps involved are detailed in this section. First, register the involved object types; then, open the stream. The following is the general form for the TDosStream and TBufStream object types:

```
<aStream>.Init(<filename>, stOpen);{ TDosStream }
<aStream>.Init(<filename>, stOpen, <buffer_size>);{ TBufStream }
```

The stOpen mode creates a new file if one does not exist.

Persistent Objects and Streams

Next, verify that the stream is properly opened, by checking the Status field or by using the SayStreamError function exported by the StrmErr library unit, as follows:

```
IF <aStream>.Status <> stOK THEN <handle_error>
IF SayStreamError(<aStream>) THEN <handle_error>
```

Move the stream pointer to a specific byte location to read or write an instance of an object type. The Seek method positions you at the specified byte location:

```
<aStream>.Seek(<byte_location>)
```

The beginning of the stream is position 0. The GetPos method enables you to query the current location:

```
I_Am_Here := <aStream>.GetPos;
```

Write an object instance in the current location in the stream, using a Put message:

```
<aStream>.Put(<PointerToObjectTypeInstance>);
```

Next, read an object instance from the current location in the stream, using a Get message:

```
<PointerToObjectTypeInstance>:=<ObjectPointerType>(<aStream>.Get);
```

Finally, close the stream when you're finished with stream I/O, as follows:

```
Dispose(<aStream>, Done);
```

The location of each instance can be stored in a dynamic array or collection.

Program MKSTRM1.PAS also demonstrates random-access stream I/O, using the data previously stored in the sequential stream I/O test. The program performs the following steps to illustrate random-access stream I/O:

1. Opens the buffered stream with an stOpen mode, as follows:

   ```
   appStream.Init(FILENAME, stOpen, BUFFER_SIZE);
   ```

2. Checks the stream status, using the function SayStreamError. If the function returns true, the program halts.

3. Marks the positions where the first byte of each instance is located, using the following FOR loop:

   ```
   FOR i := 1 TO MAX DO BEGIN
       posIndex[i] := appStream.GetPos;
       p[i] := PComplex(appStream.Get);
   END;
   ```

The Run method uses the local array posIndex to store the values returned by appStream.GetPos. The loop also retrieves the instances of TComplex in sequence.

4. Reads the second and fourth collection members. A Seek(posIndex[2]) message is sent to stream appStream, asking that it position the stream pointer to byte posIndex[2]. The p[2] instance is disposed of before a Get message is sent to appStream, to reread the second instance. A similar set of statements is used to retrieve the fourth element. The Show message is sent to the second and fourth instances, requesting that they display the values of their Xreal and Yimag data fields.

5. Overwrites the third and fifth elements with the second and fourth elements, respectively. The Seek(posIndex[3]) message is sent to stream appStream requesting that it position the stream pointer at the posIndex[3] byte location. Next, the Put(p[2]) message is sent to appStream, causing the second instance to overwrite the third instance in the stream (the third instance in the memory remains intact for now). A similar set of statements is used to overwrite the fifth element in the stream with the fourth one in memory.

6. Disposes of the instances of TComplex, using the nested procedure disposeObjects.

7. Moves the stream pointer to the beginning of the stream by sending a Seek(0) message to appStream.

8. Reads the instances from the stream in sequence, using getObjects, and displays their data using the showObjects procedure. The second and third instances now have the same data, and so do the fourth and fifth instances.

9. Disposes of the TComplex instances and closes the stream.

> **TIP**
>
> Assuming that you have EMS memory on your system, modify the MKSTRM1.PAS program to use TEmsStream.

Polymorphic Streams

Program MKSTRM1.PAS handles different instances of the same object types. The steps used for sequential or random-access stream I/O also are used for storing and retrieving instances of multiple object types. The only thing to watch out for is the fact that you're dealing with mixed types.

Listing 15.4 contains the source code for program MKSTRM2.PAS. The program declares two descendants of TObjects, T2D and T3D, that model two- and three-dimensional coordinates. The program is somewhat similar to MKSTRM1.PAS. It creates a stream with three instances of T2D and two instances of T3D, written intermittently. The program also performs random-access on the instances of T3D.

The T2D object type, which is similar to TComplex of program MKSTRM1.PAS, declares two floating-point data fields (X and Y), as well as the data field Name (a pointer to a string). The Load constructor and Store method are relevant to this example. The Store method sends a WriteStr message to stream S, to write the dynamic string Name^. The X and Y data fields are written using the Write methods presented in program MKSTRM1.PAS. The Load constructor sends a ReadStr message to stream S to obtain the dynamic string, accessed by pointer Name. Notice that the ReadStr statement does not need an explicit New or NewStr, because the dynamic allocation is performed by the message ReadStr.

The T3D object type is a descendant of T2D, adding the Z data field to model a three-dimensional point. The T3D.Store method invokes the T2D.Store method to write the data for Name^, X, and Y. The method then sends a Write(Z, SizeOf(Z)) message to the stream S to write the Z data field. Similarly, the constructor T3D.Load invokes the T2D.Load constructor to obtain the data for the Name, X, and Y fields. The method also sends a Read(Z, SizeOf(Z)) message to the stream S to read the data for the Z field.

The program supplies its own data, using the Data2D- and Data3D-typed constant arrays. The Run procedure in MKSTRM2.PAS resembles that of MKSTRM1.PAS and performs the following tasks:

1. Invokes the nested procedure initObjects to initialize the dynamic instances of T2D and T3D using the array of pointers p and q, respectively. The arrays Data2D and Data3D supply the demonstration data to create the various instances of T2D and T3D.

2. Calls the nested procedure showObjects to display the dynamic instances of T2D and T3D. The sequence of displayed instances alternates between the T2D and T3D object types.

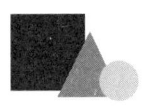

3. Creates a 1K buffered stream for input only.
4. Verifies the status of the stream using the function SayStreamError. If the function result is True, a message box appears to inform you of the error. Next, the program disposes of the dynamic instances of T2D and T3D before it halts.
5. Writes the dynamic instances of T2D and T3D to the stream by calling the nested putObjects procedure. The sequence of writing these instances alternates between the T2D and T3D object types.
6. Removes the dynamic instances of T2D and T3D from the heap space by calling the nested procedure disposeObjects.
7. Closes the stream.
8. Reopens the stream in read-only access mode to read the instances sequentially from the stream.
9. Reads the dynamic instances of T2D and T3D from the stream, in the same order they were written, by invoking the nested procedure getObjects. These instances are displayed before they are disposed of again.
10. Closes the buffered read-only mode stream.
11. Reopens the stream in a read/write access mode.
12. Uses a FOR-DO loop to obtain the position of the first byte of each instance stored in the stream. The FOR-DO loop sends Get messages to the appStream to read sequentially the instances from the stream and record their positions in the local array posIndex. When the loop terminates, the instances of T2D and T3D are removed.
13. Uses a second FOR-DO loop to read the second through the fourth instances stored on the stream. The nested procedure getAndShow seeks, obtains, shows, and then removes the i'th instance. The Seek(posIndex[i]) message is sent to the appStream to place the stream pointer at the beginning of the instance sought. Because two object types are stored in the stream, the getAndShow procedure examines whether the value of its argument (the index of the sought instance) is odd or even and, accordingly, works with the appropriate object type.
14. Swaps the second and fourth instances (both of T3D) in the streams. These file-based instances correspond to the first and second dynamic instances of T3D, accessed by q[1] and q[2]. This subtask starts with the positioning of the stream pointer at the first byte by sending a Seek(0) message to

appStream. The nested procedure getObjects then sequentially reads the instances from the stream. The Seek(posIndex[4]) message is sent to appStream to position the stream pointer at the first byte of the fourth instance. The Put(q[1]) message writes the first instance of T3D as the new fourth stored instance. Similarly, the Seek(PosIndex[2]) and Put(q[2]) messages write the second instance of T3D as the new second instance in the stream. When the swapping process is complete, the dynamic instances are removed from the heap.

15. Sequentially reads, displays, and removes the instances of T2D and T3D. This task starts with sending the Seek(0) message to appStream. The nested procedures getObjects, showObjects, and disposeObjects are invoked to perform the required task.

16. Closes the stream to conclude the program testing.

Just a reminder—the first two statements in the main program section register the T2D and T3D object types.

Listing 15.4. Program MKSTRM2.PAS, which demonstrates polymorphic streams.

```
Program Make_Stream2;

{
 This program illustrates sequential and random-access streams of
 a two-object type hierarchy. The stream in this program contains
 mixed object types. The trickiest parts are random-access writes,
 where the source and destination must be of the same type.
}

{$B-,V-,X+}

Uses Objects, Crt, StrmErr;

CONST BUFFER_SIZE = 1024;
      FILENAME    = 'MKSTRM2.STM';

TYPE
    STRING10 = STRING[10];
    { record types used by the typed constants
      that supply the program with data       }
    TwoDimRec = RECORD
        fName : STRING10;
        fX,
        fY    : REAL;
    END;
```

continues

Listing 15.4. continued

```pascal
    ThreeDimRec = RECORD
        fName : STRING10;
        fX,
        fY,
        fZ   : REAL;
    END;

    { declare object type that models a 2D point with a label }
    P2D = ^T2D;
    T2D = OBJECT(TObject)
        Name : PString;
        X,
        Y    : REAL;
        CONSTRUCTOR Init(TheName : STRING10;
                        Xval,
                        Yval    : REAL);
        CONSTRUCTOR Load(VAR S : TStream);
        PROCEDURE Show; VIRTUAL;
        PROCEDURE Store(VAR S : TStream); VIRTUAL;
    END;

    { declare object type that models a 3D point with a label }
    P3D = ^T3D;
    T3D = OBJECT(T2D)
        Z : REAL;
        CONSTRUCTOR Init(TheName : STRING10;
                        Xval,
                        Yval,
                        Zval    : REAL);
        CONSTRUCTOR Load(VAR S : TStream);
        PROCEDURE Show; VIRTUAL;
        PROCEDURE Store(VAR S : TStream); VIRTUAL;
    END;

CONST
    R2D : TStreamRec = (
        ObjType : 150;
        VmtLink : Ofs(TypeOf(T2D)^);
        Load    : @T2D.Load;
        Store   : @T2D.Store
    );

    R3D : TStreamRec = (
        ObjType : 151;
        VmtLink : Ofs(TypeOf(T3D)^);
        Load    : @T3D.Load;
        Store   : @T3D.Store
    );
```

```
    MAX_2D = 3;
    MAX_3D = 2;
    { array that internally provides data }
    Data2D : ARRAY [1..MAX_2D] OF TwoDimRec =
        ( (fName : 'P1'; fX : 1.0; fY : 1.0),
          (fName : 'P2'; fX : 2.0; fY : 2.0),
          (fName : 'P3'; fX : 3.0; fY : 3.0));
    Data3D : ARRAY [1..MAX_3D] OF ThreeDimRec =
        ( (fName : 'Q1'; fX : 1.0; fY : 1.0; fZ : 1.0),
          (fName : 'Q2'; fX : 2.0; fY : 2.0; fZ : 2.0));

{ ---------------------- T2D ---------------------- }

CONSTRUCTOR T2D.Init(TheName : STRING10;
                     Xval,
                     Yval    : REAL);
BEGIN
    Name := NewStr(TheName);
    X := Xval;
    Y := Yval;
END;

CONSTRUCTOR T2D.Load(VAR S : TStream);
BEGIN
    Name := S.ReadStr;
    S.Read(X, SizeOf(X));
    S.Read(Y, SizeOf(Y));
END;

PROCEDURE T2D.Show;
BEGIN
    WRITE(Name^, ' : ');
    IF X > 0 THEN
        WRITE(X:1:0,' + i')
    ELSE
        WRITE('(', X:1:0,') + i');
    IF Y > 0 THEN
        WRITELN(Y:1:0)
    ELSE
        WRITELN('(', Y:1:0,')');
END;

PROCEDURE T2D.Store(VAR S : TStream);
BEGIN
    S.WriteStr(Name);
    S.Write(X, SizeOf(X));
    S.Write(Y, SizeOf(Y));
END;

{ ---------------------- T3D ---------------------- }
```

continues

Listing 15.4. continued

```pascal
CONSTRUCTOR T3D.Init(TheName : STRING10;
                    Xval,
                    Yval,
                    Zval : REAL);
BEGIN
    T2D.Init(TheName, Xval, Yval);
    Z := Zval;
END;

CONSTRUCTOR T3D.Load(VAR S : TStream);
BEGIN
    T2D.Load(S);
    S.Read(Z, SizeOf(Z));
END;

PROCEDURE T3D.Show;
BEGIN
    WRITE(Name^, ' : ');
    IF X > 0 THEN
        WRITE(X:1:0,' + i')
    ELSE
        WRITE('(', X:1:0,') + i');
    IF Y > 0 THEN
        WRITE(Y:1:0, ' + j')
    ELSE
        WRITE('(', Y:1:0,') + j');
    IF Z > 0 THEN
        WRITE(Z:1:0)
    ELSE
        WRITE('(', Z:1:0,')');
    WRITELN;
END;

PROCEDURE T3D.Store(VAR S : TStream);
BEGIN
    T2D.Store(S);
    S.Write(Z, SizeOf(Z));
END;

PROCEDURE Run;

VAR aKey : CHAR;
    i, j, k : BYTE;
    p : ARRAY [1..MAX_2D] OF P2D;
    q : ARRAY [1..MAX_3D] OF P3D;
    posIndex : ARRAY [1..MAX_2D + MAX_3D] OF LONGINT;
    appStream : TBufStream;
```

```
        PROCEDURE initObjects;
        VAR i : BYTE;
        BEGIN
            FOR i := 1 TO MAX_2D DO
                WITH Data2D[i] DO
                    p[i] := New(P2D, Init(fName, fX, fY));
            FOR i := 1 TO MAX_3D DO
                WITH Data3D[i] DO
                    q[i] := New(P3D, Init(fName, fX, fY, fZ));
END;

PROCEDURE disposeObjects;
VAR i : BYTE;
BEGIN
    FOR i := 1 TO MAX_2D DO
        Dispose(p[i]);
    FOR i := 1 TO MAX_3D DO
        Dispose(q[i]);
END;

PROCEDURE showObjects;
VAR i : BYTE;
BEGIN
    WRITELN('Data is: ');
    p[1]^.Show;
    q[1]^.Show;
    p[2]^.Show;
    q[2]^.Show;
    p[3]^.Show;
    WRITELN;
END;

PROCEDURE putObjects;
BEGIN
    { alternate in storing object types }
    appStream.Put(p[1]);
    appStream.Put(q[1]);
    appStream.Put(p[2]);
    appStream.Put(q[2]);
    appStream.Put(p[3]);
END;

PROCEDURE getObjects;
BEGIN
    { must alternate in reading object types }
    p[1] := P2D(appStream.Get);
    q[1] := P3D(appStream.Get);
    p[2] := P2D(appStream.Get);
    q[2] := P3D(appStream.Get);
    p[3] := P2D(appStream.Get);
END;
```

continues

Listing 15.4. continued

```
PROCEDURE getAndShow(i : BYTE);

VAR p1 : P2D;
    q1 : P3D;

BEGIN
    appStream.Seek(posIndex[i]);
    IF (i MOD 2) = 1 THEN BEGIN
        p1 := P2D(appStream.Get);
        p1^.Show;
        Dispose(p1);
    END
    ELSE BEGIN
        q1 := P3D(appStream.Get);
        q1^.Show;
        Dispose(q1);
    END;
END;

PROCEDURE pause;
BEGIN
    WRITELN;
    WRITE('Press any key ');
    AKey := ReadKey;
    WRITELN; WRITELN;
END;

BEGIN
    ClrScr;
    { create dynamic array of T2D and T3D instances }
    initObjects;
    WRITELN('Storing data sequentially to the stream');
    showObjects;
    { open file to write data }
    appStream.Init(FILENAME, stCreate, BUFFER_SIZE);
    IF SayStreamError(appStream) THEN BEGIN
        disposeObjects;
        Halt(1);
    END;
    putObjects;
    disposeObjects;
    appStream.Done;
    { open stream for sequential input }
    appStream.Init(FILENAME, stOpenRead, BUFFER_SIZE);
    IF SayStreamError(appStream) THEN
        Halt(1);
    WRITELN('Reading data sequentially from the stream');
    getObjects;
    showObjects;
```

Persistent Objects and Streams 15

```
    disposeObjects;
    appStream.Done;
    pause;
    { open stream to random-access read }
    appStream.Init(FILENAME, stOpen, BUFFER_SIZE);
    IF SayStreamError(appStream) THEN
        Halt(1);
    { mark the position of each object in the stream }
    j := 0;
    k := 0;
    FOR i := 1 TO MAX_2D + MAX_3D DO BEGIN
        posIndex[i] := appStream.GetPos;
        IF (i MOD 2) = 1 THEN BEGIN
            INC(j);
            p[j] := P2D(appStream.Get)
        END
        ELSE BEGIN
            INC(k);
            q[k] := P3D(appStream.Get);
        END;
    END;
    disposeObjects;
    WRITELN('Reading 2nd, 3rd, and 4th members gives:');
    FOR i := 2 TO 4 DO
        getAndShow(i);
    pause;
    WRITELN('After Swapping 2nd and 4th members');
    appStream.Seek(0); { move to the beginning of the stream }
    getObjects; { get all stored objects }
    { store q[1] where q[2] used to be }
    appStream.Seek(posIndex[4]);
    appStream.Put(q[1]);
    { store q[2] where q[1] used to be }
    appStream.Seek(posIndex[2]);
    appStream.Put(q[2]);
    disposeObjects;
    { go back to the beginning of the stream }
    appStream.Seek(0);
    getObjects;
    showObjects;
    disposeObjects;
    appStream.Done;
    pause;
END;

BEGIN
    RegisterType(R2D);
    RegisterType(R3D);
    Run;
END.
```

Here's the output generated by the program in Listing 15.4:

```
[BEGIN Output]
Storing data sequentially to the stream
Data is:
P1 : 1 + i1
Q1 : 1 + i1 + j1
P2 : 2 + i2
Q2 : 2 + i2 + j2
P3 : 3 + i3

Reading data sequentially from the stream
Data is:
P1 : 1 + i1
Q1 : 1 + i1 + j1
P2 : 2 + i2
Q2 : 2 + i2 + j2
P3 : 3 + i3


Press any key

Reading 2nd, 3rd, and 4th members gives:
Q1 : 1 + i1 + j1
P2 : 2 + i2
Q2 : 2 + i2 + j2

Press any key

Q1 : 1 + i1 + j1
P2 : 2 + i2
Q2 : 2 + i2 + j2
P3 : 3 + i3


Press any key

Reading 2nd, 3rd, and 4th members gives:
Q1 : 1 + i1 + j1
P2 : 2 + i2
Q2 : 2 + i2 + j2

Press any key
```

```
After Swapping 2nd and 4th members
Data is:
P1 : 1 + i1
Q2 : 2 + i2 + j2
P2 : 2 + i2
Q1 : 1 + i1 + j1
P3 : 3 + i3


Press any key
[END Output]
```

Streams and Collections

Because both streams and collections are polymorphic, there's no reason you cannot store either a monomorphic or a polymorphic collection in a stream. In program MKSTRM2.PAS, the polymorphic stream individually stores and recalls the instances of the various object types. You can store a collection of either invariable or mixed object types in a stream, in which case you perform stream I/O on the entire collection as one item.

To illustrate stream I/O with a collection, I present programs MKSTRM3A.PAS, MKSTRM3B.PAS, and MKSTRM3C.PAS. These MKSTRM3x.PAS programs manage the collection of city and country names, using stream I/O.

The MKSTRM3A.PAS program, shown in Listing 15.5, exports items used by the MKSTRM3B.PAS and MKSTRM3C.PAS programs. These items include four constants, the STRING11 type, the StringArray type, the PSTR pointer type, the TSTR object type, the RSTR registration record, and the RegisterMkStrm3Types registration procedure. The streamable TSTR object type declares two data fields: fStr and fCode. The fStr data field stores the names of a city or country in a collection. The fCode data field is an arbitrary code; I include it to make TSTR form a collection of items that includes strings as well as nonstring data. The Load constructor uses the ReadStr and Read methods to read a string and an integer from the stream S. The string pointer is assigned to the fStr data field. The Store method uses the WriteStr and Write methods to write the dynamic string and the integer-typed fCode into the stream.

Listing 15.5. The MKSTRM3A.PAS library unit.

```pascal
Unit MkStrm3A;

{ This library unit exports items to MKSTRM3B.PAS and MKSTRM3C.PAS. }

INTERFACE

Uses Objects;

CONST
    MAX_ARRAY      = 10;
    BUFFER_SIZE    = 256;
    CITY_FILE      = 'CITY.STD';
    COUNTRY_FILE   = 'COUNTRY.STD';

TYPE
    STRING11 = STRING[11];
    StringArray = ARRAY [0..MAX_ARRAY-1] OF STRING11;
    PSTR = ^TSTR;
    TSTR = OBJECT(TObject)
        fStr : PString;
        fCode : INTEGER;
        CONSTRUCTOR Init(Astring : STRING;
                         TheCode : BYTE);
        DESTRUCTOR Done; VIRTUAL;
        CONSTRUCTOR Load(VAR S : TStream);
        PROCEDURE FreeItem(P : POINTER); VIRTUAL;
        PROCEDURE Store(VAR S : TStream); VIRTUAL;
    END;

CONST
    RSTR : TStreamRec = (
        ObjType : 150;
        VmtLink : Ofs(TypeOf(TSTR)^);
        Load : @TSTR.Load;
        Store : @TSTR.Store);

    PROCEDURE RegisterMkStrm3Types;

IMPLEMENTATION

PROCEDURE RegisterMkStrm3Types;
BEGIN
    RegisterType(RCollection);
    RegisterType(RSTR);
END;

CONSTRUCTOR TSTR.Init(Astring : STRING;
                      TheCode : BYTE);
```

```
BEGIN
    fStr := NewStr(Astring);
    fCode := TheCode;
END;

DESTRUCTOR TSTR.Done;
BEGIN
    Dispose(fStr);
END;

PROCEDURE TSTR.FreeItem(P : POINTER);
BEGIN
    DisposeStr(P);
END;

CONSTRUCTOR TSTR.Load(VAR S : TStream);
BEGIN
    fStr := S.ReadStr;
    S.Read(fCode, SizeOf(fCode));
END;

PROCEDURE TSTR.Store(VAR S : TStream);
BEGIN
    S.WriteStr(fStr);
    S.Write(fCode, SizeOf(fCode));
END;

END.
```

The MKSTRM3B.PAS program, shown in Listing 15.6, creates two collections using the TSTR object type exported by MKSTRM3A.PAS. The collections of cities and countries are stored in the CITY.STD and COUNTRY.STD files, respectively. The program uses the typed-constant arrays CityData and CountryData to supply internally the names of the cities and countries for the collections. The MKSTRM3B.PAS program declares no object types and is not a Turbo Vision application. The main program section contains all of the executable statements that perform the following tasks:

1. Registers the TCollection and TSTR object types.

2. Creates the collection to store the names of the cities.

3. Uses a FOR-DO loop to insert the names of the cities provided by CityData[I]. The arguments for the TheCode parameter are supplied by calls to the random-number generating function.

4. Creates a new buffered stream.

5. Puts the collection of city names and their numeric codes in the stream.
6. Closes the stream and deletes all the collection members.
7. Repeats steps 2 through 6 for the country names and their randomly generated numeric codes.
8. Disposes of the collection.

The program displays simple error messages if either or both files were not created.

Listing 15.6. Program MKSTRM3B.PAS to create the streams storing collections.

```
Program Make_Stream3B;

{
 This program illustrates a list box in a dialog box.
}

{$X+,V-,B-}

Uses Objects, MkStrm3A;

CONST
    CityData : StringArray = ('Paris', 'London', 'Washington',
                              'Madrid', 'Tokyo', 'Rome', 'Bern',
                              'Berlin', 'Warsaw', 'Moscow');
    CountryData : StringArray = ('France', 'U.K.', 'U.S.A.',
                              'Spain', 'Japan', 'Italy',
                              'Switzerland', 'Germany', 'Poland',
                              'U.S.S.R.');

VAR DataList : PCollection;
    I : BYTE;
    AppStream : TBufSTream;
    S : PSTR;

BEGIN
    { register object types }
    RegisterMkStrm3Types;
    Randomize;
    DataList := New(PCollection, Init(MAX_ARRAY, 1));
    FOR I := 0 TO MAX_ARRAY-1 DO BEGIN
        S := New(PStr, Init(CityData[I]), Random(100));
        DataList^.Insert(S);
    END;
    AppStream.Init(CITY_FILE, stCreate, BUFFER_SIZE);
    AppStream.Put(DataList);
```

```
    IF AppStream.Status <> stOK THEN
        WRITELN('Error in creating file ' + CITY_FILE);
    AppStream.Done;
    DataList^.DeleteAll;
    FOR I := 0 TO MAX_ARRAY-1 DO BEGIN
        S := New(PStr, Init(CountryData[I]), Random(100));
        DataList^.Insert(S);
    END;
    AppStream.Init(COUNTRY_FILE, stCreate, BUFFER_SIZE);
    AppStream.Put(DataList);
    IF AppStream.Status <> stOK THEN
        WRITELN('Error in creating file ' + COUNTRY_FILE);
    AppStream.Done;
    DataList^.DeleteAll;
    Dispose(DataList);
    WRITELN('Files created (except when notified by error messages');
END.
```

Program MKSTRM3C.PAS, shown in listing 15.7, is the version of MKCOLCT8.PAS that obtains the names of cities and countries by reading the collections stored in files CITY.STD and COUNTRY.STD. The TRApp.HandleEvent handles the cmSelectCity and cmSelectCountry commands by sending the SelectItem message with the CITY_FILE and COUNTRY_FILE arguments, respectively. These arguments, which are string constants exported by MKSTRM3A.PAS, represent the names of the files containing the collections. The highlight of the program is method SelectItem. It performs the following tasks:

1. Opens the buffer to access the stored collection of TSTR instances.

2. Checks the status of the stream; if appStream.Status is not stOK, the sought DOS file is nonexistent and the method exits after displaying an error-message box.

3. Retrieves the sought collection from the stream, using the local pointer DataCollection.

4. Closes the stream.

5. Allocates a second collection, StringCollection, to store only the strings found in DataCollection.

6. Uses a FOR-DO loop to extract the strings from DataCollection and insert them in StringCollection.

7. Creates the dialog box with its vertical bar, list box, and pushbutton. The list box inserts the StringCollection.

Object-Oriented Programming with Borland Pascal 7

8. Makes the dialog box modal and assigns its result to the local variable `Control`.

9. Examines the value of `Control` and, if it is not `cmCancel`, displays the selected string and its corresponding code. The first string is retrieved by sending a `GetText` message to the instance of the list box. The numeric code is obtained by sending an `At` message to `DataCollection`.

10. Disposes of the instances of the two collections and the dialog box.

The method `SelectItem` uses two collections—one read from the stream and the other built internally to store strings only. The latter is required by the list box. Although the presence of two collections that store common data may seem redundant at first, it represents applications in which you need to extract and display string data fields from object types that contain other data fields.

Listing 15.7. Program MKSTRM3C.PAS, which reads collections from streams.

```
Program Make_Stream3C;

{
 This program reads streams to supply data for the list boxes.
}

{$X+,V-,B-}

Uses Objects, MkStrm3A, Drivers, Views,
     Menus, Dialogs, App, MsgBox;

CONST
    cmSelectCity    = 100;
    cmSelectCountry = 101;

TYPE
    TRApp = OBJECT(TApplication)
       PROCEDURE HandleEvent(VAR Event : TEvent); VIRTUAL;
       PROCEDURE InitMenuBar; VIRTUAL;
       PROCEDURE InitStatusLine; VIRTUAL;
       PROCEDURE SelectItem(ListName : STRING);
    END;

{ TRApp }

PROCEDURE TRApp.HandleEvent(VAR Event : TEvent);
BEGIN
    TApplication.HandleEvent(Event);
    IF Event.What = evCommand THEN BEGIN
       CASE Event.Command OF
```

```
              cmSelectCity    : SelectItem(CITY_FILE);
              cmSelectCountry : SelectItem(COUNTRY_FILE);
        ELSE
         Exit;
        END;
        ClearEvent(Event);
      END;
END;

PROCEDURE TRApp.InitMenuBar;

VAR R : TRect;

BEGIN
   GetExtent(R);
   R.B.Y := R.A.Y + 1;
   MenuBar := New(PMenuBar, Init(R, NewMenu(
      NewSubMenu('~C~hoose me!', hcNoContext, NewMenu(
         NewItem('Select a c~i~ty...', 'F3', kbF3,
               cmSelectCity, hcNoContext,
         NewItem('Select a c~o~untry...', 'F4', kbF4,
               cmSelectCountry, hcNoContext,
         NewLine(
         NewItem('E~x~it', 'Alt-X', kbAltX, cmQuit, hcNoContext,
         NIL))))),
       NIL)))
    );
END;

PROCEDURE TRApp.InitStatusLine;

VAR R : TRect;

BEGIN
   GetExtent(R);
   R.A.Y := R.B.Y - 1;
   StatusLine := New(PStatusLine, Init(R,
      NewStatusDef(0, $FFFF,
         NewStatusKey('', kbF10, cmMenu,
         NewStatusKey('~Alt-X~ Exit', kbAltX, cmQuit,
         NewStatusKey('~F3~ Select a city', kbF3, cmSelectCity,
         NewStatusKey('~F4~ Select a country', kbF4, cmSelectCountry,
         NewStatusKey('~Alt-F3~ Close', kbAltF3, cmClose,
         NIL))))),
       NIL)
    ));
END;

PROCEDURE TRApp.SelectItem(ListName : STRING);
```

continues

Listing 15.7. continued

```pascal
VAR appStream : TBufStream;
   Dialog : PDialog;
   VScrollBar : PScrollBar;
   DataCollection,
   StringCollection : PCollection;
   ListBox : PListBox;
   R : TRect;
   Control : WORD;
   i : INTEGER;
   theCode : INTEGER;
   s : STRING;
   p : PSTR;
   q : PString;

BEGIN
   { build collection of data }
   appStream.Init(ListName, stOpen, BUFFER_SIZE);
   { is file ListName missing ? }
   IF appStream.Status <> stOK THEN BEGIN
      MessageBox('Cannot find file ' + ListName, NIL,
            mfError + mfOKButton);
      Exit;
   END;
   DataCollection := PCollection(appStream.Get);
   appStream.Done; { close stream }
   { allocate collection of strings }
   StringCollection := New(PCollection, Init(MAX_ARRAY, 1));
   FOR i := 0 TO DataCollection^.Count-1 DO BEGIN
     p := DataCollection^.At(i);
     q := NewStr(p^.fStr^);
     StringCollection^.Insert(q);
   END;
   { create dialog box }
   R.Assign(24, 4, 58, 17);
   Dialog := New(PDialog, Init(R, 'Geographical Selection'));
   WITH Dialog^ DO BEGIN { create various controls }
     { create the scroll bar }
     R.Assign(29, 3, 30, 9);
     VScrollBar := New(PScrollBar, Init(R));
     VScrollBar^.SetParams(0, 0, MAX_ARRAY-1, 5, 1);
     Insert(VScrollBar);
     { create list label }
     R.Assign(1, 2, 29, 3);
     Insert(New(PLabel, Init(R, '~L~ist of names', Dialog)));
     { create list and link it with the scroll bar }
```

Persistent Objects and Streams — 15

```
      R.Assign(2, 3, 29, 9);
      ListBox := New(PListBox, Init(R, 1, VScrollBar));
      ListBox^.NewList(StringCollection);
      Insert(ListBox);
      { create OK button }
      R.Assign(3, 10, 13, 12);
      Insert(New(PButton, Init(R, '~O~k', cmOK, bfDefault)));
      { create Cancel button }
      R.Assign(17, 10, 27, 12);
      Insert(New(PButton, Init(R, '~C~ancel', cmCancel, bfNormal)));
    END;
    Control := DeskTop^.ExecView(Dialog);
    IF Control <> cmCancel THEN BEGIN
       { obtain selection from list box }
       i := VScrollBar^.Value;
       s := 'You selected ' + ListBox^.GetText(i, SizeOf(s));
       IF s[Length(s)] <> '.' THEN
          s := s + '.';
       p := DataCollection^.At(i);
       theCode := p^.fCode;
       s := s + '  Its code is %d';
       MessageBox(s, @theCode, mfInformation + mfOKButton);
    END;
    { remove data collection read from stream }
    DataCollection^.DeleteAll;
    Dispose(DataCollection);
    { remove the list box collection }
    ListBox^.List^.DeleteAll;
    Dispose(Dialog, Done);
  END;

VAR RApp : TRApp;

BEGIN
 RegisterMkStrm3Types;
 RApp.Init;
 RApp.Run;
 RApp.Done;
END.
```

Figure 15.1 shows a sample session with program MKSTRM3B.EXE., and it shows the list of cities. Figure 15.2 shows a sample session with program MKSTRM3B.EXE, which displays the output dialog box.

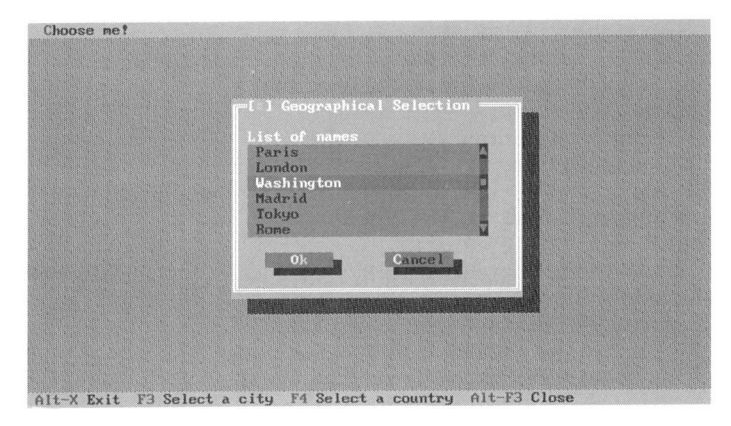

Object-Oriented Programming with Borland Pascal 7

Figure 15.1. A sample session with program MKSTRM3B.EXE, showing the the list of cities.

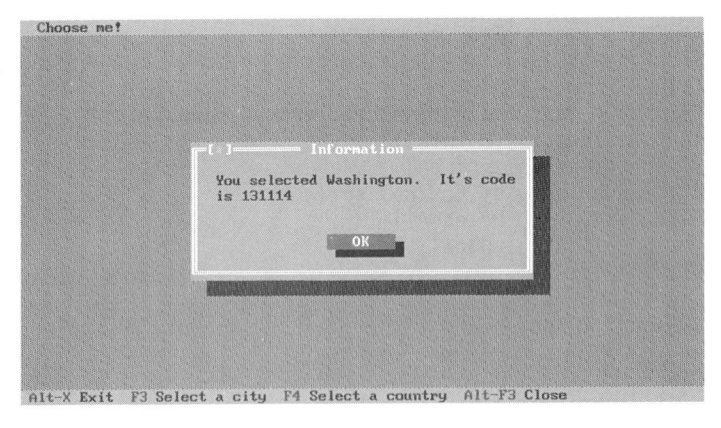

Figure 15.2. A sample session with program MKSTRM3B.EXE, showing the output dialog box.

Summary

This chapter discussed how streams can store and retrieve instances of various object types in files. You learned about the following topics:

- The ability of streams to store all of the information related to instances, including VMT data. Thus, streams can correctly write and later read instances from data files.

Persistent Objects and Streams 15

- The `TStream` subhierarchy includes the object types `TStream`, `TDosStream`, `TBufStream`, `TEmsStream`, and `TMemoryStream`. The object type `TStream` is an abstract type. Its descendants offer practical operations to store and recall instances from data files.

- The `Load` constructors and `Store` methods assist user-defined descendants of `TObject` to become streamable. The general syntax for the `Load` constructor is:

  ```
  CONSTRUCTOR <DescendantOfTObject>.Load(VAR S : TStream);
  BEGIN
    [<parentObjectType>.Load(S);]
    S.Read(<data_field_1>, SizeOf(<data_field_1>)
    S.Read(<data_field_2>, SizeOf(<data_field_2>)
       .....
    S.Read(<data_field_n>, SizeOf(<data_field_n>)
  END;
  ```

  The general syntax for the `Store` method is

  ```
  PROCEDURE <DescendantOfTObject>.Store(VAR S : TStream);
  BEGIN
    [<parentObjectType>.Store(S);]
    S.Write(<data_field_1>, SizeOf(<data_field_1>)
    S.Write(<data_field_2>, SizeOf(<data_field_2>)
       .....
    S.Write(<data_field_n>, SizeOf(<data_field_n>)
  END;
  ```

  `Write` messages are sent to the stream `S` to write the data fields to the streams. Arguments for the `Write` method resemble those for the `Read` method.

- Object-type registration, a two-step process for user-defined object types, is essential for any stream I/O. In the first step, you declare a `TStreamRec`-typed constant for the descendant of the Turbo Vision object types you create. These typed constants assign values to the first four `TStreamRec` data fields. The `ObjType` field is assigned a unique ID for the object type. The `VmtLink` is assigned the VMT offset segment to the object type. The `Load` and `Store` fields are pointers to the methods that load and store the stream (typically, `Load` and `Store`). The second step in stream registration involves calling the `RegisterType` procedure to register the various `TStreamRec`-type records.

- The `StrmErr` library unit translates the numeric codes for stream error into strings.

- Sequential stream I/O enables you to write and read instances in a serial manner in a stream. These operations use the `Get` and `Put` methods for stream I/O.

- Random-access stream I/O enables you to write and read instances in at random locations in a stream. These operations use the Seek, GetPos, Get, and Put methods for stream I/O.
- Polymorphic streams store and recall instances of different object types. This is a powerful feature that enables you to manage heterogeneous instances in the same data file.
- Streams and collections both are polymorphic. Therefore, you can store either a monomorphic or a polymorphic collection in a stream. You can store a collection of either invariable or mixed object types in a stream, in which case you perform stream I/O on the entire collection as one item.

Appendix A

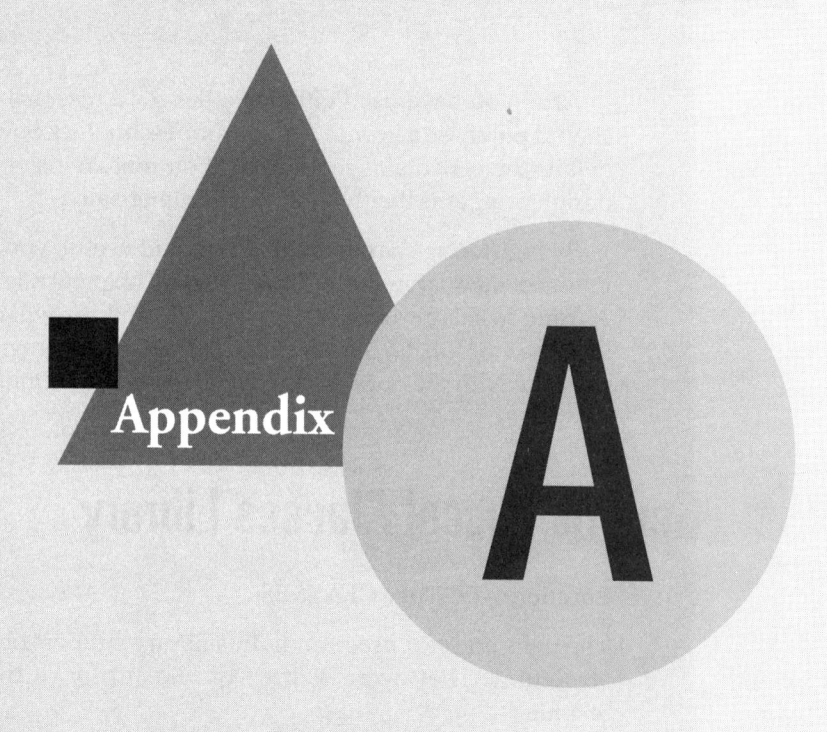

Disk Contents

The floppy disk included with this book contains the programs and library units that appear in the book, plus these bonus libraries and utilities:

- Generic Pascal classes library
- TechnoJock Object Toolkit
- TechnoJock Turbo Toolkit
- Dialog Design
- Boilerplate

Use TechnoJock's Object Toolkit and Turbo Toolkit libraries and share them freely with others; they are being distributed as shareware. You can try out the complete programs at your own pace. They are not crippled or demo copies—they are the complete working versions of the programs.

After you have used either Toolkit for a reasonable evaluation period, you should purchase a licensed copy from TechnoJock Software. The documentation details the benefits of registering. You must register if you use the Toolkits to design programs that will be sold commercially.

By registering shareware that you find useful, you will serve not only the interests of the shareware authors; you will help out all of us who program on PCs. As long as shareware works, shareware authors will continue to create and update their products. And we, the users of those programs, get to have first-rate software with the option of trying it before we commit to buying it.

Generic Pascal Classes Library

Location: \BP700P\CLASSES

The units and test program in this library support object types for generic data structures. They were written by the author of this book, Namir Clement Shammas.

These files support generic stacks, queues, arrays, rectangular matrices, jagged matrices, singly linked lists, doubly linked lists, hash tables, AVL-trees, and graphs.

TechnoJock Object Toolkit

Location: \BP700P\TOT

Documentation: The manual is broken into individual chapters, located in the \BP7OOP\TOT\DOCS directory.

This shareware package offers a library of objects that allow you to create professional-looking DOS applications. The objects in the TOT library enable you to manipulate the screen, the keys, the mouse, the display, and other aspects of a DOS program.

While writing a PC program, most people spend 80% or more of their time writing the program's user interface, and only 20% on the "meat" of the application. The Toolkit is designed to provide a set of professional user interface tools that can eliminate a great deal of development work.

The interface tools include such features as efficient screen writing, window management, menu management, full screen user input, list displaying, directory listing, and much more. These tools give programs a professional appearance, with pop-up dialog boxes, scroll-bars, and malleable windows.

Contact TechnoJock Software, Inc. at

> PO Box 820927
> Houston TX 77282, USA
> (713) 493-6354 Voice
> (713) 493-5872 Fax
> CompuServe 74017,227
> MCI Mail   TECHNOJOCK

TechnoJock Turbo Toolkit

Location: \BP700P\TTT

Documentation: MANUAL.DOC

This Toolkit is a collection of procedures and functions for Turbo Pascal programmers. The Toolkit will reduce the time taken to write applications and is designed for the novice and expert programmer alike.

The real purpose of the Toolkit is to provide easy-to-implement procedures that free the programmer from the more tedious and repetitive programming chores, such as windows, menus, user input, string formatting, directory listing, and so on. The programmer is free to focus on the main purpose of the program.

The Toolkit is designed specifically to operate with Turbo Pascal versions 5.0 and v4.0. The full source code for the entire Toolkit is included so that the code may be reviewed and modified.

See the preceding section for information on how to contact TechnoJock Software.

Dialog Design

Location: \BP700P\DIALOG

Documentation: DLGDSN.DOC

This utility takes some of the pain out of designing dialog boxes for Borland's Turbo Vision package. With Dialog Design, dialog controls can be easily added, edited, rearranged, and the dialog itself can be sized, moved, and so on.

Once the design is satisfactory, Dialog Design can produce source code to be included in your program or a resource file for use by your program.

Dialog Design was written by Dave Baldwin. You can contact Dave at the following addresses:

22 Fox Den Road
Hollis, NH 03049
(Summer Address)

144 13th Street East
Tierra Verde, FL 33715
(Winter Address)

You can also contact Dave through CompuServe; his number is 76327,53.

Boilerplate

Location: \BP700P\BOILER

Documentation: BLRPLATE.DOC

This archived file contains a utility that assists you in writing Windows applications in Turbo Pascal. The BoilerPlate utility empowers you to define your main window object and include empty (mostly) methods for the menu items and window messages you have already defined in a resource file.

The output of the BoilerPlate is a compilable program that (because of the empty methods) performs no tasks. By adding the statements to the various methods, you obtain a fully functioning Windows application.

Boilerplate was written by Dave Baldwin. You can contact Dave at the addresses listed in the preceding section.

Index

A

abstract object types
   as base types, 106-118
   in subhierarchies, 118-133
   rules, 106
abstraction, 105
AbsType1 object type, 107
accessibility
   components, 201-207
   modular objects, 195-196
accessing
   array elements, 143
   data fields, 7, 90-92
   records, random-access binary files, 375
Action function, 346
AddData function, 299

airplane malfunction simulation program, 289-292
algorithms
   linear-search, 137
   Shell-Metzner, 75, 220, 280, 327, 333-334
AllocateError data field (Boolean), 127
anArray instance, 84, 173
applications, non-OOP, 95-103
aQueue instance, 173
Ar1 instance, 129-130
Ar2 instance, 129-130
arguments
   CITY_FILE, 413
   COUNTRY_FILE, 413
Arr instance, 334
array elements, accessing, 143

array-sorting methods, 327
ARRAY1.PAS program, 32-40
ARRAY2.PAS program, 43-47
ARRAY3.PAS program, 49-57
ARRAY4.PAS program, 59-65
ARRAY5.PAS program, 84-86
ARRAY6.PAS program, 129-133
ARRAY7.PAS program, 232-241
ARRAY8.PAS program, 250-255
ARRAY9.PAS program, 270-275
ARRAY10.PAS program, 278-287
ARRAY11.PAS program, 316-317
ArrayModeEnum data type, 242
arrays
   dynamic, 49-57
      fill value, default, 33
      hybrid, 188
      modeling, 74-76
      size, specifying, 33
      unordered, 344-358
   searching, linear, 140-143
   sorting, 129
ArraySize parameter, 76
AssignVals function (Boolean), 68-69
aStack instance, 173-174
aStrFile parameter, 76
At method, 345
AtDelete function, 347
AtInsert function, 348
AtPut function, 348-349

B

Baldwin, Dave, 424
base classes, 5
base object types, 159
   abstract object types as, 106-118
behaviors, polymorphic, 76
binary files, random-access, 375
binding, deferred, 327
   implementing, 327
BinSearch function, 221, 333-334
BlockRead function, 375
BlockWrite function, 375
BoilerPlate utility, 424
Boolean
   data fields, AllocateError, 127

functions
   AssignVals, 68-69
   CalcLinReg, 299
   CopyArray, 42-49
   GetAllocateError, 26, 32, 107, 128, 144, 163
   IsEmpty, 26, 107, 144, 163
   IsEnabled, 280
   IsFull, 164
   IsGreater, 182
   IsSameLastName, 97
   Pop, 26, 108, 144, 165
   PopFront, 164
   PopScreen, 152
   PopTail, 164
   ProjectXonY, 299
   Push, 165
   PushFront, 164
   PushTail, 164
   ReadArr, 219
   Recall, 32, 75, 128, 163-164, 189, 218, 279, 312, 329
   SayStreamError, 380
   scanDueDate, 347
   SelectNewFile, 279
   Store, 32, 75, 128, 163-164, 189, 218-220, 279, 312, 329, 384-385, 389-390
   TellStreamError, 380
   WriteArr, 219
building, generic routines, 139-140

C

CalcLinReg function (Boolean), 299
CalcReg function, 304-305
calling, private components, 215-216
case-sensitive sorting, 129-130
CITY_FILE argument, 413
CITY.STD file, 411-413
classes, 3, 7
   base, 5
   declaring, 6
   inheritance, utilizing, 136-137
   records, extending, 89-90
   subclasses, 4-5
   superclasses, 5

Clear function, 26, 108, 144, 164
ClearSums function, 299, 304
client programs, selecting sorting methods, 327
cmSelectCity command, 413
cmSelectCountry command, 413
codes
    reutilizing, 136-137
    stream access, 380
    stream error, 379-380
collection object types, 343-344
collections
    index range, 345-348
    reading from streams, 414-417
    sorted, 358-369
    storing in streams, 409-418
    string, 344-358, 365-369
    Turbo Vision, 343-344
    unsorted, 344-358, 369-374
Comb sorting method, 129, 327
CombSort sort function, 333-334
commands
    cmSelectCity, 413
    cmSelectCountry, 413
common data, sharing, 310, 318-323
Compare function, 359
CompareBytes function, 141-142
CompareDate function, 69
CompareMailings function, 97
CompareNames function, 97
CompareStrings function, 141-142
comparison functions, 140-142
compilation, conditional, 84
compiler directives, $DEFINE, 84
compilers, TopSpeed Pascal (Clarion), 208
components
    modular object, accessibility, 201-207
    private, calling by object type instances, 215-216
    required for object-type implementation, 278
conditional compilation, 84
conditional instance malfunctions, 278
    single instances, 278-288

constants
    DEFAULT_CHANGEVAL, 34
    DEFAULT_FILL_PATTERN, 34
    DEFAULT_FILLVAL, 33
    DEFAULT_SIZE, 33
    TStreamRec-typed, declaring, 386
constructors, 15
    copy, 42-49
    default, 26-31
    Done, 189
    error-handling mechanisms, 58-65
    Init, 75, 188, 220, 312, 328-329
        declaring, 26
    Load, 382
        declaring, 383-385
    multiple, 32-41
    of parent object types, invoking, 49-57
    parameters, 32-34
    tasks, CONTAIN2.PAS, 188-189
    TCollection.Init, 345
    TGenStack.Init, 153
    TStrArray.Init, 188
    TStrStack.Init, 115
    TToDo.Init, 345, 359
    TToDoList.Done, 345
    TToDoList.Init, 345
    TVirtStrArray.Init, 189
    TVMStrStack.Init, 115
ContactRec object type, 92
CONTAIN1.PAS program, 181-186
CONTAIN2.PAS program, 190-194
CONTAIN3.PAS program, 195-201
CONTAIN4.PAS program, 202-207
CONTAIN5.PAS (uncompilable) program, 208-213
contained instances, disabling, 288-292
contained object types, transparent, 181, 188
containment, 179-181
    extendible records, 181-187
    modular objects
        accessibility, 201-207
        supporting, 195-201
    object-type hierarchies, 188-195
    versus multiple inheritance, 208

coordinates, 2-D/3-D (modeling), 399
copy constructors, 42-49
CopyArray function (Boolean), 42-49
copying
    instances, 42-49
        ARRAY2.PAS program, 43-47
    streams, from DOS to EMS
        memory, 383
counting, instances, 310-318
COUNTRY_FILE argument, 413
COUNTRY.STD file, 411-413
custom data types, 365
    declaring sorted collections for,
        365-368

D

data, common (sharing), 310, 318-323
data fields, 3
    accessing, 7, 90-92
    Boolean
        AllocateError, 127
        InOrder, 74
    DataPtr, 218
    declaring, 7
        TVirtStrArray object type, 279
    enablement, 276
        Boolean, 257
    ErrorInfo, 379-380
    initializing, 27
    InOrder (Boolean), 74
    MaxSize, 217
    private, declaring, 106
    ShutDown, 288-289
    Status, 379-380
    TLinReg object type, 298-308
    user-defined object types, 385
    WorkSize, 218
data members, 309
data structures, generic, 136
data types
    ArrayModeEnum, 242
    custom, 365
        declaring sorted collections for,
            365-368
    LinRegState, 298
DataPtr data field, 218

DATE1.PAS program, 68-73
DateRec object type, 181
DateTimeRec record structure, 90
deallocating, dynamic memory, 58
declaring
    classes, 6
    data fields, 7
        private, 106
        TVirtStrArray object type, 279
    Done destructor, 26
    Init constructor, 26
    Load constructors, 383-385
    methods
        as virtual, 15
        private, 106
        TBitSet object type, 318-319
    multiple inheritance, 208
    parameter lists, 68
    sorted collections for custom data
        types, 365-368
    subhierarchies, TStream, 377-379
    TComplex object type, 390-394
    TStreamRec record type, 377-379
    TStreamRec-typed constants, 386
default constructor, 26-31
DEFAULT_CHANGEVAL
    constant, 34
DEFAULT_FILL_PATTERN
    constant, 34
DEFAULT_FILLVAL constant, 33
DEFAULT_SIZE constant, 33
deferred binding, 327
    implementing, 327
    object types, testing, 333-339
$DEFINE directive, 84
Delay function, 154
DelData function, 299
DeleteAll function, 349
deleting instances of object types,
    see destructors
descendant object types, 159-160
    metamorphic, rules, 160
    private static methods, overriding,
        68-74
    pseudo-hidden methods, 256-269
descendant records, creating, 326

Index

designing
  dialog boxes, 424
  hierarchies, object type, 160
  object types, multiple inheritance, 209
destructors, 16
  Done, 16, 312
    declaring, 26
  TCollection.Done, 345
  TStrArray.Done, 189
  TToDo.Done, 345, 359
  TVirtStrArray.Done, 189
  virtual, 58
dialog boxes, designing, 424
Dialog Design utility, 424
directives
  $DEFINE, 84
  FAR, 346
disabled instances
  contained, 288-292
  single, 278-288
  types, 278
disciplined
  instances, 295-297
  object types, implementing, 296-297
disk-based
  dynamic string arrays, modeling, 76
  generic stacks, modeling, 144
DisplayArray function, 190
DisplayTasks function, 182
disposeObjects function, 395, 400
DisposeStr function, 345
Done constructor, 189
Done destructor, 16, 312
  declaring, 26
DOS files, copying streams to EMS memory, 383
downward-counting FOR loops, 316
dynamic arrays, 49-57
  fill value, default, 33
  hybrid, 188
  size, specifying, 33
  string, modeling, 74-76
  unordered, 344-358

dynamic instances
  detecting constructor errors, 59-65
  T2D/T3D object types, 399-401
dynamic memory
  deallocating, 58
  managing, 310-311
dynamic objects, 21-23
dynamic stacks, implementing, 160
dynamic-array object-type
  hierarchies, features, 217

E

EMS memory, copying streams from DOS to, 383
emulated static members, 310-311
emulating
  Oberon deferred binding, 327
  object types, Oberon, 326-327
enablement data fields, 276
  Boolean, 257
engines, state, 296
ErrorInfo data field, 379-380
errors
  constructor, 58-65
  managing, 310
  stream, 383
Expand function, 219
extendible records, 89-92
  containment, 181-187
  simulating, 90-95

F

Fail function, 58
FAR directive, 346
fatal instance malfunctions, 278
file I/O (input/output), 375-376
  polymorphic, 376
files
  CITY.STD, 411-413
  COUNTRY.STD, 411-413
  DOS, copying streams to EMS memory, 383
FillScreen function, 154
FirstThat function, 346
fixed queues, modeling, 161
fixed stacks, modeling, 161, 165

FlexUArray instance, testing, 233-234
FlexUArray_10 instance, testing, 234-235
FLY.PAS program, 289-292
FOR loops, 173-174
   downward-counting, 316
   nested, 316
FOR-DO loops, 346, 400
ForEach function, 346-347, 359
FreeItem virtual function, 365, 369-370
functionality, descendant object types, 159-160
functions
   BinSearch, 221, 333-334
   Boolean
      AssignVals, 68-69
      CalcLinReg, 299
      CopyArray, 42-49
      GetAllocateError, 26, 32, 107, 128, 144, 163
      IsEmpty, 26, 107, 144, 163
      IsEnabled, 280
      IsFull, 164
      IsGreater, 182
      IsSameLastName, 97
      Pop, 26, 108, 144, 165
      PopFront, 164
      PopScreen, 152
      PopTail, 164
      ProjectXonY, 299
      Push, 165
      PushFront, 164
      PushTail, 164
      ReadArr, 219
      Recall, 32, 75, 128, 163-164, 189, 218, 279, 312, 329
      SayStreamError, 380
      scanDueDate, 347
      SelectNewFile, 279
      Store, 32, 75, 128, 163-164, 189, 218-220, 279, 312, 329, 384-385, 389-390
      TellStreamError, 380
      WriteArr, 219
   Action, 346
   AddData, 299

At, 345
AtDelete, 347
AtInsert, 348
AtPut, 348, 349
BlockRead, 375
BlockWrite, 375
CalcReg, 304-305
Clear, 26, 108, 144, 164
ClearSums, 299, 304
Compare, 359
CompareBytes, 141-142
CompareDate, 69
CompareMailings, 97
CompareNames, 97
CompareStrings, 141-142
comparison, 140-142
constructors, 15
Delay, 154
DelData, 299
DeleteAll, 349
DisplayArray, 190
DisplayTasks, 182
disposeObjects, 395, 400
Expand, 219
Fail, 58
FillScreen, 154
FirstThat, 346
ForEach, 347, 359
GenSearch, 140-143
Get, 389-396
GetComponents, 202
GetMaxSize, 75, 128, 163, 189, 218, 280, 312, 329
GetNumInstances, 312
getObjects, 395
GetPos, 397
GetSize, 32
GetStreamError, 380
GetVals, 96-97
GetWorkSize, 75, 128, 163, 189, 218, 280, 312, 329
HeapErrorHandler, 27
IndexOf, 348
InitArray, 190
InitializeTasks, 182
Insert, 359

Index

KeyOf, 360
LastThat, 347
linear search, 139
LinSearch, 218, 333-334
Load, 389-390
MoveDn, 164
MoveUp, 164
NewStr, 345
Project, 304, 305
Push, 26, 108, 144
Put, 389-396
putObjects, 395, 400
RecallDate, 69
RegisterMkStrm3Types, 409
RegisterXXXX, Turbo Vision object types, 386-388
Run, 394, 399-401
SayStreamError, 395-397, 400
Search, 76, 128-129, 280, 329
SearchDosFileName, 139
SearchInteger, 138
SearchString, 137-138
Seek, 397
SelectItem, 413-414
SetComponents, 202
SetSearchMethod, 329
SetSortMethod, 329
SetVals, 96-97
ShowArray, 34-40
showElement, 346
showObject, 395
Sort, 75, 129, 329
SortArray, 190
SortTasks, 182
Test, 346
TestInstance, 280-281
TToDoList.Run, 345
viewAll, 346
virtual, 14-21
   FreeItem, 365, 369-370
   GetItem, 365
   KeyOf, 358-359
   parameter list, 16
   PutItem, 365
   Search, 358-360
   setting up, 15

TSortedCollection.Compare, 358
UnSafeRecall, 75-77, 218-219, 280
UnSafeStore, 75-77, 218, 279
see also methods

G

generic data structures, 136
generic object types, 135-136
Generic Pascal Classes Library, 422
generic programming, 135-136
generic routines, building, 139-140
generic stack object types, 143-156
   disk-based, 144
   GenStack library unit, 143-156
   heap-based, 144
GenSearch function, 140-143
GenStack library unit
   generic stack object types, implementing, 143-156
   testing, 153-156
Get function, 389-396
GetAllocateError function (Boolean), 26, 32, 107, 128, 144, 163
GetComponents function, 202
GetItem virtual function, 365
GetMaxSize function, 75, 128, 163, 189, 218, 280, 312, 329
GetNumInstances function, 312
getObjects function, 395
GetPos function, 397
GetSize function, 32
GetStreamError function, 380
GetVals function, 96-97
GetWorkSize function, 75, 128, 163, 189, 218, 280, 312, 329
graphs, mathematical, 296

H

heap-based dynamic string arrays, modeling, 74
heap-based generic stacks, modeling, 144
HeapErrorHandler function, 27
hierarchies
   extendible record, simulating, 92-95

object-type, 7-14, 180-181
　abstract object types, 106-133
　containment, 188-195
　creating by pseudo-private
　　methods, 256-269
　designing, 160
　metamorphic, 161-162
　modeling, 216-217
　stack, implementing, 107-118
　static members, 311
record, Oberon, 326
Turbo Vision, 343-344
　streams, 376
　TStream subhierarchy, 377-383
hybrid dynamic arrays, 188

I

I/O (input/output)
　file, 375-376
　　polymorphic, 376
　stream
　　object-type registration, 386-388
　　random-access, 390-398
　　sequential, 388-396
implementing
　deferred binding, 327
　hierarchies, stack object-type,
　　107-118
　members, static, 311
　object types, 278
　　disciplined, 296-297
　stacks, dynamic, 160
IndexOf method, 348
indices, out-of-range, 345-348
inheritance, 4-5, 136, 179
　extendible records, 92
　multiple, 208-213
　single, 208
INHERITED keyword, 10-13
inherited methods, overriding, 67
Init constructor, 15, 75, 188, 220, 312,
　328-329
　declaring, 26
　parameters, 33
Init2 constructor, parameters, 33-40
Init3 constructor, parameters, 33

InitArray function, 190
InitializeTasks function, 182
initializing
　data fields, 27
　object-variables, 15
　statistical summations, 297
initSum state, 297-299
Insert function, 359
instance-counting object types,
　testing, 316-317
instances, 3
　AnArray, 84
　anArray, 173
　aQueue, 173
　Ar1, 129-130
　Ar2, 129-130
　Arr, 334
　aStack, 173-174
　contained, disabling, 288-292
　copying, 42-49
　　ARRAY2.PAS program, 43-47
　disabled, types, 278
　disciplined, 295, 296-297
　dynamic
　　constructor errors, detecting,
　　　59-65
　　T2D/T3D object types, 399-401
　object type
　　communication through static
　　　members, 311
　　counting, 310-318
　　private components, calling,
　　　215-216
　　sequentially reading from/
　　　writing to streams, 388-389
　　testing, 232-244
　privileged, 216-217
　　testing, 232-241
　　utilizing, 241-256
　S, 114-115, 153-154
　single, disabled, 278-288
　state, 3
　static, detecting constructor errors,
　　59-65
　VS, 114-115, 153-154
　see also objects

Index

integers
    dynamic arrays of, 49-57
    long, manipulating, 26-31
interface tools, TechnoJock Object
  Toolkit library, 422-423
intrinsic routines, Move, 140
invoking, constructors of parent
  object types, 49-57
IsEmpty function (Boolean), 26, 107, 144, 163
IsEnabled function (Boolean), 280
IsFull function (Boolean), 164
IsGreater function (Boolean), 182
IsSameLastName function
  (Boolean), 97
iterator methods, ForEach, 346

K

KeyOf virtual method, 358-360
keywords
    INHERITED, 10-13
    OBJECT, 6
    PRIVATE, 7
    PUBLIC, 7
    VIRTUAL, 15, 208

L

languages, programming
    generic programming support, 136
    Oberon, 325-327
LastThat method, 347
late binding, *see* deferred binding
libraries
    Generic Pascal Classes, 422
    Object Toolkit (TechnoJock), 421-423
    Turbo Toolkit (TechnoJock), 421-423
library units
    LinReg, 297
    PolyMorf, 188
linear object-type hierarchies, creating
  by pseudo-private methods, 256-269
linear regression, states, 297-298
linear search functions, 139
linear searches, arrays, 140-143

linear-search algorithms, 137
linking object types in different
  hierarchies, *see* containment
LinRegRec record, data fields, 298
LinRegState data type, 298
LinSearch function, 218, 333-334
listings
    1.1. PRGMSHAP.PAS, 10-14
    1.2. SHAPES library unit, 17-20
    1.3. TSSHAPE1.PAS, 20-21
    1.4. TSSHAPE2.PAS, 22-23
    2.1. STACK1.PAS, 26-31
    2.2. ARRAY1.PAS, 32-40
    2.3. ARRAY2.PAS, 43-47
    2.4. ARRAY3.PAS, 49-57
    2.5. ARRAY4.PAS, 59-65
    3.1. DATE1.PAS, 70-73
    3.2. UNIT Polymorf, 77-83
    3.3. ARRAY5.PAS, 84-86
    4.1. RECOBJ1.PAS, 93-95
    4.2. RECOBJ2.PAS, 97-103
    5.1. UNIT AbsStack, 108-114
    5.2. STACK2.PAS, 115-118
    5.3. Unit AbsArray, 119-127
    5.4. ARRAY6.PAS, 130-133
    6.1. SearchString function, 137-138
    6.2. SearchInteger function, 138
    6.3. SearchDosFileName, 139
    6.4. GenSearch function, 142-143
    6.5. UNIT GenStack, 145-151
    6.6. UNIT ScrnStak, 152-153
    6.7. STACK3.PAS, 154-156
    7.1. Unit MetaMorf, 165-172
    7.2. TSMTMRF.PAS, 174-175
    8.1. CONTAIN1.PAS, 182-186
    8.2. CONTAIN2.PAS, 190-194
    8.3. CONTAIN3.PAS, 197-201
    8.4. CONTAIN4.PAS, 203-207
    8.5. CONTAIN5.PAS
      (uncompilable), 209-213
    9.1. UNIT Polymrf 2 source code, 222-232
    9.2. ARRAY7.PAS, 235-240
    9.3 UNIT Polymrf3 source code, 242-250
    9.4. ARRAY8.PAS, 251-255

9.5. UNIT Polymrf4, 260-269
9.6. ARRAY9.PAS, 270-275
10.1. ARRAY10.PAS, 281-287
10.2. FLY.PAS, 290-292
11.1 Unit LinReg source code, 300-304
11.2. TSSTAT.PAS, 305-307
12.1. UNIT Static1, 313-315
12.2. ARRAY11.PAS, 316-317
12.3. UNIT Static2 source code, 319-321
12.4. TSBITS.PAS, 321-323
13.1. UNIT Oberon source code, 330-333
13.2. TSOBERON.PAS, 335-339
14.1. MKCOLCT1.PAS, 349-355
14.2. MKCOLCT2.PAS, 360-364
14.3. MKCOLCT3.PAS, 366-368
14.4. MKCOLCT4.PAS, 370-373
15.1. TStream subhierarchy declaration, 377-379
15.2. STRMERR.PAS library unit, 380-382
15.3. MKSTRM1.PAS, 390-394
15.4. MKSTRM2.PAS, 401-407
15.5. MKSTRM3A.PAS library unit, 409-411
15.6. MKSTRM3B.PAS, 412-413
15.7. MKSTRM3C.PAS, 414-417
Load constructor, 382
   declaring, 383-385
Load method, 389-390
long integers, manipulating, 26-31
loops
   FOR, 173-174
      downward-counting, 316
   FOR-DO, 346, 400

M

macros, VM_ARRAY, 84
MailingRec object type, 92
malfunctions
   instance
      conditional, 278
      fatal, 278
      partial, 278
      single, 278-288
   object variable, disabling, 288-292
management, dynamic memory, 310-311
mathematical graphs, 296
MaxSize data field, 217
members
   data, 309
   static, 309-310
      implementing, 311
      utilization, 310-311
memory
   dynamic
      deallocating, 58
      managing, 310-311
      EMS, copying streams from DOS to, 383
message abstraction, 5
messages, 4
MetaMorf library unit
   program, 165-172
   testing, 172-177
   TStrArray object type, 162-163
   TStrFixedQue object type, 163-164
metamorphic object types, 160
   rules, 160
metamorphic object-type hierarchy, 161-162
methods, 4
   array-sorting, 327
      Comb, 327
      QuickSort, 327
      Shell-Metzner, 327
   containment, 180-181
   declaring
      as virtual, 15
      private, 106
      TBitSet object type, 318-319
   headers, 7
   iterator, ForEach, 346
   nested method calls, 14-21
   overriding, 67
      static, 68-74
      TSortedCollection object type, 358
      virtual, 74-86

Index

pseudo-hidden, descendant object types, 256-269
pseudo-private, 216
  object-type hierarchies, creating, 256-269
redundant, 222
sorting, Comb, 129
static, 14-21
  parameter list, 16
TCollection.Error, 345-348
testing, TCollection object type, 349-355
see also functions
MKCOLCT1.PAS program, 344-355
MKCOLCT2.PAS program, 359-364
MKCOLCT3.PAS program, 366-368
MKCOLCT4.PAS program, 369-373
MKSTRM1.PAS program, 390-396, 399
  random-access stream I/O, 397-398
MKSTRM2.PAS program, 399-407
MKSTRM3A.PAS library unit program, 410-411
MKSTRM3B.PAS program, 409-413
MKSTRM3C.PAS program, 409, 413-417
modeling
  2-D/3-D coordinates, 399
  arrays, dynamic, 74-76
  generic stacks
    disk-based, 144
    heap-based, 144
  object-type hierarchies, 216-217
  queues, fixed, 161
  stacks, fixed, 161, 165
modes, stCreate, 388
Modula-2 programming language, 136
modular objects
  components, accessibility, 201-207
  containment, 195-201
monomorphic collections, storing in streams, 409-418
Move intrinsic routine, 140
MoveDn function, 164
MoveUp function, 164

multiple constructors, 32-41
multiple inheritance, 208-213
multiple parent object types, 208

N

NameRec object type, 92
nested
  FOR loops, 316
  method calls, 14-21
  procedures
    disposeObjects, 395, 400
    getObjects, 395
    putObjects, 395, 400
    showObject, 395
NewStr function, 345
NIL objects, placing in streams, 390
non-OOP applications, using object types as extendible records, 95-103
normalization, 68

O

Oberon programming language, 325
  extendible records, 326
  object types, emulating, 326-327
object instances, sequentially reading from/writing to streams, 388-389
OBJECT keyword, 6
Object Toolkit library (TechnoJock), 421-423
object type hierarchies, designing, 160
object type instances, calling private components, 215-216
object types, 7
  abstract
    as base types, 106-118
    in subhierarchies, 118-133
    rules, 106
  AbsType1, 107
  as extendible records, non-OOP applications, 95-103
  base, 159
  collection, 343-344
  ContactRec, 92
  contained, transparent, 181, 188
  DateRec, 181
  descendant, 159-160

metamorphic, rules, 160
private static methods,
  overriding, 68-74
pseudo-hidden methods,
  256-269
design, multiple inheritance, 209
disciplined, implementing, 296-297
emulating, Oberon programming
  language, 326-327
exported by UNIT Static2
  testing, 321-323
extendible record hierarchies,
  simulating, 92-95
generic, 135-136
generic stack, 143-156
  GenStack library unit, 143-156
hierarchies, 7-14
implementing, 278
instances
  communication through static
    members, 311
  copying, 42-49
  counting, 310-318
  creating, *see* constructors
  deleting, *see* destructors
  testing, 232-244
MailingRec, 92
metamorphic, 160
NameRec, 92
parent
  constructors, invoking, 49-57
  multiple, 208
pointers to, 21-23
T2D, 399
T3D, 399
TAbsSortArray, 119, 128-129
TAbsStack, 107-108, 143-144
TArray, 119, 127-128, 242
  testing, 250-256
TaskRec, 181
TBitSet, 318-319
TBufStream, 383
  reading object instances from
    streams, 389
  registering, 396
  writing object instances to
    streams, 388-389

TCircle, 7-14
TCollection (Turbo Vision), 344-358
TComplex
  declaring, 390-394
  registering for stream I/O, 394
  rendering streamable, 384
TCPU, 196
TCylinder, 8-14
TDate, 68-69
TDosStream, 383
  reading object instances from
    streams, 389
  registering, 396
  writing object instances to
    streams, 388-389
TEmsStream, 383, 398
testing, Metamorf library unit,
  172-177
TFlexOArray, 221, 259
TFlexOArray_IO, 221, 259
TFlexUArray, 219, 258
TFlexUArray_IO, 220, 259
TFrmtDate, 68-69
TGenStack, 143-144, 151
TGenVMstack, 143-144, 151
THardDisk, 196
THollowCylinder, 9-14
THybStrArray, 190, 208
  data fields, declaring, 188
TimeRec, 181
TIntArray, 49-57
TLinReg, 297
  data fields, 298
  methods, 299-300
  testing, 305-307
TMailing, 96
TMailingObj, 96-103
TMemory, 196
TName, 96
TNameObj, 96-103
TNocaseSortArray, 119, 129
TOArray, 220-221, 259
TOArray_IO, 221
TObject, 344
  rendering descendants
    streamable, 383-385
TPC, 196, 202

TRandIntArray, 49-57
TRealArray, 32-49
TScreenStack, 151
TSortArray, 119, 129
TSortedCollection (Turbo Vision), 358-360
TSortedRandIntArray, 49-57
TSphere, 8-14
TStack, 26-31
TSTR, 409-411
TStrArray, 74-77, 161-163
TStream, declaring, 377-383
TStrFixedQue, 161-164
TStrFixedStack, 161, 165
TStringCollection (Turbo Vision), 365
TStrStack, 107-114
TTaskCollection (Turbo Vision), declaring, 359
TToDo, 344
TToDoList, 344
TUArray, 217-219, 258
    testing, 232
TUArray_IO, 219, 258-259
    testing, 233
TUnorderedStringCollection, 369-370
Turbo Vision, 343-344
    RegisterXXXX procedures, 386-388
    StreamRec-typed constants, declaring, 386
TVirtStrArray, 74-77, 279-280
TVMscreenStack, 151
TVMStrStack, 107-114
user-defined
    data fields, 385
    rendering streamable, 383-385
object variables, 7
object-oriented programming, 2
    generic object types, creating, 136-137
object-oriented streams, 376
object-type hierarchies, 180-181
    abstract object types, placement, 106-118
    containment, 188-195
    modeling, 216-217
    static members, 311
    with extendible records, 96-103
    with internal abstract object types, 118-133
object-type registration, 386-388
objects, 3, 7
    dynamic, 21-23
    functionality, 3
    modular, containment, 195-201
    NIL, placing in streams, 390
    persistent, 376
    state, 3
OOP (object-oriented programming), 2
out-of-range indices, 345-348
overriding, methods, 67
    static, 68-74
    TSortedCollection object type, 358
    virtual, 74-86

P

parameter lists
    declaring, 68
    GenSearch function, 140
    of static methods, 16
parameters
    ArraySize, 76
    aStrFile, 76
    constructor, 33-34
parent object types, constructors, invoking, 49-57
partial instance malfunctions, 278
partially functioning abstract object types, 106
PCs, accessibility of modular objects, 196
persistent objects, 376
pointers
    generic routines, 140
    to contained instances, 202-207
    to object types, 21-23
PolyMorf library unit, 188
polymorphic behaviors
    overriding virtual method support of, 74
    resources, conserving, 76

polymorphic collections, storing in streams, 409-418
polymorphic file I/O, 376
polymorphic streams, 399-409
polymorphism, 5-6
Polymrf4 library unit, testing, 270-276
Pop function (Boolean), 26, 108, 144, 165
PopFront function (Boolean), 164
PopScreen function (Boolean), 152
PopTail function (Boolean), 164
PRGMSHAPE.PAS program, 10-14
private
   components, calling (object type instances), 215-216
   data fields, declaring, 106
   methods
      declaring, 106
      static, overriding (descendant object types), 68-74
      virtual, overriding, 74-86
   virtual functions
      UnSafeRecall, 218, 280
      UnSafeStore, 218, 279
PRIVATE keyword, 7
privileged instances, 216-217
   testing, 232-241
   utilizing, 241-256
procedural types, implementing deferred binding, 327
procedures, *see* functions
programming
   generic, 135-136
   object-oriented, creating generic object types, 136-137
   structured, 2
programming languages
   generic programming support, 136
   Oberon, 325
      extendible records, 326
      object types, emulating, 326-327
programs
   airplane malfunction simulation, 289-292
   ARRAY1.PAS, 32-40
   ARRAY2.PAS, 43-47
   ARRAY3.PAS, 49-57
   ARRAY4.PAS, 59-65
   ARRAY5.PAS, 84-86
   ARRAY6.PAS, 129-133
   ARRAY7.PAS, 232-241
   ARRAY8.PAS, 250-255
   ARRAY9.PAS, 270-275
   ARRAY10.PAS, 278-287
   ARRAY11.PAS, 316-317
   client, selecting sorting methods, 327
   CONTAIN1.PAS, 181-186
   CONTAIN2.PAS, 190-194
   CONTAIN3.PAS, 197-201
   CONTAIN4.PAS, 203-207
   CONTAIN5.PAS (uncompilable), 209-213
   DATE1.PAS, 68-73
   FLY.PAS, 289-292
   MKCOLCT1.PAS, 344-355
   MKCOLCT2.PAS, 359-364
   MKCOLCT3.PAS, 366-368
   MKCOLCT4.PAS, 369-373
   MKSTRM1.PAS, 390-396, 399
      random-access stream I/O, 397-398
   MKSTRM2.PAS, 399-407
   MKSTRM3A.PAS library unit, 409-411
   MKSTRM3B.PAS, 409-413
   MKSTRM3C.PAS, 409, 413-417
   PRGMSHAP.PAS, 10-14
   RECOBJ1.PAS, 92-95
   RECOBJ2.PAS, 96-103
   routines, reusing, 136-137
   STACK1.PAS, 26-31
   STACK2.PAS, 114-118
   STACK3.PAS, 153-156
   STRMERR.PAS library unit, 380-382
   TSBITS.PAS, 321-323
   TSMTMRF.PAS, 172-175
   TSOBERON.PAS, 333-339
   TSSHAPE1.PAS, 20-21
   TSSHAPE2.PAS, 22-23
   TSSTAT.PAS, 304-307
   Unit AbsArray, 119-127
   UNIT AbsStack, 107-114

Index

UNIT GenStack, 143-151
Unit LinReg source code, 300-304
Unit MetaMorf, 165-172
UNIT Oberon source code, 330-333
UNIT Polymorf, 74-83
UNIT Polymrf 2 source code, 222-232
UNIT Polymrf3 source code, 242-250
UNIT Polymrf4, 260-269
UNIT ScrnStak, 151-153
UNIT Static1, 313-315
UNIT Static2 source code, 319-321
Project function, 304-305
ProjectXonY function (Boolean), 299
pseudo-hidden methods, descendant object types, 256-269
pseudo-private methods, 216
  object-type hierarchies, creating, 256-269
PUBLIC keyword, 7
purely abstract object types, 106
Push function (Boolean), 165
Push function, 26, 108, 144
PushFront function (Boolean), 164
PushTail function (Boolean), 164
Put function, 389-396
PutItem virtual function, 365
putObjects function, 395, 400

Q

queues, fixed (modeling), 161
QuickSort function, 327

R

random-access binary files, 375
random-access stream I/O, 390-398
ReadArr Boolean function, 219
reading, collections from streams, 414-417
readyForLinReg state, 297-299
readyForProject state, 297-299
rebinding, 327
Recall function (Boolean), 32, 75, 128, 163-164, 189, 218, 279, 312, 329
RecallDate function, 69

RECOBJ1.PAS program, 92-95
RECOBJ2.PAS program, 96-103
record structures, DateTimeRec, 90
record types, TStreamRec, 377-379
records
  descendent, creating, 326
  extendible, 89-92
    containment, 181-187
    Oberon programming language, 326
    simulating, 90-95
  LinRegRec, data fields, 298
  registration, RSTR, 409
  storage/access, random-access binary files, 375
redundant methods, 222
registering
  object types
    TBufStream, 396
    TDosStream, 396
  shareware, 422
RegisterMkStrm3Types registration procedure, 409
RegisterXXXX procedures, Turbo Vision object types, 386-388
registration, 376
  object-type, 386-388
  procedures, RegisterMkStrm3Types, 409
  records, RSTR, 409
regression, linear, 297-298
routines
  CONTAIN1.PAS, 182
  CONTAIN2.PAS, 189-194
  DisposeStr, 345
  generic, building, 139-140
  intrinsic, Move, 140
  reusing, 136-137
  see also procedures
RSTR registration record, 409
rules
  abstract object types, 106
  descendant metamorphic object types, 160
  metamorphic object types, 160
  Turbo Vision, 365
Run function, 394, 399-401

439

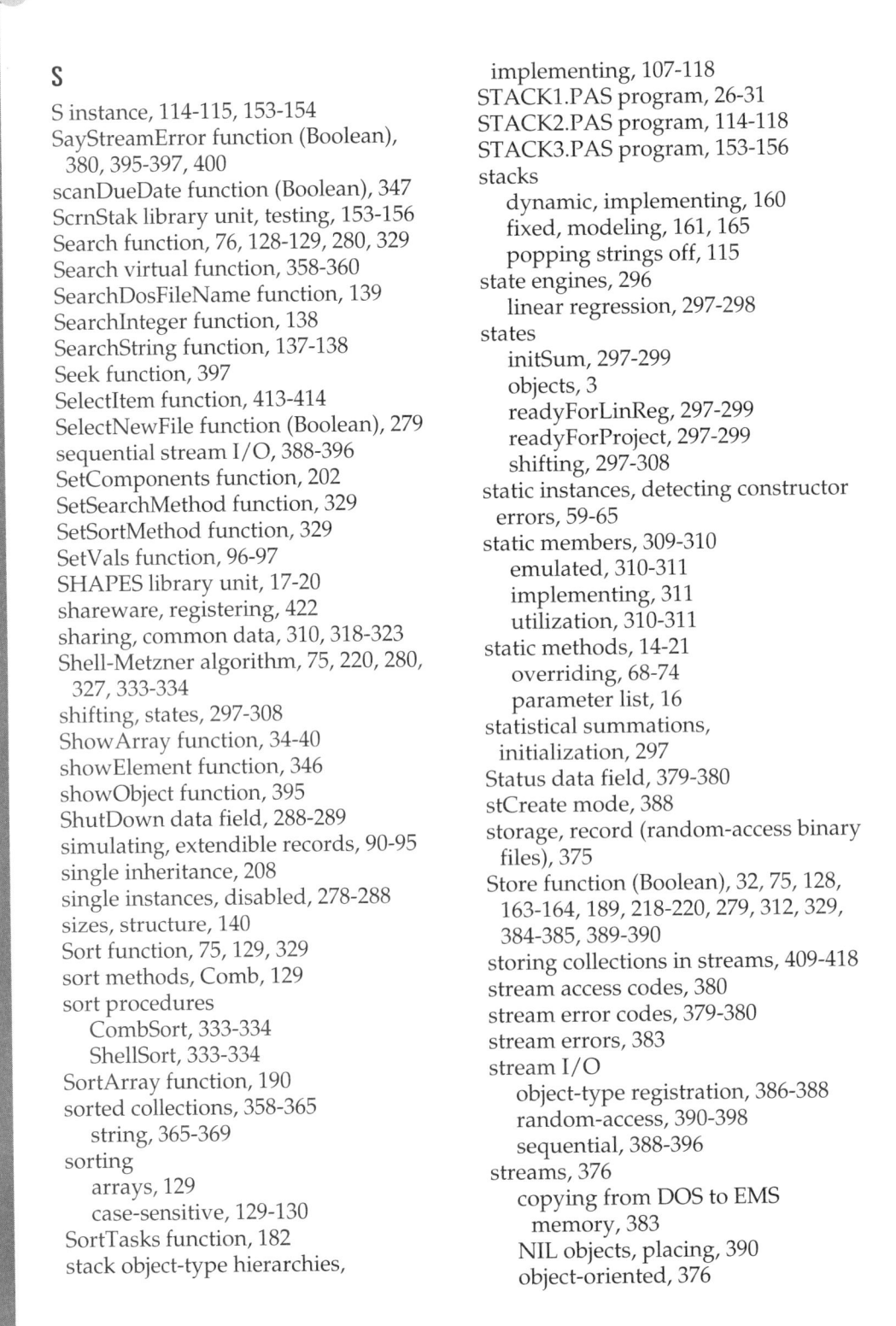

S

S instance, 114-115, 153-154
SayStreamError function (Boolean), 380, 395-397, 400
scanDueDate function (Boolean), 347
ScrnStak library unit, testing, 153-156
Search function, 76, 128-129, 280, 329
Search virtual function, 358-360
SearchDosFileName function, 139
SearchInteger function, 138
SearchString function, 137-138
Seek function, 397
SelectItem function, 413-414
SelectNewFile function (Boolean), 279
sequential stream I/O, 388-396
SetComponents function, 202
SetSearchMethod function, 329
SetSortMethod function, 329
SetVals function, 96-97
SHAPES library unit, 17-20
shareware, registering, 422
sharing, common data, 310, 318-323
Shell-Metzner algorithm, 75, 220, 280, 327, 333-334
shifting, states, 297-308
ShowArray function, 34-40
showElement function, 346
showObject function, 395
ShutDown data field, 288-289
simulating, extendible records, 90-95
single inheritance, 208
single instances, disabled, 278-288
sizes, structure, 140
Sort function, 75, 129, 329
sort methods, Comb, 129
sort procedures
    CombSort, 333-334
    ShellSort, 333-334
SortArray function, 190
sorted collections, 358-365
    string, 365-369
sorting
    arrays, 129
    case-sensitive, 129-130
SortTasks function, 182
stack object-type hierarchies,
    implementing, 107-118
STACK1.PAS program, 26-31
STACK2.PAS program, 114-118
STACK3.PAS program, 153-156
stacks
    dynamic, implementing, 160
    fixed, modeling, 161, 165
    popping strings off, 115
state engines, 296
    linear regression, 297-298
states
    initSum, 297-299
    objects, 3
    readyForLinReg, 297-299
    readyForProject, 297-299
    shifting, 297-308
static instances, detecting constructor errors, 59-65
static members, 309-310
    emulated, 310-311
    implementing, 311
    utilization, 310-311
static methods, 14-21
    overriding, 68-74
    parameter list, 16
statistical summations, initialization, 297
Status data field, 379-380
stCreate mode, 388
storage, record (random-access binary files), 375
Store function (Boolean), 32, 75, 128, 163-164, 189, 218-220, 279, 312, 329, 384-385, 389-390
storing collections in streams, 409-418
stream access codes, 380
stream error codes, 379-380
stream errors, 383
stream I/O
    object-type registration, 386-388
    random-access, 390-398
    sequential, 388-396
streams, 376
    copying from DOS to EMS memory, 383
    NIL objects, placing, 390
    object-oriented, 376

Index

polymorphic, 399-409
    reading collections from, 414-417
    storing collections in, 409-418
    Turbo Vision, 376
string arrays, dynamic (modeling), 74-76
string collections
    sorted, 365-369
    unsorted, 369-374
strings
    ordered lists, maintaining, 365-368
    popping off stacks, 115
STRMERR.PAS library unit program, 380-382
structured programming, 2
structures
    data, generic, 136
    sizes, 140
subclasses, 4-5
subhierarchies
    abstract object types in, 118-133
    TStream, declaring, 377-379
summations, statistical (initialization), 297
superclasses, 5

T

T2D object type, 399
    dynamic instances, 399-401
T3D object type, 399
    dynamic instances, 399-401
TAbsSortArray object type, 119, 128-129
TAbsStack object type, 107-108, 143-144
TArray object type, 119, 127-128, 242
    testing, 250-256
TaskRec object type, 181
tasks, 181
    constructor, CONTAIN2.PAS, 188-189
    MKSTRM2.PAS program, 399-401
TBitSet object type, 318-319
    methods, declaring, 318-319
TBufStream object type, 383
    object instances

        reading from streams, 389
        writing to streams, 388-389
    registering, 396
TCircle object type, 7-14
TCollection object type (Turbo Vision), 344-358
    methods, testing, 349-355
TCollection.Done destructor, 345
TCollection.Error function, 345-348
TCollection.Init constructor, 345
TComplex object type
    declaring, 390-394
    registering for stream I/O, 394
    rendering streamable, 384
TCPU object type, 196
TCylinder object type, 8-14
TDate object type, 68-69
TDosStream object type, 383
    object instances
        reading from streams, 389
        writing to streams, 388-389
    registering, 396
TellStreamError function (Boolean), 380
TEmsStream object type, 383, 398
Test function, 346
testing
    GenStack library unit, 153-156
    instances, privileged, 232-241
    MetaMorf library unit, 174-175
    methods, TCollection object type, 349-355
    object types
        deferred binding, 333-339
        instance-counting, 316-317
        instances, 232-244
        Metamorf library unit, 172-177
        TArray, 250-256
        TLinReg, 305-307
        TUArray, 232
    object types exported by UNIT Static2, 321-323
    Polymrf4 library unit, 270-276
    ScrnStak library unit, 153-156
TestInstance procedure, 280-281
tests, ARRAY10.PAS program, 280-281

441

TFlexOArray object type, 221, 259
TFlexOArray_IO object type, 221, 259
TFlexUArray object type, 219, 258
TFlexUArray_IO object type, 220, 259
TFrmtDate object type, 68-69
TGenStack object type, 143-144, 151
TGenStack.Init constructor, 153
TGenVMstack object type, 143-144, 151
THardDisk object type, 196
THollowCylinder object type, 9-14
three-dimensional coordinates, modeling, 399
THybStrArray object type, 190, 208
   data fields, declaring, 188
TimeRec object type, 181
TIntArray object type, 49-57
TLinReg object type, 297
   data fields, 298
   methods, 299-300
   testing, 305-307
TMailing object type, 96
TMailingObj object type, 96-103
TMemory object type, 196
TName object type, 96
TNameObj object type, 96-103
TNocaseSortArray object type, 119, 129
TOArray object type, 220-221, 259
TOArray_IO object type, 221
TObject object type, 344
   rendering descendants streamable, 383-385
tools, interface (TechnoJock Object Toolkit library), 422-423
TopSpeed Pascal compiler (Clarion), 208
TOT library, *see* Object Toolkit (TechnoJock)
TPC object type, 196, 202
TRandIntArray object type, 49-57
transparent contained object types, 181, 188
TRApp.HandleEvent, 413
TRealArray object type, 32-49

TSBITS.PAS program, 321-323
TScreenStack object type, 151
TSMTMRF.PAS program, 172-175
TSOBERON.PAS program, 333-339
TSortArray object type, 119, 129
TSortedCollection object type, 358-360
TSortedCollection.Compare virtual function, 358
TSortedRandIntArray object type, 49-57
TSphere object type, 8-14
TSSHAPE1.PAS program, 20-21
TSSHAPE2.PAS program, 22-23
TSSTAT.PAS program, 304-307
TStack object type, 26-31
TSTR object type, 409-411
TStrArray object type, 74-77, 161-163
   deferred binding, testing, 333-339
   instances, counting, 312-318
TStrArray.Done destructor, 189
TStrArray.Init constructor, 188
TStream object type, declaring, 377-383
TStream subhierarchy, 377-383
   declaring, 377-379
TStreamRec record type, declaring, 377-379
TStreamRec-typed constants, declaring, 386
TStrFixedQue object type, 161-164
TStrFixedStack object type, 161, 165
TStringCollection object type (Turbo Vision), 365
TStrStack object type, 107-114
TStrStack.Init constructor, 115
TTaskCollection object type, declaring, 359
TToDo object type, 344
TToDo.Done destructor, 345, 359
TToDo.Init constructor, 345, 359
TToDoList object type, 344
TToDoList.Done constructor, 345
TToDoList.Init constructor, 345
TToDoList.Run method, 345
TUArray object type, 217-219, 258
   testing, 232

Index

TUArray_IO object type, 219, 258-259
    testing, 233
TUnorderedStringCollection object
    type, 369-370
Turbo Pascal
    version 5.0, 423
    version v4.0, 423
Turbo Toolkit library (TechnoJock),
    421- 423
Turbo Vision
    rules, 365
    stream access codes, 380
    stream error codes, 379-380
    TCollection object type, 344-358
    TSortedCollection object type,
        358-360
    TStringCollection object types, 365
    TTaskCollection object type,
        declaring, 359
Turbo Vision hierarchy
    streams, 376
    TStream subhierarchy, 377-383
Turbo Vision object types
    RegisterXXXX procedures, 386-388
    StreamRec-typed constants,
        declaring, 386
    TVirtStrArray object type, 74-77
        functions, declaring, 279-280
        instances, enabling, 279
TVirtStrArray.Done destructor, 189
TVirtStrArray.Init constructor, 189
TVMscreenStack object type, 151
TVMStrStack object type, 107-114
TVMStrStack.Init constructor, 115
two-dimensional coordinates,
    modeling, 399
types, procedural (deferred binding,
    implementing), 327

U

UArray instance, testing, 232
UArray_10 instance, testing, 233
Unit AbsArray program, 119-127
UNIT AbsStack program, 107-114
UNIT GenStack program, 143-151

Unit LinReg source code, 300-304
Unit MetaMorf program, 165-172
UNIT Oberon source code, 330-333
UNIT Polymorf program, 74-83
UNIT Polymrf 2 source code, 222-232
UNIT Polymrf3 source code, 242-250
UNIT Polymrf4 source code, 260-269
UNIT ScrnStak program, 151-153
UNIT Static1 program, 313-315
    instance-counting object types,
        testing, 316-317
UNIT Static2 object types, testing,
    321-323
UNIT Static2 source code, 319-321
unordered collections, 344-358
unordered dynamic arrays, managing, 344-358
UnSafeRecall virtual function, 75-77,
    218-219, 280
UnSafeStore virtual function, 75-77,
    218, 279
unsorted string collections, 369-374
user-defined object types
    data fields, 385
    object-type registration, 386-388
    rendering streamable, 383-385
utilities
    BoilerPlate, 424
    Dialog Design, 424

V

viewAll procedure, 346
virtual
    Boolean functions
        Pop, 108
        Recall, 128, 218, 279, 329
        Store, 128, 218, 279, 312, 329
    destructors, 58
    functions, 14-21,
        Clear, 26, 108, 144
        FreeItem, 365, 369-370
        GetItem, 365
        KeyOf, 358-359
        overriding, 74-86
        parameter list, 16

Push, 26, 108, 144
PutItem, 365
Search, 128-129, 358-360
setting up, 15
Sort, 129
UnSafeRecall, 75-77, 218, 219, 280
UnSafeStore, 75-77, 218, 279
TSortedCollection.Compare, 358
VIRTUAL keyword, 15, 208
Virtual Method Table (VMT), 15, 376
VM_ARRAY macro, 84
VMT (Virtual Method Table), 376
VS instance, 114-115, 153-154

W-Z

Wirth, Nicklaus, 325
WorkSize data field, 218
WriteArr function (Boolean), 219
writing, comparison functions, 141-142

Add to Your Sams Library Today with the Best Books for Programming, Operating Systems, and New Technologies

The easiest way to order is to pick up the phone and call
1-800-428-5331
between 9:00 a.m. and 5:00 p.m. EST.
For faster service please have your credit card available.

ISBN	Quantity	Description of Item	Unit Cost	Total Cost
0-672-30150-4		Visual C++ Object-Oriented Programming (Book/Disk)	$39.95	
0-672-30300-0		Real-World Programming for OS/2 2.1 (Book/Disk)	$39.95	
0-672-30309-4		Programming Sound for DOS & Windows (Book/Disk)	$39.95	
0-672-30240-3		OS/2 2.1 Unleashed (Book/Disk)	$34.95	
0-672-30288-8		DOS Secrets Unleashed (Book/Disk)	$39.95	
0-672-30298-5		Windows NT: The Next Generation	$22.95	
0-672-30269-1		Absolute Beginner's Guide to Programming	$19.95	
0-672-30326-4		Absolute Beginner's Guide to Networking	$19.95	
0-672-30341-8		Absolute Beginner's Guide to C	$16.95	
0-672-27366-7		Memory Management for All of Us	$29.95	
0-672-30190-3		Windows Resource & Memory Management (Book/Disk)	$29.95	
0-672-30249-7		Multimedia Madness! (Book/Disk/CD-ROM)	$44.95	
0-672-30248-9		FractalVision (Book/Disk)	$39.95	
0-672-30229-2		Turbo C++ for Windows Programming for Beginners (Book/Disk)	$39.95	
0-672-30317-5		Your OS/2 2.1 Consultant	$24.95	
0-672-30145-8		Visual Basic for Windows Developer's Guide (Book/Disk)	$34.95	
0-672-30040-0		Teach Yourself C in 21 Days	$24.95	
0-672-30324-8		Teach Yourself QBasic in 21 Days	$24.95	

❏ 3 ½" Disk

❏ 5 ¼" Disk

Shipping and Handling: See information below.

TOTAL

Shipping and Handling: $4.00 for the first book, and $1.75 for each additional book. Floppy disk: add $1.75 for shipping and handling. If you need to have it NOW, we can ship product to you in 24 hours for an additional charge of approximately $18.00, and you will receive your item overnight or in two days. Overseas shipping and handling adds $2.00 per book and $8.00 for up to three disks. Prices subject to change. Call for availability and pricing information on latest editions.

11711 N. College Avenue, Suite 140, Carmel, Indiana 46032

1-800-428-5331 — Orders   1-800-835-3202 — FAX   1-800-858-7674 — Customer Service

Book ISBN 0-672-30333-7

What's on the Disk

- Complete source code for the author's programs and library units
- The author's generic Pascal classes library
- TechnoJock Software's Object Toolkit (shareware)
- TechnoJock Software's Turbo Toolkit (shareware)
- Dialog Design
- Boilerplate

For more information about these utilities, see Appendix A, "Disk Contents."

Installing the Floppy Disk

The software included with this book is stored in compressed form. You cannot use the software without first installing it to your hard drive.

> To install the files, you'll need at least 3.6M of free space on your hard drive.

1. From a DOS prompt, change to the drive that contains the installation disk. For example, if the disk is in drive A:, type **A:** and press Enter.

2. Type **INSTALL** *drive* (where *drive* is the drive letter of your hard drive), and press Enter. For example, if your hard drive is drive C:, type **INSTALL C:** and press Enter.

This installs all the files to a directory called \BP7OOP on your hard drive. You'll find the file README.TXT in this directory—be sure to read it for more information on the installed software.